FIFTH EDITION

GROUNDWORK FOR COLLEGE READING

FIFTH EDITION

GROUNDWORK FOR COLLEGE READING

JOHN LANGAN

TP

Books in the Townsend Press Reading Series

Groundwork for College Reading with Phonics
Groundwork for College Reading
Ten Steps to Building College Reading Skills
Ten Steps to Improving College Reading Skills
Ten Steps to Advancing College Reading Skills
Ten Steps to Advanced Reading

Books in the Townsend Press Vocabulary Series

Vocabulary Basics
Groundwork for a Better Vocabulary
Building Vocabulary Skills
Building Vocabulary Skills, Short Version
Improving Vocabulary Skills
Improving Vocabulary Skills, Short Version
Advancing Vocabulary Skills
Advancing Vocabulary Skills, Short Version
Advanced Word Power

Supplements Available for Most Books

Instructor's Edition
Instructor's Manual and Test Bank
Online Exercises
PowerPoint Slides

Copyright © 2016 by Townsend Press, Inc.
Printed in the United States of America
9 8 7 6 5 4 3 2 1

ISBN (Student Edition): 978-1-59194-472-0
ISBN (Instructor's Edition): 978-1-59194-473-7

Send book orders and requests for desk copies or supplements to:
Townsend Press Book Center
439 Kelley Drive
West Berlin, New Jersey 08091

For even faster service, contact us in any of the following ways:
By telephone: 1-800-772-6410
By fax: 1-800-225-8894
By e-mail: cs@townsendpress.com
Through our website: www.townsendpress.com

Contents

Part Two

Part Three

Appendixes

Preface: To the Instructor

We all know that many students entering college today do not have the reading and thinking skills needed to do effective work in their courses. For any one of a number of reasons, their background in reading is limited. At the same time, their concerns and interests are those of other college students. These students need to develop their reading skills through the use of adult-level materials.

Groundwork for College Reading, Fifth Edition, is designed to develop effective reading and clear thinking. To do so, the book is divided into three parts, each described below.

Part One begins with a chapter on basic matters: having the right attitude, learning key study skills, and developing a reading habit. The nine chapters that follow present a sequence of skills that are widely recognized as essential for sound comprehension:

- Knowing how to use the dictionary
- Understanding vocabulary in context
- Recognizing main ideas
- Identifying supporting details
- Locating main ideas in different parts of a passage
- Understanding relationships that involve addition and time
- Understanding relationships that involve examples, contrast, and cause and effect
- Making inferences
- Evaluating arguments

In every chapter in Part One, the key aspects of a skill are explained and illustrated clearly and simply. Explanations are accompanied by a series of practices, and each chapter ends with three review tests. The last review test consists of a reading selection so that students can apply the skill just learned to real-world reading materials.

Following each chapter in Part One are **six mastery tests for the skill in question.** The tests progress in difficulty, giving students the additional practice and challenge they may need to learn a skill.

Part Two consists of ten additional readings that will improve students' reading and thinking skills. Each reading is followed by *Vocabulary Questions* and *Reading Comprehension Questions* so that students can practice all of the skills presented in Part One. In addition, an *Outlining, Mapping,* or *Summarizing* activity after each reading helps students think carefully about the basic content and organization of a selection. *Discussion Questions* then afford instructors one more opportunity to engage students in a variety of reading and thinking skills and to deepen their understanding of a selection.

Part Three consists of a set of five relationships tests and a series of fifteen combined-skills tests that review skills in Part One and help students prepare for the standardized reading test that may be a requirement at the end of a semester.

Finally, the **Appendixes** include writing assignments for each of the ten reading selections in Part One and the ten reading selections in Part Two. These assignments will help students understand that reading, writing, and thinking are closely connected skills.

Important Features of the Book

- **Focus on the basics.** The book seeks to explain, in an extremely clear, step-by-step way, the essential elements of each skill. Many examples are provided to ensure that students understand each point. In general, the focus is on *teaching* the skills—not just on explaining them and not just on testing them.

- **Frequent practice and feedback.** In the belief that progress is made largely through abundant practice and careful feedback, this book includes numerous activities. Students can get immediate feedback on the practice exercises in Part One by turning to the limited answer key at the back of the book. The answers to the review and mastery tests in Part One, the reading questions in Part Two, and the relationships tests and combined-skills tests in Part Three are in the *Instructor's Manual.*

    The limited answer key increases the active role that students take in their own learning. They are likely to use the answer key in an honest and positive way if they know they will be tested on the many activities and selections for which answers are not provided. (Answers not in the book can be easily copied from the *Instructor's Edition* or the *Instructor's Manual* and passed out at the teacher's discretion.)

- **High interest level.** Dull and unvaried readings and exercises work against learning. Students need to experience genuine interest and enjoyment in what they read. Teachers as well should be able to take pleasure in the selections, for their own good feeling about them can carry over favorably into class work. The readings in the book, then, have been chosen not only for the appropriateness of their reading level but also for their compelling content. They should appeal to a wide range of students—developmental students, students for whom English is a second language, and Adult Basic Education students. They also take into account the diverse backgrounds of such students.

- **Ease of use.** The logical sequence in each chapter—from explanation to example to practice to review tests to mastery tests—helps make the skills easy to teach. The book's organization into distinct parts also makes for ease of use. Within a single class, for instance, instructors can work on a particular skill in Part One, review another skill with a mastery test, and provide variety by having students read one of the selections in Part Two. The limited answer key at the back of the book also makes for versatility: it means that an instructor can assign parts of each chapter for self-teaching. Finally, the mastery tests—each on its own tear-out page—and the combined-skills tests make it a simple matter for a teacher to test and evaluate student progress.

- **Integration of skills.** Students do more than learn the skills individually in Part One. They also learn to apply the skills together through the reading selections in Parts One and Two and the relationships tests and combined-skills tests in Part Three. They become effective readers and thinkers by means of a good deal of practice in applying a combination of skills.

- **Integrated online resources.** Through the use of TP's acclaimed Learning Center, *Groundwork for College Reading*, Fifth Edition, features powerful online components to enhance learning, including:

    1 **Online practice exercises and mastery tests.** Each chapter of the book features additional practice exercises *and* online versions of the book's mastery tests. These materials can be used to reinforce skills taught in the chapter *or* to assess students' learning.

    2 **Helpful PowerPoint files.** A comprehensive collection of PowerPoint files covering the book's ten skills chapters is available for immediate downloading.

3   **Downloadable supplements.** Electronic (PDF) versions of the instructor's manual and test bank can be downloaded directly from the Learning Center. These files give you the resources you need whenever and wherever you are—24 hours a day.

4   **Class management controls.** The Learning Center allows you to control which assignments and tests your students can access. It also allows you to create unique assignments for each class you teach, track students' progress, and simplify grading. To learn more, e-mail **cs@townsendpress.com** or visit the Learning Center at **www.townsendpress.net.**

● **Thinking activities.** Thinking activities—in the form of outlining, mapping, and summarizing—are a distinctive feature of the book. While educators agree that such organizational abilities are important, these skills are all too seldom taught. From a practical standpoint, it is almost impossible for a teacher to respond in detail to entire collections of class outlines or maps. This book, then, presents activities that truly involve students in outlining, mapping, and summarizing—in other words, that truly make students think—and yet enable a teacher to give quick feedback. Again, it is through continued practice and feedback on challenging material that a student becomes a more effective reader and thinker.

   In addition, the final chapter in Part One, "The Basics of Argument," provides extensive explanation of and practice in the concepts of point and support that are central to critical thinking.

● **Supplementary materials.**

Print Supplement

An *Instructor's Edition*—chances are that you are holding it in your hand—is identical to the student book except that it also provides hints for teachers (see the front of the book), answers to all the practices and tests, and comments on most answers. *No other book on the market has such detailed and helpful annotations.* The IE can be obtained quickly by writing or calling Townsend Press (439 Kelley Drive, West Berlin, NJ 08091; 1-800-772-6410), by sending a fax to 1-800-225-8894, or by e-mailing Customer Service at **cs@townsendpress.com.**

Online Supplements

Three online supplements are available through the TP website by going to the "Supplements" area for instructors at **www.townsendpress.net**.

1 A combined *Instructor's Manual and Test Bank* includes suggestions for teaching the course, a model syllabus, and readability levels for the text and the reading selections, as well as a complete answer key. The test bank contains **four** additional mastery tests for each of the ten skills and **four** additional combined-skills tests—all on letter-sized sheets so they can be copied easily for use with students.

2 PowerPoint presentations.

3 Online exercises.

● **One of a sequence of books.**

    Groundwork for College Reading with Phonics and *Groundwork for College Reading* are the basic texts in the series. They are suitable for ESL students and basic adult learners.

    Ten Steps to Building College Reading Skills is often the choice for a first college reading course.

    Ten Steps to Improving College Reading Skills is an intermediate text appropriate for the core developmental reading course offered at most colleges.

    Ten Steps to Advancing College Reading Skills is a higher-level developmental text than the *Improving* book. It can be used as the core text for a more advanced class, as a sequel to the intermediate book, or as a second-semester alternative to it.

    Finally, *Ten Steps to Advanced Reading* is the most advanced text in the series. It can also be used as a sequel (or a second-semester alternative) to either the *Improving* or the *Advancing* text.

    A companion set of vocabulary books, listed on the copyright page, has been designed to go with the *Ten Steps* books. Recommended to accompany this book is *Groundwork for a Better Vocabulary*.

    Together, the books and all their supplements form a sequence that should be ideal for any college reading program.

To summarize, *Groundwork for College Reading,* Fifth Edition, provides a sequence of key reading skills to help developmental students become independent readers and thinkers. Through an appealing collection of readings and a carefully designed series of activities and tests, students receive extensive guided practice in the skills. The result is an integrated approach to learning that will, by the end of a course, produce better readers and stronger thinkers.

xii PREFACE: TO THE INSTRUCTOR

Changes in the Fifth Edition

Following are changes in this edition of the book:

- **A full-color design.** Color has been carefully used throughout, not as window dressing but to add clarity and readability to the different parts of the book.

- **Numerous cartoons and other graphics.** Because so many students today are visual learners, over fifty illustrations have been added to help introduce or reinforce points made in the book.

- **Four new readings** (pages 316, 351, 370, and 446) as well as **five updated readings** (pages 216, 337, 380, 413, and 432).

- **A set of five relationships tests** (page 457) that will help strengthen students' reading and thinking skills.

- **Added combined-skills tests** (page 467).

- An expanded offer for **free books** (page 25).

- And a freshening of practice materials throughout.

In addition, the book will be available in electronic as well as print format, and online support for the book has been expanded.

Acknowledgments

I am grateful for the helpful suggestions provided by all the educators who have used the book over the first four editions. And at Townsend Press, I thank Bill Blauvelt, Eliza Comodromos, Denton Cairnes, Steve Farmer, Akisia Grigsby, Paul Langan, and Tanya Savory for help they provided along the way. I also owe special thanks to two TP editors who brought their exceptional talents to this revision. Barbara Solot is responsible for a layout and full-color text design that are as clear as they are inviting. The result of her artistry is a strikingly attractive book that both students and teachers will appreciate. Janet Goldstein has provided design input along with her usual superb editorial skills. Her insights, coupled with her many years of classroom teaching, have strengthened the clarity and pedagogy of the book. Her talents have also enabled the creation of the *Instructor's Edition*, complete with answers, that accompanies the book.

It is always a special pleasure to work with people who aspire toward excellence. With help from my colleagues in the teaching profession and at Townsend Press, I have been able to create a much better book than I could have managed on my own.

John Langan

How to Become a Better Reader and Thinker

The chances are that you are not as good a reader as you should be to do well in college. If so, it's not surprising. You live in a culture where people watch an average of *over five hours of television every day!* All that passive viewing does not allow much time for reading. And when you add the time spent online—for example, using Facebook and other social media, texting, surfing the Net, playing games on your smartphone—that total rises to *over eight hours a day!* Reading is a skill that must be actively practiced. The simple fact is that people who do not read very often are not likely to be strong readers.

- How much television do you think you watch on an average day? _____ hours

- How much time do you think you spend online on an average day? _____ hours

Another reason for not reading much is that you may have a lot of responsibilities. You may be going to school and working at the same time. You may have a lot of family duties as well. If you have free time, you may feel too tired to read. It might seem easier to turn on the TV than to pick up a book.

- Do you do any regular reading—for example, a daily newspaper or a weekly magazines? _____

- When are you most likely to do your reading? _____

A third reason for not reading is that reading may not have been a pleasant experience in school. You may not have been good at reading, or you may not have enjoyed what you were given to read. As a result, you may have concluded that reading in general is not for you.

- Do you think that school made you dislike reading, rather than enjoy it?

_____

If you feel you need to improve your reading, *Groundwork for College Reading,* Fifth Edition, should help you a lot. The book will help you build a solid foundation in the most important skills you need to become a better reader. To find out just how this book can help, read the next several pages and do the brief activities as well. The activities are easily completed and will give you a quick, helpful overview of the book.

How the Book is Organized

The book is organized into three main parts:

Part One: Ten Steps to College Reading (pages 7–334)

The ten steps to college reading are listed in the table of contents starting on page v. Turn to that page to fill in the steps missing below:

1 Getting Started

2 _____

3 Vocabulary in Context

4 _____

5 Supporting Details

6 Finding Main Ideas

7 Signal Words I

8 _____

9 Inferences

10 _____

Each chapter is developed in the same way.

First of all, clear explanations and examples help you *understand* the chapter. Practices then give you the "hands-on" experience needed to *learn* the content of the chapter.

● How many practices are there in the third chapter, "Vocabulary in Context" (pages 75–96)? _____

Closing each chapter are three review tests. The first one reviews the information presented in the chapter.

● On which page is Review Test 1 for "Vocabulary in Context"? _____

The second review test consists of activities that help you practice the skill presented in the chapter.

- On which pages is Review Test 2 for "Vocabulary in Context"? _____

The third review test centers on a reading selection that both gets you reading and gives you practice in the skill you learned in the chapter.

- What is the title of the reading selection in the "Vocabulary in Context" chapter? _____

Following each chapter are six mastery tests that gradually increase in difficulty.

- On what pages are the mastery tests for the "Vocabulary in Context" chapter? _____

The tests are on tear-out pages that can be easily removed and handed in to your instructor. So that you can track your progress, there is a score box at the top of the first page of each test. Your score can also be entered into the "Reading Performance Chart" on the inside back cover of the book.

Part Two: Ten Reading Selections (pages 335–454)

The ten reading selections that make up Part Two are followed by activities that give you practice in all of the skills studied in Part One. Each reading begins in the same way. Look, for example, at "Rosa: A Success Story," which starts on page 393. What are the headings of the two sections that come before the reading itself?

- _____

- _____

Note that the vocabulary words in "Words to Watch" are followed by the numbers of the paragraphs in which the words appear. Look at the first page of "Rosa: A Success Story" and explain how each vocabulary word is marked in the reading itself.

- _____

Activities Following Each Reading Selection

After each selection, there are four kinds of activities to improve the reading and thinking skills you learned in Part One of the book.

1 The first activity consists of **vocabulary questions**—questions involving vocabulary in context as well as "Words to Watch."

● Look at the vocabulary questions for "Rosa: A Success Story" on pages 397–398. The first five questions deal with understanding vocabulary in context. How many questions then help you learn words taken from "Words to Watch"? _____

2 The second activity consists of ten **reading comprehension questions**—questions involving vocabulary in context, main ideas, supporting details, signal words, inferences, and argument.

● Look at the questions for "Rosa: A Success Story" on pages 399–400. Note that the questions are labeled so you know which skill you are practicing in each case. How many questions deal with the central point and main ideas? _____

3 The third activity involves **outlining, mapping,** or **summarizing**. Each of these activities will sharpen your ability to get to the heart of a selection and to think logically and clearly about what you read.

● What kind of activity is provided for "Rosa: A Success Story" on page 401? _____

● What kind of activity is provided for "The Fist, the Clay, and the Rock" on page 368? _____

● What kind of activity is provided for "The Lady, or the Tiger?" on pages 410–411? _____

Note that a **map**, or diagram, is a visual way of organizing material. Like an outline, it shows at a glance the main parts of a selection.

4 The fourth activity consists of **discussion questions**. These questions provide a chance for you to deepen your understanding of each selection.

● How many discussion questions are there for "Rosa: A Success Story" (page 402)—and for every other reading? _____

Part Three: Relationships and Combined Skills (pages 455–498)

This part of the book provides a series of relationships and combined-skills tests that help you practice a number of the skills in the book.

- How many "Relationships Tests" are there on pages 457–466? _____
- How many "Combined-Skills Tests" are there on pages 467–498? _____

These tests are made up of short passages that closely resemble the ones typically found in standardized tests.

Appendixes (pages 499–526)

The first section in the "Appendixes" is a pronunciation guide. It tells you how to use the information provided for pronouncing the vocabulary words in this book.

The second section is "Writing Assignments." Reading and writing are closely connected skills, and writing practice will improve your ability to read closely and think carefully.

- How many assignments are offered for each reading? _____

Also included in the appendixes is a limited answer key.

Helpful Features of the Book

1 The book centers on *what you really need to know* to become a better reader and thinker. It presents key comprehension skills and explains the most important points about each one.

2 The book gives you *lots of practice*. We seldom learn a skill only by hearing or reading about it; we make it part of us by repeated practice. There are, then, many activities in the text. They are not "busywork" but carefully designed materials that should help you truly learn each skill.

   Notice that after you learn each skill in Part One, you go on to the next step: review tests and mastery tests that ask you to apply the skill. And as you move from one skill to the next, you continue to practice and reinforce the ones already learned.

3 The selections throughout the book are *lively and appealing*. Dull and unvaried readings work against learning, so subjects have been carefully chosen for their high interest level. All the selections here are good examples of how what we read can capture our attention. For example, start reading "One Less Sucker Lives" (page 91) or the timeless short story "The Lady, or the Tiger?" (page 403) or the account, with photographs, of an abused woman (page 413)—and try to *stop* reading.

How to Use the Book

1   A good way to proceed is to read—and reread—the explanations and examples in a chapter in Part One until you feel you understand the ideas presented. Then carefully work through the practices. As you finish each one, check your answers with the "Limited Answer Key" that starts on page 521.

For your own sake, *don't just copy in the answers without trying to do the practices!* The only way to learn a skill is to practice it first and then use the answer key to give yourself feedback. Also, take whatever time is needed to figure out just why you got some answers wrong. By using the answer key to help teach yourself the skills, you will prepare yourself for the review and mastery tests at the end of each chapter as well as the other reading tests in the book. Your instructor can supply you with answers to those tests.

If you have trouble catching on to a particular skill, stick with it. In time, you will learn each skill.

2   Read the selections first with the intent of simply enjoying them. There will be time afterward for rereading each selection and using it to develop your comprehension skills.

3   Keep track of your progress. Fill in the charts at the end of each chapter in Part One and each reading in Part Two. And in the "Reading Performance Chart" on the inside back cover, enter your scores for the review tests and mastery tests as well as the reading selections. These scores can give you a good view of your overall performance as you work through the book.

In summary, *Groundwork for College Reading, Fifth Edition,* has been designed to interest and benefit you as much as possible. Its format is straightforward, its explanations are clear, its readings are appealing, and its many practices will help you learn through doing. *It is a book that has been created to reward effort,* and if you provide that effort, you will make yourself a better reader and a stronger thinker. I wish you success.

John Langan

Part One

Ten Steps to College Reading

1 Getting Started

This Chapter in a Nutshell

- You must truly want to succeed in college and be willing to work at it.

- You must go to class, take notes, and make good use of your time.

- You must develop the reading habit.

© 1998 Randy Glasbergen. www.glasbergen.com

GLASBERGEN

"It's not enough to be in her class.
She actually expects you to *learn* something."

Hello, and welcome to the book. The chapters that follow will help you learn important reading skills. This first chapter is going to cover three other keys to success. I'll discuss your attitude about the course in which you are using this book, basic study skills, and your reading habits.

Your Attitude about this Course

The course in which you are using this book can help you become a better reader and writer. It can also help you get off to a strong start in college. But as the above cartoon suggests, it's not enough to just *be* in this course, or to just be in college. Instead, you must have the attitude that you are going to work hard and learn as much as you can.

You need to believe in the saying, "No pain, no gain." You must be ready to work hard in this course to improve your language skills. The heart of the matter is not the speed at which you will learn. The heart of the matter is your determination that "I *will* learn."

Discovering the Need to Work

I have seen a number of students over the years who have acted more like zombies in class than like live people. Such students are their own worst enemies. It's clear they regard themselves as unlikely to succeed in school. They walk into the classroom carrying defeat on their shoulders the way other students carry textbooks under their arms.

I'd look at them slouching in their seats and staring into space and think, "What terrible things have gone on in their lives that they've quit already? They have so little faith in their ability to learn that they're not even trying." Such students often suddenly disappear one day. Sadly, no one pays much attention because they had already disappeared in spirit long before.

When I have seen such students with defeat in their eyes, I have wanted to shake them by the shoulders and say, "You are not dead. Be proud and pleased that you have brought yourself this far. Don't give up now." Such people should not let self-doubt stop them from trying. They should roll up their sleeves and get to work. They should decide to try to learn.

What I have seen happen is that a spark will catch fire. Students will discover the meaning that school can have in their lives.

Here is one student's account of such a discovery:

> My present feeling about college is that it will improve my life. My first attitude was that I didn't need it. I had been bored by high school where it seemed we spent grades 9 to 12 just reviewing everything we had learned up through grade 8.
>
> When I entered college in January, I thought it was fun but that's all. I met a lot of people and walked around with college textbooks in my hand, playing the game of being a college student. Some weeks I went to class, and other weeks I didn't go at all and went off on trips instead. I didn't do much studying. I really wasn't into it but was just going along with the ball game. Sometimes kids would be going to an early class when I would be be getting home from an all-night party.
>
> Then two things happened. My sociology class was taught by a really cool person who would ask us a lot of questions, and they began getting to me. I started asking myself questions and looking at myself and thinking, "What's goin' on with me? What do I want and what am I doing?" Also I discovered I could write. I wrote a paragraph about my messy brother that was read in class and everyone roared. Now I'm really putting time into my writing and my other courses as well.

Just the other day my writing teacher asked me, "What is the point at which you changed? Was there a moment of truth when the switch turned to 'On' in your head?" I don't know the exact moment, but it was just there, and now it seems so real I can almost touch it. I know this is my life and I want to be somebody and college is going to help me do it. I'm here to improve myself, and I'm going to give it my best shot.

Evaluating Your Attitude toward School

Take a moment to think about your own attitude toward learning. Put a check (✓) by the item or items that apply to you. (If you agree with some sentences in an item but not others, cross out the ones you do not agree with.)

_____ School has never really turned me on. I feel I can start to study if I need to, but I don't want to. What's wrong with being a bit lazy? Life is supposed to be about enjoying yourself and having some fun. I want to take it easy and have as many good times as I can for now.

_____ I want to do more in school, but I'm afraid of really giving it a good effort. What if I try my best and I still get lousy grades? People will just laugh at me. I don't want to look foolish, so I'm probably just going to drift along and not call any attention to myself.

_____ I'm not ready to learn a lot of stuff that is not going to be of any value to me as far as I can see. Why should I study stuff that has no interest for me?

_____ I'm not an active student who tries my best all the time. But I'm not a zombie either. I do some studying, just not as much as other people would like me to. I should probably do more, and I'm going to work on that and try to do a better job of taking charge of my studies.

_____ I'm on the move, and I have taken charge of my life. There is something inside me that is strong and determined to succeed. I feel in my heart of hearts that nothing is going to stop me. It's my life, and I'm going to work hard and respect myself and gain success and happiness.

If you have a chance, share your answers with other students. Spend some time talking with each other about what your attitude is and how you can improve it.

Two Basic Study Skills

There are two basic study skills that are sure to make you a better student. After teaching first-year college students for many years, I know just how important these skills are.

Skill 1: Go to Class and Take Lots of Notes

More than anything else, here is what you must do to succeed in school:

1 Go to class.

2 Take good notes.

Why You Must Attend Class

The instructor will use class time to present the key ideas of the course. If you are not in class to hear and write down these ideas, you are not going to learn anything. Also, you greatly increase your chances of failing the course!

There are only two alternatives to class attendance. You can read and study the textbook and hope to learn the key ideas of the course from it. But textbook study will take you many hours. Even then, you still won't know which ideas the teacher feels are most important. Those ideas are the ones most likely to appear on exams.

You can also use the notes of another student. However, those notes cannot make up for the experience of actually being in class and hearing the instructor talk about key ideas. At best, the notes of another student can help you fill in any missing information in your own notes.

Why You Must Take Notes

You must write down the material presented in class because forgetting begins almost immediately! Studies have shown that within two weeks, you will probably forget a good deal of what you have heard in class.

- In fact, how much class material do you think most people do forget in just two weeks? Check (✓) the answer you think is correct:

  ____ 20 percent is forgotten within two weeks.

  ____ 40 percent is forgotten within two weeks.

  ____ 60 percent is forgotten within two weeks.

  ____ 80 percent is forgotten within two weeks.

Studies have shown that within two weeks, most people forget 80% of what they have heard!

- Now see if you can guess how much class material people typically forget within four weeks:

  ____ 85 percent is forgotten within four weeks.

  ____ 90 percent is forgotten within four weeks.

  ____ 95 percent is forgotten within four weeks.

The fact is that within four weeks, people typically forget 95% of the information they have heard in class! So the reality of the matter is that, no matter how carefully you listen to a classroom lecture, you forget very quickly—and you forget a great deal. To guard against forgetting, you should write down much of the information presented in class. If you just listen and don't write, you're heading for trouble. The point bears repeating: *you should get a written record of what an instructor presents in class.*

- How many notes do you typically take in class?

  ____ A lot

  ____ Some

  ____ Very few

If you have not checked "A lot," make it your intention to take a lot of notes from now on.

Skill 2: Organize Your Time

Do you consider yourself an organized person or a disorganized one? Check the description below that applies to you:

____ *I'm organized.* I get to places on time, I keep up with school work, I'm always ready for tests, and I allow plenty of time for planning and working on papers.

____ *I'm somewhere in the middle* between organized and disorganized.

____ *I'm disorganized.* I'm often late for appointments or forget them, I miss classes, I work on papers and cram for tests at the last minute.

If you have not checked the first item above, you need to learn more about how to control your time. The skillful use of time will help you enormously in school and in life.

Here are three steps to take to control your time:

1 First, pay close attention to the course outline, or **syllabus**, that your instructors will probably give you during the first week of class. That syllabus will most likely give you the dates of exams and tell you when papers or reports are due.

2 Second, move all those dates onto a **large monthly calendar**—a calendar that has a good-sized block of white space for each date. Hang the calendar in a place where you'll be sure to see it every day—perhaps above your desk or on a bedroom wall.

OCTOBER

Sunday	Monday	Tuesday	Wednesday	Thursday	Friday	Saturday
			1	2	3	4
5	6 English paper	7	8	9 Math test	10	11
12	13	14	15 History test	16	17	18
19	20	21 Math test	22	23	24	25
26	27	28	29	30 Speech report	31	

3 Third, buy a small notebook and write down every day a **"to do" list** of things that need to get done that day. Decide which items are most important, and handle them first. (If you have classes that day, going to those classes will be "A" priority items. Other items may be a "B" or a "C" in importance.) Carry your list with you during the day, referring to it every so often and checking off items as you complete them.

● Look at the "to do" list on the next page. Place an A, B, or C in front of each item, depending on how important you think it is.

> ## ✳ To Do ✳
>
> **Monday**
> 1. Go to History and English class.
> 2. Study for math test tomorrow.
> 3. Cash check at bank.
> 4. Meet Ben for lunch.
> 5. Check e-mail.
> 6. Pick up drinks and snacks for later.
> 7. Call Mom.
> 8. Recharge phone tonight.

● Answer these questions:

1. Of the three steps for organizing time, which is the most important one for you, and why?

   _____

   _____

2. Which step is the second most important for you, and why?

   _____

   _____

Your Reading Habits

Recently I was at a conference that featured a panel of first-year college students. They were asked, "If you could give just one bit of advice to high-school kids, what would it be?" One student answered, "I can answer that in one word: **Read.** Read everything you can. The more you read, the better off you're going to be." Up and down the panel, heads nodded. No one disagreed with this advice.

All these students agreed because they had learned the truth about reading—that it is at the very heart of education. They had been in college long enough to know that the habit of regular reading is needed for success in school and life. Here are four specific reasons why you should become a regular reader:

1 Real Pleasure. Chances are that you have done little reading for pleasure in your life. Perhaps you grew up in a home like mine where a television set was the center of the household. Perhaps you got off to a bad start in reading in school and never seemed to catch up. Or maybe you were eager to learn about reading when you began school but didn't like what you had to read. You may then have decided that reading wasn't for you.

The truth is that reading can open the door to a lifetime of pleasure and adventure. Take the time to walk through that door. You may learn that one of the great experiences of life is the joy of reading for its own sake.

2 **Language Power.** Research has shown beyond any question that regular reading improves your vocabulary, writing, and thinking skills—as well as your reading skills. If you want more language power in your life, reading is the way to get it.

3 **Job Power.** Regular reading will increase your chances for job success. In today's world more than ever before, jobs involve the processing of words and information. Studies have found that the better your command of words, the more success you are likely to have. Nothing will give you a command of words like regular reading.

There are countless stories about people who went on to successful careers after developing the reading habit. One is the story of Ben Carson, who as a boy believed that he was "the dumbest kid" in his fifth-grade class. After he started reading two books a week, at his mother's insistence, his entire world changed. Within two years he had moved to the head of his class, and he was later to become Dr. Benjamin Carson, a world-famous neurosurgeon at Johns Hopkins University Hospital.

4 **Human Power.** Reading enlarges the mind and the heart. It frees us from the narrow limits of our own experience. Knowing how other people view important matters helps us decide what we ourselves think and feel. Reading also helps us connect with others and realize our shared humanity. Someone once wrote, "We read in order to know that we are not alone." We become less isolated as we share the common experiences, emotions, and thoughts that make us human. We grow more sympathetic and understanding because we realize that others are like us.

How to Become a Better Reader

I can make my point here by asking you two questions:

- What is the best way to learn how to become a good cook?

  _____ A. Study cookbooks.

  ___ B. Take a class on how to cook.

  ___ C. Watch films of good cooks.

  ___ D. Help out a good cook.

  ___ E. Practice cooking.

You know the answer. The best way to become a good cook is to practice cooking. We become good at a skill by practicing the skill.

- What, then, is the best way to become a better reader?

Based on question 1, you can probably guess. Write your answer here:

_____

The best way to become a better reader is to do a lot of reading. In this book, you will do a good amount of reading at the same time you learn and practice key reading skills. All the reading and practice are sure to make you a better reader.

At the same time, I strongly recommend that you not limit your reading to what is in this book. I know from my many years of working with students that you should read even more. It's like becoming a good cook: the more you cook, the better you become. The more you read, the better you become.

A Question, and a Challenge

- How many books would you guess you have read in your life? _____

I have had many students say they have never read a single book from cover to cover in their lives. At most they read a book or two in school, but their memories of such books are seldom pleasant ones. They often describe that reading as a kind of forced death march—a chapter at a time with lots of worksheets and quizzes. Such experiences are not true reading experiences.

- Are you willing to take on this challenge: To read at least one outside book at the same time you are using this textbook?

  ___ Yes   ___ No   ___ Maybe

If you have answered "Yes," here are some ways to proceed:

- Go to the Townsend Press website at **www.townsendpress.com** and click on "Special Offers" from Townsend Press. You'll see that in Offer 4 you'll be able to download two free books.

- Get book suggestions from friends, family, or your instructor. Then visit a bookstore or library to find a book that interests you and read it.

- Take advantage of the special offer on page 25.

CHAPTER REVIEW

In this chapter, you learned the following:

- Your attitude about school is a key to your success. You must be determined to do the hard work needed to do well in your courses.

- If you don't go to class and take notes, you may be wasting your time in college.

- Take control of your time by using a monthly calendar and a "to do" list.

- Regular reading will improve your reading, vocabulary, writing, and thinking skills. If you want more language power in your life, reading is the way to get it.

The next chapter—Chapter 2—will show you how you can use context, rather than a dictionary, to figure out the meaning of a word.

REVIEW TEST 1

To review what you've learned in this chapter, answer the following questions by writing the letter of each correct answer.

_____ 1. To do well in school, you must
      A. have the ability to learn quickly.
      B. be determined to work hard.
      C. have respect for teachers.
      D. seek help from others.

_____ 2. To become a better reader, you must
      A. read more.
      B. study more.
      C. write more.
      D. take a course in reading.

_____ 3. Regular reading can
      A. increase your chances for job success.
      B. give you more language power.
      C. help you grow as a person.
      D. all of the above.

_____ 4. After you make up a "to do" list, you should
      A. hang it on your wall.
      B. mark down dates when papers or reports are due.
      C. decide on which items are most important.
      D. check it at least once a week.

REVIEW TEST 2

To review what you've learned in this chapter, answer the following questions by writing the letter of each correct answer.

_____ 1. How determined are you to do the **hard work** needed to succeed in school? On the following scale of *Passive* to *Determined*, where would you rate yourself?

Passive   1   2   3   4   5   6   7   8   9   10   *Determined*

Comment here on the rating you have given yourself:

_____

_____

_____

_____ 2. How good a job have you done **managing time** in your life so far? On the following scale of *Little or no time control* to *Strong time control*, rate your degree of success.

Little or no time control   **1   2   3   4   5   6   7   8   9   10**   *Strong time control*

Comment here on the rating you have given yourself:

_____

_____

_____

_____ 3. How much of a **reader** have you been in your life so far? On the following scale of *Nonreader* to *Active reader*, where would you put yourself?

Nonreader   **1   2   3   4   5   6   7   8   9   10**   *Active reader*

Comment here on the rating you have given yourself:

_____

_____

_____

_____ 4. On the basis of your ratings above, what will be your biggest challenge in school, and why will it be such a challenge?

_____

_____

_____

REVIEW TEST 3

The selection that follows is about a mother who wants to do as much as she can for her children. But it turns out she is not doing one important thing that she should. Read the selection carefully. Then answer the questions that follow to check your general understanding of the material.

Words to Watch

Below are some words in the reading that do not have strong context support. Each word is followed by the number of the paragraph in which it appears and its meaning there. These words are indicated in the selection by a small circle (°).

mollified (7): quieted; calmed
launched (16): started
skepticism (20): doubt

A PARENT GETS A READING LESSON
Lucia Herndon

1   The woman rushed into the school, out of breath. She hurried up to the reading teacher who was seated next to me at a table of books.

2   "What's this I hear about the kids not having reading books?" she demanded of the teacher.

3   It was back-to-school night at a local elementary school, and parents were there for a first chat with their children's teachers. I was there to tell people about an after-school program available at my church, located only a block away.

4   This parent had heard that the school was not making reading books available to students this year, and she was furious.

5   "I want my kids to read!" she said, her voice getting louder. "I tell them all the time they have to read. How can they do that if the school doesn't give them a book?"

6   The reading teacher tried to relieve her fears by telling her that each grade had reading books and showed her examples of the books her children would receive in their class.

7   The woman was somewhat mollified°, but still had a full head of steam. "I tell my kids all the time that they have to read, but they just want to tear the books up," she said. "So I don't let them have books at home. I expect the school to have books for them."

8   She went on to say how hard she works—indeed, she was wearing a uniform that evening, having rushed from work to make it to school; she hadn't had a chance to go home to change.

9   "And when I'm not working, I'm home cooking and cleaning, washing their clothes," she said.

10   I had been sitting there quietly while the tirade went on. She hadn't been speaking to me, although it was clear she wanted everyone within earshot to know how hard she was working to provide for her children.

11   Finally I could contain myself no longer.

12   "Do you read to your children?" I asked.

13   She looked at me as if I hadn't just heard her say how hard she worked.

14   "I don't have time to read to them," she said. "I'm working all the time. When I get home, I'm tired. I tell them to go read by themselves."

15   "Well, do you read for your own pleasure?" I asked. "Do your children see you reading a book when you have a spare moment?"

16   She launched° into another explanation about being too busy or tired to do any reading.

17   "So your children think of reading as a chore or punishment," I said quietly. "It's not something they see you do or enjoy."

18   She opened her mouth again, and I waited for what I expected was more elaboration on how hard she worked to provide a home for her children.

19   "You're saying they'll read if they see me read?" she asked. "Yes," I said, a smile on my face. "You've got it! You know kids will do what they see you do. If you take five minutes before bedtime and read to them all, you might find you have as much fun as

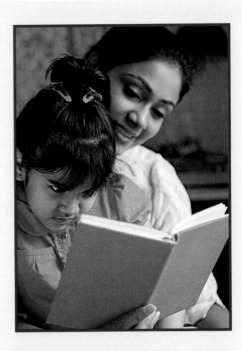

they do. You're relaxing, but you're working hard for your kids."

20   She nodded her head, although with some skepticism°.

21   "Try it once," I said. "Might be good."

22   So what was I trying to say to this harried mother? First, that everyone can appreciate hard work. But children require other things as well—some of a parent's time and attention and care. That parents can be teachers by modeling the behavior they want their children to adopt as their own. And that parents have such power over their children it can be frightening if used poorly.

23   I don't know if I convinced this mother to try something new.

24   Have I convinced you?

Questions about the Reading

For each question, write the letter of your answer in the space provided.

_____ 1. In the sentence below, the word *tirade* (tī′rād′) probably means
    A. an angry speech.
    B. an apology.
    C. a meeting.
    D. an interview.

       "I had been sitting there quietly while the tirade went on." (Paragraph 10)

_____ 2. In the sentence below, the word *elaboration* (ĭ-lăb′ər-ā′shən) probably means
    A. confusion.
    B. jokes.
    C. difficult questions.
    D. added details.

       "She opened her mouth again, and I waited for what I expected was more elaboration on how hard she worked to provide a home for her children." (Paragraph 18)

_____ 3. In the sentences below, the word *harried* (hăr′ēd) probably means
    A. mild and pleasant.
    B. annoyed and overworked.
    C. bright and questioning.
    D. passive and lazy.

       "So what was I trying to say to this harried mother? First, that everyone can appreciate hard work. But children require other things as well. . . ." (Paragraph 22)

_____ 4. Which statement best expresses the main idea of the entire selection?
    A. Parents who work too hard are cheating their kids.
    B. It is the school's responsibility to teach kids to love reading.
    C. Reading should not be seen as a chore or a punishment.
    D. Parents need to model the behavior that they want for their children.

_____ 5. When the mother arrived at back-to-school night, she
    A. was very late.
    B. seemed unconcerned.
    C. was wearing a uniform.
    D. had her children with her.

_____ 6. The author was at back-to-school night because
   A. she had a child in the teacher's class.
   B. she knew the angry mother would be there and wanted to talk with her.
   C. she was a teacher at the school.
   D. she wanted to tell parents about an after-school program.

_____ 7. The mother probably
   A. thought she was doing everything right for her children.
   B. was worried that the teacher didn't like her.
   C. had only one child.
   D. had loved to read when she was young.

_____ 8. The mother seemed to believe that
   A. reading is a waste of time.
   B. it is the job of the school, not the parents, to encourage reading.
   C. her children were being treated unfairly by their teachers.
   D. it was too late to teach her children to like reading.

_____ 9. The author probably
   A. thought the woman was a terrible mother.
   B. did not believe that the woman worked hard.
   C. had met the mother on other occasions.
   D. believed the woman needed to show, not just say, that reading was important.

_____ 10. The author suggests that the mother
   A. may not change her attitude about reading with her children.
   B. will certainly go home and begin reading to her children.
   C. does not really care if her children read or not.
   D. should quit her job to spend more time with her children.

Discussion Questions

1. Why does the mother say she does not let the children have their own books at home? What effect do you think this decision has had on her children?

2. What are some ways that a parent can encourage a child to love reading?

3. Educating a child is a big responsibility. Who should play a greater role—the school or the parent? Is there anything the parent can do that the school cannot?

Note: Writing assignments for this selection appear on page 505.

Check Your Performance

GETTING STARTED

Activity	Number Right	Points	Score
Review Test 1 (4 items)	_____	× 5 =	_____
Review Test 2 (4 items)	_____	× 5 =	_____
Review Test 3 (10 items)	_____	× 6 =	_____
		TOTAL SCORE =	_____ %

Enter your total score into the **Reading Performance Chart: Review Tests** on the inside back cover.

A Special Offer

To promote your reading growth, Townsend Press will send you five books at no charge except for postage and handling. Here are the five books:

Use the order form below, enclosing five dollars to cover the cost of shipping and handling. You'll then be sent these five very readable books.

ORDER FORM

YES! Please send me copies of *Great Stories of Suspense and Adventure*, *Rosa Parks and the Bus to Freedom*, *Ten Real-Life Stories*, *Rod Sutton: My Story*, and *Maria Cardenas: My Story*. Enclosed is five dollars to help cover the shipping and handling of the books.

Please PRINT the following very clearly. It will be your shipping label.

Name _____

Address _____

City _____ State _____ Zip _____

MAIL TO: TP Book Center, 439 Kelley Drive, West Berlin, NJ 08091.

GETTING STARTED: Mastery Test 1 (Your Attitude)
Looking Inside Yourself

1. Here is a list of some of the reasons that students are in college. Check (✓) those that apply to you. Use the space provided to add others that may apply.

_____ To prepare for a specific career.

_____ To please my parents.

_____ To set an example for my children or my brothers or sisters.

_____ To be with friends who are in college.

_____ To help me figure out just what I want to do with my life.

_____ To help me speak English better and adjust to life in America.

_____ To educate myself.

_____ To fill in time and have some fun before getting a job.

_____ To help me get a promotion at work.

_____ To take advantage of VA benefits or other special funding.

_____ Other: _____

_____

_____ Other: _____

_____

_____

2. What are some of the personal **strengths** that will help you as a student?

_____

_____

_____

3. What are some of the personal **challenges** that you must overcome to be a good student?

_____

_____

_____

(Continues on next page)

4. For many students, a main reason for being in college is to prepare for a career—the specific kind of work they intend to do in life. What is your long-term career goal—or what do you think might be your career goal?

_____

_____

_____

_____

_____

_____

5. There is a familiar saying that the longest journey begins with a single step. To achieve a long-term career goal, you must set and work toward a series of short-term goals. In the space below, list your short-term goals for this semester in college. What specifically do you want to achieve *this semester*?

_____

_____

_____

_____

_____

_____

GETTING STARTED: Mastery Test 2 (Your Attitude)

Escape Habits

Here are some of the habits that people practice to avoid working hard in school. Read about each habit and use a check (✓) to rate yourself.

If you see yourself in any of these situations, you need to know it. Once you are aware of a problem, you can begin to deal with it.

1. **"I Can't Do It."**

Some people will let themselves be discouraged by bad grades. They'll think, "There's no use trying. I'm just not any good at this." But the only way people will really know that they cannot do something is by first trying—giving it their best shot. If you think you "can't do it," the reason may be that you have given up far too soon.

My use of this habit: _____ Often   _____ Sometimes   _____ Never

2. **"I'm Too Busy."**

Some people make themselves too busy. Perhaps they work more hours on a part-time job than they need to. Perhaps they spend too much time with family or friends. They create excuses for not taking the time to study hard.

My use of this habit: _____ Often   _____ Sometimes   _____ Never

3. **"I'll Do It Later."**

Everyone tends at times to put things off. But some students, time and time again, put off what needs to be done so they can watch TV, talk to a friend, take naps, go to the movies, play cards, or do any one of a hundred other things. These students often wind up cramming for tests and writing last-minute papers. Then they seem surprised and angry at their low grades.

My use of this habit: _____ Often   _____ Sometimes   _____ Never

4. **"I'm Bored with the Subject."**

Students sometimes explain that they are doing poorly in a course because the instructor or the subject matter is boring. But on the whole, courses and instructors balance out: Some are boring; some are exciting; many are in between. If a course is not interesting, students should work even harder so that they can leave the course behind once and for all.

My use of this habit: _____ Often   _____ Sometimes   _____ Never

(Continues on next page)

5. **"I'm Here, and That's What Counts."**

   Some students spend their first weeks in college lost in a dangerous kind of dream. They feel, "All will be well, for here I am in college. I have a student ID in my pocket, classes to go to, and textbooks under my arm. All this proves I am a college student. I have made it." Such students imagine they will get something for nothing. But such a hope is a false one. Life seldom gives us something for nothing—and school won't either.

   My use of this habit: _____ Often   _____ Sometimes   _____ Never

6. Of the five habits listed here, which ones (if any) do you think will be the greatest challenge for you? Why?

   _____

   _____

   _____

   _____

   _____

   _____

GETTING STARTED: Mastery Test 3 (Study Habits)

A. Making a Daily "To Do" List

A "to do" list is a written list—on paper—of things that need to get done. It is a very powerful tool for organizing one's life and making the best use of one's time. Successful people in all walks of life use the "to do" list. With a pen and a piece of paper, you can have exactly the same tool to organize and manage your life.

Use the space below to make up your own "to do" list for tomorrow. Here are some examples of entries: "Do journal entry for English class"; "Study for math quiz"; "Call Mom"; "Do laundry."

After you list all the items, label them A, B, or C in importance. Making the best use of your time means paying most attention to "A" and "B" items. If need be, "C" items can carry over to another day.

❋ **To Do** ❋

(Continues on next page)

B. Using a Large Monthly Calendar

You should buy or make a large monthly calendar. Be sure your calendar has a good-sized block of white space for each date. Then write on the calendar the important things you have to do as well as the dates for papers and tests.

Place the calendar in a place where you will see it every day. It allows you, in one quick glance, to get a clear picture of what you need to do during each month of the semester.

Use the calendar below to write in important dates in your life for this month.

Sunday	Monday	Tuesday	Wednesday	Thursday	Friday	Saturday

GETTING STARTED: Mastery Test 4 (Study Skills)

A. To get a better sense of how much time you have each day, fill out the weekly study schedule below and on the next page. Include your meals, travel time, courses, study times, hours of any job, as well as "R&R" (rest, relaxation, time with friends, and the like).

To begin, add the word TRAVEL to the appropriate time blocks. Then add the word MEAL. Then add the names of your COURSES. Then add JOB (if any). Then add STUDY in the blocks where you see time for study and which you intend to use for study. Finally, add R&R (for "rest and relaxation"), as time permits.

Time	Monday	Tuesday	Wednesday	Thursday	Friday	Saturday	Sunday
6–7 am							
7–8 am							
8–9 am							
9–10 am							
10–11 am							
11 am–12 noon							
12–1 pm							
1–2 pm							
2–3 pm							
3–4 pm							
4–5 pm							
5–6 pm							
6–7 pm							
Subtotal Study Hrs							

(Carry these hours forward to the next page)

(Continues on next page)

Time	Monday	Tuesday	Wednesday	Thursday	Friday	Saturday	Sunday
7–8 pm							
8–9 pm							
9–10 pm							
10–11 pm							
11 pm–12 mid							
12–1 am							
1–2 am							
Subtotal from p. 33							
Total Study Hrs							

B. On the basis of your weekly study schedule, what is the total number of study hours you can schedule each week?

_____

GETTING STARTED: Mastery Test 5 (Reading)

Think about and then write out your answers to the questions that follow.

1. What was the attitude toward reading in your home? Was it positive or negative? Explain.

_____

_____

_____

_____

_____

_____

2. How did your family's attitude toward reading affect your development as a reader? Did you do a lot of reading—or very little reading?

_____

_____

_____

_____

_____

_____

3. What about your friends and brothers or sisters? Were they readers or nonreaders? How did their attitude affect your attitude toward reading?

_____

_____

_____

_____

_____

_____

(Continues on next page)

4. How much attention was given to reading in the school or schools you went to? Did school help you develop a positive attitude toward reading—or a negative one? Explain.

_____

_____

_____

_____

_____

_____

5. TV, movies, music, video games, and the Internet are all distractions in everyday life that keep people from reading. Do such distractions limit your reading? How much?

_____

_____

_____

_____

_____

_____

GETTING STARTED: Mastery Test 6 (Reading)

Here are some ways to become a regular reader. Check (✓) the way or ways that you think would work for you.

___ 1. Create a half hour or an hour of reading in your daily schedule. That time might be during your lunch hour, or late afternoon before dinner, or the half hour or so before you turn off your light at night. Find a time that is possible for you, and make reading then a habit.

● What time would probably best fit your schedule? _____

___ 2. Subscribe to a daily newspaper (or visit it online) and read the sections that interest you. Keep in mind that it is not *what* you read that matters—for example, you should not feel that you must read the editorial section if opinion columns are not your interest. What does matter is *the very fact that you read*. Feel perfectly free to read whatever you like: the sports page, the fashion section, movie reviews, front-page stories—even the comics.

● What sections are you most likely to read?

_____

_____

_____

___ 3. Subscribe to one or more magazines. Browse in the magazine section of your library or a local bookstore; chances are you'll find some magazines that interest you. You may want to consider a weekly news magazine, such as *U.S. News and World Report;* a weekly general-interest magazine, such as *People*; or any number of special-interest monthly magazines, such as *Glamour, Sports Illustrated, Essence,* or *Health*. Many of these magazines, and others like them, are available online.

You'll find subscription cards within most magazines. Also, on many college bulletin boards you'll see display cards offering a wide variety of magazines at discount rates for students.

● Do you already subscribe to any magazine(s)? Which one(s)?

_____

_____

(Continues on next page)

___ 4. Read aloud to children in your family, whether younger brothers or sisters or sons or daughters or nephews or nieces. Alternatively, have a family reading time when you and the children take turns reading.

● Do you already read aloud to any young person in your family?

_____

___ 5. Read books on your own. This is the most important step on the road to becoming a regular reader. Reading is most enjoyable when you get drawn into the special world created by a book. You can travel in that world for hours, unmindful of everyday concerns. Too many people are addicted to smoking or drugs or television; you should try, instead, to get hooked on books.

What should you read? Select anything that interests you. That might be comic books, fantasies or science fiction, horror and mystery stories, romances, adventure or sports stories, biographies and autobiographies, or how-to books. To select a book, browse in a bookstore, library, or reading center. Find something you like and begin reading. If you stick to it and become a regular reader, you may find that you have done nothing less than change your life.

● Look at the list of Townsend Library books by going to **www.townsendpress.com**. What are the titles of several books you might like to read on your own?

_____

_____

_____

_____

_____

2 Dictionary Use

This Chapter in a Nutshell

- You should own both a paperback and a hardbound dictionary.

- You can use a computer to visit online dictionaries.

- Use spelling hints to help you look up in the dictionary a word you cannot spell.

- A dictionary entry will tell you how a word is spelled and pronounced and give you the various meanings of the word. It will also provide other helpful information about the word.

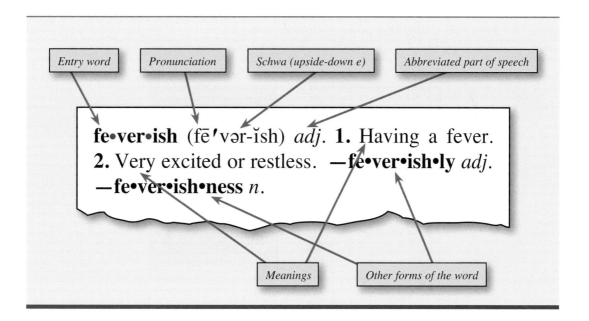

The dictionary is a valuable tool. To help you use it, this chapter explains in a clear and detailed way what you need to know about dictionaries and the information they provide.

Owning Your Own Dictionaries

You can benefit greatly by owning two dictionaries. The first dictionary you should own is a paperback edition you can carry with you. Any of the following would be a good choice:

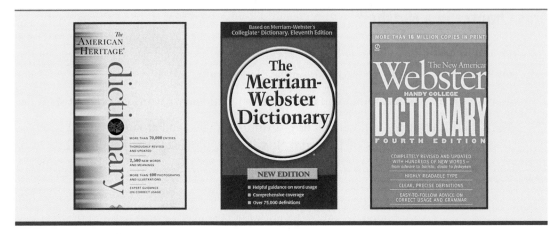

The second dictionary you should own is a desk-sized, hardcover edition, which should be kept in the room where you study. Here are two good hardbound dictionaries:

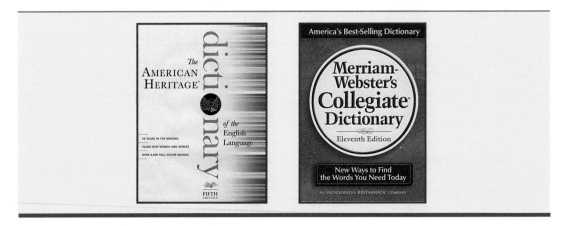

Hardbound dictionaries contain a good deal more information than the paperback editions. For instance, a hardbound dictionary defines far more words than a paperback dictionary. And there are more definitions for each word, as well. They are worth the extra cost.

If you can, invest in a new dictionary so you will have up-to-date information on old and new words. A dictionary is easily among the best investments for learning that you will ever make.

Online Dictionary

If your computer is connected to the Internet, you may find it easy to check words online. Here is one dictionary site you can go to:

www.merriam-webster.com

For example, if you go online to **www.merriam-webster.com** and type in the word *confront*, you will see something like this:

---

confront 🔊

verb   con·front   \kən-ˈfrənt\

: to oppose or challenge (someone) especially in a direct and forceful way
: to directly question the action or authority of (someone)
: to deal with (something, such as a problem or danger); *especially* : to deal with (something) in an honest and direct way

Full Definition of CONFRONT
transitive verb

1 : to face especially in challenge : oppose
   <*confront* an enemy>
2 **a** : to cause to meet : bring face-to-face
      <*confront* a reader with statistics>
   b : to meet face-to-face : **ENCOUNTER**
      <*confronted* the possibility of failure>
   — con·front·al 🔊 \-ˈfrən-tᵊl\   *noun*
   — con·front·er   *noun*

See confront defined for English-language learners
See confront defined for kids

Examples of CONFRONT

They *confronted* the invaders at the shore.

She *confronted* him about his smoking.

(continued)

The country is reluctant to *confront* its violent past.

The photographs *confront* the viewer with images of desperate poverty.

I *confronted* her with the evidence.

Origin of CONFRONT

Middle French *confronter* to border on, confront, from Medieval Latin *confrontare* to bound, from Latin *com-* + *front-, frons* forehead, front
First Known Use: circa 1568

Related to CONFRONT

Synonyms
beard, brave, brazen, breast, face, dare, defy, outbrave, outface
Antonyms
dodge, duck, funk, shirk, sidestep

[+] more

Rhymes with CONFRONT

affront, beachfront, bowfront, breakfront, cold front, drag bunt, drop front, fly front, forefront, home front, housefront, lakefront, man...

[+] more

By permission. From *Merriam-Webster's Collegiate® Dictionary, 11th Edition* © 2015 by Merriam-Webster, Incorporated (www.merriam-webster.com).

Notice the speaker icon next to the word *confront*. **If you click on this icon, the word will be pronounced for you.**

This site will also give you information on **synonyms** (words with similar meanings to the word you have looked up) and **antonyms** (words with opposite meanings to the word you have looked up). Synonyms and antonyms are explained further on pages 53 and 79–83.

Note: Some computer programs come with a built-in dictionary. For example, if you use Microsoft Word on a Mac, click on "Tools" and then choose "Dictionary." If you are using Word for Windows, highlight a word in your document, scroll down to "Look Up," and then click on one of the dictionaries listed.

Finding Words in the Dictionary

Using Guidewords to Find a Word

One way to find a given word in a dictionary is to use **guidewords**—the pair of words at the very top of each dictionary page. Shown below are the top and bottom parts of a page in one paperback dictionary.

---

155   **cluster • cobra**

²**cluster** *vb* : to grow or gather in a cluster

¹**clutch** \ˈkləch\ *vb* : to grasp with or as if with the hand

²**clutch** *n* **1** : the claws or a hand in the act of grasping; *also* : CONTROL, POWER **2** : a device for gripping an object **3** : a coupling used to connect and disconnect a driving and a driven part of a mechanism; *also* : a lever or pedal operating such a coupling **4** : a crucial situation

nous coal and used in dyes and drugs

co‧an‧chor \ˈkō-ˈaŋ-kər\ *n* : a newscaster who shares the duties of head broadcaster

coarse \ˈkȯrs\ *adj* **coars‧er; coars‧est 1** : of ordinary or inferior quality **2** : composed of large parts or particles ⟨∼ sand⟩ **3** : CRUDE ⟨∼ manners⟩ **4** : ROUGH, HARSH — **coarse‧ly** *adv* — **coarse‧ness** *n*

coars‧en \ˈkȯrs-ᵊn\ *vb* : to make or become coarse

---

coal gas *n* : gas from coal; *esp* : gas distilled from bituminous coal and used for heating

co‧a‧li‧tion \ˌkō-ə-ˈli-shən\ *n* : UNION; *esp* : a temporary union for a common purpose — **co‧a‧li‧tion‧ist** *n*

coal oil *n* : KEROSENE

coal tar *n* : tar distilled from bitumi-

hastily

cob‧bler \ˈkä-blər\ *n* **1** : a mender or maker of shoes **2** : a deep-dish fruit pie with a thick crust

cob‧ble‧stone \ˈkä-bəl-ˌstōn\ *n* : a naturally rounded stone larger than a pebble and smaller than a boulder

co‧bra \ˈkō-brə\ *n* [Pg *cobra* (de

The first guideword tells what the first word is on that page; the second guideword tells what the last word is on the page. All the word entries on the page fall alphabetically between the two guidewords.

 PRACTICE 1

Following are five pairs of dictionary guidewords followed by other words. Underline the **three** words in each series that would be found on the page with the guidewords.

1. **camp / candidate**

   camera   campus   canary   cancer   candle

2. **hoax / holiness**

   holdup   history   hollow   holiday   hog

3. **lesson / lever**

length	letter	liberty	lettuce	level

4. **raft / rake**

railroad	radio	raise	raincoat	ranch

5. **shame / shaving**

sharp	shapely	shallow	shampoo	sheep

Finding a Word You Can't Spell

"If I can't spell a word," you might ask, "how can I find it in the dictionary?" The answer is that you have to guess what the letters might be.

Guessing is not too difficult with certain sounds, such as the sounds of *b* and *p*. But other sounds are more difficult to pin down because they can belong to more than one letter. And that's where the guessing comes in. Here are three hints to help in such cases:

Hints for Finding Words

Hint 1: If you're not sure about the vowels in a word, you will simply have to experiment. Vowels often sound the same. So try an *i* in place of an *a*, an *i* in place of an *e*, and so on. If, for example, you don't find a word that sounds as if it begins with *pa*, try looking under *pe*, *pi*, *po*, *pu* or *py*.

Hint 2: Below are groups of letters or letter combinations that often sound alike. If your word isn't spelled with one of the letters in a pair or group shown below, it might be spelled with another in the same pair or group. For example, if it isn't spelled with a *k*, it may be spelled with a *c*.

c / k	c / s	f / v / ph	g / j	qu / kw / k	s / c / z
sch / sc / sk	sh / ch	shun / tion / sion		w / wh	able / ible
ai / ay	al / el / le	ancy / ency	ate / ite	au / aw	ea / ee
er / or	ie / ei	ou / ow	oo / u	y / i / e	

Hint 3: Consonants are sometimes doubled in a word. If you can't find your word with a single consonant, try doubling it.

PRACTICE 2

For this practice, you will need a dictionary. Try using your ear, the hints on this page, and guidewords to help you find the correct spelling of the following words. Write each correct spelling in the answer space.

1. revize _____

2. kiddnap _____

3. pleeze _____

4. beleive _____

5. realy _____

6. skoolteacher _____

7. writting _____

8. libary _____

9. definately _____

10. acros _____

Learning from a Dictionary Entry

Each entry word in a dictionary is in **boldface type**. Here is a sample entry:

Sample Dictionary Entry

> **dis•tress** (dĭ-strĕs′) *n.* Extreme anxiety or pain. 2. In need of immediate assistance: *The police helped the motorist in distress.* —*v.* -tressed, -tress•ing, -tress•es. To cause anxiety or pain: *I didn't mean to distress you.*

All of the following information may be provided in a dictionary entry:

1 Spelling and syllables

2 Pronunciation symbols and accent marks

3 Parts of speech

4 Irregular forms of words

5 Definitions

6 Synonyms

The rest of this chapter will look at each kind of information above.

1   Spelling and Syllables

The dictionary first gives the correct spelling and syllable breakdown of a word. Dots separate the words into syllables. Each syllable is a separate sound, and each sound includes a vowel. In the entry shown above, *distress* is divided into two syllables.

How many syllables are in each of the following words?

harsh   **ru•mor**   **ex•cep•tion**   **in•stall•ment**

The dots tell you that *harsh* has one syllable, *rumor* has two syllables, and *exception* and *installment* have three syllables each.

 PRACTICE 3

Use your dictionary to separate the following words into syllables. Put a large dot (•) between the syllables. Then write down the number of syllables in each word. The first one is done for you as an example.

Example: con•for•mi•ty   ___4___ syllables

1. f r a g m e n t   _____ syllables

2. i n j e c t i o n   _____ syllables

3. c o m p l i c a t e   _____ syllables

4. i n s e n s i t i v e   _____ syllables

5. c o m m u n i c a t i o n _____ syllables

2   Pronunciation Symbols and Accent Marks

A dictionary entry word is followed by information in parentheses, as in the entry for *distress*:

dis•tress (dĭ-strĕs′)

The information in parentheses shows you how to pronounce the word. It includes two kinds of symbols: pronunciation symbols and accent marks. Following are explanations of each.

Pronunciation Symbols

The **pronunciation symbols** tell the sounds of the consonants and the vowels in
a word. The sounds of the consonants are probably familiar to you, but you may
find it helpful to review the vowel sounds. Vowels are the letters *a, e, i, o,* and *u*.
(Sometimes *y* is also a vowel, as in *myself* and *copy*.) To know how to pronounce
the vowel sounds, use the pronunciation key in your dictionary. Here is a sample
pronunciation key:

Pronunciation Key

ă hat	ā pay	âr care	ä card	ĕ ten	ē she	ĭ sit
ī hi	îr here	ŏ lot	ō go	ô all	oi oil	ou out
o͝o look	yo͝o cure	o͞o cool	yo͞o use	ŭ up	ûr fur	th thick
th then	ə ago, item, easily, gallop, circus					

To use the above key, match the symbol (**ă, ā,** and so on) with the letter or
letters in **bold print** in the short word that follows the symbol. For instance, **ă**
(also called "short *a*") sounds like the *a* in *hat*.

You can pronounce the *i* in *distress* by first finding the matching symbol
within the parentheses. Note that the matching symbol for *i* is **ĭ**. Then look for
that symbol in the Pronunciation Key. It shows you that the *i* has the sound of *i*
in the short word *sit*. You can also use the Pronunciation Key to pronounce the *e*
in *distress*. It shows you that the **ĕ** is pronounced like the *e* in *ten*.

A long vowel (a vowel with a line over it) has the sound of its own
name. Long *a* (**ā**) sounds like the *a* in *pay*; long *e* (**ē**) sounds like the *e* in *she*;
and so on.

Finally, note that the last pronunciation symbol in the key looks like an
upside-down e: **ə**. This symbol is known as the **schwa**. As you can see by the
words that follow it, the schwa has a very short sound that sounds like "uh" (as
in *ago, gallop,* and *circus*) or "ih" (as in *item* and *easily*). It usually sounds much
like the "uh" a speaker makes when pausing.

PRACTICE 4

Refer to the pronunciation key on the facing page to answer the questions about the following ten words. In the space provided, write the letter of each of your answers.

_____ 1. *contest* (kŏn'tĕst')
       The *o* in *contest* is pronounced like the *o* in
       A. *lot.*   B. *go.*

_____ 2. *impress* (ĭm-prĕs')
       The *i* in *impress* is pronounced like the *i* in
       A. *sit.*   B. *hi.*

_____ 3. *evident* (ĕv'ĭ-dənt)
       The first *e* in *evident* is pronounced like the *e* in
       A. *ten.*   B. *she.*

_____ 4. *betray* (bĭ-trā')
       The *a* in *betray* is pronounced like the *a* in
       A. *hat.*   B. *pay.*

_____ 5. *poker* (pō'kər)
       The *o* in *poker* is pronounced like the *o* in
       A. *lot.*   B. *go.*

_____ 6. *humane* (hyōo-mān')
       The *u* in *humane* sounds like the *yoo* in
       A. *cure.*   B. *use.*

_____ 7. *license* (lī'səns)
       The *i* in *license* sounds like the *i* in
       A. *sit.*   B. *hi.*

_____ 8. *mastery* (măs'tə-rē)
       The *a* in *mastery* is pronounced like the *a* in
       A. *hat.*   B. *pay.*

_____ 9. *remedy* (rĕm'ĭ-dē)
       The *y* in *remedy* is pronounced like the *e* in
       A. *ten.*   B. *she.*

_____ 10. *disappear* (dĭs'ə-pîr')
       The first *a* in *disappear* sounds like the
       A. *a* in *hat.*   B. schwa in the word *ago.*

PRACTICE 5

Below are pronunciation symbols for five common words. Write in the word in each case and also the number of schwa sounds in each word. The first item has been done for you as an example.

Pronunciation symbols	*Word itself*	*Number of schwas*
1. (ĭn′stənt)	instant	1
2. (mĭr′ə-kəl)	_____	_____
3. (ə-fĕns′)	_____	_____
4. (ĭn-tĕl′ə-jənt)	_____	_____
5. (rĭ-lī′ə-bəl)	_____	_____

Accent Marks

Notice the black marks in the pronunciation guide (the information shown in parentheses) for the word *information*. The marks look a little like apostrophes.

    in•for•ma•tion (ĭn′fər-mā′shən)

The darker line (′) is a bold accent mark, and it shows which syllable has the strongest stress. That means the third syllable in *information* is pronounced a little louder than the other three. Syllables without an accent mark are unstressed. Some syllables—like the first syllable in *information*—are in between, and they are marked with a lighter accent mark (′).

Say *information* to yourself. Can you hear that the strongest accent is on *ma*, the third syllable? Can you hear that the first syllable, *in*, is also accented, but not as strongly? If not, say the word to yourself again until you hear the differences in accent sounds.

Here are some familiar words with syllable divisions and accent marks shown in parentheses. Use those guides to help you pronounce the words to yourself.

- bat•tle (băt′l)
- dis•gust (dĭs-gŭst′)
- ap•prov•al (ə-pro͞o′vəl)
- fa•vor•a•ble (fā′vər-ə-bəl)
- ex•am•i•na•tion (ĭg-zăm′ə-nā′shən)

PRACTICE 6

Answer the questions following each of the five words below.

1. **mag•net** (măg′nĭt)

   A. How many syllables are in *magnet*? _____

   B. Which syllable is most strongly accented? _____

2. **en•cour•age** (ĕn-kûr′ĭj)

   A. How many syllables are in *encourage*? _____

   B. Which syllable is more strongly accented? _____

3. **grat•i•tude** (grăt′ĭ-tōōd′)

   A. How many syllables are in *gratitude*? _____

   B. Which syllable is most strongly accented? _____

4. **re•li•a•ble** (rĭ-lī′ə-bəl)

   A. How many syllables are in *reliable*? _____

   B. Which syllable is more strongly accented? _____

5. **a•pol•o•gize** (ə-pŏl′ə-jīz′)

   A. How many syllables are in *apologize*? _____

   B. Which syllable is most strongly accented? _____

3   Parts of Speech

Every word in the dictionary is either a noun, a verb, an adjective, or another part of speech. In dictionary entries, the parts of speech are shown by letters in italics. In the entry below for *progress,* for example, the abbreviations *n.* and *v.* tell us that *progress* is both a noun and a verb.

> **pro•gress** (prŏg′rĕs′) *n.* Movement toward a goal; steady advance.
> —*v.* (prə-grĕs′). To move along; advance.

When a word is more than one part of speech, the dictionary gives the definitions for each part of speech separately. In the above entry for *progress*, the abbreviation telling us that *progress* is a noun comes right after the pronunciation symbols; the definitions of the noun follow. When the noun meaning ends, the abbreviation *v.* tells us that the verb pronunciation and definitions will follow.

Parts of speech are abbreviated in order to save space. Following are the most common abbreviations for parts of speech:

n. — noun	*v.* — verb
pron. — pronoun	*conj.* — conjunction
adj. — adjective	*prep.* — preposition
adv. — adverb	*interj.* — interjection

Note: Many dictionaries use the abbreviations *tr.* and *intr.* (or *vt* and *vi*) to indicate two types of verbs, not other parts of speech. The abbreviations *tr.* and *vt* stand for a transitive verb (one that has a direct object); the abbreviations *intr.* and *vi* stand for an intransitive verb (one that does not have a direct object).

PRACTICE 7

Use your dictionary to list the parts of speech for each of the following words. Each word has more than one part of speech.

Parts of speech

1. attack   A. _____   B. _____

2. wonder   A. _____   B. _____

3. pinch   A. _____   B. _____

4. respect   A. _____   B. _____

5. quiet   A. _____   B. _____

4 Irregular Forms of Words

Look at the following two words and the forms that follow them in most dictionaries.

draw (drô) *v.* **drew** (dro͞o), **drawn**, **draw•ing**

la•zy (lā′zē) *adj.* **la•zi•er**, **la•zi•est**

When other forms of a word are spelled in an irregular way (differently from the main form of the word), those forms are shown. As you can see in the examples above, those forms are given after the part of speech in an entry. With irregular verbs, the dictionary gives the past tense (*drew*) and the past participle (*drawn*), as well as the present participle (*drawing*). With adjectives, the dictionary gives the comparative (*lazier*) and superlative (*laziest*) forms.

Plural forms of irregular spellings are also included in this spot in an entry. For example, the entry for *city* begins:

cit•y (sĭt′ē) *n., pl.* **cities**

After the part of speech of *city* (*n.* for noun), the entry shows the irregular form of the plural (*pl.*) of *city: cities*.

Finally, comparative forms of adjectives and adverbs are also given at this point in an entry. Here are two examples:

good (gŏŏd) *adj.* **bet•ter** (bĕt′ər), **best** (bĕst)

high (hī) *adj.* **-er, -est**

PRACTICE 8

Use your dictionary to answer the following questions.

1. What is the plural spelling of the noun *party*? _____

2. What are the past tense and past participle forms of the verb *write*?

   _____   _____

3. What is the plural spelling of the noun *life*? _____

4. What are the past tense and past participle forms of the verb *speak*?

   _____   _____

5. What are the comparative forms of the adjective *little*?

   _____   _____

5 Definitions

Words often have more than one meaning. When they do, their **definitions** (meanings) may be numbered in the dictionary. You can tell which definition of a word fits a given sentence by the meaning of the sentence. For example, the following are three of the definitions of the noun form of *judgment* given in most dictionaries.

 1. A decision made in a court of law.
 2. The ability to think carefully about something.
 3. An opinion or conclusion.

Which of these definitions best fits the sentence below?

> The parents showed good judgment in refusing to put a television in their son's room.

The answer is definition 2: The parents thought carefully about whether to give their son a personal television and then decided against it.

PRACTICE 9

Below are three words and their dictionary definitions. A sentence using each word is also given. Choose the dictionary meaning that best fits each sentence.

 1. **suspect:**   **1.** To regard as likely or probable.
                   2. To distrust or doubt.
                   3. To think of as guilty without proof.

 Which definition of *suspect* fits the sentence below? _____

 I *suspect* the exam is going to be all essay questions.

 2. **quick:**   **1.** Very fast; rapid.
                 2. Thinking or learning fast.

 Which definition of *quick* fits the following sentence? _____

 My boss has a *quick* temper.

 3. **instruct:**   **1.** To teach a subject or skill.
                    2. To give orders to; direct.

 Which definition of *instruct* fits the following sentence? _____

 The doctor *instructed* the nurse to take my blood pressure.

6 Synonyms

A **synonym** is a word whose meaning is similar to that of another word. For instance, two synonyms for the word *help* are *aid* and *assist*.

Dictionary entries sometimes end with synonyms. For example, the word *forgive* in some dictionaries ends with the synonyms *excuse* and *pardon*. A hardbound dictionary, in particular, will provide synonyms for a word and explain the differences in meaning among the various synonyms.

More information on synonyms as well as **antonyms** (words with opposite meanings) can be found in a **thesaurus** (thĭ-sôr′əs), which is a collection of synonyms and antonyms. If you have access to the Internet, you can find a free thesaurus online by going to

www.merriam-webster.com or **www.thesaurus.com**

Or check on your computer to see if it has a built-in thesaurus. For example, if you use Microsoft Word on a Mac computer, just click on "Tools" and then choose "Thesaurus." (If you are using Word for Windows, click on "Review" and then "Thesaurus," or right-click a word in your document and then click "Synonyms.")

Or you may want to buy a paperback thesaurus, which you can find in almost any bookstore. Here are three good ones:

CHAPTER REVIEW

In this chapter, you learned the following:

- It helps to own two dictionaries. One should be a small paperback you can carry with you. The other should be a large hardbound version for use at home.

- If you have a computer, you can easily find a dictionary online.

- Guidewords and the spelling hints on page 43 will help you find a word in the dictionary.

- A dictionary entry will tell you: (1) how a word is spelled and broken into syllables; (2) how the word is pronounced; (3) the word's part (or parts) of speech; (4) other forms of the word; (5) definitions of the word. Some dictionaries will also list synonyms—words that mean nearly the same as the word.

The next chapter—Chapter 3—will show you how you can use context, rather than a dictionary, to figure out the meaning of a word.

On the Web: If you are using this book in class, you can visit our website for additional practice in using the dictionary. Go to **www.townsendpress.com** and click on "Learning Center."

REVIEW TEST 1

To review what you've learned in this chapter, answer the following questions by writing the letter of each correct answer.

_____ 1. Use the guidewords at the top of every dictionary page to help you
     A. pronounce a word in a dictionary.
     B. find a word in a dictionary.
     C. define a word in a dictionary.

_____ 2. In a pronunciation key, a dark accent mark shows
     A. which syllable has the strongest stress.
     B. which syllable has the weakest stress.
     C. that the word has only one syllable.

_____ 3. TRUE OR FALSE? A schwa usually sounds like the "uh" a speaker makes when pausing.

_____ 4. Dictionary entries will show you all of the following **except**
     A. how to spell a word.
     B. how to pronounce a word.
     C. the meaning or meanings of a word.
     D. common spelling errors of a word.

REVIEW TEST 2

A. Below are three pairs of dictionary guidewords followed by a series of other words. In the space provided, write the letter of the **one** word in each series which would be found on the page with the guidewords.

_____ 1. **fountain / fracture**
     A. fragment   B. found   C. fourteen

_____ 2. **midnight / military**
     A. middle   B. million   C. midterm

B. Use your dictionary and the spelling hints on page 43 to find the correct spelling of the following words.

3. busness _____

4. vizitor _____

5. sirprise _____

6. realy _____

C. Use your dictionary to put dots between the syllables in each word. Then write out the word with the correct pronunciation symbols, including the accent mark or marks.

7. m i c r o s c o p e _____

8. p r o n u n c i a t i o n _____

D. Answer the questions about the two words below. The pronunciation key on page 46 will help you answer the questions.

_____ 9. In **ca•ble** (kā′bəl), the *a* is pronounced like the *a* in what common word?
  A. *hat*   B. *pay*   C. *card*

_____ 10. In **hes•i•tate** (hĕz′ĭ-tāt), the first *e* is pronounced like the *e* in what common word?
  A. *ten*   B. *she*   C. *item*

REVIEW TEST 3

Here is a chance to apply your understanding of dictionary use to a full-length reading. This selection is a true story about Malcolm X, an African-American civil rights leader in the 1950s and 1960s. In this excerpt from his autobiography, Malcolm X (with his coauthor, Alex Haley) explains how he used his time in jail to become "truly free." Read the selection and then answer the questions that follow.

Words to Watch

Following are some words in the reading that do not have strong context support. Each word is followed by the number of the paragraph in which it appears and its meaning there. These words are indicated in the reading by a small circle (°).

> *painstaking* (5): very careful
> *ragged* (5): uneven
> *burrowing* (6): digging
> *succeeding* (7): following
> *word-base* (8): vocabulary
> *bunk* (8): bed

DISCOVERING WORDS

Malcolm X with Alex Haley

1 It was because of my letters [which Malcolm X wrote to people outside while he was in jail] that I happened to stumble upon starting to acquire some kind of a homemade education.

2 I became increasingly frustrated at not being able to express what I wanted to convey in letters that I wrote. . . . And every book I picked up had few sentences which didn't contain anywhere from one to nearly all the words that might as well have been in Chinese. When I skipped those words, of course, I really ended up with little idea of what the book said. . . .

3 I saw that the best thing I could do was get hold of a dictionary— to study, to learn some words. I requested a dictionary along with some tablets and pencils from the Norfolk Prison Colony school.

4 I spent two days just riffling uncertainly through the dictionary's pages. I'd never realized so many words existed! I didn't know which

words I needed to learn. Finally, just to start some kind of action, I began copying.

5   In my slow, painstaking°, ragged° handwriting, I copied into my tablet everything printed on that first page, down to the punctuation marks. I believe it took me a day. Then, aloud, I read back to myself everything I'd written on the tablet. Over and over, aloud, to myself, I read my own handwriting.

6   I woke up the next morning, thinking about those words— immensely proud to realize that not only had I written so much at one time, but I'd written words that I never knew were in the world. Moreover, with a little effort, I also could remember what many of these words meant. I reviewed the words whose meanings I didn't remember. Funny thing, from the dictionary's first page right now, that *aardvark* springs to my mind. The dictionary had a picture of it, a long-tailed, long-eared, burrowing° African mammal, which lives off termites caught by sticking out its tongue as an anteater does for ants.

7   I was so fascinated that I went on—I copied the dictionary's next page. And the same experience came when I studied that. With every succeeding° page, I also learned of people and places and events from history. Actually, the dictionary is like a miniature encyclopedia. Finally, the dictionary's A section had filled a whole tablet—and I went on into

Malcolm X in 1964

the B's. That was the way I started copying what eventually became the entire dictionary. It went a lot faster after so much practice helped me to pick up handwriting speed.

8   I suppose it was inevitable that as my word-base° broadened, I could for the first time pick up a book and read and now begin to understand what the book was saying. Anyone who has read a great deal can imagine the new world that opened. Let me tell you something: From then until I left the prison, in every free moment I had, if I was not reading in the library, I was reading on my bunk°. You couldn't have gotten me out of books with a wedge. Months passed without my even thinking about being imprisoned. In fact, up to then, I never had been so truly free in my life.

Dictionary Questions

Answer the dictionary questions that follow about words in this selection. Use your dictionary when needed.

_____ 1. *Stumble* (in "I happened to stumble upon starting to acquire some kind of a homemade education") would be found on the dictionary page with which guidewords?
A. **strongbox / study**
B. **success / sufficient**
C. **student / style**
D. **stock / store**

_____ 2. Below are dictionary definitions of *stumble*. Choose the meaning that best fits *stumble* in "I happened to stumble upon starting to acquire some kind of a homemade education."
A. To strike the foot against something
B. To walk unsteadily
C. To discover accidentally

_____ 3. Below are dictionary definitions of *acquire*. Choose the meaning that best fits *acquire* in "I happened to stumble upon starting to acquire some kind of a homemade education."
A. To buy (an object)
B. To learn or develop (a skill, habit, or quality)
C. To achieve (a reputation)

_____ 4. Below are dictionary definitions of *convey*. Choose the meaning that best fits *convey* in "I became increasingly frustrated at not being able to express what I wanted to convey in letters that I wrote. . . ."
A. To carry, bring, or take from one place to another
B. To communicate
C. To lead or conduct

5. Malcolm says, "I suppose it was inevitable that as my word-base broadened, I could for the first time pick up a book and read and now begin to understand what the book was saying."

Use your dictionary to find the definition of *inevitable* and write the meaning here: _____

_____

6. How many syllables are in *inevitable*, and which syllable is accented?

_____   _____

7. What part of speech is *inevitable*? _____

8. *Aardvark* was a word on the first page of Malcolm X's dictionary. Select a word on the first page of your dictionary. The word should have two or more syllables.

Write the word and its definition(s) here: _____

_____

9. Use your dictionary to write out the word again, this time putting dots between the syllables in the word.

_____

10. Finally, write out the pronunciation of the word (which often appears in parentheses), showing pronunciation symbols and including the accent mark or marks.

_____

Questions about the Reading

For each question, write the letter of your answer in the space provided.

_____ 1. In the excerpt below, the word *riffling* (rĭf′lĭng) probably means
   A. flipping.
   B. writing.
   C. destroying.
   D. laughing.

   "I spent two days just riffling uncertainly through the dictionary's pages." (Paragraph 4)

_____ 2. In the sentence below, the word *wedge* (wĕj) probably means
   A. page.
   B. magazine.
   C. tool used to separate objects.
   D. tool used to press objects together.

   "You couldn't have gotten me out of books with a wedge." (Paragraph 8)

_____ 3. Which sentence best expresses the main idea of the entire selection?
   A. Increasing his vocabulary opened Malcolm's mind in exciting ways.
   B. When he arrived in prison, Malcolm's vocabulary was poor.
   C. Reading the dictionary is the best way to learn new vocabulary words.
   D. Malcolm used his time in prison constructively.

_____ 4. What seems to be the main idea of paragraph 2?
   A. While in prison, Malcolm liked to write letters.
   B. A lot of the words Malcolm saw in books might as well have been written in Chinese.
   C. When Malcolm came to a word he didn't understand, he skipped it.
   D. Malcolm's poor vocabulary began to frustrate him as he tried to read and write.

_____ 5. Malcolm requested a dictionary so that
   A. he could improve his spelling.
   B. he could learn what an aardvark was.
   C. he could have something to read.
   D. he could learn new words.

_____ 6. Malcolm's work with the dictionary went faster after he
   A. learned to write more quickly.
   B. got an assistant to help him.
   C. got a typewriter.
   D. learned shorthand.

_____ 7. How much of the dictionary did Malcolm eventually copy?
   A. The A's
   B. The A's and B's
   C. A through P
   D. All of it

_____ 8. Malcolm compared the dictionary to
   A. the Bible.
   B. a miniature encyclopedia.
   C. a novel.
   D. a magazine.

_____ 9. Malcolm probably
    A. was very intelligent, but did not have a lot of education.
    B. was a college graduate.
    C. wanted to become a professional writer.
    D. stopped reading much after he was released from prison.

_____ 10. The selection suggests that
    A. becoming a reader transformed Malcolm's life.
    B. Malcolm was innocent of the crime that had sent him to prison.
    C. Malcolm expected other prisoners to follow his example.
    D. Malcolm hoped to shorten his prison sentence by studying.

Discussion Questions

1. What is your impression of Malcolm X? After reading this short selection, what kind of person do you think he was?

2. At the end of the selection, Malcolm X says that even though he was still in jail, he "never had been so truly free" in his life. What does he mean by that? What is it that makes you feel free?

3. Malcolm X decided to improve his vocabulary in order to express himself better in letters. What was it that made you decide to continue your education? What do you hope to do with the knowledge you are gaining?

Note: Writing assignments for this selection appear on pages 505–506.

Check Your Performance   **DICTIONARY USE**

Activity	Number Right	Points	Score
Review Test 1 (4 items)	_____	× 5 =	_____
Review Test 2 (10 items)	_____	× 2 =	_____
Review Test 3 (20 items)	_____	× 3 =	_____
		TOTAL SCORE =	_____%

Enter your total score into the **Reading Performance Chart: Review Tests** on the inside back cover.

DICTIONARY USE: Mastery Test 1

A. Below are two pairs of dictionary guidewords followed by a series of other words. On the answer line, write the letter of the **one** word in each series which would be found on the page with the guidewords.

_____ 1. **coverage / crab**

      A. court   B. coward   C. cracked

_____ 2. **gate / gear**

      A. general   B. gasoline   C. gather

B. Use your dictionary and the spelling hints on page 43 to find the correct spelling of the following words.

3. bycicle _____

4. takeing _____

5. hury _____

6. beleive _____

C. Use your dictionary to put dots between the syllables in each word. Then write out the word with the correct pronunciation symbols, including the accent marks.

7. c i r c u m s t a n c e _____

8. i n s i g n i f i c a n t _____

(Continues on next page)

D. Use the following pronunciation key to answer the questions below.

Pronunciation Key

ă hat	ā pay	âr care	ä card	ĕ ten	ē she	ĭ sit
ī hi	îr here	ŏ lot	ō go	ô all	oi oil	ou out
ŏŏ look	yŏŏ cure	ōō cool	yōō use	ŭ up	ûr fur	th thick
th then	ə ago, item, easily, gallop, circus					

9. In *dignity* (dĭg′nĭ-tē), the *y* is pronounced like the *e* in what common word?

    _____

10. In *dignity* (dĭg′nĭ-tē), the *i*'s are pronounced like the *i* in what common word? _____

DICTIONARY USE: Mastery Test 2

A. Below are two pairs of dictionary guidewords followed by a series of other words. On the answer line, write the letter of the **one** word in each series which would be found on the page with the guidewords.

_____ 1. **prize / process**

      A. private   B. problem   C. professor

_____ 2. **snowy / soccer**

      A. soak   B. social   C. snob

B. Use your dictionary and the spelling hints on page 43 to find the correct spelling of the following words.

    3. lable _____

    4. froun _____

    5. acshun _____

    6. ordurly _____

C. Use your dictionary to put dots between the syllables in each word. Then write out the word with the correct pronunciation symbols, including the accent marks.

    7. e n e r g e t i c _____

    8. d e m o n s t r a t i o n _____

(Continues on next page)

D. Use the following pronunciation key to answer the questions below.

Pronunciation Key

ă hat	ā pay	âr care	ä card	ĕ ten	ē she	ĭ sit
ī hi	îr here	ŏ lot	ō go	ô all	oi oil	ou out
ŏŏ look	yŏŏ cure	ōō cool	yōō use	ŭ up	ûr fur	th thick
th then	ə ago, item, easily, gallop, circus					

9. In *firetrap* (fīr′trăp), the *i* is pronounced like the *i* in what common word?

   _____

10. In *firetrap* (fīr′trăp), the *a* is pronounced like the *a* in what common word?

    _____

DICTIONARY USE: Mastery Test 3

A. Below are two pairs of dictionary guidewords followed by a series of other words. On the answer line, write the letter of the **one** word in each series which would be found on the page with the guidewords.

_____ 1. **flavor / flexible**

     A. flesh   B. flatter   C. float

_____ 2. **jeweler / job**

     A. jingle   B. jealous   C. join

B. Use your dictionary and the spelling hints on page 43 to find the correct spelling of the following words.

    3. dicide _____

    4. komplete _____

C. Use your dictionary to put dots between the syllables in each word. Then write out the word with the correct pronunciation symbols, including the accent marks.

    5. f u n d a m e n t a l _____

    6. a p p r o x i m a t e _____

(Continues on next page)

D. Use the following pronunciation key to answer the questions below.

Pronunciation Key

ă hat	ā pay	âr care	ä card	ĕ ten	ē she	ĭ sit
ī hi	îr here	ŏ lot	ō go	ô all	oi oil	ou out
ŏŏ look	yŏŏ cure	ōō cool	yōō use	ŭ up	ûr fur	th thick
th then	ə ago, item, easily, gallop, circus					

7. In *shallow* (shăl′ō), the *a* is pronounced like the *a* in what common word?

    _____

8. In *shallow* (shăl′ō), the *o* is pronounced like the *o* in what common word?

    _____

9. In *precise* (prĭ-sīs′), the first *e* is pronounced like the *i* in what common word?

    _____

10. In *precise* (prĭ-sīs′), the *i* is pronounced like the *i* in what common word?

    _____

DICTIONARY USE: Mastery Test 4

Answer the following questions about the dictionary entries for *verdict* and *maintain*. Use the pronunciation key below for help as needed.

Pronunciation Key

ă hat	ā pay	âr care	ä card	ĕ ten	ē she	ĭ sit
ī hi	îr here	ŏ lot	ō go	ô all	oi oil	ou out
ŏŏ look	yŏŏ cure	ōō cool	yōō use	ŭ up	ûr fur	th thick
th then	ə ago, item, easily, gallop, circus					

ver•dict (vûr′dĭkt) *n.* **1.** The finding of a jury in a trial. **2.** A judgment, opinion, or conclusion that is expressed about something.

_____ 1. Which syllable in *verdict* is accented?
   A. The first   B. The second

_____ 2. The *e* in *verdict* is pronounced like the
   A. *e* in *ten*.   B. *u* in *fur*.

_____ 3. What part of speech is *verdict*?
   A. Noun   B. Verb   C. Adjective

_____ 4. Which definition of *verdict* best fits the sentence below—1 or 2?

   Tim's verdict on the new video game was that it was well worth the money.

_____ 5. Which definition of *verdict* best fits the sentence below—1 or 2?

   When the guilty verdict was announced, the defendant began to sob.

(Continues on next page)

main•tain (mān-tān') *v.* **1.** To carry on; continue. **2.** To keep in good repair. **3.** To provide for; support. **4.** To defend against criticism. **5.** To declare to be true. —**main•tain'a•ble** *adj.* —**main'te•nance** *n.*

_____ 6. Both *a*'s in *maintain* sound like the
   A. *a* in *hat*.   B. *a* in *pay*.

_____ 7. How many syllables are in the word *maintainable*?

_____ 8. What part of speech is *maintenance*?
   A. Noun   B. Verb   C. Adjective

_____ 9. Which definition of *maintain* best fits the sentence below—1, 2, 3, 4, or 5?

   It can be costly to properly maintain a house.

_____10. Which definition of *maintain* best fits the sentence below—1, 2, 3, 4, or 5?

   My grandmother maintains that Ronald Reagan was one of our greatest presidents.

DICTIONARY USE: Mastery Test 5

Answer the following questions about the dictionary entries for *linger* and *solitary*. Use the pronunciation key below for help as needed.

Pronunciation Key

ă hat	ā pay	âr care	ä card	ĕ ten	ē she	ĭ sit
ī hi	îr here	ŏ lot	ō go	ô all	oi oil	ou out
ŏŏ look	yŏŏ cure	ōō cool	yōō use	ŭ up	ûr fur	th thick
th then	ə ago, item, easily, gallop, circus					

ling•er (lĭng′gər) *v.* **1.** To put off leaving a place because you are reluctant to go. **2.** To remain alive, although very weak, while gradually dying. **3.** To take longer than usual to do something, usually because you are enjoying yourself. **4.** To persist: *an aftertaste that lingers.* —**lin′ger•er** *n.* —**lin′ger•ing•ly** *adv.*

_____ 1. Which syllable in *linger* is accented?
    A. The first   B. The second

_____ 2. The *i* in *linger* is pronounced like the *i* in
    A. *hi.*   B. *sit.*

_____ 3. What part of speech is *lingerer*?
    A. Noun   B. Verb   C. Adjective

_____ 4. Which definition of *linger* best fits the sentence below—1, 2, 3, or 4?
    Joan liked to linger in the garden when the roses were in bloom.

_____ 5. Which definition of *linger* best fits the sentence below—1, 2, 3, or 4?
    It was sad to watch Phil's grandfather linger in the hospital while slowly dying of lung cancer.

(Continues on next page)

sol•i•tar•y (sŏl′ĭ-tĕr′ē) *adj.* **1.** Done without the company of other people. **2.** Preferring to be or live alone. **3.** In a remote location; secluded. **4.** Existing as the only one of its kind. — **sol′i•tar′i •ness** *n.*

_____ 6. The *o* in *solitary* sounds like the
    A. *o* in *go*.   B. *o* in *lot*.

_____ 7. How many syllables are in the word *solitary*?

_____ 8. What part of speech is *solitariness*?
    A. Noun   B. Verb   C. Adjective

_____ 9. Which definition of *solitary* best fits the sentence below — 1, 2, 3, or 4?

    Deep in the woods, we came upon a solitary cabin.

_____10. Which definition of *solitary* best fits the sentence below — 1, 2, 3, or 4?

    Surfing the Internet is usually a solitary pastime.

DICTIONARY USE: Mastery Test 6

A. Answer the following questions about the dictionary entries for *assert* and *interfere*. Use the pronunciation key below for help as needed.

Pronunciation Key

ă hat	ā pay	âr care	ä card	ĕ ten	ē she	ĭ sit
ī hi	îr here	ŏ lot	ō go	ô all	oi oil	ou out
ŏŏ look	yŏŏ cure	ōō cool	yōō use	ŭ up	ûr fur	th thick
th then	ə ago, item, easily, gallop, circus					

as•sert (ə-sûrt′) *v.* **1.** To state something as being true. **2.** To keep or defend. **3.** To put (oneself) forward boldly or forcefully. —**as•ser′tive** *adj.* —**as•ser′tive•ly** *adv.* —**as•ser′tive•ness** *n.*

_____ 1. Which syllable in *assert* is accented?
    A. The first   B. The second

_____ 2. The *e* in *assert* is pronounced like the
    A. *u* in *up*.   B. *u* in *fur*.

_____ 3. What part of speech is *assertive*?
    A. Noun   B. Verb   C. Adjective

_____ 4. Which definition of *assert* best fits the sentence below—1, 2, or 3?

When the bully pushed ahead of me in line, I asserted myself by pushing him back.

_____ 5. Which definition of *assert* best fits the sentence below—1, 2, or 3?

My English teacher likes to assert that everyone should read Shakespeare.

(Continues on next page)

B. in•ter•fere (ĭn′tər-fîr′) *v.* **in•ter•fered, in•ter•fer•ing 1.** To delay, hinder, or obstruct the natural or desired course of something. **2.** To intrude in the affairs of others; meddle. **3.** To cause electronic interference. **4.** To obstruct, block, or hinder illegally an opponent in sport. —**inter•fer′ence** *n.* —**inter•fer′er** *n.*

_____ 6. The *i* in *interfere* sounds like the *i* in

      A. *hi.*   B. *sit.*

_____ 7. How many syllables are in the word *interfered*?

_____ 8. What part of speech is *interference*?

      A. Noun   B. Verb   C. Adjective

_____ 9. Which definition of *interfere* best fits the sentence below—1, 2, 3, or 4?

      Carol didn't like it when her best friend tried to interfere with her relationship with Kevin.

_____ 10. Which definition of *interfere* best fits the sentence below—1, 2, 3, or 4?

      An accident at rush hour interfered with the flow of traffic along the expressway.

C. Use your dictionary to find the correct spelling of the following words. (Feel free to use the spelling hints on page 43.)

    11. instructer _____

    12. practis _____

    13. recieve_____

    14. impresion _____

    15. eazy_____

D. Use your dictionary to put dots between the syllables in each word. Then write out the word with the correct pronunciation symbols, including the accent marks.

    16. a b r u p t _____

    17. f a t i g u e _____

    18. e x t r a v a g a n t_____

    19. e s s e n t i a l _____

    20. m i s i n t e r p r e t _____

3 Vocabulary in Context

This Chapter in a Nutshell

- You don't always have to use a dictionary to learn the meanings of new words in your reading. You can often use context clues to figure out the meaning of a word.
- There are four kinds of context clues:
  - Examples of the new word
  - Synonyms (words that mean the same as the new word)
  - Antonyms (words that mean the opposite of the new word)
  - The rest of the sentence or the passage

Do you know the meaning of the word *jeopardize*? Look at the following cartoon and see if the context helps you choose the correct answer.

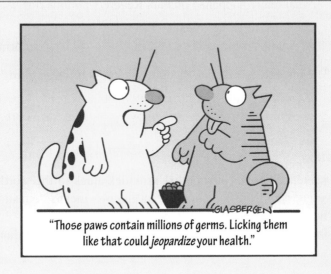

"Those paws contain millions of germs. Licking them like that could *jeopardize* your health."

_____ *Jeopardize* (jĕp′ər-dīz) means
A. to play with.
B. to take into account.
C. to put in danger.

The **context**—the words surrounding the unfamiliar word—tells us that *jeopardize* means "to put in danger." In this chapter, you will learn how to use context to figure out the meanings of words.

Understanding Vocabulary in Context

Do you know the meaning of the word *queries*? How about the word *tedious*? Or the word *transmit*?

You may be having trouble coming up with the meanings of these words. However, you will be more likely to know what they mean when you see them in complete sentences. Read each sentence below and see if you can understand the meaning of the word in *italics*. In the space provided, write the letter of the meaning you think is correct. Then read the explanation.

_____ 1. Julia was nervous about answering the detective's *queries*. Why was he asking so many questions, anyway?

   Queries (kwîr′ēz) are
   A. charges.   B. questions.   C. statements of fact.

_____ 2. Most of my history teacher's lectures were *tedious*, but the one about what really happened on Paul Revere's famous ride was very interesting.

   Tedious (tē′dē-əs) means
   A. interesting.   B. long.   C. boring.

_____ 3. Mosquitoes *transmit* sleeping sickness through biting.

   Transmit (trăns-mĭt′) means
   A. spread.   B. enjoy.   C. cure.

Explanation

In each sentence above, the context provides clues to the word's meaning. You may have guessed from the context that *queries* means "questions," that *tedious* means "boring," and that *transmit* means to "spread."

Using context clues to understand the meaning of unfamiliar words will help you in two ways:

1 It will save you time when reading. You will not have to stop to look up words in the dictionary. (Of course, you won't *always* be able to understand a word from its context, so you should have a dictionary nearby as you read.)

2 It will improve your "working vocabulary"—words you recognize as you read and will eventually be able to use when you speak and write.

Types of Context Clues

Here are four common types of context clues:

1 Examples
2 Synonyms
3 Antonyms
4 General Sense of the Sentence or Passage

In the following sections, you will read about and practice each type of clue. The practices will sharpen your skills in recognizing and using context clues and help you add new words to your vocabulary.

Remember *not* to use a dictionary for these practices. Their purpose is to help you develop the skill of figuring out what words mean *without* using a dictionary. Pronunciations are provided in parentheses for the words, and a guide to pronunciation is on pages 501–502.

1   Examples

An unfamiliar word may appear with examples that reveal what the word means. Look at the cartoon below and see if the example helps you choose the correct meaning of the word *commitment:*

"You have a 30-year mortgage, a 5-year car lease, and a lifetime gym membership . . . but you're afraid of *commitment?*"

_____ *Commitment* (kə-mĭt′mənt) means

A. a promise to do something.   C. an opinion about something.
B. an opportunity for something.

The three examples of commitment—a 30-year mortgage, a 5-year car lease, and a lifetime gym membership—help you understand that *commitment* means "a promise to do something."

Check Your Understanding

Now read the items that follow. An *italicized* word in each sentence is followed by examples that serve as context clues for that word. These examples, which are **boldfaced**, will help you figure out the meaning of each word. On each line, write the letter of the answer you think is correct.

Note that examples are often introduced with signal words and phrases like *for example, for instance, including,* and *such as.*

_____ 1. *Assets* (ăs′ĕts′) such as **good health**, **a loving family**, and **an enjoyable job** make life rewarding.

   Assets are

   A. things of value.   B. rewards on the job.   C. helpful people.

   Hint: Remember that in the exercises in this chapter, you can insert into each sentence the word you think is the answer. For example, substitute *things of value, rewards on the job,* or *helpful people* into sentence 1 in place of *assets* to see which one fits.

_____ 2. A coyote's *prey* (prā) includes **squirrels, rabbits,** and **mice.**

   Prey means

   A. friends.   B. victims.   C. replacement.

_____ 3. The sports car had *defects* (dē′fĕkts′)—for example, **a dented fender** and **torn seats**—but I didn't care. I had wanted a Corvette for years, and I was going to buy it.

   Defects are

   A. faults.   B. out-of-date features.   C. foreign qualities.

Explanation

1. The correct answer is A. The examples given—good health, a loving family, and a job you enjoy—show that assets are "things of value."

2. The correct answer is B. The examples—squirrels, rabbits, and mice—reveal that prey are "victims."

3. The correct answer is A. The examples—a dented fender and torn seats—show that defects are "faults."

PRACTICE 1: Examples

Read each item below and then do two things:

1. Underline the examples that suggest the meaning of the word in *italics*.
2. Then write the letter of the word's meaning on the answer line.

_____ 1. We often communicate what we mean by using *gestures* such as the thumbs-up sign, hands on the hips, and a shrug of the shoulders.

Gestures (jĕs′chərs) are
A. motions of the body.   B. good feelings.   C. hand signals.

_____ 2. Newspaper reporters have been fired for *fictitious* reporting that included quotations which were never said and events that never occurred.

Fictitious (fĭk-tĭsh′əs) means
A. true-life.   B. unknown.   C. not real.

_____ 3. *Obnoxious* behavior in a movie theater—for instance, burping, loud talking, or playing around—is considered childish by most people.

Obnoxious (ŏb-nŏk′shəs) means
A. very unpleasant.   B. acceptable.   C. funny.

_____ 4. For better health and a longer life, doctors recommend *wholesome* activities, including exercising daily and eating nutritious foods.

Wholesome (hōl′səm) means
A. boring.   B. skillful.   C. healthy.

_____ 5. Examples of *distractions* that always seem to occur during an important test include coughing, sighing, and scraping of chairs.

Distractions (dĭ-străkt′shənz) are things that
A. are friendly.   B. take away   C. increase your
                        your attention.   ability to perform.

2 Synonyms

Context clues are often found in the form of **synonyms**: one or more words that mean the same or almost the same as the unknown word. Look again at the sentence on page 76: "Julia was nervous about answering the detective's *queries*. Why was he asking so many questions, anyway?" Here the synonym *questions* tells you the meaning of *queries*.

Now look at the cartoon about a boy talking to his mother.

Notice that the synonym for *humiliate*—expressed in the words of the young man who says "I feel worthless enough already"—helps you understand that *humiliate* (hyōo′mĭl′ē-āt′) means "to make (someone) feel ashamed."

 ## Check Your Understanding

Each item below contains a word or phrase that is a synonym of the *italicized* word. Underline the synonym in each sentence. Then read the explanation that follows.

1. Hal was a *mediocre* (mē′dē-ō′kər) student. He was an average baseball player, as well.

2. It is hard to believe that my millionaire cousin was once *indigent* (ĭn′dĭ-jənt), so poor that he walked the streets without knowing where his next meal would come from.

3. Most companies have a *regulation* (rĕg′yə-lā′shən) allowing new mothers to take three months off from work. Some firms also have a rule allowing fathers the same time off.

Explanation

In each sentence, the synonym probably helped you understand the meaning of the word in italics:

1. Someone who is *mediocre* at something is "average."
2. Someone who is *indigent* is "poor."
3. A *regulation* is a "rule."

PRACTICE 2: Synonyms

Each item below includes a synonym of the *italicized* word. Write each synonym in the space provided.

_____ 1. Some people hate to admit an error. My boss, for instance, will never *concede* (kən-sēd′) that he might be wrong.

_____ 2. You may be *reluctant* (rĭ-lŭk′tənt) to give a speech now, but the more speaking practice you get, the less unwilling you will be.

_____ 3. The *absurd* (əb-sûrd′) idea that people from outer space live among us is as ridiculous as the belief that the Earth is flat.

_____ 4. Students are often *apprehensive* (ăp′rĭ-hĕn′sĭv) of final exams, but with the right study skills, they don't have to be fearful.

_____ 5. The belief that you can drink and then drive safely is a *fallacy* (făl′ə-sē); unfortunately, this false idea is held by many people.

3 Antonyms

Antonyms—words and phrases that mean the opposite of a word—are also useful as context clues. For example, *soft* is the opposite of *hard*, and *worried* is the opposite of *relieved*. Antonyms are often signaled by words such as *unlike, but, however, instead of, in contrast,* or *on the other hand.*

Look again at the sentence on page 76: "Most of my history teacher's lectures were *tedious*, but the one about what really happened on Paul Revere's famous ride was very interesting." Here the word *but* helps suggest that *tedious* must be the opposite of *interesting*.

Look also at the cartoon below about a married couple doing household chores.

—GLASBERGEN

"Before the kids, we had nothing to do.
Now we're *overwhelmed*."

Notice that the antonym "nothing to do" helps you figure out that *overwhelmed* (ō′vər-hwĕlmd′) must mean "having too much to do."

✓ Check Your Understanding

In each of the following sentences, underline the word or phrase that means the opposite of the *italicized* word. Then, on the answer line, write the letter of the meaning of the italicized word. Finally, read the explanation that follows.

_____ 1. The *adverse* weather conditions forced us to stay inside for most of our vacation. The day the weather finally turned nice, we had to leave.

Adverse (ăd-vûrs′) means

A. nice.   B. bad.   C. summer.

_____ 2. I thought it was difficult to *ascend* the mountain, but I discovered that climbing down it was even worse.

Ascend (ə-sĕnd′) means

A. climb up.   B. walk around.   C. climb down.

_____ 3. After years of *defying* my parents, I decided life might be better if I tried agreeing with them once in a while.

Defying (dĭ-fī′yĭng) means

A. avoiding.   B. obeying.   C. opposing.

Explanation

1. The correct answer is B. *Adverse* weather conditions are the opposite of "nice" ones—they are bad.

2. The correct answer is A. To *ascend* is the opposite of "climbing down"—when you ascend, you climb up.

3. The right answer is C. *Defying* one's parents is the opposite of "agreeing with them." When you defy people, you oppose what they say.

PRACTICE 3: Antonyms

Each item below includes a word or phrase that is an antonym of the *italicized* word. Underline each of these antonyms. Then, on the line, write the letter of the meaning of the italicized word.

_____ 1. Your science project is much more *elaborate* than mine. In fact, mine looks very simple compared with yours.

Hint: What would be the opposite of *elaborate*?

Elaborate (ĭ-lăb′ər-ĭt) means
  A. plain.   B. large.   C. complicated.

_____ 2. Gordon's family worried that he would remain an *obscure* author all his life. However, he believed that someday he would be famous.

Obscure (ŏb-skyŏor′) means
  A. unknown.   B. well-known.   C. good.

_____ 3. The attorney introduced facts she felt were *relevant* to the case. But the judge said the facts were unrelated to the trial.

Relevant (rĕl′ə-vənt) means
  A. legal.   B. related.   C. known.

_____ 4. When providing directions, give the steps *in sequence*. If they are out of order, anyone trying to follow the directions will become confused.

In sequence (sē′kwəns) means
  A. all at once.   B. in order.   C. in a confusing way.

_____ 5. The teacher *commended* two students on the outstanding work they were doing. Then he criticized the rest of the class for doing so poorly.

Commended (kə-mĕnd′ed) means
  A. blamed.   B. graded.   C. praised.

4   General Sense of the Sentence or Passage

Often, the context of a new word contains no examples, synonyms, or antonyms. In such cases, you must do a bit of detective work and try to make a guess based on any clues provided.

Look at the cartoon below about a job interview.

"Allen is an incredible, wonderful, fun, generous, exciting, kind, loving, brilliant, very special human being. This personal reference from your mother is quite *impressive*."

The glowing reference (from the job applicant's mother!) helps you realize that *impressive* (ĭm-prĕs′ĭv) means "very favorable."

Check Your Understanding

In each sentence below, look for general clues to the meaning of the word in *italics*. Then write the letter of the answer you feel is the meaning of the italicized word.

_____ 1. Elena thought she had *ample* time to review her notes before the afternoon exam. Then she discovered her watch was incorrect—she was actually late for the test!

   Ample (ăm′pəl) means

   A. no.   B. plenty of.   C. little.

_____ 2. At the animal shelter, Rita fell in love with a poodle, but Dan couldn't resist a collie. So they felt that there was no *alternative* but to keep both animals.

   An *alternative* (âl-tûr′nə-tĭv) is a

   A. choice.   B. reason.   C. mystery.

_____ 3. As a *consequence* of his bad report card, my brother could not watch TV until his grades improved.

A *consequence* (kŏn′sĭ-kwĕns) is a

A. right.   B. result.   C. chance.

Explanation

1. The correct answer is B. *Ample* means "plenty of." Elena mistakenly thought she had plenty of time to prepare for the exam.

2. The right answer is A. An alternative is a "choice." Rita and Dan felt they had no choice but to take both dogs home.

3. The correct answer is B. A consequence is a "result." The result of the brother's bad report card was not being able to watch TV until his teachers reported that he had improved.

PRACTICE 4: General Sense of the Passage

Figure out the meaning of the word in *italics* by looking for general clues. Then, on the line, write the letter of the meaning you think is correct.

_____ 1. My brother felt it would be *futile* to try to make the basketball team. The other players were all at least eight inches taller than he was.

Futile (fyo͞ot′l) means

A. easy.   B. useless.   C. expensive.

_____ 2. The *impact* of the crash was so great that you couldn't tell the make of either car. Both were totally destroyed.

Impact (ĭm′păkt) means

A. force.   B. time.   C. place.

_____ 3. The young eagle was clearly a *novice* at flying. As he tried to land, he got himself caught in a thornbush.

A *novice* (nŏv′ĭs) is a

A. bird.   B. success.   C. beginner.

_____ 4. At a party given by a company for its clients, employees are expected to *mingle with* the guests to make the guests feel more comfortable.

Mingle (mĭng′gəl) *with* means

A. bother.   B. mix with.   C. sell things to.

_____ 5. Big band music was popular during the 1940s. It then disappeared from the music scene, but has been *revived* in recent years.

Revived (rĭ-vīvd′) means

A. lost.   B. brought back to life.   c. destroyed.

An Important Point about Textbook Definitions

You don't always have to use context clues or the dictionary to find definitions. Very often, textbook authors provide definitions of important terms. They usually follow a definition with one or more examples to make sure that you understand the word being defined.

Here is a short textbook passage that includes a definition and an example. Note that the term to be defined is set off in **boldface** type, and the definition then follows.

> [1]**Phobias** are fears that are out of proportion to the actual danger in a situation. [2]Some people, for example, have a fear of riding in elevators. [3]But there is almost no chance that a cable could break and that the elevator would suddenly plunge to the ground. [4]Other people may have a phobia about spiders, dogs, driving over a bridge, or being trapped in a confined space. [5]In all such cases, there is an unreasonable desire to avoid the feared activity or object.

Textbook authors, then, often do more than provide context clues: they set off their definitions in *italic* or **boldface** type, as above. When they take the time to define and give examples of a term, you should assume that the material is important enough to learn.

More about textbook definitions and examples appears on pages 241–242 in the "Signal Words II" chapter.

CHAPTER REVIEW

In this chapter, you learned the following:

- To save time when reading, you should try to figure out the meanings of unfamiliar words. You can do so by looking at their *context*—the words surrounding them.

- There are four kinds of context clues: **examples** (marked by words like *for example, for instance, including,* and *such as*); **synonyms** (words that mean the same as unknown words); **antonyms** (words that mean the opposite of unknown words); and **general sense of the sentence** (clues in the sentence or surrounding sentences about what words might mean).

- Textbook authors typically set off important words in *italic* or **boldface** type and define those words for you, often providing examples as well.

The next chapter—Chapter 4—will introduce you to the most important of all comprehension skills: finding the main idea.

 On the Web: If you are using this book in class, you can visit our website for additional practice in understanding vocabulary in context. Go to **www.townsendpress.com** and click on "Learning Center."

REVIEW TEST 1

To review what you've learned in this chapter, answer the following questions by writing the letter of each correct answer.

_____ 1. The context of a word is
   A. its meaning.
   B. its opposite.
   C. the words around it.

_____ 2. Which type of context clue often follows signal words like *including, such as,* and *for instance*?
   A. Example
   B. Synonym
   C. Antonym

_____ 3. In the sentence below, which type of context clue is provided for the italicized word?
   A. Example
   B. Synonym
   C. Antonym

   Students often prefer a *lenient* teacher to a strict one, but they may learn more from the strict teacher.

_____ 4. Often, when textbook authors introduce a new word, they provide a definition and help make the meaning of the word clear by including one or more
   A. examples.
   B. synonyms.
   C. antonyms.

REVIEW TEST 2

A. Look at the cartoon below and then answer the question that follows.

"Why do I struggle so much and you *cope* so well?"

_____ 1. Using the context clues in the cartoon, write the letter of the best
meaning of *cope* (kōp) in the space provided.
A. deal effectively   B. fail to relate   C. try harder

B. Using context clues for help, write the letter of the best meaning for each italicized
word.

_____ 2. Judges are supposed to be *impartial*, but the judge in the trial didn't
seem fair to me.

Impartial (ĭm-pär′shəl) means
A. not listening.   B. not honest.   C. not favoring one
side or the other.

_____ 3. After standing empty for fifteen years, the old mansion had
deteriorated. The wood was decaying, the plaster was peeling, and
most of the windows had been broken.

Deteriorate (dĭ-tîr′ē-ə-rāt′) means to
A. become older.   B. become worse.   C. become empty.

_____ 4. Successful students have learned that if they *adhere* to a schedule, they
accomplish more. When they don't stick to a set routine, they get less
done.

Adhere (ăd-hîr′) to means
A. faithfully follow.   B. avoid.   C. buy.

_____ 5. At an accident scene, police must determine whose version of the accident *distorts* the events and whose tells it just as it happened.

Distorts (dĭ-stôrts′) means
A. explains.   B. describes falsely.   C. forgets.

_____ 6. If you are pushed and have your books knocked to the floor, you may find it hard to *refrain* from yelling at the person who caused the accident.

Refrain (rĭ-frān′) means
A. continue.   B. hold back.   C. take.

_____ 7. Olga always comes up with quick *retorts* to people's comments, but I can never think of a clever answer until it's too late.

A *retort* (rĭ-tôrt′) is a
A. clever reply.   B. dumb remark.   C. kind response.

_____ 8. Experts say exercise makes the appetite *diminish*. So wanting to lose weight provides another good reason to exercise.

Diminish (dĭ-mĭn′ĭsh) means
A. grow larger.   B. get smarter.   C. get smaller.

_____ 9. Antonio made a *pretense* of writing the answers to the essay test, but he was just scribbling. He hadn't studied for the test at all.

Pretense (prē′tĕns′) means
A. intelligent attempt.   B. false show.   C. slow effort.

_____10. Twins separated early in life often lead *parallel* lives. For instance, many study the same subjects, get similar jobs, and marry the same kind of person.

Parallel (păr′ə-lĕl′) means
A. vastly different.   B. matching.   C. boring.

REVIEW TEST 3

Here is a chance to apply the skill of understanding vocabulary in context to a full-length reading. If you have ever been cheated by someone, you will probably understand the feelings that motivated the author to write her essay. After reading it, answer the vocabulary and reading questions that follow.

Words to Watch

Below are some words in the reading that do not have strong context support. Each word is followed by the number of the paragraph in which it appears and its meaning there. These words are indicated in the selection by a small circle (°).

acute (1): severe, extreme
skeptical (9): doubting
scurried (12): rushed
deceit (21): dishonesty
cynical (24): believing that people are motivated only by selfishness

ONE LESS SUCKER LIVES

Jeanne R. Smith

1   The thing that struck me most about him was his acute° discomfort.

2   He approached the door of the newspaper office timidly, opened it, and stood on the threshold as if uncertain about the kinds of creatures he would face inside.

3   He wore regular work clothes. There was nothing extraordinarily distinguishing about him. He just looked nervous and uncomfortable.

4   He'd never done anything like this in his life, he told me as he timidly neared my desk.

5   He didn't even know how to go about it . . . but if I would just bear with him, maybe he could get his story out.

6   He was just so embarrassed.

7   He was a driver for the Arnold

Baking Company, he said. His truck had broken down up the highway, filled with his day's delivery of breadstuffs. He'd gladly give our office staff a few loaves of our favorite bread if only someone could lend him eight dollars to catch a bus back to his company to get a substitute truck.

8   Oh, this was just so embarrassing.

9   Seeing what might have been a slightly skeptical° look on my face, he produced a wad of credit and identification cards. One in particular, an Arnold ID card, had his picture on it. He was who he said he was. And he really did need help.

10   He just sat there looking woebegone while I pondered whether or not to help my fellow man in distress. He seemed overjoyed when I pulled

out my wallet, searched for eight bucks, and handed the money to him.

11   He was so grateful. After all, this had been so embarrassing.

12   He scurried° out the door, promising English muffins as a thank-you when he returned before our office closed at five.

13   I never saw him again.

14   In fact, when I called the Arnold Baking Company the next day to inquire about their poor driver with all the truck trouble, I found that they never heard of him.

15   Indeed, someone from Arnold's called back to warn me that this same man had pulled the same scam on someone in Cherry Hill . . . the same story . . . the same ID cards . . . the same eight bucks.

16   Everyone ribbed me about being too trusting. I got kind advice from the local police department when I reported the flim-flam so others could be alerted to the perpetrator's method.

17   But no one taught me as valuable a lesson as the con artist himself. And, thanks to him, someday, some person who is really in need will find a deaf ear when he or she approaches me for help. At least when it comes to money, anyway.

18   That's really very sad.

19   We were brought up to believe in the virtue of helping one's neighbor. One of the greatest commandments given by the Almighty involves the way we should treat each other.

20   Just try it.

After the incident, I pondered 21 what it was about the whole thing that really stuck in my craw. Was it the money? Or was it the lie? . . . the deceit°? . . . the con?

It really wasn't the money. Had 22 the guy come into the office, poured out his heart about being out of work, with sick kids and nowhere else to turn, I probably would have given him the money to help out. At least before yesterday I might have.

It was the lie and the deliberate 23 attempt to cheat me out of money that really angers me.

It's probably true that there's 24 a sucker born every minute. But yesterday, one sucker died. And a wiser, more cynical° person emerged.

There's the pity of it all. 25

Vocabulary in Context Questions

For each question, write the letter of your answer in the space provided.

_____ 1. In the sentences below, the word *timidly* (tĭm′ĭd-lē) means
  A. confidently.   C. loudly.
  B. shyly.   D. on schedule.

"He approached the door of the newspaper office timidly, opened it, and stood on the threshold as if uncertain about the kinds of creatures he would face inside. . . . He just looked nervous and uncomfortable." (Paragraphs 2–3)

_____ 2. In the sentences below, the word *woebegone* (wō′bĭ-gôn) means
  A. pleased.   C. unhappy.
  B. healthy.   D. confident.

"Oh, this was just so embarrassing. . . . He just sat there looking woebegone while I pondered whether or not to help my fellow man . . . and seemed overjoyed when I pulled out my wallet." (Paragraphs 8 and 10)

_____ 3. In the sentence below, the word *wad* (wŏd) means
  A. story.   C. lack.
  B. large number.   D. photograph.

"Seeing what might have been a slightly skeptical look on my face, he produced a wad of credit and identification cards." (Paragraph 9)

_____ 4. In the sentence below, the word *pondered* (pŏn′dərd) means
  A. thought about.   C. forgot about.
  B. remembered.   D. knew.

"He just sat there looking woebegone while I pondered whether or not to help my fellow man." (Paragraph 10)

_____ 5. In the sentence below, the word *scam* (skăm) means
  A. practical joke.   C. agreement.
  B. anger.   D. dishonest scheme.

"Indeed, someone from Arnold's called back to warn me that this same man had pulled the same scam on someone in Cherry Hill . . . the same story . . . the same ID cards . . . the same eight bucks." (Paragraph 15)

_____ 6. In the sentence below, the word *flim-flam* (flĭm'flăm') means
   A. truck trouble.   C. cheating.
   B. embarrassment.   D. credit cards.

   "I got kind advice from the local police department when I reported the flim-flam so others could be alerted to the perpetrator's method." (Paragraph 16)

_____ 7. In the sentence below, the word *perpetrator* (pŭr'pĭ-trāt'ər) means
   A. someone who committed a crime.   C. citizen.
   B. beginner.   D. witness.

   "I got kind advice from the local police department when I reported the flim-flam so others could be alerted to the perpetrator's method." (Paragraph 16)

_____ 8. In the sentences below, the words *stuck in my craw* (krô) mean
   A. delighted me.   C. informed me.
   B. destroyed me.   D. troubled me.

   "After the incident, I pondered what it was about the whole thing that really stuck in my craw. Was it the money? Or was it the lie?" (Paragraph 21)

_____ 9. In the sentence below, the word *deliberate* (dĭ-lĭb'ər-ĭt) means
   A. easy.   C. planned.
   B. fair.   D. weak.

   "It was the lie and the deliberate attempt to cheat me out of money that really angers me." (Paragraph 23)

_____ 10. In the sentences below, the word *emerged* (ĭ-mûrjd') means
   A. disappeared.   C. died.
   B. took advantage.   D. appeared.

   "It's probably true that there's a sucker born every minute. But yesterday, one sucker died. And a wiser, more cynical person emerged." (Paragraph 24)

Questions about the Reading

For each question, write the letter of your answer in the space provided.

_____ 1. A central idea in "One Less Sucker Lives" is that the author
   A. realizes that most people are dishonest.
   B. feels grateful to the con man for teaching her a lesson.
   C. is glad that she reported the con man to the police.
   D. regrets that she has lost her trust in people as a result of being cheated.

_____ 2. The main idea of paragraphs 1–6 is that
  A. the author is not used to being approached by strange–looking men.
  B. there is nothing extraordinarily distinguished about the man.
  C. the author is most impressed by the man's acute discomfort.
  D. the author works in a busy newspaper office.

_____ 3. The main idea of paragraph 9 is that
  A. the man had an Arnold Baking identification card.
  B. the writer was skeptical of the man's story.
  C. the man seemed to really be who he said he was.
  D. the man had credit cards.

_____ 4. The writer worked at
  A. a police station.
  B. a newspaper office.
  C. an office of the Arnold Baking Company.
  D. a truck stop.

_____ 5. In return for her help, the man promised the writer
  A. to pay back her money with interest.
  B. to help someone in need himself someday.
  C. to bring her some English muffins.
  D. to write her a thank-you letter.

_____ 6. The author realizes she has been cheated when
  A. the man does not call her later that day.
  B. she reads a local newspaper story about a con man operating in the area.
  C. she receives a call from the local police department warning her of a scam.
  D. someone from the Arnold Baking Company calls to warn her about the con man.

_____ 7. We can guess that the man
  A. wants others to feel sorry for him.
  B. is genuinely needy.
  C. regrets having to cheat other people.
  D. is not very intelligent.

_____ 8. The man probably
  A. was going from place to place pretending to be someone he wasn't.
  B. was an employee of the Arnold Baking Company.
  C. felt very bad about lying to the writer.
  D. had never cheated anyone out of money before.

_____ 9. We can assume that the writer
  A. is really grateful for what the man taught her.
  B. feels bitter and sad about the lesson she learned.
  C. thinks that the man who asked her for money should be arrested.
  D. wishes she had given the man more money.

_____10. The next time someone tells the writer a hard-luck story, she will most likely
  A. listen sympathetically.
  B. call the police.
  C. not give the person anything.
  D. demand that the person give her eight dollars.

Discussion Questions

1. When people on the street ask you for money, do you ever give them anything? Why or why not? If you sometimes do, how do you decide which person to help?

2. What was the "lesson" the writer learned from the incident? If the incident had happened to you, would you feel you had learned the same lesson? Why or why not?

3. Have you ever had to ask a stranger for help? What were the circumstances? How did the stranger respond?

Note: Writing assignments for this selection appear on page 506.

Check Your Performance		**VOCABULARY IN CONTEXT**		
Activity	*Number Right*	*Points*	*Score*	
Review Test 1 (4 items)	_____	× 5 =	_____	
Review Test 2 (10 items)	_____	× 4 =	_____	
Review Test 3 (20 items)	_____	× 2 =	_____	
	TOTAL SCORE	=	_____	%

Enter your total score into the **Reading Performance Chart: Review Tests** on the inside back cover.

VOCABULARY IN CONTEXT: Mastery Test 1

A. Look at the cartoon below, and then answer the questions that follow.

"I wish I were an *extrovert* like you. I love the way you happily jump up on people and kiss them every time you see them."

_____ 1. Using the context clues in the cartoon, write the letter of the best meaning of *extrovert* (ĕk′strə-vûrt) in the space provided.

    A. a supporter of causes   C. a friendly person
    B. a timid person

_____ 2. Which kind of context clue helps you understand the meaning of *extrovert?*

    A. Examples clue   C. Antonym clue
    B. Synonym clue

B. For the item below, underline the **examples** that suggest the meaning of the italicized word. Then, on the answer line, write the letter of the meaning of that word.

_____ 3. The students showed all the signs of *apathy*, including scribbling instead of taking notes, constantly looking at the clock, and writing messages to one another.

    Apathy (ăp′ə-thē) means
    A. lack of interest.   C. curiosity.
    B. attention.   D. surprise.

C. Each item below includes a word that is a **synonym** of the italicized word. Write the synonym of the italicized word in the space provided.

_____ 4. It is not *appropriate* (ə-prō′prē-ĭt) to wear cut-off jeans to most job interviews. Nor is it suitable to smoke during an interview.

(Continues on next page)

_____ 5. When people are angry with each other, a frank (frăngk) discussion can be helpful. An honest exchange of ideas can lead to an understanding of the other person's point of view.

_____ 6. The ultimate (ŭl′tə-mĭt) reward for working hard at school is earning a degree. Similarly, the greatest reward for working hard on the job is a big promotion.

D. Each item below includes a word that is an **antonym** of the italicized word. Underline the antonym of each italicized word. Then, on the answer line, write the letter of the meaning of the italicized word.

_____ 7. College students often complain that a course is either overly *complex* or too simple.

Complex (kəm-plĕks′) means
A. interesting.   C. difficult.
B. dull.   D. crowded.

_____ 8. Although Juan's efforts to get back together with Margarita were truly *earnest*, she thought he was being dishonest.

Earnest (ûr′nĭst) means
A. successful.   C. amazing.
B. pleasing.   D. honest.

E. Use the **general sense of each sentence** to figure out the meaning of each italicized word. Then, on the answer line, write the letter of the meaning of the italicized word.

_____ 9. Some people have a *phobia* about heights. They can't look down from the top of a tall building without feeling as if they are about to fall.

Phobia (fō′bē-ə) means
A. humorous situation.   C. pleasant experience.
B. fear.   D. determination.

_____10. Tidal waves sometimes *accelerate* until they reach a speed of 450 miles an hour.

Accelerate (ăk-sĕl′ə-rāt) means
A. slow down.   C. bend.
B. speed up.   D. destroy.

VOCABULARY IN CONTEXT: Mastery Test 2

A. For each item below, underline the **examples** that suggest the meaning of the italicized term. Then, on the answer line, write the letter of the meaning of that word.

_____ 1. *Remote* areas such as the deserts of Arizona and the wilderness of Alaska appeal to people who want to get away for a while.

Remote (rĭ′mōt) means
A. populated.   C. wealthy.
B. fancy.   D. out-of-the-way.

_____ 2. *Traits*—including height, eye color, and hair color—are passed on from generation to generation.

Traits (trātz) are
A. features.   C. rights.
B. materials.   D. suggestions.

_____ 3. *Awkward* movements are common for infants learning to walk. Sometimes they will fall backward; at other times they will move sideways instead of going forward.

Awkward (ôk′wərd) means
A. correct.   C. silly.
B. clumsy.   D. expected.

B. Each item below includes a word or words that are a **synonym** of the italicized word. Write the synonym of the italicized word in the space provided.

_____ 4. I can't *comprehend* (kŏm′prĭ-hĕnd′) how a computer works, but at least I understand how to use it.

_____ 5. A good prison *reforms* (rē-fôrms′) inmates. If it makes them better people, they are less likely to return to prison.

_____ 6. Travel by jet has *altered* (ôl-tərd) the way people experience the world. For many, the "wide" world has changed into a much smaller place.

(Continues on next page)

C. Each item below includes a word that is an **antonym** of the italicized word. Underline the antonym of each italicized word. Then, on the answer line, write the letter of the meaning of the italicized word.

_____ 7. The idea that certain people can communicate with the dead is an *illusion*. The truth is that people who claim to be speaking with the dead are making up the "messages" as they go along.

   Illusion (ĭ-lōo′zhən) means

   A. stupidity.   C. fun.
   B. false idea.   D. example.

_____ 8. It is important to keep *alert* in class. If you are sleepy, you may miss a key point.

   Alert (ə-lûrt′) means

   A. notes.   C. positive.
   B. quiet.   D. wide awake.

D. Use the **general sense of each sentence** to figure out the meaning of each italicized word or group of words. Then, on the answer line, write the letter of the meaning of the italicized word(s).

_____ 9. Certain foreign officials in this country have *immunity from* our laws; they can't be arrested even for murder.

   Immunity (ĭ-myōo′nĭ-tē) *from* means

   A. protection from.   C. fear of.
   B. punishment for.   D. lack of respect for.

_____ 10. If you were in the *vicinity* when the gasoline tank exploded, you must have heard the roar and seen smoke pouring into the sky.

   Vicinity (vĭ-sĭn′ĭ-tē) means

   A. area.   C. amount.
   B. country.   D. land.

VOCABULARY IN CONTEXT: Mastery Test 3

Using context clues for help, write the letter of the best meaning for each italicized word.

_____ 1. No one likes a *chronic* complainer like Simon, who criticizes everything all the time.

Chronic (krŏn′ĭk) means

A. rare.   C. messy.

B. constant.   D. educated.

_____ 2. In a hospital emergency room, it is common to see such *gruesome* sights as burned skin and bleeding wounds.

Gruesome (gro͞o′səm) means

A. horrible.   C. false.

B. common.   D. amazing.

_____ 3. "Your paper needs to be more *coherent*," my English teacher wrote. "In places, it is poorly organized and lacking in logic."

Coherent (kō-hîr′ənt) means

A. disorganized.   C. organized and logical.

B. detailed.   D. critical.

_____ 4. Some people believe that they need to *supplement* their diet with large amounts of vitamins and minerals. The addition of these vitamins and minerals, they believe, is what keeps them in good health.

Supplement (sŭp′lə-mənt) means

A. substitute.   C. flavor.

B. add to.   D. vary.

_____ 5. Sometimes people with *contrary* qualities are attracted to each other. For example, a shy person may go out with someone who likes to talk.

Contrary (kŏn′trĕr′ē) means

A. similar.   C. opposite.

B. unusual.   D. respectable.

(Continues on next page)

_____ 6. To *prolong* your life, you should consider getting married. Married people tend to live longer than people who stay single.

Prolong (prə-lông′) means to
A. make shorter.
B. make longer.
C. make duller.
D. make more exciting.

_____ 7. Common *transactions* include buying food and clothing, going to the bank, and getting gas for the car.

Transactions (trăn-săk′shəns) are
A. reasons.
B. business deals.
C. thrills.
D. ways to relax.

_____ 8. Many cities have decided to *initiate* a recycling program so that their old newspapers, bottles, and cans will be re-used instead of dumped.

Initiate (ĭ-nĭsh′ē-āt′) means to
A. cancel.
B. apologize for.
C. start.
D. finish.

_____ 9. There is a special chair that eases the *ordeal* of giving birth. Most women who use the chair say they feel less pain and give birth more quickly than when lying down.

An *ordeal* (ôr-dēl′) is
A. a difficult experience.
B. an enjoyable experience.
C. a very short experience.
D. an educational experience.

_____ 10. On a warm summer day, you may say, "It is my opinion that the level of heat has gone beyond what I am able to consider comfortable." A *concise* way to say the same thing is "I'm hot."

Concise (kən-sīs′) means
A. different.
B. confusing.
C. brief and clear.
D. funny.

VOCABULARY IN CONTEXT: Mastery Test 4

Using context clues for help, write the letter of the best meaning for each italicized word.

_____ 1. Checking e-mail seems to be as *vital* to some people as food and air.

      Vital (vīt′l) means

      A. difficult.   C. unimportant.

      B. free.   D. necessary.

_____ 2. When an Asian volcano erupted in 1883—the largest volcanic explosion in modern history—the sound was *audible* 3,000 miles away.

      Audible (ô′də-bəl) means

      A. able to be seen.   C. able to be felt.

      B. able to be heard.   D. talked about.

_____ 3. A headache can be so *severe* that it keeps a person from being able to work.

      Severe (sə′vīr) means

      A. serious.   C. mild.

      B. new.   D. unusual.

_____ 4. One usually *rational* football fan became so crazy when his favorite team lost the Super Bowl that he shot the TV.

      Rational (răsh′ə-nəl) means

      A. insane.   C. reasonable.

      B. very popular.   D. determined.

_____ 5. It was said that no *obstacle*—whether extreme heat, snow, or rocky land—could keep the Pony Express from delivering the mail on time. Once, when Indians *killed* the rider, the horse went on to deliver the mail alone.

      Obstacle (ŏb′stə-kəl) means

      A. something that gets in the way.   C. animal.

      B. temperature.   D. adventure.

(Continues on next page)

_____ 6. Ice is harder than most people think; its hardness is *comparable* to that of concrete.

Comparable (kŏm'pər-ə-bəl) *to* means

A. as thick as.
B. similar to.
C. different from.
D. not at all like.

_____ 7. My sister is such an *inept* cook that she never needs to call the family to supper. We just come to the table when the smoke alarm goes off.

Inept (ĭn-ĕpt') means

A. excellent.
B. slow.
C. unskilled.
D. experienced.

_____ 8. When my friend asked, "Do you feel all right?" she *implied* that I did not look well.

Implied (ĭm-plīd') means

A. suggested.
B. asked.
C. forgot.
D. pretended.

_____ 9. The small store had many hip-hop and rock recordings, but not much in the *category* of country music.

Category (kăt'ĭ-gôr'ē) means

A. goal.
B. feeling.
C. group.
D. plan.

_____ 10. During Mardi Gras in New Orleans, people like to dress up in *extravagant* costumes. Some wear silk or satin along with feathers and colorful beads.

Extravagant (ĭk-străv'ə-gənt) means

A. showy.
B. plain.
C. athletic.
D. businesslike.

VOCABULARY IN CONTEXT: Mastery Test 5

A. Using context clues for help, write the letter of the best meaning for each italicized word.

_____ 1. My plants did poorly in the living room, but in the sunny kitchen window, they have *thrived*.

Thrived (thrīvd) means

A. needed more care.　　　　C. grown very well.

B. grown weaker.　　　　　　D. become overgrown.

_____ 2. Sometimes people in online personal ads are not very *candid*. They will say that they're attractive, slender, and young when they're really average-looking, overweight, and middle-aged.

Candid (kăn′dĭd) means

A. pleasing.　　　　　　　　C. honest.

B. happy.　　　　　　　　　 D. attractive.

_____ 3. People who *encounter* a wild animal in the woods should stay calm and try to back away as soon as possible.

Encounter (ĕn-koun′tər) means

A. admire.　　　　　　　　　C. get away from.

B. meet.　　　　　　　　　　D. try to save.

_____ 4. A complicated lecture can be *clarified* with logical examples and down-to-earth explanations.

Clarified (klăr′ə-fīd′) means

A. made clear.　　　　　　　C. confused.

B. practiced.　　　　　　　　D. shortened.

_____ 5. After a *thorough* search of my car, I finally found my contact lens.

Thorough (thûr′ō) means

A. quick.　　　　　　　　　　C. exciting.

B. careful.　　　　　　　　　D. enjoyable.

(Continues on next page)

B.   Read the entire paragraph below. Then, using context clues, write the letter of the meaning of each word in italics.

> ¹We have long known that dolphins are intelligent. ²Research has shown that they may be far more intelligent than we *initially* thought. ³To begin with, except for humans, dolphins have the largest brain-to-body size in the animal kingdom. ⁴That large brain allows them to be self-aware—a *characteristic* that has been observed only in apes and humans. ⁵In other words, dolphins can look in a mirror and realize they are looking at themselves, not another dolphin. ⁶Another *indicator* of intelligence is the dolphin's ability to make tools. ⁷Researchers have observed dolphins breaking sea sponges apart. ⁸They then wear the sponges on their noses for protection as they *probe* the rocky sea floor for fish. ⁹Finally, dolphins have a *prominent* sense of curiosity and playfulness. ¹⁰They will respond to images on a television screen with excitement or even fear. ¹¹Also, dolphins have often been observed making underwater rings by blowing air bubbles. ¹²Not only do they then play with these rings; they often gather other dolphins together to view their "artwork."

_____   6. *Initially* (ĭ-nĭsh′əl-lē) means
        A. falsely.   C. never.
        B. first.   D. happily.

_____   7. *Characteristic* (kăr′ək-tə-rĭs′tĭk) means
        A. quality.   C. trick.
        B. danger.   D. problem.

_____   8. *Indicator* (ĭn′dĭ-kā′tər) means
        A. sign.   C. reason.
        B. miracle.   D. strangeness.

_____   9. *Probe* (prōb) means
        A. destroy.   C. search.
        B. prepare.   D. listen to.

_____ 10. *Prominent* (prŏm′ə-nənt) means
        A. annoying.   C. funny.
        B. troubling.   D. noticeable.

VOCABULARY IN CONTEXT: Mastery Test 6

A. Using context clues for help, write the letter of the best meaning for each italicized word.

_____ 1. It is hard to be *neutral* when you listen to two people arguing. Usually you want to take one person's side.

Neutral (noo′trəl) means
- A. interested.
- B. friendly.
- C. not favoring one side over another.
- D. disgusted.

_____ 2. Many students begin college because they see only two *options*: either go to college and get a good-paying job, or work for minimum wages the rest of their life.

Options (ŏp′shəns) means
- A. choices.
- B. wishes.
- C. habits.
- D. opportunities.

_____ 3. Rob's *tolerance* for dogs that slobber, bark, and jump up on people is very low. He prefers well-behaved dogs, or cats.

Tolerance (tŏl′ər-əns) means
- A. dislike.
- B. worry.
- C. acceptance.
- D. experience.

_____ 4. Recently a college student had a choice of studying for a final or going out for pizza with her friends. She chose to study, and that turned out to be a *prudent* decision. She got an A on the exam, while her friends all got D's.

Prudent (prood′nt) means
- A. generous.
- B. wise.
- C. unfortunate.
- D. tricky.

_____ 5. If a prisoner shows no *remorse* at committing a crime, the judge is likely to sentence him to the longest possible prison term.

Remorse (rĭ-môrs′) means
- A. regret.
- B. pleasure.
- C. purpose.
- D. surprise.

(Continues on next page)

B. Read the entire paragraph below. Then, using context clues, write the letter of the meaning of each word in italics.

¹In several *locales* around the country, the United States Postal Service has set up a special room where postal clerks have an *extraordinary* job: they open and read your mail. ²This room is called the "Dead Letter Office." ³Reading people's mail is permitted because the clerks are trying to find out where the mail is supposed to go or who sent it. ⁴Millions of letters each year are sent with incorrect addresses, no return addresses, or both. ⁵Others are written in a scribble that must be *comprehended* or in a foreign language that must be translated. ⁶Some envelopes are completely blank. ⁷Specially trained clerks spend their time opening letters and packages to discover whether or not they can be sent to the intended *recipient* or returned to the sender. ⁸Estimates are that only 30 percent of the mail that ends up at the Dead Letter Office *ultimately* finds its way to the sender or receiver.

_____ 6. *Locales* (lō-kălz′) means

    A. places.

    B. targets.

    C. people.

    D. boxes.

_____ 7. *Extraordinary* (ĭk-strôr′dn-ĕr′ē) means

    A. boring.

    B. very unusual.

    C. common.

    D. dangerous.

_____ 8. *Comprehended* (kŏm′prĭ-hĕnd′ĭd) means

    A. taken seriously.

    B. ignored.

    C. understood.

    D. listed.

_____ 9. A *recipient* (rĭ-sĭp′ē-ənt) is a

    A. letter carrier.

    B. clerk.

    C. writer.

    D. receiver.

_____ 10. *Ultimately* (ŭl′tə-mĭt-lē) means

    A. strangely.

    B. finally.

    C. illegally.

    D. sadly.

4 Main Ideas

This Chapter in a Nutshell

- Recognizing a writer's **main idea**, or point, is the most important reading skill.

- Learn to think as you read by asking yourself, "What is the writer's point?"

- The main idea is a general idea supported by specific ideas and details.

What Is the Main Idea?

College was not going well.

"**W**hat's the point?" People ask this question when they want to know what idea is being presented. Sometimes a main idea is clear right away, as in the cartoon above. What is the point of the cartoon?

Explanation

The main idea is that "College was not going well." The support for the main idea is the list of specific grades showing on the student's grade report.

When you read, get in the habit of asking "What is the main point the writer is trying to make?" Recognizing the **main idea,** or point, is the most important key to better reading.

✓ Check Your Understanding

For example, read the following paragraph, asking yourself as you do, "What is the writer's point?"

> [1]Certain basic fears are part of our lives. [2]For one thing, we fear being disrespected. [3]Bullies play on this fear. [4]They cruelly tease their victims and take away their self-respect. [5]And we feel hurt and disrespected when someone doesn't return our phone calls or walks past us without saying hello. [6]Another of our deepest fears is being alone. [7]No matter how tough we act, we know that the poet who wrote "No man is an island" was telling the truth. [8]We need each other. [9]Not having other people in our lives makes us feel empty inside. [10]A third basic fear is of growing old. [11]Every year, Americans use plastic surgery to try to turn back the clock. [12]And our magazines and TV shows and movies are full of beautiful young people. [13]We do not want to be reminded that the clock keeps ticking.

Here is a good two-step way to find an writer's point, or main idea:

1 Look for a general statement.

2 Decide if that statement is supported by most of the other material in the paragraph. If it is, you have found the main idea.

Below are four statements from the passage about basic fears. Pick out the general statement that is supported by the other material in the passage. Write the letter of that statement in the space provided. Then read the explanation that follows.

Four statements from the passage

A. We fear being disrespected.

B Another of our deepest fears is being alone.

C. A third basic fear is of growing old.

D. Certain basic fears are part of our lives.

The general statement that expresses the main idea of the passage is: _____

Explanation

Sentences A, B, and C all refer to specific fears that we have in life: being disrespected, being alone, and growing old. Only sentence D is a general statement that covers all of the specific fears described in the paragraph. Sentence D, then, is the sentence that expresses the main idea of the passage.

The Main Idea as an "Umbrella" Idea

Think of the main idea as an "umbrella" idea. The main idea is the writer's general point. The other material of the paragraph fits under the general point. That other material is made up of specific **supporting details**—evidence such as examples, reasons, or facts. The diagram below shows the relationship:

The explanations and activities on the following pages will deepen your understanding of the main idea.

General Versus Specific Ideas

You saw in the paragraph on basic fears that the main idea is a *general* idea that is supported by *specific* ideas. To improve your skill at finding main ideas, then, it will be helpful to practice separating general from specific ideas.

Check Your Understanding

See if you can do the following brief exercises. Then read the explanations that follow.

1. *Fish* is a general term. Write the names of three specific kinds of fish.

    _____   _____   _____

2. *Countries* is a general term. Write the names of three specific countries.

    _____   _____   _____

3. *Household chores* is a general term. Write three specific chores you sometimes have to do in your house or apartment.

    _____   _____   _____

4. Finally, *a bad day* is a general term. Write three specific reasons why you might say, "Today was a really bad day for me."

    _____

    _____

    _____

Explanation

Three specific kinds of fish might be flounder, salmon, and tuna. Three specific countries might be the United States, Mexico, and Korea. Three specific chores might be preparing a meal, washing dishes, and taking out the trash. Finally, three specific reasons for a bad day might be "My cat died," "I came down with a cold," and "I missed the bus and was late for class."

Now do the practices that follow, which will give you more experience in telling the difference between general and specific ideas.

PRACTICE 1

Each cluster of words below consists of one general idea and three specific ideas. The general idea includes all the specific ideas. Identify each general idea with a **G** and the specific ideas with an **S**. Look first at the example.

Example   _S_   anger
             _S_   love
             _S_   fear
             _G_   emotion
             _S_   envy

(*Emotion* is the general idea because it includes anger, love, fear, and envy, which are specific kinds of emotions.)

1. ___ goldfish
   ___ parakeet
   ___ pet
   ___ dog
   ___ cat

2. ___ square
   ___ circle
   ___ triangle
   ___ shape
   ___ diamond

3. ___ up
   ___ down
   ___ direction
   ___ sideways
   ___ north

4. ___ soda
   ___ beer
   ___ orange juice
   ___ beverage
   ___ water

5. ___ high-risk job
   ___ astronaut
   ___ firefighter
   ___ policeman
   ___ miner

6. ___ sleeping bag
   ___ sheet
   ___ pillow
   ___ blanket
   ___ bedding

7. ___ "hello"
   ___ greeting
   ___ a wave
   ___ "hi"
   ___ open arms

8. ___ screech
   ___ noise
   ___ crash
   ___ off-key music
   ___ sirens

9. ___ jump
   ___ command
   ___ stop
   ___ move
   ___ sit down

10. ___ jail
    ___ hanging
    ___ suspension
    ___ fine
    ___ punishment

PRACTICE 2

In each item below, one idea is general and one is specific. The general idea includes the specific idea. In the spaces provided, write two more specific ideas that are covered by the general idea.

Example   *General idea:*   containers

                  Specific ideas: box, _____can_____, _____bottle_____

                (*Containers* is the general idea; *box* is a specific kind of container. *Can* and *bottle* are also specific kinds of containers.)

1. *General idea:* movie stars
   Specific ideas: Denzel Washington, _____, _____

2. *General idea:* wild animals
   Specific ideas: gorilla, _____, _____

3. *General idea:* furniture
   Specific ideas: rocking chair, _____, _____

4. *General idea:* desserts
   Specific ideas: ice cream, _____, _____

5. *General idea:* U.S. cities
   Specific ideas: Los Angeles, _____, _____

6. *General idea:* holidays
   Specific ideas: Thanksgiving, _____, _____

7. *General idea:* ball games
   Specific ideas: baseball, _____, _____

8. *General idea:* birds
   Specific ideas: hawk, _____, _____

9. *General idea:* vegetables
   Specific ideas: spinach, _____, _____

10. *General idea:* planets
    Specific ideas: Earth, _____, _____

Note: You will have more practice with general and specific ideas in "The Basics of Argument" on pages 303–322.

The Topic and Main Idea

To find the main idea of a selection, you can look first for a general statement. If that statement is supported by most of the other material in the selection, you've found the main idea. Another approach to finding the main idea is to look for the topic of the selection.

The **topic** is the general subject of a selection. It can often be expressed in several words. Recognizing the topic can lead you to the writer's main point about that topic. To find the topic of a selection, ask this simple question:

Who or what is the selection about?

Then, to find the main idea, ask:

What is the main point being made about the topic?

 Check Your Understanding

For example, read the paragraph below and see if you can answer the questions that follow.

> ¹Spanking is a bad idea. ²First of all, think about the lesson that a child learns when he is spanked. ³He learns that physical violence is a way to deal with a problem. ⁴Spanking tells him that bigger, stronger people are allowed to hit smaller, weaker people. ⁵Secondly, a spanking often has more to do with a parent's emotions than with the child's behavior. ⁶Parents under stress may spank a child to ease their own problems and frustrations. ⁷And finally, spanking is just not effective discipline. ⁸Children should be taught through careful and consistent explanations to behave in a certain way. ⁹They will develop better self-control than children who behave only to avoid getting hit.

_____ 1. Write the letter of the *topic* of the paragraph. To find the topic, ask yourself what the paragraph is about.

    A. Spanking

    B. Lessons

    C. Children's behavior

_____ 2. Write the number of the sentence that states the *main idea* of the paragraph. In other words, what point is the writer making about the topic? (Remember that the main idea will be supported by the other material in the paragraph.)

Explanation

As the first sentence of the paragraph suggests, the topic is "spanking." Continuing to read the paragraph, you see that, in fact, everything in it is about spanking. And the main idea is clearly sentence 1: "Spanking is a bad idea." This is a general idea that sums up what the entire paragraph is about. It is the "umbrella" statement under which all the other material in the paragraph fits. The parts of the paragraph could be shown as follows:

Topic: Spanking.

Main idea: Spanking is a bad idea.

Supporting details:
1. Spanking teaches physical violence.
2. Spanking often has more to do with the parent than with the child.
3. Spanking is not effective discipline.

The following practices will sharpen your sense of the difference between a topic, the point about the topic (the main idea), and the supporting details.

 PRACTICE 3

Below are groups of four items. In each group, one item is the topic, one is the main idea, and two are details that support and develop the main idea. Label each item with one of the following:

    T — for the **topic** of the paragraph
    MI — for the **main idea**
    SD — for the **supporting details**

Note that an explanation is provided for the first group; reading it will help you do this practice.

Group 1

_____ A. Binge buyers go shopping on a regular basis to buy huge numbers of things.

_____ B. Daily shoppers cannot miss a single day at the stores or on online shopping sites.

_____ C. Shopping addicts.

_____ D. There are two types of shopping addicts.

Explanation

All of the statements in Group 1 involve shopping addicts, so item C must be the topic. (A topic is expressed in a single word or short phrase and is not a complete sentence.) Statements A and B each describe one specific type of shopping addict. Statement D is a general statement: that there are two types of shopping addicts. Therefore, it is the main idea.

Group 2

_____ A. Headaches can be caused by changes in the supply of blood to the head.

_____ B. Headaches can result from muscle tension.

_____ C. Headaches can have two main causes.

_____ D. Causes of headaches.

Group 3

_____ A. Remedies for too much sun.

_____ B. You can soothe a case of sunburn by spreading plain yogurt over the burnt area for ten minutes.

_____ C. Several remedies for too much sun can be found in your kitchen.

_____ D. If your eyes have been irritated by the sun, cover them for five minutes with chilled tea bags or a paper towel soaked in milk.

Group 4

_____ A. Drinking excessively can lead to problems other than alcoholism.

_____ B. Excessive drinking.

_____ C. People who drink too much often develop liver disease.

_____ D. Damage to brain cells results from heavy drinking.

PRACTICE 4

Following are four paragraphs. Read each paragraph and then choose what you think are the correct topic and main idea for that paragraph.

Here is how to proceed:

1   Ask yourself, "What seems to be the topic of the paragraph?" (It often helps to look for and even circle a word or idea that is repeated in the paragraph.)

> **Hint:** When looking for the topic, make sure you do not pick one that is either **too broad** (covering a great deal more than is in the selection) or **too narrow** (covering only part of the selection). The topic and the main idea of a selection must include everything in that selection—no more and no less.

2   Next, ask yourself, "What point is the writer making about this topic?" This will be the main idea. In this practice, it is stated in one of the sentences in the paragraph.

3   Then test what you think is the main idea by asking, "Is this statement supported by all or most of the other material in the paragraph?"

Paragraph 1

¹Male and female children are sometimes treated and viewed differently from birth on. ²First, boys get a blue blanket and girls get pink. ³Also, although more male than female babies fall ill, studies say a number of parents are more likely to consider a baby strong if it is male. ⁴Similarly, such parents urge boys to take part in rough-and-tumble play. ⁵But these parents prefer that girls watch and talk rather than be physically active. ⁶When questioned, the parents say they want their sons to be successful and independent, and they want their daughters to be loving and well-behaved.

_____   1. The topic of the paragraph is
      A. males and females.
      B. male and female children.
      C. childhood illness.

_____   2. Write the number of the sentence that states the main idea of the paragraph.

Paragraph 2

¹An enlarged heart can be a sign that the heart is having trouble pumping blood. ²This condition could be caused by a bad heart valve or by high blood pressure. ³An enlarged heart could also be caused by a high level of exercise. ⁴Athletes such as long-distance runners frequently have larger than average hearts. ⁵However, their hearts operate at a high rate of efficiency. ⁶An enlarged heart, then, can be a sign of bad health or good health.

_____ 3. The topic of the paragraph is
   A. pumping blood.
   B. athletes and their hearts.
   C. an enlarged heart.

_____ 4. Write the number of the sentence that states the main idea of the paragraph.

Paragraph 3

¹Researchers who do surveys depend on what people tell them. ²People who are surveyed, however, sometimes lie. ³In one survey, for instance, people were asked if they used seat belts. ⁴Later, researchers checked to see how many people really did use their seat belts. ⁵It turned out that almost 40 percent of those who said they buckled up did not. ⁶Also, researchers once asked people about their smoking habits. ⁷Then they tested the people's saliva to find a chemical that is found in the mouths of smokers. ⁸The tests showed that 6 percent of the women and 8 percent of the men had lied about smoking.

_____ 5. The topic of the paragraph is
   A. researchers.
   B. people who are surveyed.
   C. people who are surveyed about smoking.

_____ 6. Write the number of the sentence that states the main idea of the paragraph.

Paragraph 4

¹As you speak with someone, you can gather clues as to whether he or she understands you. ²Then you can adjust what you say accordingly. ³But when you write, you must try to predict the reader's reactions without such clues. ⁴You also have to give stronger evidence in writing than in conversation. ⁵A friend may accept an unsupported statement such as "My boss is awful." ⁶But in most writing, the reader would expect you to back up such a statement with proof. ⁷Obviously, effective writing requires more attention to detail than everyday conversation does.

_____ 7. The topic is
  A. proof.
  B. conversation.
  C. effective writing versus conversation.

_____ 8. Write the number of the sentence that states the main idea of the paragraph.

A Note on the Central Point

In selections made up of many paragraphs, the overall main idea is called the **central point**. You can find a central point in the same way that you find a main idea. First, identify the topic (which is often suggested by the title of the selection). Then look at the supporting material. The paragraphs within the longer reading will provide supporting details for the central point.

CHAPTER REVIEW

In this chapter, you learned the following:

- The main idea is the key to good comprehension. The main idea is a general "umbrella" idea. The specific details of a passage fit under it.

- To find the main idea, look for a general statement that is supported by specific details in a passage.

- The topic—the general subject of a selection—can also help lead you to the main idea. Ask yourself, "What point is being made about the topic?"

The next chapter—Chapter 5—will increase your understanding of the specific details that writers use to support and develop their main ideas.

On the Web: If you are using this book in class, you can visit our website for additional practice in recognizing main ideas. Go to **www.townsendpress.com** and click on "Learning Center."

REVIEW TEST 1

To review what you've learned in this chapter, answer each of the following questions by filling in the blank or writing the letter of the correct answer.

1. The supporting details are always more *(general or specific?)* _____ than the main idea.

2. The umbrella statement that covers all of the material in a paragraph is the *(topic or main idea?)* _____ .

3. To help yourself find the *(topic or main idea)* _____ of a paragraph, ask yourself, "Who or what is this paragraph about?"

_____ 4. TRUE OR FALSE? To help you decide if a certain sentence is the main idea of a paragraph, ask yourself, "Is this sentence supported by all or most of the other material in the paragraph?"

REVIEW TEST 2

A. Each group of words below consists of one general idea and four specific ideas. The general idea includes all the specific ideas. Underline the general idea in each group.

1. uncle   sister   relative   cousin   grandmother

2. vanilla   flavor   chocolate   strawberry   butterscotch

3. poker   baseball   hide and seek   game   Monopoly

4. sandals   boots   sneakers   footwear   high heels

B. In each item below, one idea is general and one is specific. In the spaces provided, write two more specific ideas that are covered by the general idea.

5–6. *General idea:* means of transportation
     Specific ideas: train,   _____, _____

7–8. *General idea:* musical instruments
     Specific ideas: guitar,   _____, _____

C. (9–16.) Below are groups of four items. In each case, one item is the topic, one is the main idea, and two are details that support and develop the main idea. Label each item with one of the following:

    T — for the **topic** of the paragraph
    MI — for the **main idea**
    SD — for the **supporting details**

Group 1

_____ A. Single children have their problems.

_____ B. Single children have little privacy from their parents.

_____ C. Single children.

_____ D. Single children can be lonely without the companionship of brothers and sisters.

Group 2

_____ A. Television can be educational, with news programs and nature shows.

_____ B. Television is relaxing and entertaining after a stressful day.

_____ C. Television has its good points.

_____ D. Television.

D. Following are two paragraphs. Read each paragraph, and then choose what you think are the correct topic and main idea for that paragraph.

Paragraph 1

¹The crocodile and a small bird called the plover have a surprisingly friendly relationship. ²A crocodile's jaws are strong, and its teeth are razor sharp. ³Yet the plover dares to step inside the croc's mouth. ⁴You see, after eating, the crocodile opens his mouth. ⁵This allows his "living toothbrush" to step in and clean uneaten food from his teeth. ⁶In return for his service, the plover gets a free meal.

_____ 17. The topic is
    A. the crocodile's habits.
    B. the crocodile and the plover.
    C. friendly relationships between animals.

_____ 18. Write the number of the sentence that states the main idea of the paragraph.

Paragraph 2

¹It's well known that trees provide shade, beauty, and wind protection. ²However, there are also two lesser-known benefits of trees. ³First, trees clean the air. ⁴Their leaves actually filter out pollution in the air. ⁵One large sugar maple, for example, can remove as much pollution as is put in the air by cars burning a thousand gallons of gas. ⁶The second lesser-known benefit of trees is that they reduce stress. ⁷Experiments show that people relax more when they are shown scenes with trees than when they are shown city scenes without natural greenery.

_____ 19. The topic is
   A. nature.
   B. lesser-known benefits of trees.
   C. anti-stress benefits of trees.

_____ 20. Write the number of the sentence that states the main idea of the paragraph.

REVIEW TEST 3

Here is a chance to apply your understanding of main ideas to a full-length reading. This selection tells you about a study skill that can mean the difference between success and failure in college. Read it and then answer the questions that follow.

Words to Watch

Below are some words in the reading that do not have strong context support. Each word is followed by the number of the paragraph in which it appears and its meaning there. These words are indicated in the selection by a small circle (°).

concepts (4): ideas
vividly (4): in a clear and lively way
legible (8): easily read
global warming (11): an increase in the world's temperatures

CLASSROOM NOTETAKING

Robin White

1 How would you feel if you were forced to spend 1800 hours—the equivalent of 75 days in a row—sitting in a hard-backed chair, eyes wide open, listening to the sound of someone else's voice? You wouldn't be allowed to sleep, eat, or smoke. You couldn't leave the room. To make matters worse, you'd be expected to remember every important point the speaker made, and you'd be punished for forgetting. And, to top it off, you'd have to pay many thousands of dollars for the experience.

2 Sound like a torture scene from a spy movie? Actually, it's nothing of the kind. It's what all college students do who take a full load of five courses for four years. Those 1800 hours are the time they'll spend listening in class.

3 Unfortunately, many students *do* regard these hours as torture. Many of them will let their attention wander. They'll spend a lot of time daydreaming or scribbling on the edges of their notebooks. Maybe they'll sit in the back of the room and prepare for some other class or jot a note to a friend. Some students will reduce the pain to a minimum by not even coming to class. These students do not realize that if they don't listen in class—and take notes—they're putting their college life in danger.

WHY TAKE CLASS NOTES?

4 One reason you should take class notes is that the information in the classroom adds to what you might find in textbooks. Good teachers keep up to date with their subjects and can include the latest facts and ideas in their presentations. They needn't wait for the next edition of the book to come out. They can provide additional examples or simplify difficult concepts°, making it easier for you to master hard material. And the best teachers combine knowledge with showmanship. They can make any subject, from world history to computers, leap vividly° to life.

5 True, you say, but isn't it good enough just to listen to these wonderful people without writing down what they say? Actually, it isn't, which leads us to another reason for taking lecture notes. Studies have shown that after two weeks, you'll forget 80 percent of what you heard. And you didn't come to the lecture room just to be entertained. You came to learn. The only way to keep the material in your head is to get it down in permanent form—in the form of class notes.

HOW TO TAKE CLASS NOTES

6 There are three steps to mastering the art of taking good lecture notes: getting yourself to the classroom, taking good notes, and reviewing those notes.

Getting to Class

7 Your attitude should be, "Here I am in college. So I've got to go to class and learn all I can." Remember, you're not going to class to be bored, tortured,

or entertained; you're going there to learn. Get to class on time and get a good seat near the front of the room. You'll hear better there and be less tempted to let your mind wander.

Taking Good Notes

8   When you take class notes, always use 8½" × 11" paper, preferably in a looseleaf notebook so you can insert handouts. Write on only one side of the paper. Later, you might want to spread all your notes out in front of you. Have a pen to write with rather than a pencil, which moves more slowly across a page and is not as legible°.

9   Be prepared to do a good deal of writing in class. A good rule of thumb for taking notes is "When in doubt, write it down." After class, you will have time to go over your notes and make decisions about what is important enough to study and what is not. But during a lecture, you don't always have time to decide what is really important and what is not. You don't want to miss getting down a valuable idea that the instructor might not repeat later.

10   Be sure to *always* write down what the instructor puts on the board. If he or she takes the time to write something on the board, the material is probably important. And don't fall into the trap that some students fall into. They write down what is on the board, but nothing more. They just sit and listen while the instructor explains all the connections between those words that have been chalked on the board. Everything may be

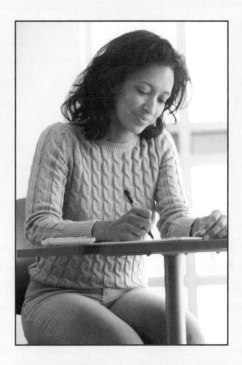

perfectly clear to a student at that moment. However, several days later, chances are that all the connecting material will be forgotten. If you write down the explanations in class, it will be much easier for you to make sense of the material and to study it later.

11   As much as possible, organize your notes by starting main points at the margin. Indent secondary points under the main points, and indent examples even further. Skip lines between main sections. Wherever possible, number the points. If the instructor explains three reasons for poverty, or four results of global warming°, make sure you number each of those reasons or results. The numbers help organize the material and make it easier for you to study and remember it.

12   Here are some other hints for taking good classroom notes:

13   • **If you miss something, don't panic.** Leave space for it in your notes and keep going. Later, get the missing information from a classmate or your textbook.

14   • **Be alert for signals of importance.** If you get a definition with an example, that is important. If you get a numbered list of items, it is probably important. If your instructor says, "The point I am trying to make is . . . ," that point is important. Get all such things down in your notes.

15   • **Use abbreviations in order to save time.** Put a key for abbreviated words in the top margin of your notes. For instance, in a business class, *com* could stand for *communication*; *info* for *information*. In a psychology class, *beh* could stand for *behavior*; *mot* for *motivation*. You can also abbreviate certain common words, using a "+" for *and*, a *"w/"* for *with*, and an *"ex"* for *example*.

16   • **Finally, don't ignore the very beginning and end of class.** Often, instructors spend the first five minutes of a class either reviewing material they've already covered or giving a preview of the day's lecture. The last five minutes of a class may be a summary of the important ideas covered that day. Don't spend the first five minutes of class getting your materials out and the last five minutes putting them away. If you do, you'll probably miss something important.

Reviewing Class Notes

17   If you have taken good notes, you're ready to really learn the material back at home.

18   As soon as you have time, sit down and reread your notes. Fill in anything unclear or missing while it's still fresh in your mind. Then, in the left-hand column of each page, write a few key words and phrases from the day's notes. Cover your notes, and, using only these key words, try to recall as much of the material as you can. This review will help you remember the material and prepare for exams.

19   To sum all this up, be prepared to go into class and be an active notetaker. Going to class and taking good notes while you are there are keys to success in college.

Questions about the Reading

For each question, write the letter of your answer in the space provided.

_____ 1. In the sentences below, the word *showmanship* (shō′mən-shǐp) means
    A. dramatic skill.
    B. handwriting.
    C. research ability.
    D. popularity.

"And the best lecturers combine knowledge with showmanship. They can make any subject, from world history to computers, leap vividly to life." (Paragraph 4)

_____ 2. Which subject is the topic of the entire selection?
   A. Students
   B. Success in school
   C. College lectures
   D. Taking lecture notes

_____ 3. Which sentence expresses the selection's central point (the main idea of the entire reading)?
   A. Students can learn more from lectures than from reading textbooks.
   B. Taking lecture notes is an important skill involving three main steps.
   C. College lectures are more than just entertainment.
   D. There are various ways to achieve success in school.

_____ 4. The main idea of paragraph 4 is stated in its
   A. first sentence.   C. third sentence.
   B. second sentence.   D. last sentence.

_____ 5. Which sentence expresses the main idea of paragraph 18?
   A. Notetaking allows you to bring a copy of the lecture home with you.
   B. Always fill in the blanks in your notes as soon as class ends.
   C. Completing and reviewing lecture notes soon after class will help you remember the material.
   D. Reread your notes soon after class.

_____ 6. According to the author, good teachers
   A. include material in their lectures that is not found in the textbook.
   B. organize their lectures so clearly that notetaking is not necessary.
   C. write everything on the blackboard.
   D. are careful not to say anything important at the beginning or end of class.

_____ 7. A good general rule for taking notes is:
   A. Write down only what is written on the board.
   B. Listening carefully is more important than taking notes.
   C. Write your notes in one big paragraph.
   D. When in doubt, write it down.

_____ 8. Which of the following is **not** recommended by the author?
   A. Take notes with a pen, not a pencil.
   B. Take notes on only one side of the paper.
   C. Tape record your instructor's lectures.
   D. Use abbreviations in your notes.

9. From reading this selection, you can guess that
   A. many students can do well in a class without taking notes.
   B. even if you listen carefully, it is almost impossible to remember everything you hear in a lecture.
   C. students who sit in the back row are less distracted by activity in the classroom.
   D. students who take good notes do not need to read their textbooks.

 10. Which of the following statements might the author agree with?
   A. Good notetaking can make the difference between low and high grades.
   B. Taking notes in class is not as important as listening to the lecture.
   C. It is the instructor's responsibility to make sure that each student learns.
   D. If you've done a good enough job taking notes, you should not ever have to review them.

Discussion Questions

1. How would you rate yourself as a classroom notetaker? Would you give yourself an A, a B, a C, or a failing grade? Explain why.

2. According to the reading, part of a student's preparation for classroom notetaking should be to examine his or her attitude (paragraph 7). Why do you think the author feels examining one's attitude is so important?

3. Of all the advice in this selection, which three points will probably be the most helpful for you to use?

   Note: Writing assignments for this selection appear on page 507.

Check Your Performance   **MAIN IDEAS**

Activity   *Number Right*   *Points*   *Score*

Review Test 1   (4 items)   _____   × 5 =   _____

Review Test 2   (20 items)   _____   × 2 =   _____

Review Test 3   (10 items)   _____   × 4 =   _____

                                    TOTAL SCORE   =   _____%

Enter your total score into the **Reading Performance Chart: Review Tests** on the inside back cover.

MAIN IDEAS: Mastery Test 1

A. Each group of words below consists of one general idea and four specific ideas. The general idea includes all the specific ideas. Underline the general idea in each group.

1. jazz	blues	rap	music	rock
2. coffee maker	dishwasher	microwave	household appliance	clothes dryer
3. fry	boil	cook	bake	steam
4. protection	burglar alarm	guard dog	insurance	suntan lotion
5. Detroit	New Orleans	Boston	Cleveland	city
6. murder	crime	stealing	speeding	kidnapping
7. steel	copper	iron	metal	silver
8. newspaper	editorials	sports	comics	classified ads

(Continues on next page)

B. In each item below, one idea is general and one is specific. In the spaces provided, write **two** more specific ideas that are covered by the general idea.

9–10. *General idea:* sandwich
Specific ideas:
peanut butter and jelly, _____, _____

11–12. *General idea:* singer
Specific ideas: Beyoncé, _____, _____

13–14. *General idea:* flowers
Specific ideas: tulip, _____, _____

15–16. *General idea:* tools
Specific ideas: drill, _____, _____

17–18. *General idea:* floor coverings
Specific ideas: carpet, _____, _____

19–20. *General idea:* TV or radio talk show
Specific ideas:
The Tonight Show, _____, _____

MAIN IDEAS: Mastery Test 2

A. Each group of words below consists of one general idea and four specific ideas. The general idea includes all the specific ideas. Underline the general idea in each group.

1. helmet   turban   head covering   baseball cap   sombrero

2. granola   oatmeal   raisin bran   cereal   bran flakes

3. debt   credit-card bill   mortgage   child support   car loan

4. burnt toast   minor problems   flat tire   boring date   a cold

5. poker   card game   canasta   hearts   blackjack

6. Dracula   Wolfman   monster   Frankenstein   King Kong

7. silk   nylon   wool   cotton   fabric

8. microwaves   take-out food   time savers   high-speed trains   express mail

(Continues on next page)

B. In each item below, one idea is general and one is specific. In the spaces provided, write two more specific ideas that are covered by the general idea.

9–10. *General idea:*   fruit
Specific ideas: apple, _____, _____

11–12. *General idea:*   sports
Specific ideas: basketball, _____, _____

13–14. *General idea:*   relaxing activities
Specific ideas:
listening to music, _____, _____

15–16. *General idea:*   medicine
Specific ideas: cough syrup, _____, _____

17–18. *General idea:*   ways to pay
Specific ideas: check, _____, _____

19–20. *General idea:*   sources of stress
Specific ideas: poor health, _____, _____

MAIN IDEAS: Mastery Test 3

Below are groups of four items. In each case, one item is the topic, one is the main idea, and two are details that support and develop the main idea. Label each item with one of the following:

T — for the **topic** of the paragraph
MI — for the **main idea**
SD — for the **supporting details**

Group 1

_____ A. I think I am getting the flu.

_____ B. The flu.

_____ C. I have a fever of 102.

_____ D. My throat is sore and my nose keeps running.

Group 2

_____ A. Some people are active and find a way to deal with conflict.

_____ B. People deal with conflict in different ways.

_____ C. Some people are passive and hope the conflict will go away on its own.

_____ D. Conflict.

Group 3

_____ A. Good teachers often leave teaching because of low salaries.

_____ B. Problems in schools.

_____ C. Children who are troublemakers can prevent other students from learning in class.

_____ D. There are many problems in our schools.

(Continues on next page)

Group 4

_____ A. Some foods may protect against certain diseases.

_____ B. Some fish oils contain a substance that may lower blood pressure.

_____ C. Protective foods.

_____ D. A substance in garlic and onions appears to reduce cholesterol.

Group 5

_____ A. Working mothers, students, and older people find work-sharing positions very practical.

_____ B. Work sharing—full-time jobs shared by two or more workers—can benefit both employees and employers.

_____ C. Employers are pleased that the turnover rate is lower and productivity is high.

_____ D. Work sharing.

MAIN IDEAS: Mastery Test 4

Following are five paragraphs. Read each paragraph and do two things:

1. Choose what you think is the correct topic of the paragraph.
2. Write the number of the sentence that states the main idea of the paragraph.

A. ¹Men are more likely than women to have health problems. ²In almost all parts of the world, men die at an earlier age than women do. ³In America, men are more likely than women to die from lung disease or heart disease. ⁴Men are also more likely to deal with diseases in which stress is a factor—diseases such as ulcers and asthma. ⁵In addition, men go to the hospital for mental illness far more often than women. ⁶Men are also three times more likely to take their own life than women are.

_____ 1. The topic is
   A. health problems.
   B. men and women.
   C. health problems in men.

_____ 2. Write the number of the sentence that states the main idea of the paragraph.

B. ¹Although people dream of being celebrities, the disadvantages of fame are great. ²First, these famous people are expected to look perfect all the time. ³There's always someone ready to photograph a celebrity looking dumpy in old clothes. ⁴Famous people also give up their privacy. ⁵Their divorces and other problems end up on the evening news and in headlines. ⁶Even worse, celebrities are often in danger. ⁷They get threatening letters and are sometimes attacked.

_____ 3. The topic is
   A. the dangers of fame.
   B. the disadvantages of fame.
   C. the advantages and disadvantages of fame.

_____ 4. Write the number of the sentence that states the main idea of the paragraph.

(Continues on next page)

C.   [1]Where do ideas for new products come from? [2]Surprisingly, a number of products we use every day were discovered by accident. [3]While trying to invent a substance to replace rubber in the 1800s, a chemist stumbled upon the first chewing gum. [4]Coca-Cola was developed as a medicine to treat headaches and anxiety. [5]However, patients really enjoyed its flavor. [6]Before long, Coke became a popular drink. [7]And Listerine was created 133 years ago for surgeons to use as an antiseptic. [8]Somewhere along the line, dentists started using it to kill oral germs. [9]The first mouthwash was born.

_____ 5. The topic is
    A. ideas for new products.
    B. products discovered by accident.
    C. chewing gum and Coca-Cola.

_____ 6. Write the number of the sentence that states the main idea of the paragraph.

D.   [1]Flea markets and garage sales appeal to people for a couple of reasons. [2]First, of course, a used item costs less than a new one. [3]Many people on a budget have wonderful wardrobes they have assembled with good used clothing. [4]Second, many who shop at flea markets and garage sales are collectors. [5]There are people who collect old hats, 1950s toasters, salt and pepper shakers, comic books, and just about anything else you can think of.

_____ 7. The topic is
    A. collecting old hats.
    B. flea markets and garage sales.
    C. places to shop.

_____ 8. Write the number of the sentence that states the main idea of the paragraph.

E.   [1]Secondhand smoke—smoke from someone else's cigar or cigarette—can cause breathing illnesses and even lung cancer. [2]According to the government, the dangers of secondhand smoke can be avoided in a few ways. [3]First, don't allow smoking at all in your home. [4]Second, if someone smokes outdoors, it should not be in areas where nonsmokers pass by. [5]Third, in restaurants that still allow smoking, ask to be seated as far away from the smoking area as possible.

_____ 9. The topic is
    A. smoking.
    B. the smoking area in restaurants.
    C. secondhand smoke.

_____10. Write the number of the sentence that states the main idea of the paragraph.

MAIN IDEAS: Mastery Test 5

Following are five paragraphs. Read each paragraph and do two things:
1. Choose what you think is the correct topic of the paragraph.
2. Write the number of the sentence that states the main idea of the paragraph.

A. ¹Many employees steal small items from their workplaces. ²The most common stolen goods are office supplies. ³People who would never steal a pen from a supermarket shelf think nothing of taking one home from work. ⁴Also, many office workers consider personal use of the office copying machine a benefit of the job. ⁵And then there are specialists. ⁶One famous story concerns an appliance plant worker. ⁷He regularly helped himself to parts from the assembly line. ⁸Eventually, he had enough to build his own refrigerator.

_____ 1. The topic is
    A. crime.
    B. employee theft.
    C. employee theft of office supplies.

_____ 2. Write the number of the sentence that states the main idea of the paragraph.

B. ¹It is estimated that 50 percent of all dog owners buy their dogs Christmas and birthday presents. ²Of course we do a lot for our dogs, but you may be surprised to learn how much our dogs do for us. ³Small children who live with dogs learn responsibility and kindness early on. ⁴Studies show that teens have better self-esteem and are more thoughtful when they've grown up with a dog. ⁵For adults and the elderly, the company of a dog can lower blood pressure and prevent depression and loneliness.

_____ 3. The topic is
    A. dogs.
    B. dog owners.
    C. how dogs help us.

_____ 4. Write the number of the sentence that states the main idea of the paragraph.

C.   ¹Harmful chemicals are often found around the house. ²However, harmful household chemicals can be replaced with safer ones. ³For instance, baking soda can be used in place of harsh oven cleaners and stain removers. ⁴Instead of a chemical cleaner, a mixture of vinegar and water can be used to clean windows and glass. ⁵Vinegar and salt can remove mildew. ⁶And skim milk can be used to polish linoleum floors.

_____ 5. The topic is
   A. skim milk.
   B. the love of the environment.
   C. harmful household chemicals.

_____ 6. Write the number of the sentence that states the main idea of the paragraph.

D.   ¹Motion sickness is caused by mixed messages sent by the eyes and ears to the brain. ²When a vehicle is moving, the body moves up and down. ³The eyes usually sense this and send the brain a message that everything is okay. ⁴But the ears may not be so sure, and can send the brain a worry message. ⁵The brain relays these messages to the rest of the body. ⁶When the messages reach the stomach, sickness results.

_____ 7. The topic is
   A. the stomach.
   B. motion sickness.
   C. a moving vehicle.

_____ 8. Write the number of the sentence that states the main idea of the paragraph.

E.   ¹Twenty years ago, most dentists advised patients not to chew gum. ²It was thought that chewing gum would increase tooth decay. ³Ten years ago, chewing gum became more accepted by dentists. ⁴Today, there is evidence that chewing gum can actually assist in the fight against tooth decay. ⁵As a result, more dentists are recommending that their patients chew gum daily. ⁶Over the years, then, dentists' advice on chewing gum has changed greatly.

_____ 9. The topic is
   A. dentists.
   B. tooth decay.
   C. dentists' advice on chewing gum.

_____10. Write the number of the sentence that states the main idea of the paragraph.

MAIN IDEAS: Mastery Test 6

Following are five paragraphs. Read each paragraph and do two things:
1. Choose what you think is the correct topic of the paragraph.
2. Write the number of the sentence that states the main idea of the paragraph.

A. ¹Fairy tales are often thought to be charming and lovely stories for children. ²Yet the original versions of some familiar fairy tales are shockingly violent. ³"Cinderella" is the story of a handsome prince who searched for Cinderella with a glass slipper worn by Cinderella at a ball. ⁴In the original version, Cinderella's sisters cut off their toes to make the slipper fit. ⁵"Little Red Riding Hood" is another familiar fairy tale that has become less shocking. ⁶In the original version, a wicked queen sent a hunter to kill Red Riding Hood and bring back her heart and lungs.

_____ 1. The topic is
   A. fairy tales.
   B. original versions of some fairy tales.
   C. "Little Red Riding Hood."

_____ 2. Write the number of the sentence that states the main idea of the paragraph.

B. ¹The EPA (Environmental Protection Agency) estimates that American cars use over 200 million gallons of motor oil per year. ²Only 10 percent of this is recycled. ³The rest is dumped. ⁴It eventually makes its way into streams, rivers, lakes, and oceans. ⁵The amount of motor oil dumped is ten times more than the worst oil spill this country has ever known. ⁶Recycling the motor oil your car uses, then, is a very good way to help the environment.

_____ 3. The topic is
   A. motor oil.
   B. the EPA.
   C. oil spills.

_____ 4. Write the number of the sentence that states the main idea of the paragraph.

C. ¹It's human nature to want to talk to others. ²And the extent to which we "talk" electronically is amazing. ³The number of words posted on Twitter each day would fill a million-page book. ⁴Also, 30 million different users update their Facebook statuses more than 45 million times a day. ⁵These updates get many millions of responses. ⁶But perhaps most astonishing is our love of texting. ⁷Worldwide, nearly a quarter of a million texts are sent every *second!*

_____ 5. The topic is
     A. talking to others.
     B. talking electronically.
     C. our love of texting.

_____ 6. Write the number of the sentence that states the main idea of the paragraph.

D. [1]Children who don't read during summer vacation will lose six months of their reading level by September. [2]There are several things parents can do to help children maintain their reading levels during summer vacation. [3]First, turn the TV off when it is not being watched. [4]Second, set up a daily reading time for children. [5]Third, be a role model by reading novels, magazines, or newspapers. [6]Leave them around the house so that children will see these reading materials. [7]Fourth, show an interest in what your child is reading by asking questions or by taking turns reading out loud. [8]Also, remember that writing and reading go together. [9]Leave notes for your child that require a written response. [10]Buy a notebook for children in which they can record their daily activities and thoughts.

_____ 7. The topic is
     A. reading.
     B. children's reading levels.
     C. reading out loud.

_____ 8. Write the number of the sentence that states the main idea of the paragraph.

E. [1]Biologists recently discovered that the common field mouse has a surprisingly complicated social structure. [2]Among California field mice, for instance, males and females stay with each other for as long as they both live. [3]In addition, a chemical produced by the female encourages the male to take care of the young. [4]Finally, older siblings take care of younger ones. [5]When the female gives birth to one litter, she immediately gets pregnant, and another litter is born soon thereafter. [6]Those born in the first litter take care of the next generation.

_____ 9. The topic is
     A. biology.
     B. the common field mouse.
     C. field-mouse siblings.

_____10. Write the number of the sentence that states the main idea of the paragraph.

5 Supporting Details

This Chapter in a Nutshell

- Supporting details are the evidence—such as reasons or examples—that backs up main ideas. Those details help you understand main ideas.

- Outlines and maps can show you a main idea and its major and minor supporting details at a glance.

Look at the following cartoon and see if you can answer the questions that follow.

© 1997 Randy Glasbergen.
www.glasbergen.com

"First my ball rolled under the sofa, then my water dish was too warm, then the squeaker broke on my rubber pork chop. I've had a horrible day and I'm totally stressed out!!!"

- What is the dog's main idea, or point?
- What is his support for his point?

Explanation

The dog's main idea, or point, is that he has had a horrible day and is stressed out. He supports his point by providing three examples (lost ball, warm water dish, and broken squeaker toy) of just why the day was so terrible for him.

What Are Supporting Details?

Supporting details are reasons, examples, facts, or other kinds of evidence that explain a main idea, or point.

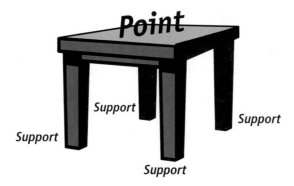

In the model paragraph in Chapter 4, the supporting details appear as a series of reasons:

> ¹Certain basic fears are part of our lives. ²For one thing, we fear being disrespected. ³Bullies play on this fear. ⁴They cruelly tease their victims and take away their self-respect. ⁵And we feel hurt and disrespected when someone doesn't return our phone calls or walks past us without saying hello. ⁶Another of our deepest fears is being alone. ⁷No matter how tough we act, we know that the poet who wrote "No man is an island" was telling the truth. ⁸We need each other. ⁹Not having other people in our lives makes us feel empty inside. ¹⁰A third basic fear is of growing old. ¹¹Every year, Americans use plastic surgery to try to turn back the clock. ¹²And our magazines and TV shows and movies are full of beautiful young people. ¹³We do not want to be reminded that the clock keeps ticking.

 Check Your Understanding

See if you can complete the basic outline below by writing in the three examples that support the main idea. The first one has been added for you.

Main idea: Certain basic fears are part of our lives.

Supporting detail 1: Being disrespected

Supporting detail 2: _____

Supporting detail 3: _____

Explanation

You should have added "Being alone" and "Growing old" as the two other supporting details. Notice that the supporting details provide the added information—specific examples of basic fears—that is needed to fully understand the main idea. To read effectively, then, you must recognize both main ideas and the details that support those ideas.

In the previous paragraph about basic fears, the supporting details are *examples*. Now look at the paragraph below, in which the main idea is explained by *reasons*. In the outline provided, write in the main idea and the three reasons that serve as supporting details.

¹My wife and children love our dog Punch, but I have several reasons for wanting to get rid of him. ²First of all, Punch hates me. ³Every time I walk past him, he gives me an evil look and curls his top lip back to show me his teeth. ⁴The message is clearly, "Someday, I'm going to bite you." ⁵Another reason to get rid of Punch is his shedding. ⁶Every surface in our house is covered with white Punch hair. ⁷I spend more time brushing it off my clothes than I do mowing the lawn. ⁸Finally, Punch is an early riser, while I am not. ⁹Even on weekends, he starts barking and whining to go outside at 7 a.m. ¹⁰Somehow or other, I seem to be the only family member that hears him. ¹¹When I told my family that I had a list of reasons for getting rid of Punch, they said they would make up a list of reasons to get rid of Dad.

Main idea: _____

   Supporting detail 1: _____

   Supporting detail 2: _____

   Supporting detail 3: _____

Explanation

The main idea is that the writer wants to get rid of the family's dog, and the supporting details are the three reasons that he gives (Punch hates him, sheds everywhere, and wakes him up early).

PRACTICE 1

Each group of items below includes a main idea and two supporting details. In the space provided, label each item with one of the following:

MI — for the **main idea**
SD — for a **supporting detail**

Group 1

_____ A. In Italian, the word for "mother" is "madre."

_____ B. The word for "mother" is similar in many languages.

_____ C. In Mandarin Chinese, the word for "mother" is "ma."

Group 2

_____ A. School uniforms make it easy and worry-free for students to get dressed every day.

_____ B. When students wear uniforms, it eliminates competition over who is better dressed.

_____ C. Requiring students to wear school uniforms has definite advantages.

Group 3

_____ A. People who do not exercise regularly after age 30 suffer the consequences.

_____ B. Inactive people lose nearly one pound of muscle each year after age 30.

_____ C. After age 30, inactive people lose about 5 percent of their strength every decade.

Group 4

_____ A. Some parents have tried to ban *The Adventures of Huckleberry Finn* from the classroom.

_____ B. Attempts have been made to ban *To Kill a Mockingbird* from schools.

_____ C. Efforts have been made to ban many great American novels from school libraries.

Outlining

Preparing an outline of a passage will help you see clearly the relationship between a main idea and its supporting details. Notice how the outlines on this page and the next page help you see and understand material at a glance.

Outlines begin with a main idea, followed by supporting details. There are often two levels of supporting details—major and minor. The **major details** explain and develop the main idea. In turn, the **minor details** help fill out the major details and make them clear.

Once you know how to outline, you can use this skill to prepare very useful study notes. Instead of studying fact after fact in sentence after sentence, you can organize the material into outlines. Good outlines tie ideas together clearly, making them easier to understand and remember.

Below is a more detailed outline of the paragraph on basic fears. This outline shows both major and minor details:

> ¹Certain basic fears are part of our lives. ²For one thing, we fear being disrespected. ³Bullies play on this fear. ⁴They cruelly tease their victims and take away their self-respect. ⁵And we feel hurt and disrespected when someone doesn't return our phone calls or walks past us without saying hello. ⁶Another of our deepest fears is being alone. ⁷No matter how tough we act, we know that the poet who wrote "No man is an island" was telling the truth. ⁸We need each other. ⁹Not having other people in our lives makes us feel empty inside. ¹⁰A third basic fear is of growing old. ¹¹Every year, Americans use plastic surgery to try to turn back the clock. ¹²And our magazines and TV shows and movies are full of beautiful young people. ¹³We do not want to be reminded that the clock keeps ticking.

Main idea: Certain basic fears are part of our lives.

Major detail: 1. Being disrespected
Minor details: a. Bullies tease us.
                  b. We're hurt when phone calls are not returned or people don't say hello.

Major detail: 2. Being alone
Minor details: a. "No man is an island."
                  b. Not having other people in our lives makes us feel empty inside.

Major detail: 3. Growing old
Minor details: a. We use plastic surgery to turn back the clock.
                  b. Our magazines, TV shows, and movies are full of beautiful young people.

The main idea is supported and explained by the major details, and in turn, the major details are supported and explained by the minor details. For example, the major detail of "being disrespected" is supported by the details about the teasing by bullies and people not calling or saying hello.

Check Your Understanding

See if you can fill in the missing major and minor supporting details in the outline of the following paragraph.

> ¹Clapping and applause serve a number of purposes. ²First of all, sometimes people clap to show encouragement. ³For example, think of a child nervously walking onto a stage to perform a magic trick for an audience. ⁴Often, audience members will clap in support even before the child begins to perform. ⁵A second reason people clap is out of joy or excitement. ⁶This can be seen, for instance, at concerts when people begin to suddenly clap in time with the music. ⁷Another reason for applause is as a sign of respect. ⁸Famous and admired people usually receive big rounds of applause simply for being introduced. ⁹Last of all, people clap to show appreciation. ¹⁰After a speaker has delivered a talk or a performer has sung or played, people will applaud to show their gratitude.

Main idea: Clapping and applause serve a number of purposes.

  1. To show encouragement
     Ex.—Supporting a child performer

  2. _____
     Ex.—Clapping in time to music at a concert

  3. _____
     Ex.— _____

  4. _____
     Ex.— _____

Explanation

You should have added three major details: (2) out of joy or excitement; (3) as a sign of respect; (4) to show appreciation. And for the third and fourth major supporting details, you should have added minor details in the form of examples. As a sign of respect, people applaud when famous or admired people are introduced. To show appreciation, people applaud after a talk or performance.

Notice that just as the main idea is more general than its supporting details, major details are more general than minor ones.

Outlining Tips

The following tips will help you prepare outlines:

 TIP 1 **Look for words that tell you a list of details is coming**. Here are some common list words:

List Words

several kinds of	various causes	a few reasons
a number of	a series of	three factors
four steps	among the results	several advantages

For example, look again at the main ideas in two of the paragraphs already discussed, and circle the list words:

- Certain basic fears are part of our lives.
- Clapping and applause can serve a number of purposes.

Explanation

In the main ideas above, the words *certain basic fears* and *a number of purposes* tell us that a list of major details is coming. You will not always be given such helpful signals that a list of details will follow. However, be ready to take advantage of them when they are present. Such list words can help you quickly understand the basic organization of a passage.

 TIP 2 **Look for words that signal major details.** Such words are called **addition words**; they tell us writers are adding to their thoughts. Here are some common addition words:

Addition Words

one	to begin with	in addition	last
first	another	next	last of all
first of all	second	moreover	final
for one thing	also	furthermore	finally

For example, look again at the selection on basic fears, shown on the following page, and answer the questions that follow.

¹Certain basic fears are part of our lives. ²For one thing, we fear being disrespected. ³Bullies play on this fear. ⁴They cruelly tease their victims and take away their self-respect. ⁵And we feel hurt and disrespected when someone doesn't return our phone calls or walks past us without saying hello. ⁶Another of our deepest fears is being alone. ⁷No matter how tough we act, we know that the poet who wrote "No man is an island" was telling the truth. ⁸We need each other. ⁹Not having other people in our lives makes us feel empty inside. ¹⁰A third basic fear is of growing old. ¹¹Every year, Americans use plastic surgery to try to turn back the clock. ¹²And our magazines and TV shows and movies are full of beautiful young people. ¹³We do not want to be reminded that the clock keeps ticking.

● Which words signal the first major detail? _____

● Which word signals the second major detail? _____

● Which word signals the third major detail? _____

Look also at the selection on clapping and applause, shown below, and answer the questions that follow.

¹Clapping and applause serve a number of purposes. ²First of all, sometimes people clap to show encouragement. ³For example, think of a child nervously walking on to a stage to perform a magic trick for an audience. ⁴Often, audience members will clap in support even before the child begins to perform. ⁵A second reason people clap is out of joy or excitement. ⁶This can be seen, for instance, at concerts when people begin to suddenly clap in time with the music. ⁷Another reason for applause is as a sign of respect. ⁸Famous and admired people usually receive big rounds of applause simply for being introduced. ⁹Last of all, people clap to show appreciation. ¹⁰After a speaker has delivered a talk or a performer has sung or played, people will applaud to show their gratitude.

● Which words signal the first major detail? _____

● Which word signals the second major detail? _____

● Which word signals the third major detail? _____

● Which words signal the fourth major detail? _____

Explanation

In the first selection, on basic fears, the addition word signals are *For one thing*, *Another*, and *third*. In the second selection, on clapping and applause, the addition word signals are *First of all*, *second*, *Another*, and *Last of all*.

TIP 3   In your outline, put all supporting details of equal importance at the same distance from the margin. In the outline of the paragraph on basic fears (page 145), the three major supporting details all begin at the same distance from the left margin. Likewise, the minor supporting details are all indented at a slightly greater distance from the margin. You can therefore see at a glance the main idea, the major details, and the minor details.

PRACTICE 2

Read each passage. Then complete the outline that follows by filling in the missing major and minor details. Finally, answer the questions that follow each outline.

Passage 1

¹There are different ways to handle embarrassing moments. ²One way is not to make a big deal of your mistake. ³For instance, if you spill your coffee, just casually clean it up and continue your conversation. ⁴Another way is to respond with humor. ⁵After spilling the coffee, say something like "And for my next trick, I'll knock over a water glass!" ⁶And a third way to handle an embarrassing moment is to get help, without making a big fuss. ⁷For example, if you spill a cup of coffee at a restaurant, don't crawl under the table to clean it up yourself. ⁸Just politely tell the waiter, "Sorry; I need some help cleaning up here."

Main idea: There are different ways to handle embarrassing moments.

1. _____

   Ex.—If you spill coffee, clean it up and keep talking.

2. _____

   Ex.—Say "And for my next trick, I'll knock over a water glass!"

3. _____

   Ex.—_____

Questions about the passage

● Which words in the main idea tell you that a list is coming?

   _____

● Which word signals the first major detail?_____

● Which word signals the second major detail? _____

● Which word signals the last major detail? _____

Passage 2

¹In high school, almost every student belongs to one of three subcultures, or social groups, within the student body. ²The first subculture is the delinquent group, the least popular of the subcultures. ³Members of this group dislike authority figures and hate school in general. ⁴The next step up the ladder of popularity is the academic subculture. ⁵These students are known for their high regard for education. ⁶They also have the reputation of being hard-working students. ⁷Last of all, the most popular group is the fun subculture. ⁸Members of this group are interested in their social status at the school. ⁹They also focus on material things like clothes and cars.

Main idea: In high school, almost every student belongs to one of three subcultures.

1. _____

    a. Dislike authority figures
    b. Hate school in general

2. _____

    a. Known for high regard for education
    b. Known as hard-working

3. _____

    a. _____

    b. _____

Questions about the passage

● Which words in the main idea tell you that a list of details is coming?

    _____

● Which word signals the first major detail? _____

● Which word signals the second major detail? _____

● Which words signal the third major detail? _____

Preparing Maps

Students sometimes find it helpful to use maps rather than outlines. **Maps,** or diagrams, are highly visual outlines in which circles, boxes, or other shapes show the relationship between main ideas and supporting details. Each major detail is connected to the main idea. If minor details are included, each is connected to the major detail it explains.

Check Your Understanding

Read the following passage, and then see if you can complete the map and answer the questions that follow.

¹In our busy lives, there are different steps we take to save time. ²First, we use modern inventions to help us do more in less time. ³For instance, we use the GPS on our phone to find a nearby place to eat. ⁴Or we use the self-checkout option at the grocery store rather than waiting for a cashier. ⁵We also save time by doing more than one thing at a time. ⁶For example, a student may finish writing a paper while eating breakfast. ⁷Or we may take a shower and brush our teeth at the same time. ⁸Finally, of course, we may simply rush. ⁹We may save time simply by gulping a meal or running to catch to a bus.

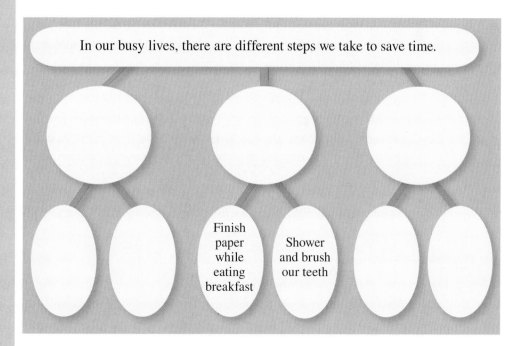

Questions about the passage

● Which words in the main idea tell you that a list of details is coming?

_____

● Which word signals the first major detail? _____

● Which word signals the second major detail? _____

● Which word signals the third major detail? _____

Explanation

The first major detail is "Use modern inventions," and the minor details are "Phone GPS" and "Self-checkout option." The second major detail is "Do more than one thing at a time." The third major detail is "Rush," and the minor details are "Gulp a meal" and "Run to catch a bus."

PRACTICE 3

Read each passage. Then complete the map that follows by filling in the missing major and minor details. Finally, answer the questions that follow each map.

Passage 1

¹A recent poll identified Americans' four most popular hobbies. ²The number one hobby enjoyed by Americans is reading. ³Fiction is the favorite category. ⁴Readers enjoy new thrillers as well as classics such as *To Kill a Mockingbird*. ⁵Biographies of famous people are next in line. ⁶The second favorite hobby is photography. ⁷Thanks to phone cameras and selfies, more and more Americans are taking pictures. ⁸The next most popular hobby is gardening. ⁹From growing roses to raising their own tomatoes, Americans like playing in the dirt. ¹⁰The final favorite hobby is listening to music. ¹¹The average American spends $500 to $1000 a year on downloads, CDs, concert tickets, and listening devices. ¹²What are we listening to the most? ¹³Rock and R&B.

A recent poll identified Americans' four
most popular hobbies.

	Photography		

Fiction				Tomatoes		

Questions about the passage

● Which words in the main idea tell you that a list of details is coming?

_____

● Which word signals the first major detail? _____

● Which word signals the second major detail? _____

● Which word signals the third major detail? _____

● Which word signals the fourth major detail? _____

Passage 2

¹Here are several suggestions to help you do better on tests. ²To begin with, go to class and take a lot of notes. ³Teachers tend to base their exams on the material they present in class. ⁴You must be there and write down that material. ⁵Another key suggestion is to study regularly. ⁶Learn new material on a daily basis. ⁷At the same time, review everything often. ⁸Finally, use test-taking strategies. ⁹Answer the easier questions on an exam first; then go back and tackle the hard ones. ¹⁰Also, for an essay question, make a brief outline before beginning to write.

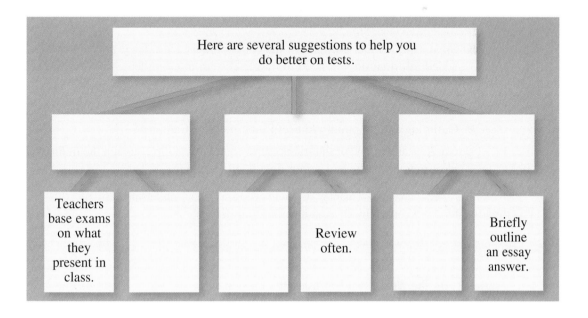

Questions about the passage

● Which words in the main idea tell you that a list of details is coming?

_____

● Which words signal the first major detail? _____

● Which word signals the second major detail? _____

● Which word signals the third major detail? _____

A Final Note

This chapter has looked at supporting details in well-organized paragraphs. But keep in mind that supporting details are part of readings of any length, including selections that may not have an easy-to-follow list of one major detail after another. Starting with the reading at the end of this chapter (page 157), you will be given practice in answering questions about key supporting details. These questions will develop your ability to pay close, careful attention to what you are reading.

CHAPTER REVIEW

In this chapter, you learned the following:

● Supporting details go hand in hand with main ideas. They provide the added information you need to make sense of a main idea.

● List words and addition words can help you to find major and minor supporting details.

● Outlining and mapping are useful note-taking strategies.

● Outlines and maps, or diagrams, show the relationship between the main idea, major details, and minor details of a passage.

The next chapter—Chapter 6—will deepen your understanding of the relationship between main ideas and supporting details.

 On the Web: If you are using this book in class, you can visit our website for additional practice in identifying supporting details. Go to **www.townsendpress. com** and click on "Learning Center."

REVIEW TEST 1

To review what you've learned in this chapter, fill in the blank or write the letter of your answer.

1. Supporting details are reasons, examples, facts, steps, or other kinds of evidence that explain a _____.

2. A _____ is a visual outline; it shows at a glance the relationship between a main idea and its supporting details.

_____ 3. Words such as *several reasons, a number of causes,* and *three steps* tell you that a series of details is coming; such words are known as
   A. addition words.
   B. list words.

_____ 4. Words such as *first, also, another,* and *finally* often tell you that a new supporting detail is being introduced; such words are known as
   A. addition words.
   B. list words.

REVIEW TEST 2

A. (1–6.) Complete the outline below by filling in the missing major and minor details. Then answer the questions that follow the outline.

> [1]Good speakers "talk" with their bodies in several ways. [2]For one thing, they use eye contact. [3]Looking directly into people's eyes helps speakers build a warm bond with the audience. [4]Eye contact can also tell speakers whether or not they are keeping the audience's interest. [5]Head and face motions are another way speakers use their bodies. [6]A shaking of one's head can show dislike for an idea. [7]A nod or a smile can show acceptance of a concept. [8]Finally, good speakers can use hand movements to accent what is being said. [9]Upraised hands can put a positive emphasis on one's words. [10]And a clenched fist can demonstrate anger.

Main idea: **Good speakers "talk" with their bodies in several ways.**

1. _____

    a. Looking directly into people's eyes helps speakers build a warm bond with the audience.

    b. Eye contact tells speakers if they are keeping the audience's interest.

2. _____

    a. Head shaking can show dislike for an idea.

    b. _____

3. _____

    a. _____

    b. _____

B. Now answer the following questions about the passage you have outlined.

7. Which words tell you that a list of details is coming?

_____

8. Which words introduce the first major detail? _____

9. Which word signals the second major detail? _____

10. Which word signals the third major detail? _____

REVIEW TEST 3

Here is a chance to apply your understanding of supporting details to a full-length reading. Job interviews, like final exams, can cause self-doubt and upset stomachs. You may feel that interviews are even worse than finals since you can't prepare for them. In the selection below, however, the author explains that there is much you can do to get ready for job interviews. You can make yourself stand out from the crowd of other applicants.

Read the selection and then answer the questions that follow. You'll find questions on vocabulary in context and main ideas as well as on supporting details.

Words to Watch

Below are some words in the reading that do not have strong context support. Each word is followed by the number of the paragraph in which it appears and its meaning there. These words are indicated in the selection by a small circle (°).

personable (1): friendly
conservative (4): traditional
flustered (5): nervously confused
potential (14): possible

WINNING THE JOB INTERVIEW GAME
Marcia Prentergast

1 Few things in everyday life are dreaded more than going to a job interview. First you have to wait in an outer room, which may be filled with other people all applying for the same job you want. You look at them and they look at you. Everyone knows that only one person is going to get the job. Then you are called into the interviewer's office, where you have to sit in front of a complete stranger. You have to try to act cool and personable° while you are asked all sorts of questions. The questions are highly personal, or confusing, or both. "What are your strengths and weaknesses?" "Where do you see yourself in five years?" The interview may take twenty minutes, but it may seem like two hours. Finally, when you're done, you get to go home and wait a week or so to find out if you got the job.

2 The job-interview "game" may not be much fun, but it is a game you can win if you play it right. The name

of the game is standing out from the crowd—in a positive way. If you go to the interview in a Bozo the Clown suit, you may stand out from the crowd, all right, but not in a way that is likely to get you hired.

3   A few basic hints can help you play the interview game to win:

4   **1. Dress like you're in charge.** That means wearing business clothing: usually a suit and tie or a conservative° dress or suit. Don't dress casually or sloppily, but don't overdress— remember, you're going to a business meeting, not a social affair. Business attire will impress the interviewer. More than that, it will actually help you to feel more businesslike, more in charge. As the old saying goes, the clothes make the man (or woman).

5   **2. Plan to arrive early.** This will keep you from getting hurried and flustered°, and also help you avoid the disaster of being late. Give yourself a few minutes to catch your breath and mentally go over your application or resumé.

6   **3. Expect to do some small talk first.** Knowing what to expect can put you ahead of the game. When the interviewer calls you in, you will probably spend a minute or so in small talk before getting down to the actual interview questions. This small talk is a good time to make a positive impression, though. Follow the interviewer's lead, and if he or she

wants to discuss the weather, let's say, by all means do so for a little bit.

4. Be prepared. Certain questions   7 come up regularly in job interviews. You should plan for all these questions in advance! Here are common questions, what they really mean, and how to answer them:

• *"Tell me about yourself."* This   8 question is raised to see how organized you are. If you give a wandering, aimless answer, the interviewer may put you down as a scatterbrain. You might talk briefly about where you were born and raised, where your family lives now, where you went to school, what jobs you've had, and how you happen to be here now looking for the challenge of a new job. You should have planned and rehearsed your answer, so you can present this basic information about yourself quickly and smoothly.

9 This question can also give you a chance to show that you're right for the job. If you're applying for a sales job, for example, you might want to point out that you like being around people.

10 • *"What are your weaknesses?"* This question is asked to put you off your guard, perhaps making you reveal things you might not want to. A good ploy is to admit to a "weakness" that employers might actually like—for example, admit to being a workaholic or a perfectionist.

11 • *"Why did you leave your last job?"* This can be a "killer" question, especially if you were fired, or if you quit because you hated your boss. According to the experts, never badmouth anyone when asked this question. If you were fired, talk about personality conflicts, but without blaming anyone. If you hated your boss, say you quit for some other reason—to find a position with more growth opportunities, for example.

12 • *"Why did you apply for this job?"* This question is really asking how eager an employee you will be. The simple answer might be "I need the money"—but that is not what job interviewers and employers want to hear. They want employees who will work hard and stay with the company. So be honest, but give a suitable response. You might say that this is the sort of work you've always wanted to do, or that you see this company as the kind of place where you would like to create a career.

13 Other typical questions are pure softball—if you're ready. If you are asked, "Are you creative?" or "Are you a leader?" give some examples to show that you are. For instance, you may want to discuss your organizational role in one of your college clubs. Perhaps you helped recruit new members or came up with ideas to increase attendance at events. If you are asked, "What are your greatest strengths?" be ready to talk about your abilities that fit the job. Perhaps you'll mention your ability to learn quickly, your talent for working with others, your skill with organizing time efficiently, or your ability to solve problems.

14 No amount of preparation is ever going to make job interviews your favorite activity. But if you go in well-prepared and with a positive attitude, your potential° employer can't help but think highly of you. And the day will come when you will be the one who wins the job.

Questions about the Reading

Vocabulary in Context

_____ 1. In the sentences below, the word *attire* (ə-tīr′) means
   A. notes.
   B. answers.
   C. clothing.
   D. posture.

   "Business attire will impress the interviewer. . . . As the old saying goes, the clothes make the man (or woman)." (Paragraph 4)

_____ 2. In the sentence below, the word *ploy* (ploi) means
   A. question.
   B. mistake.
   C. approach.
   D. wish.

   "A good ploy is to admit to a 'weakness' that employers might actually like—for example, admit to being a workaholic or a perfectionist." (Paragraph 10)

_____ 3. In the sentences below, the word *badmouth* (băd′mouth′) means
   A. answer.
   B. criticize.
   C. recognize.
   D. imitate.

   "'Why did you leave your last job?' . . . According to the experts, never badmouth anyone when asked this question. If you were fired, talk about personality conflicts, but without blaming anyone." (Paragraph 11)

Central Point and Main Ideas

_____ 4. Which statement best expresses the central point of the selection?
   A. Interviewers may ask some difficult and highly personal questions.
   B. When going to an interview, dress in business clothing, mentally go over your application or resumé, and go in with a positive attitude.
   C. There are several things you can do to make yourself stand out in a positive way at job interviews.
   D. Employers may ask you why you left your last job.

_____ 5. Which sentence best expresses the main idea of paragraph 1?
   A. First sentence
   B. Second sentence
   C. Third sentence
   D. Last sentence

Supporting Details

_____ 6. According to the author, some advantages of arriving early to an interview are
   A. you will not be flustered or late, and you'll have time to review your application or resumé.
   B. you will have time for small talk with the interviewer.
   C. you will have time to see all the other people applying for the same job.
   D. you will have time to check your appearance and to speak to the interviewer's secretary.

7–10. Complete the following outline of "Winning the Job Interview Game" by filling in the main idea and the missing major and minor details, which are listed below in random order.

Items Missing from the Outline

- Tell me about yourself.
- There are ways to do well at job interviews.
- What are your greatest strengths?
- Plan to arrive at the interview a few minutes early.

Main idea: _____

1. To look like you're in charge, dress in business clothing.

2. _____

3. Expect to do some small talk at the beginning of the interview.

4. Be prepared to answer certain questions that are often asked in job interviews.

   a. _____
   b. What are your weaknesses?
   c. Why did you leave your last job?
   d. Why did you apply for this job?
   e. Are you creative?
   f. Are you a leader?
   g. _____

Discussion Questions

1. Have you ever had a job interview? What did you learn from it?

2. If you were asked by a job interviewer, "What is your greatest weakness?" and "What is your greatest strength?" how would you answer?

3. In terms of a career, where do you see yourself in five years? How are you preparing for that goal?

Note: Writing assignments for this selection appear on page 507.

Check Your Performance   **SUPPORTING DETAILS**

Activity	Number Right	Points		Score
Review Test 1 (4 items)	_____	× 5	=	_____
Review Test 2 (10 items)	_____	× 4	=	_____
Review Test 3 (10 items)	_____	× 4	=	_____
	TOTAL SCORE		=	_____%

Enter your total score into the **Reading Performance Chart: Review Tests** on the inside back cover.

SUPPORTING DETAILS: Mastery Test 1

A. (1–6.) Each group of items below includes a main idea and two major supporting details. In the space provided, label each item with one of the following:

MI — for the **main idea**
SD —for a **supporting detail**

Group 1

_____ 1. There are far more deaths in automobile accidents than in airplane accidents.

_____ 2. The fear of flying is not based in reality.

_____ 3. Six times as many people die in train wrecks as in commercial airline crashes.

Group 2

_____ 1. American families have changed a great deal during the last few decades.

_____ 2. Since 1970, single-parent families have increased by more than 300 percent.

_____ 3. In 1970, over 40 percent of American households were made up of married parents with children; today fewer than 25 percent of them are.

(Continues on next page)

B. (7–10.) In the spaces provided, complete the outline of the paragraph by filling in the **two** missing major details. Then answer the questions that follow the outline.

> ¹Many people continue to work after "retiring." ²There are two main reasons many senior citizens continue to work. ³The first reason, of course, is for the money. ⁴Many senior citizens need to add to what they receive from Social Security and pensions. ⁵According to one survey, one-third of older workers fall into this category. ⁶The other reason many senior citizens continue to work is that they like to. ⁷One retiree, a former mechanic, loves his $5.15-an-hour job at a fast-food restaurant because it gives him the chance to meet people. ⁸And a teacher who had always wanted to be a doctor went into medicine after her retirement. ⁹She went back to school to become a nurse.

Main idea: There are two main reasons many senior citizens continue to work.

1. _____

2. _____

9. Which word signals the first major detail?

_____

10. Which word signals the second major detail?

_____

SUPPORTING DETAILS: Mastery Test 2

A. (1–6.) Each group of items below includes a main idea and two major supporting details. In the space provided, label each item with one of the following:

> MI — for the **main idea**
> SD —for a **supporting detail**

Group 1

_____ 1. To make sure your application is easy to read, use a pen and print or write clearly.

_____ 2. Come prepared to fill in the details of your educational and employment backgrounds.

_____ 3. There are certain things to remember when filling out a job application.

Group 2

_____ 1. At the time of the Civil War, the average adult male was 5 feet 7 inches tall; today the average adult male is nearly 5 feet 10 inches.

_____ 2. The average American male is much bigger than the average American male was at the time of the Civil War.

_____ 3. Today the average adult male weighs about 190 pounds; at the time of the Civil War, the average adult male weighed less than 150 pounds.

(Continues on next page)

B. (7–9.) In the spaces provided, complete the outline of the paragraph by filling in the **three** missing major details. Then answer the question that follows the outline.

> ¹When you die, what will happen to your body? ²Most people end up underground in a metal coffin. ³But a traditional burial is expensive and takes up valuable land. ⁴Fortunately, there are less costly ways than a traditional burial to dispose of your remains. ⁵One popular option is cremation. ⁶This low-priced option involves burning your body until it is reduced to ashes. ⁷Your ashes can be kept by loved ones or sprinkled in a special spot. ⁸Another option is natural burial. ⁹In this case, your body is buried in a cardboard box or cloth blanket that decays rapidly in soil, leaving no metals or chemicals in the ground. ¹⁰A final option is to donate your body to science. ¹¹This option is free and allows you to contribute to medical science and to the welfare of humankind long after your death.

Main idea: **There are less costly ways than a traditional burial to dispose of your remains.**

1. _____

2._____

3._____

10. Which word signals the second major detail?

_____

SUPPORTING DETAILS: Mastery Test 3

A. Read the paragraph and answer the questions that follow. In the space provided, write the letter of each answer.

To help you focus on the supporting details of the paragraph, the main idea has been boldfaced.

> **¹Parts of our environment affect the way we behave and feel.** ²For one thing, there is temperature. ³Most of us prefer temperatures in the 70s. ⁴When it is hotter than the 70s, we become less active and less alert. ⁵Lighting also affects us. ⁶In the classroom or on the job, bright light encourages work. ⁷In contrast, the low lighting of a restaurant relaxes us and encourages informal conversation. ⁸Last is color. ⁹For example, red is felt as exciting, blue as calming, and yellow as cheerful.

_____ 1. As the main idea in the first sentence suggests, the major details of this paragraph are
   A. various temperatures.
   B. places where we work and relax.
   C. parts of our environment that affect our behavior and moods.

_____ 2. Specifically, the major details of this paragraph are
   A. cool, hot, and just-right temperatures.
   B. the classroom, the job, and the restaurant.
   C. temperature, lighting, and color.

_____ 3. The addition words that introduce the major details are
   A. *for one thing, also,* and *last.*
   B. *most, when,* and *and.*
   C. *in contrast, for example,* and *as.*

_____ 4. According to the paragraph, most people become less alert
   A. in bright light.
   B. in temperatures greater than the 70s.
   C. in restaurants with low lighting.

_____ 5. The last sentence of the paragraph provides
   A. a major detail.
   B. minor details.
   C. both major and minor details.

(Continues on next page)

B. Read the paragraph and answer the questions that follow. In the space provided, write the letter of each answer.

To help you focus on the supporting details of the paragraph, the main idea has been boldfaced.

> [1]**Intelligence includes several basic mental abilities.** [2]One is language skill. [3]People who have this ability do well on reading tests and have large vocabularies. [4]Another such ability is a quick memory. [5]People with this skill may learn the words to a popular song after hearing it only once or twice. [6]A third basic mental skill allows us to make sense of visual information. [7]People who have this ability are skilled at reading maps or understanding diagrams.

_____ 6. The major details of this paragraph are types of
    A. mental abilities.
    B. language abilities.
    C. similarities and differences.

    7. Fill in the blank: The addition words that introduce the major details are *one*, *another*, and _____.

_____ 8. According to the paragraph, the ability to learn the words to a popular song quickly shows a strong
    A. language ability.
    B. memorizing ability.
    C. visual ability.

_____ 9. According to the paragraph, the ability to make sense of maps and diagrams shows a strong
    A. language ability.
    B. memorizing ability.
    C. visual ability.

_____ 10. Write the letter of the better outline of the paragraph.

    A. Intelligence
      1. Doing well on reading tests
      2. Having large vocabularies
      3. Quickly learning the words to a popular song
      4. Seeing similarities and differences between designs and pictures

    B. Some basic mental abilities that make up intelligence
      1. Language skill
      2. A quick memory
      3. The ability to make sense of visual information

SUPPORTING DETAILS: Mastery Test 4

A. (1–4.) Complete the map of the following paragraph. First complete the main idea sentence at the top, and then fill in the **three** missing major details.

¹Heart disease is the number one killer of Americans. ²The American Heart Association has identified the major causes of heart disease. ³Up until recently, it had listed three factors. ⁴Smoking was the number one cause. ⁵It was closely followed by high blood levels of cholesterol. ⁶The next most common cause of heart disease was high blood pressure. ⁷Recently a fourth cause was identified. ⁸Inactivity was added because evidence showed that people need to move to keep the heart stimulated.

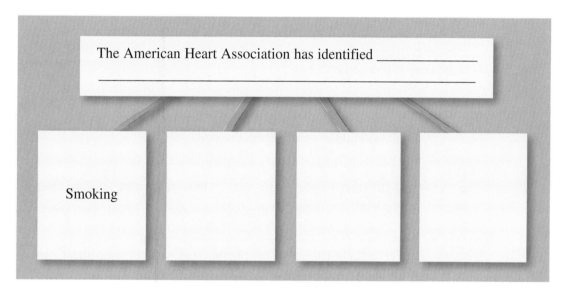

The American Heart Association has identified _____
_____

Smoking

5. What words in the main idea tell you that a list of details is coming?

_____

(Continues on next page)

B. (6–10.) Complete the outline of the following paragraph by filling in the missing major and minor details.

> ¹Storytelling can be a good way to calm down a restless child. ²Here are some tips on how to involve your child in a story you are telling. ³First, grab the child's interest from the start. ⁴If the story is imaginary, you might start with "Once upon a time, . . ." ⁵If the story is true, you might begin with "Many years ago, . . ." or "Before you were born, . . ." ⁶Second, have a setting for your story. ⁷For a fictional story, a phrase such as "in the forest" gives children a useful frame of reference. ⁸For a nonfiction story, even something like "outside of town" gives children a frame of reference. ⁹Third, appeal to the senses. ¹⁰Describe how things look. ¹¹For instance, you might mention colors that characters are wearing. ¹²Or imitate the sounds of parts of your story—for instance, a train whistle or a birdcall. ¹³When appropriate, also include descriptions of how things smelled and felt. ¹⁴Finally, don't worry if the child appears to be daydreaming as you tell the story—he or she may be imagining the story as you speak.

Main idea: Here are some tips on how to involve your child in a story you are telling.

1. Grab the child's interest from the start.

   a. _____

   b. If the story is true, begin with "Many years ago, . . . " or "Before you were born, ..."

2. _____

   a. For a fictional story, a phrase such as "in the forest" gives children a useful frame of reference.

   b. _____

   _____

3. _____

   a. _____

   b. Imitate the sounds of parts of your story.

   c. When appropriate, also include descriptions of how things smelled and felt.

4. Don't worry if the child appears to be daydreaming as you tell the story—he or she may be imagining the story as you speak.

SUPPORTING DETAILS: Mastery Test 5

A. (1–4.) Fill in the major details needed to complete a map of the following passage.

¹A respectful parent guides and instructs more than he or she punishes. ²To be a respectful parent, there are several "don'ts" you should remember. ³First, don't yell a lot at children. ⁴Yelling will tell a child that the parent is out of control. ⁵Or it will result in a shouting match that loses respect. ⁶Second, don't make too many rules. ⁷Growing up is not a boot camp. ⁸Too many rules will prevent children from understanding what is really important. ⁹Third, don't show disrespect to a child. ¹⁰This will create resentment. ¹¹Fourth, don't order children around. ¹²They will not learn responsibility if they feel they have to do what you want at the instant you command it. ¹³Finally, don't neglect to acknowledge good behavior. ¹⁴Praise and hugs work wonders in promoting responsibility and respect.

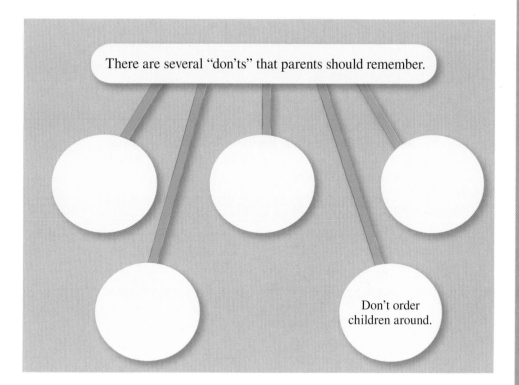

(Continues on next page)

B. (5–10.) Complete the outline of the following paragraph by filling in the missing major and minor details.

> ¹Certain kinds of employee behavior are likely to lead to dismissal. ²First is dishonesty. ³For example, if a boss thinks an employee is lying, that employee is not likely to be on the job long. ⁴Similarly, if a worker is believed to be stealing, he or she may not last long. ⁵A second type of unacceptable behavior is irresponsibility. ⁶For instance, most bosses dislike workers taking too many breaks. ⁷Just as bad is an employee doing personal business during the workday. ⁸Finally, a poor attendance record can lead to dismissal. ⁹Employees cannot afford to be absent frequently. ¹⁰And on some jobs, an employee who is even fifteen minutes late will have some serious explaining to do.

Main idea: Certain kinds of employee behavior are likely to lead to dismissal.

1. _____

   a. Lying

   b. _____

2. _____

   a. _____

   b. Doing personal business during the workday

3. Poor attendance

   a. _____

   b. _____

SUPPORTING DETAILS: Mastery Test 6

A. (1–5.) Read the paragraph and answer the questions that follow. In the space provided, write the letter of each answer.

To help you focus on the supporting details of the paragraph, the main idea has been boldfaced.

> [1]**The National Board of Medical Examiners released a number of alarming facts about doctors.** [2]To begin with, the amount of time doctors spend examining patients is down dramatically from previous years. [3]Twenty years ago, doctors spent eleven minutes with patients. [4]Today they take only seven minutes. [5]Next, it was found that a large number of patients have been switching doctors. [6]In one recent year, for instance, 25 percent of patients reported changing doctors. [7]The most common reason given was that patients did not feel comfortable with the doctor they left. [8]Finally, medical students' reasons for wanting to become a doctor were unexpected. [9]The most common reason given was to make a good living. [10]Working with people ranked third.

_____ 1. The opening words that tell you a list of details is coming are
  A. "The National Board of Medical Examiners."
  B. "a number of alarming facts about doctors."
  C. "the amount of time doctors spend examining patients."

_____ 2. The first major supporting detail is signaled by the words
  A. *a number of.* B. *previous years.* C. *to begin with.*

_____ 3. The second major detail is introduced in sentence
  A. 3.   B. 5.   C. 6.

_____ 4. The third major detail is introduced in sentence
  A. 7.   B. 8.   C. 9.

_____ 5. Write the letter of the better outline of the paragraph.

  A. **Main idea:** The National Board of Medical Examiners recently released a number of alarming facts about doctors.

   1. Twenty years ago, doctors spent eleven minutes examining patients.
   2. Today, on the average, doctors spend seven minutes examining patients.
   3. Within the past year, 25 percent of patients reported changing doctors, in most cases because of discomfort with the doctor.
   4. The reasons medical students give for wanting to become a doctor were unexpected.

(Continues on next page)

    B. **Main idea:** The National Board of Medical Examiners recently released a number of alarming facts about doctors.

      1. Doctors today spend less time examining patients than they did twenty years ago.

      2. A large number of patients have been switching doctors.

      3. Medical students rank making a good living as a more important reason to become a doctor than working with people.

B. (6–9.) In the spaces provided, complete the map of the paragraph by filling in the four missing major details. Then answer the question that follows the map.

    ¹Very often, the more mysterious something is, the more false ideas there are surrounding it. ²There are several incorrect ideas about the human brain, a mysterious object. ³One false idea is that the brain itself is firm and gray. ⁴In reality, the living brain is deep red, darker than blood, and is soft and shaky like jelly. ⁵Next, the idea that new brain cells can't be created after damage or loss is not true. ⁶Cells continue to reproduce throughout one's life, and the ability to learn and create is unending. ⁷A third false idea is that humans use only 10 percent of their brains. ⁸Since this idea first appeared in the early 1900s, scientists have gone on to show that we use all of our brains. ⁹The final mistaken idea is that we have "right brain" and "left brain" abilities. ¹⁰It is true that some abilities are located in specific areas of the brain. ¹¹However, most skills are spread out equally on both sides. ¹²In fact, if one side of the brain in injured at a young age, skills often just transfer to the other side of the brain.

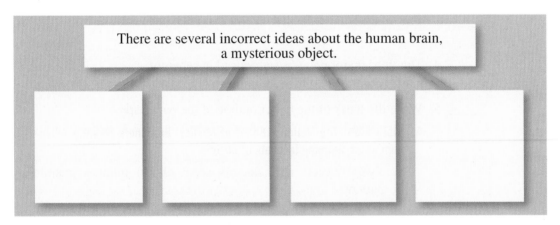

There are several incorrect ideas about the human brain, a mysterious object.

10. What words in the main idea tell you that a list of details is coming?

_____

6 Finding Main Ideas

This Chapter in a Nutshell

- The main idea most often appears in the first sentence of a paragraph.

- The main idea may include such list words as *various kinds* and *a number of.* Supporting details may be introduced with such addition words as *first of all, next,* and *finally.*

- Sometimes the first sentence or two of a paragraph act only as an introduction to the main idea. The main idea then appears in the second or third sentence. Often a word like *but* or *however* signals such a main idea.

- The main idea may also appear in the middle or at the end of a paragraph.

In real estate, no words are more important than "Location, location, location." In a paragraph, location is also important, as you will learn in this chapter.

In the previous chapters, most of the main ideas were in the first sentence of each paragraph. But the main idea may appear elsewhere in the paragraph as well. This chapter begins by describing common locations of the main idea. The chapter will then give you practice in finding the main idea in a series of paragraphs.

As you work through this chapter, remember what you have already learned about finding main ideas:

1   Look for a **general idea** and ask yourself, "Is this idea supported by all or most of the other material in the paragraph?"

2   See if you can decide on the **topic**—the general subject of the paragraph—and then ask, "What point is the paragraph making about this topic?"

3   Look for **list words** such as *several reasons* or *various factors* or *three steps*; such words often appear in the main idea sentence. (See page 147.) Also, look for **addition words** such as *first, another, also,* and *finally*; such words may introduce details that support the main idea. (See page 147.)

Main Idea at the Beginning

Writers often begin a paragraph with the main idea. The rest of the paragraph then supports the main idea with details.

 ## *Check Your Understanding*

See if you can underline the main idea in the following paragraph.

¹My desk is well organized. ²I keep pencils and pens in the top left drawer. ³Printer paper and note pads are in the middle left drawer. ⁴The bottom left drawer has all the other supplies I might need, from paper clips to staples. ⁵The top of the desk is clear, except for a study lamp and a stapler. ⁶The right side of the desk has two drawers. ⁷The bottom one is a file drawer, where I keep my notes for each class. ⁸And in the top drawer? ⁹That's where I keep nuts, raisins, small pretzels, and M&M's that I snack on while I work.

Explanation

This paragraph follows a very common pattern: The main idea is presented in the *first* sentence. The following sentences support the main idea with details of just how the desk is organized.

But a main idea does not always appear in the very first sentence of a passage. See if you can underline the main idea in this paragraph:

> [1]Many people say they have a problem sleeping. [2]But in many cases, sleep problems can be avoided by following a few simple guidelines. [3]First, don't drink alcoholic beverages or drinks with caffeine close to bedtime. [4]Next, do not exercise within three hours of bedtime. [5]Finally, plan a sleep routine. [6]Every day, go to bed at the same time and get up at the same time.

Explanation

In the above paragraph, the main idea is stated in the *second* sentence. The first sentence introduces the topic (sleeping problems), but it is the idea in the second sentence—that sleep problems can be avoided by following a few simple guidelines—that is supported in the rest of the paragraph. So keep in mind that the first sentence may simply introduce or lead into the main idea of a paragraph. **Very often, a word like *but* or *however* then signals the main idea.** In the above paragraph, the word but *helps* mark the main idea.

Main Idea in the Middle

Sometimes the first few sentences of a paragraph act as an introduction to the main idea. The main idea then appears in the middle of the paragraph.

Check Your Understanding

Here is an example of a paragraph in which the main idea is somewhere in the middle. Try to find and underline it. Then read the explanation that follows.

> ¹Today we take world-wide communication for granted. ²Through TV and radio, we learn almost instantly what happens throughout the world. ³In Roman times, however, military leaders communicated with each other through a more down-to-earth method—pigeons. ⁴Homing pigeons have a strong instinct to return home from just about anywhere. ⁵The birds were kept in cages at the military camps. ⁶When a message had to be sent, a soldier strapped it to the bird's leg. ⁷The bird was then released, and it flew home, delivering the message.

Explanation

If you thought the third sentence contains the main idea, you were correct. The two sentences before the main idea introduce the topic: communication. Then the writer presents the main idea, which is that in Roman times pigeons were used for military communications. The rest of the paragraph develops that idea with supporting details that explain just how the pigeons were used.

Main Idea at the End

Sometimes all the sentences in a paragraph will lead up to the main idea, which is stated at the end.

Check Your Understanding

See if you can underline the main idea in the following paragraph.

> ¹One common belief is that damp weather or a "chill" causes people to catch a cold. ²The truth is that exposure to a cold virus—not weather—is what causes the sickness. ³A related idea is that vitamin C can help prevent the common cold. ⁴While

vitamin C can help with other conditions, there is no evidence that it stops or relieves colds. [5]Another medical myth is that chocolate causes acne. [6]Researchers who have studied this skin condition have not been able to connect acne to a diet rich in chocolate. [7]Finally, many people believe they should drink eight glasses of water a day for good health. [8]But the only result you can expect from this much water is a need to visit the bathroom. [9]Many popular ideas about health are simply false.

Explanation

Here the supporting details (beliefs and ideas about health) appear first, and the point of the supporting details—that many popular ideas about health are false—appears at the end.

PRACTICE 1

The main idea may appear at any place within each of the four paragraphs that follow. Write the number of each main idea sentence in the space provided.

> *Hints:* Remember the three ways to find main ideas:
>
> **1** Look for a general idea and ask yourself, "Is this idea supported by all or most of the other material in the paragraph?"
>
> **2** See if you can decide on the topic—the general subject of the paragraph—and then ask, "What point is the paragraph making about this topic?"
>
> **3** Look for list words such as *several reasons* or *various factors* or *three steps*; such words often appear in the main idea sentence. Also, look for addition words such as *first, another, also,* and *finally*; such words may introduce details that support the main idea.

_____ 1. [1]What you consider a "normal" diet depends upon where you live. [2]For example, horse meat is on the menu in many French restaurants. [3]In Korea, dogs are raised to be eaten. [4]Rabbits are popular food in Italy. [5]Fried grasshoppers are eaten in rural Mexico. [6]In much of Asia, giant waterbugs are roasted and eaten whole. [7]Sheep's head is popular in Norway, lizards are eaten in South America, and whale blubber is consumed in the Arctic. [8]While we may think these foods are unusual or even disgusting, remember that people of the Hindu religion think it is disgusting that we eat beef.

_____ 2. [1]If you are like seventy million Americans, you don't get enough sleep. [2]Lack of sleep affects people in a number of harmful ways. [3]For one thing, too little sleep affects our concentration and judgment. [4]We are more likely to make mistakes, whether taking a test or driving a car. [5]Also, lack of sleep harms our body. [6]Our level of stress increases and our immune system weakens, leaving us at risk for illness. [7]Last, lack of sleep has negative psychological effects, such as irritability, impatience, and an increased risk of depression. [8]The good news: these effects can be erased—with about eight hours of sleep a night.

_____ 3. [1]Shooting deaths are all too common on our city streets. [2]And after the shooting, bystanders often say, "I didn't see anything." [3]The sad truth is that witnesses to a crime are often afraid to speak up, even if they know who pulled the trigger. [4]Some feel that what happens in the neighborhood is nobody else's business. [5]Others stay silent because they don't want to be seen as "snitches," helping the police or other authorities. [6]A few even fear that if they do say something, they will become the next victims. [7]And so their neighborhood continues to be a hopeless and dangerous place, where killers are allowed to walk freely.

_____ 4. [1]Robotic surgeons are becoming a reality. [2]One of the most promising surgical robots is called the Da Vinci. [3]It is a 1,200-pound, $1.5 million gadget that already sits in some operating rooms. [4]A human surgeon works at a nearby control board to guide Da Vinci's multiple arms. [5]Those arms are so long, slender, and flexible that they can reach deep into a patient's body, perform difficult tasks, and withdraw, leaving only a tiny scar. [6]Other surgical robots that are even "smarter" than the Da Vinci are being developed.

 PRACTICE 2

The main idea may appear at any place within each of the four paragraphs that follow. Write the number of each main idea sentence in the space provided.

_____ 1. [1]In the deep South, where it is often very hot, people tend to speak slowly. [2]They draw out their words, making a one-syllable word like "down" sound as if it has two syllables. [3]On the other hand, people living in the New England states, where it gets very cold, often speak quickly.

[4]Sometimes they clip their words as though they are in a hurry to get out of an icy wind blowing around them. [5]Meanwhile, people living in parts of the country that don't usually have extreme temperatures, such as the West Coast and the Midwest, are often said to have no accent at all. [6]They just talk "regular." [7]It seems possible that the climate in an area actually influences how the local residents speak.

_____ 2. [1]America should put an end to the death penalty. [2]There is no evidence that the death penalty stops people from committing crimes. [3]A person about to murder another person does not stop to think, "No, I might be executed for this." [4]Also, the death penalty is unfairly applied. [5]Poor or minority people are put to death far more often than wealthier white people. [6]The more well-off people can pay for better lawyers and therefore escape the death penalty. [7]Last, the death penalty is immoral. [8]The Bible says, "Thou shalt not kill," and our society should honor that commandment.

_____ 3. [1]There is much that people can do for their pets. [2]But the opposite is also true—numerous studies have shown that owning a pet can improve a person's mental and physical well-being. [3]A pet that a person feels attached to improves the owner's frame of mind. [4]In addition, a pet gives a feeling of being needed to the person who takes care of it. [5]Pets also give an unconditional love that makes coming home after a rotten day more bearable. [6]Even being in the same room as a pet can lower one's blood pressure and heart rate.

_____ 4. [1]Several kinds of changes can warn that a teenager is considering suicide. [2]Some changes are physical. [3]The youngster may have no energy or may show a sudden gain or loss in weight. [4]Other changes are emotional. [5]There can be unexpected outbursts, usually for no obvious reason. [6]Also, the youngster may stop communicating with family or may even withdraw from people in general. [7]The most dramatic signs of suicide are changes in old habits and interests. [8]These signs often include new sleeping patterns and giving away favorite possessions.

CHAPTER REVIEW

In this chapter, you learned the following:

- The first place to check for the main idea is the first sentence. But the main idea can appear anywhere within a paragraph.

- At times the first sentence or two serve as an introduction to the main idea, which then appears in the second or third sentence. In such cases, a word like *but* or *however* often signals the main idea.

The next two chapters—Chapter 7 and Chapter 8—explain how writers use signal words to connect their ideas.

On the Web: If you are using this book in class, you can visit our website for additional practice in finding main ideas. Go to **www.townsendpress.com** and click on "Learning Center."

REVIEW TEST 1

To review what you've learned in this chapter, complete each of the following sentences.

1. The main idea appears most often in the (*first, second, final*) _____ sentence of a paragraph.

2. Sometimes the first sentence or so of a paragraph may simply introduce or lead into the _____, which may appear in the second or third sentence.

3. When a sentence early in a paragraph begins with a word such as *however* or _____, look closely at that sentence to see if it is the main idea.

4. The main idea may occur at the beginning, in the middle, or at the _____ of a paragraph.

REVIEW TEST 2

The main idea may appear at any place within each of the four paragraphs that follow. Write the number of each main idea sentence in the space provided.

_____ 1. ¹Wood was once the only material used in a home's framework. ²However, some homebuilders now have good reasons for using steel in constructing house frames. ³First, wood is not always available. ⁴Also, the cost of steel is often 20 percent less than that of wood. ⁵Furthermore, unlike wood, steel is termite-proof. ⁶Steel will not shrink, warp, or split. ⁷Steel will not catch on fire, as wood will. ⁸And steel is stronger and more durable than wood.

_____ 2. ¹Highway maintenance workers must be prepared to clean up just about any mess you can think of. ²Once, twenty thousand gallons of molasses leaked from a tanker truck. ³Highway workers spent hours scraping up the gooey mess. ⁴Another time, a load of live chickens escaped from an overturned truck. ⁵Workers ran all over trying to catch the birds. ⁶Some escaped and are still living in bushes near the accident site. ⁷One highway crew had to stop traffic to pick up a safe that someone had dropped. ⁸A highway crew in California reported that in one month they picked up fifty mattresses, twenty ladders, fifteen chairs, ten refrigerators, and three bathtubs.

_____ 3. ¹Lightning usually strikes outdoors. ²We've all heard about people who were struck by lightning while walking or working outside. ³But lightning can be harmful inside as well as outside. ⁴It can come in through an open window or door and then bounce around a room until it finds a way outside again. ⁵Also, any electrical appliance which conducts electricity can act as a magnet for dangerous lightning. ⁶Lightning can even be conducted through telephone wires and strike a person talking on the phone.

_____ 4. ¹It is becoming more and more common for single women to bear children. ²In 1960, only 5.3 percent of children had single moms. ³By 2013, that figure had increased to 40.6 percent. ⁴Among ethnic groups, African-American women are most likely to have children outside of marriage. ⁵Sixty-seven percent of African-American children are born to single mothers. ⁶Next are American Indian and native Alaskan women. ⁷Fifty-two percent of births to those women are outside of marriage. ⁸Forty-two percent of births to Hispanic women are to single women. ⁹Twenty-five percent of babies born to non-Hispanic white women are to single moms. ¹⁰And 17 percent of births to Asian or Pacific Island women are to unmarried women.

REVIEW TEST 3

Here is a chance to apply your understanding of signal words to a full-length reading. This selection was written by a former community college student who has strong opinions about what students really need to know as they begin their college careers. Read the selection and then answer the questions that follow. You'll find questions on vocabulary in context, main ideas, and supporting details.

Words to Watch

Below are some words in the reading that do not have strong context support. Each word is followed by the number of the paragraph in which it appears and its meaning there. These words are indicated in the selection by a small circle (°).

> *paralegal assistant* (7): a person trained to assist a lawyer
> *persist* (10): continue on
> *endured* (13): carried on in spite of hardship
> *projected* (22): gave the impression of

LEARNING SURVIVAL SKILLS
Jean Coleman

1   For four years I was a student at a community college. I went to night school as a part-time student for three years, and I was able to be a full-time student for one year. My first course was a basic writing course because I needed a review of grammar and the basics of writing. I did well in that course, and that set the tone for everything that followed.

2   It is now eleven years since I started college, and I have a good job with a Philadelphia accounting firm. When I was invited to write this article, the questions put to me were "What would you want to say to students who are just starting out in college?

What advice would you give? What experiences would it help to share?" I thought a lot about what it took for me to be a successful student. Here, then, are my secrets for survival in college and, really, for survival in life as well.

"Be Realistic."

3   The first advice that I'd give to beginning students is this: "Be realistic about how college will help you get a job." Some students believe that once they have college degrees, the world will be waiting on their doorsteps, ready to give them wonderful jobs. But the chances are that unless they've planned, there will be nobody on their doorsteps.

4   I remember the way my teacher in a study skills course dramatized this point in class. He played a student who had just been handed a college degree. He opened up an imaginary door, stepped through, and peered around in both directions outside. There was nobody to be seen. I understood the point he was making immediately. A college degree in itself isn't enough. We've got to prepare while we're in college to make sure our degree is a marketable one.

5   At that time I began to think seriously about (1) what I wanted to do in life and (2) whether there were jobs out there for what I wanted to do. I went to the counseling center and said, "I want to learn where the best job opportunities will be in the next ten years." The counselor gave me some ideas. If I had that question today, I'd just go to the Internet. Using the search engine Google, I'd type in "best jobs," and I would quickly have plenty of information about good future jobs.

6   The result of my personal career planning was that I eventually graduated from community college with a degree in accounting. I then got a job almost immediately, for I had chosen an excellent employment area. The firm that I work for paid my tuition as I went on to get my bachelor's degree. It is now paying for my work toward becoming a certified public accountant, and my salary increases regularly.

7   By way of contrast, I know a woman named Sheila who earned a bachelor's degree with honors in French. After graduation, she spent several unsuccessful months trying to find a job using her French degree. Sheila eventually wound up going to a specialized school where she trained for six months as a paralegal assistant°. She then got a job on the strength of that training—but her years of studying French were of no practical value in her career at all.

8   I'm not saying that college should serve only as a training ground for a job. People should take some courses just for the sake of learning. At the same time, they should take courses with a career in mind.

9   In my own case, I started college at the age of twenty-seven. I was divorced, had a six-year-old son to care for, and was working full time as a hotel night clerk. I was in school getting ready for the solid job I desperately needed. I am saying, then, that students must be realistic. If they will need a job soon after graduation, they should be sure to study in an area where jobs are available.

"Persist."

10 The older I get, the more I see that life lays on us some hard experiences. There are times for each of us when simple survival becomes a deadly serious matter. We must then learn to persist°—to struggle through each day and wait for better times to come—as they always do.

11 I think of one of my closest friends, Neil. After graduating from high school with me, Neil spent two years working as a stock boy at a local department store in order to save money for college tuition. He then went to the guidance office at the small college in our town. Incredibly, the counselor there told him, "Your IQ is not high enough to do college work." Thankfully, Neil decided to go anyway and earned his degree in five years—with a year out to care for his father, who had had a stroke one day at work.

12 Neil then got a job as a manager of a regional beauty supply firm. He met a woman who owned a salon, got married, and soon had two children. Three years later he found out that his wife was having an affair. I'll never forget the day Neil came over and sat at my kitchen table and told me what he had learned. He always seemed so much in control, but that morning he lowered his head into his hands and cried. "What's the point?" he kept saying in a low voice over and over to himself.

13 But Neil has endured°. He divorced his wife, won custody of his children, and learned how to be a single parent. Recently, Neil and I got letters informing us of the twentieth reunion of our high-school graduating class. Included was a short questionnaire for us to fill out that ended with this item: "What has been your outstanding accomplishment since graduation?" Neil wrote, "My outstanding accomplishment is that I have survived." I have a feeling that many of our high-school classmates, twenty years out in the world, would have no trouble understanding the truth of his statement.

14 I can think of people who started college with me who had not yet learned, like Neil, the basic skill of endurance. Life hit some of them with unexpected low punches and knocked them to the floor. There was Alan, whose girlfriend broke off their relationship. Alan stopped coming to class, and by the end of the semester, he was failing most of his courses. I also recall Nelson, whose old car kept breaking down. After Nelson put his last $200 into it, the brakes failed and needed to be replaced. Overwhelmed by his continuing car troubles, Nelson dropped out of school. And there was Rita, discouraged by her luck of the draw with teachers and courses. In sociology, she had a teacher who wasn't able to express ideas clearly. She also had a math teacher who talked too fast and seemed not to care at all about whether his students learned. To top it off, Rita's adviser had enrolled her in an economics course that put her to sleep. Rita told me she had expected college to be an exciting place, but instead she was getting

busywork assignments and trying to cope with hostile or boring teachers. Rita decided to drop her math course, and that must have set something in motion in her head, for she soon dropped her other courses as well.

15   In my experience, younger students seem more likely to drop out than do older students. I think some younger students are still in the process of learning that life slams people around without warning. I'm sure they feel that being knocked about is especially unfair because the work of college is hard enough without having to cope with other hardships.

16   In some situations, withdrawing from college may be the best response. But there are going to be times in college when students—young or old—must simply decide, "I am going to persist." They should remember that there are many other people out there who are quietly having hard times. I think of Dennis, a boy in my introductory psychology class, who lived mostly on peanut butter and discount-store loaves of white bread for almost a semester in his freshman year. And I remember Estelle, who came to school because she needed a job to support her sons when her husband, who was dying of leukemia, would no longer be present.

"Grow."

17   I don't think that people really have much choice about whether to grow in their lives. To not be open to growth is to die a little each day. Grow or die— it's as simple as that.

I have a friend, Jackie, who, when   18 she's not working, can almost always be found at home or at her mother's. Jackie eats too much and watches TV too much. I sometimes think that when she swings open her apartment door in response to my knock, I'll be greeted by her familiar chubby body with an eight-inch-screen television set occupying the place where her head used to be.

Jackie seems quietly desperate.   19 There is no growth or plan for growth in her life. I've said to her, "Go to school and study for a job you'll be excited about." She says, "It'll take me forever." Once Jackie said to me, "The favorite time of my life was when I was a teenager. I would lie on my bed listening to music and I would dream. I felt I had enormous power, and there seemed no way that life would stop me from realizing my biggest dreams. Now that power doesn't seem possible to me anymore."

I feel that Jackie must open some   20 new windows in her life. If she does not, her spirit is going to die. There are many ways to open new windows, and college is one of them. For this reason, I think people who are already in school should stay long enough to give it a chance. No one should turn down lightly such an opportunity for growth.

"Enjoy."

For all its challenges, college is often   21 a wonderful experience. If school had not been something I really enjoyed, I would not have made it.

22   In high school I felt I was shy, clumsy, and average. But in college, I was free to present myself in any way I chose. I decided from my first week in school that my college classmates and instructors were going to see the new, improved Jean. I projected° a confidence I didn't always feel. I sat near the front in every class. I took part in discussions. Instead of slipping away after class, I made a point to chat with my teachers and invite other students to have coffee with me. Soon I realized that my "act" had worked. People saw me as a confident, outgoing woman. I really liked this new image of myself as a successful college student.

23   Another of the pleasures of college was the excitement of walking into a class for the first time. As it turned out, some courses were more memorable than others. However, I rarely had a course that didn't have some real rewards to offer me.

24   I even enjoyed the physical preparation for a new class. I loved going to the bookstore and finding the textbooks I'd need. I liked to sit down with them, crack open their bindings, and smell their new-book scent. I made a habit of buying a new spiral-bound notebook for each of my classes. Writing the new course's name on the notebook cover and seeing those fresh, blank sheets waiting inside helped me feel organized and ready to tackle a new challenge.

25   One of the best parts of college was the people I've met. Some of them became friends I hope I'll keep forever. Even the ones I just knew briefly helped make my life richer. One of my best friends was Charlotte. Like me, she came back to school after her marriage broke up. When I first met Charlotte, she was scared to death. She was sure that she could never keep up with the younger students. She felt she would be over her head in returning to college. I'll never forget one day about three weeks into the term when she turned to me and broke into a silly grin. "You know, Jean," she said, "I'm doing as well in class as anyone else!" Seeing Charlotte's growing confidence helped me believe in my own ability to succeed.

26   Getting to know my instructors was a pleasure as well. I had more of a relationship with them than with my high-school teachers. They weren't perfect or all-knowing—but they were mostly good people who really cared about helping me get where I wanted to go.

In Conclusion

27   College helped me make it. I now have a secure job future. My son is doing well in school. I have friends. I am proud and happy. I still have my fears and my problems, but I have survived and done more than survive. I'm in control of my life. I believe college can do the same for you.

Questions about the Reading

Vocabulary in Context

_____ 1. In the sentences below, the word *peered* (pîrd) means
   A. joked.
   B. looked.
   C. raced.
   D. hid.

> "He opened up an imaginary door, stepped through, and peered around in both directions outside. There was nobody to be seen." (Paragraph 4)

_____ 2. In the sentence below, the word *overwhelmed* (ō-vər-hwĕlmd′) means
   A. overlooked.
   B. strengthened.
   C. defeated.
   D. unconcerned.

> "Overwhelmed by his continuing car troubles, Nelson dropped out of school." (Paragraph 14)

Central Point and Main Ideas

_____ 3. Which sentences best expresses the central point of the selection?
   A. All people experience great problems in the course of their lives.
   B. Following certain guidelines will help you succeed in school and in life.
   C. Divorce can be the beginning of a new and better life.
   D. Certain survival skills can help you become a successful accountant.

_____ 4. Which sentence best expresses the main idea of paragraphs 3–8?
   A. Students should make sure that college prepares them for a career that they will enjoy and in which jobs are available.
   B. If the author was planning her career today, she would simply check the Internet for good job opportunities.
   C. The author's friend Sheila ended up with a job that had nothing to do with her college degree.
   D. The author is now working as an accountant and also toward becoming a certified public accountant.

_____ 5. Which sentence best expresses the main idea of paragraphs 11–13?
A. Neil's story makes the point that sometimes the most important thing in life is to simply continue on.
B. The author's friend, Neil, suffered through some very hard times.
C. The author and Neil have kept in touch long after graduating together.
D. Even if someone tells you that you shouldn't go to college, you should still go.

_____ 6. Which sentence best expresses the main idea of paragraphs 18–20?
A. The author believes that her friend, Jackie, eats too much and watches too much TV.
B. The author's friend, Jackie, has lost her belief that she will realize her biggest dreams.
C. The author realizes that attending college is simply one way to grow as a person.
D. The author believes that her friend, Jackie, should stop sitting around the house and go to college in order to grow as a person.

_____ 7. Which sentence best expresses the main idea of paragraph 26?
A. The author realized that her college instructors had private lives of their own.
B. The author enjoyed working with and getting to know her college instructors.
C. In high school, the author thought her teachers had no private lives.
D. The author realized that most of her college instructors weren't perfect.

Supporting Details

_____ 8. The author
A. took a straight liberal arts curriculum.
B. switched from being a French major to an accounting major.
C. took accounting classes and ended up with a degree in art.
D. took some general interest classes, but ended up with a degree in accounting.

_____ 9. The author saw herself as shy, clumsy, and average, but decided to
A. project a confidence she didn't always feel.
B. sit in the middle of the class so no one would notice her.
C. get involved in school clubs.
D. drop out of any classes that seemed worthless.

_____10. The author states in paragraphs 14–16 that successful students
   A. have better luck with teachers than unsuccessful students.
   B. are often younger students.
   C. face fewer hardships than unsuccessful students.
   D. make up their minds to keep trying despite hardships.

Discussion Questions

1. The author's "secrets" for survival in college and in life are "be realistic," "persist," "grow," and "enjoy." Which of these points do you feel are most important for you to remember, and why?

2. Jean Coleman gives a lot of advice to students just starting college. Is there anything she does *not* mention that you think beginning students need to know? What is it?

3. The author suggests that students should find out what jobs will be available in the future and then get a degree in a related field. What type of career do you think you'd be interested in, and why? What degree will help you enter that field?

Note: Writing assignments for this selection appear on page 508.

Check Your Performance   **FINDING MAIN IDEAS**

Activity	Number Right	Points	Score
Review Test 1 (4 items)	_____	× 5 =	_____
Review Test 2 (4 items)	_____	× 5 =	_____
Review Test 3 (10 items)	_____	× 6 =	_____
		TOTAL SCORE =	_____%

Enter your total score into the **Reading Performance Chart: Review Tests** on the inside back cover.

FINDING MAIN IDEAS: Mastery Test 1

The main idea may appear at any place within each of the five paragraphs that follow. Write the number of each main idea sentence in the space provided.

_____ 1. ¹In many homes, the refrigerator door is the family bulletin board. ²On it, people place things they don't want to lose. ³These may include the phone number of the local police or of a favorite baby sitter. ⁴Also kept there are reminders, including notes about social events. ⁵In addition, the refrigerator is a favorite spot to display things, such as a child's art work.

_____ 2. ¹The first frost in Montana occurs around September 15. ²Colorado gets its first frost about October 1. ³Oklahoma's first frost is near the end of October. ⁴Louisiana can expect a frost around the middle of November. ⁵And Florida can look for a frost about the middle of December. ⁶Clearly, the farther south you go, the later the first frost date is likely to be.

_____ 3. ¹Have you ever wondered why we are attracted to certain people as friends and lovers? ²Several factors help explain our attraction to other people. ³One key is physical closeness. ⁴We are more likely to be interested in people we see often. ⁵What we think of as good looks is also important. ⁶We tend to like people we find physically attractive. ⁷In addition, we are drawn to people with whom we share similar backgrounds, interests, and values.

_____ 4. ¹Marta is fourteen years old and lives in a village in San Salvador. ²As in most peasant families there, every day the women prepare tortillas, thin round pancakes made from mashed corn. ³In San Salvador, the tortillas are made in a few steps, the same way they were made hundreds of years ago. ⁴Marta collects the corn and puts it in a pot of water to soak. ⁵The next day, she puts the wet corn through a hand grinder. ⁶Her mother then puts the ground corn on a block of stone and mashes it back and forth many times until it is a pasty dough. ⁷This dough is then patted into tortillas, which are cooked on a flat griddle over an open fire. ⁸They are eaten with salt and a portion of beans.

(Continues on next page)

_____ 5. [1]When people think of "Frankenstein," they usually think of a dangerous monster with a stitched-on head. [2]However, the original creature, presented in the 1818 novel by Mary Shelley, was nothing like the modern Hollywood version. [3]First of all, his appearance is described as "hideous" in the novel, but he doesn't have a flat head or bolts sticking out of his neck. [4]In addition, the creature in the book is to be pitied, not feared. [5]He sits and cries over the fact that people reject him. [6]He is ultimately driven to violence because he wants to be loved, and no one will love him. [7]He has human emotions even though he is not a human. [8]Finally, "Frankenstein" isn't even the monster's name. [9]Dr. Frankenstein is the scientist who created the monster. [10]The novel is named after him, not his creation.

FINDING MAIN IDEAS: Mastery Test 2

The main idea may appear at any place within each of the five paragraphs that follow. Write the number of each main idea sentence in the space provided.

_____ 1. ¹Many of us might think that only children believe in ghosts and spirits. ²However, believing in ghosts is actually quite common among adults. ³In a recent study of 1000 adults, 45 percent said that they believe ghosts are real and that the dead can and do come back to visit us. ⁴Most did not think these spirits could actually hurt us, but they did believe that some spirits come back to frighten the living. ⁵A majority of the adults in the study said they had never seen a ghost. ⁶Still, most believed "they might" at some point in the future.

_____ 2. ¹Being a judge may be an important job, but judges often face the down-to-earth problem of fighting off sleepiness during a long trial. ²One reason is that arguments made by attorneys are usually routine. ³They are also often long and boring. ⁴Another reason is that judges must remain seated throughout a trial. ⁵This can slow the body down, especially after lunch. ⁶Also, courtrooms are usually stuffy. ⁷Air circulation is poor, there are no windows, and lighting is dim.

_____ 3. ¹As people get older, their physical and mental capabilities decline. ²Yet research has shown that as people age, they are likely to feel happier. ³One poll found that two-thirds of people over 65 were happy with their lives. ⁴In contrast, only about half of the people between the ages of 18 and 49 said that they were pleased with their lives.

_____ 4. ¹Some foreign students are uncomfortable with the casual relationship that exists between American teachers and students. ²In many countries, students treat teachers much more formally. ³In addition, foreign students have the language problem to deal with. ⁴Their English classes may not have prepared them to understand fast-paced conversations filled with slang expressions. ⁵Foreign students' social lives can be difficult as well. ⁶Having a background so different from that of other students can make it hard to find friends. ⁷Obviously, life in America can be hard on foreign students.

(Continues on next page)

_____ 5. [1]Aron Ralston is a mountain climber with an amazing story. [2]In 2003, Ralston was climbing down a canyon when a large boulder fell and pinned his arm against the canyon wall. [3]Within minutes, Ralston knew that he would not be able to free his arm from beneath the 800-pound rock. [4]Ralston was hiking alone and had not told anyone where he was going. [5]With only 12 ounces of water and little food, Ralston assumed he was going to die. [6]However, on his fifth day trapped in the canyon, Ralston realized how he could save his life. [7]He could cut off his arm! [8]Using only a dull two-inch knife, Aron was able to amputate his arm in about 90 minutes. [9]He then hiked eight miles in the desert sun until he found other hikers, who called for help.

FINDING MAIN IDEAS: Mastery Test 3

The main idea may appear at any place within each of the five paragraphs that follow. Write the number of each main idea sentence in the space provided.

_____ 1. [1]Velcro is a fastening tape that was first seen as a replacement for the zipper. [2]The ease in opening and closing Velcro has given it some interesting uses. [3]For instance, astronauts have used it to keep objects — and themselves—from floating off into space. [4]They also have had small pieces of Velcro stuck inside their helmets so they could scratch an itchy nose. [5]Today, the fabric is used to fasten the fireproof suits of race-car drivers. [6]This allows a driver to jump out of a suit in seconds if necessary. [7]Velcro is also used to join two parts of the artificial heart.

_____ 2. [1]According to a medical journal, there are some important guidelines for having your ears or other body parts pierced. [2]First, let a professional who uses sterile instruments perform the task. [3]Second, do not pierce your ears if you have a serious medical condition, including heart disease, blood disorder, or diabetes. [4]Also, for six weeks, do not wear rings that contain nickel or a gold alloy or that are gold-plated. [5]Next, avoid the risk of infection by washing the pierced area twice a day with cotton dipped in rubbing alcohol. [6]Finally, if the area becomes red, swollen, or sore, see a doctor immediately.

_____ 3. [1]Every week, guns kill several hundred Americans. [2]To cut down on these deaths, some say we should change the background check waiting period from three days to 10. [3]This would give the FBI time to complete checks. [4]Others suggest passing laws that would ban all assault weapons and guns that can fire more than 10 rounds without reloading. [5]Finally, many Americans agree that we simply need more research on what actually *could* stop gun violence. [6]These are just a few of many ideas on how to reduce the dangers of guns in America.

(Continues on next page)

_____ 4. ¹A single computer chip can hold a great deal of information. ²For several reasons, veterinarians are implanting computer microchips under the skin of pets. ³First, the chips can be used to recognize an animal that has been lost or stolen. ⁴Second, they can be used to identify purebred animals that have come from breeders. ⁵Breeders who guarantee that an animal is free from defects can identify the animal later in life. ⁶And third, the animal's history can be kept on the chip. ⁷This means that if a pet changes vets, the new doctor can see what treatments the animal has undergone.

_____ 5. ¹The ways people stay informed about important events in the world have changed in the past few decades. ²People still do read newspapers and magazines and watch the news. ³However, many people now use their computers to read online news sites during the day. ⁴These sites change almost the instant news happens. ⁵Others keep informed by using news apps on their phones, making it easy to scan headlines and read stories no matter where they are. ⁶Still others engage in or view news-related conversations and debates on social media. ⁷Many people find that they learn the most about current events when they discuss them with other people.

FINDING MAIN IDEAS: Mastery Test 4

The main idea may appear at any place within each of the five paragraphs that follow. Write the number of each main idea sentence in the space provided.

_____ 1. ¹Before much was known about germs, doctors unknowingly caused much illness and death by spreading germs. ²Before the 20th century, doctors did not wash their hands between tasks. ³Little was known about germs and how they were spread. ⁴Doctors would finish one operation, then immediately start on another. ⁵Then they would examine patients, never realizing that they were carrying bacteria from one person to another. ⁶In many cases, they seriously infected the very people they were trying to cure.

_____ 2. ¹Instincts are animal behaviors that don't need learning. ²One example of instinct is the way birds build nests. ³Birds don't stop to think about which type of nest to build. ⁴All robins, for instance, build their nests the same way. ⁵Also, ants don't think about how to get food. ⁶Without lessons, they gather food in the same way that every other ant in the hill does. ⁷A third example is that all cats lick themselves clean without learning to do so.

_____ 3. ¹Husbands once had more power in marriages: they earned more, were better educated, and had jobs with more prestige. ²But as more women finish college, get better jobs, and earn more, they gain power at home. ³Another factor in the balance of power is whether or not both partners care equally about the marriage. ⁴If the husband, for example, cares more about staying married than the wife does, the wife will have more power. ⁵That is because the husband will do more to please her. ⁶Thus the power structure of marriage has become more complicated in recent years.

(Continues on next page)

_____ 4. [1]What steps can you take if you turn an ankle or strain a muscle? [2]Many sports physicians recommend the "RICE" formula for sprains and strains: Rest, Ice, Compression, and Elevation. [3]First, rest the joint or muscle that hurts. [4]Secondly, apply ice to the injured area. [5]Ice may be used at regular times for two days. [6]A compression bandage, such as an Ace bandage, will also ease the pain. [7]Finally, elevating an injured ankle or knee will keep pressure off it and prevent further damage. [8]Of course, if the pain continues or if the injury swells, you should see a doctor at once.

_____ 5. [1]Sometimes it's hard to remember that cats and dogs are descended from wild animals. [2]Even though these house pets have been tame for many centuries, they still have some leftover wild qualities. [3]For example, watch a cat when she drinks water. [4]You'll notice that her ears are turned around to listen for any sounds behind her. [5]This is the result of a wild cat's (lions, tigers, leopards) instinct of listening for approaching animals while drinking at a water hole. [6]Or perhaps you've seen a dog turn around and around before settling down for a nap. [7]Wild dogs (wolves, coyotes, foxes) are often observed trotting around in circles in order to flatten out resting spots in tall grasses and scratchy weeds. [8]Although Rover may actually be preparing to stretch out on the sofa, this old instinct still remains.

FINDING MAIN IDEAS: Mastery Test 5

The main idea may appear at any place within each of the five paragraphs that follow. Write the number of each main idea sentence in the space provided.

_____ 1. ¹There are six major problems that students bring into the high-school classroom, says the National Education Association. ²First, about a quarter of all students smoke marijuana regularly, and more than two-thirds use alcohol. ³Also, 40 percent of today's fourteen-year-old girls will get pregnant in their teens, and 80 percent of these will drop out of high school. ⁴A third problem is that 30 percent of all students now in high school will drop out. ⁵In addition, one out of three girls and one out of eight boys under eighteen years old have reported being sexually abused. ⁶Fifth, 15 percent of girls will suffer an eating disorder during part or all of their teenage years. ⁷Finally, suicide is the second most common cause of death among fifteen- through nineteen-year-olds.

_____ 2. ¹In California, a "Victim's Bill of Rights" law was passed recently. ²This law broadened the type of evidence that could be used in court. ³The idea was to keep criminals from going free because of legal loopholes. ⁴But defense lawyers soon learned that they, too, could use this law. ⁵In rape trials especially, the new law could be used to move part of the blame onto the victim. ⁶This was done by presenting evidence, not permitted before, that the victim was careless or sexually "loose." ⁷Therefore, a law intended to protect crime victims turned out to have just the opposite effect.

_____ 3. ¹The far inland parts of Antarctica seem more like a different planet than part of our Earth. ²Because this area of Antarctica is at the very bottom of the world, the temperatures often fall below -100 degrees. ³Sustained winds of 80 miles per hour or more can howl across the icy land for days on end. ⁴There are no trees, buildings, or hills to block or slow down the winds. ⁵Obviously, there are no signs of any kind of life present, and total darkness covers the land from April to October! ⁶And although there is land in Antarctica, most of it is buried more than a mile beneath the ever-present snow and ice. ⁷Because temperatures always remain well below freezing, some of this ice pack that makes up the strange land of Antarctica is estimated to be more than a million years old.

(Continues on next page)

_____ 4. [1]Our life stages—for example, birth, puberty, death—may be set by biology. [2]However, how we view those stages is shaped by society. [3]During the Middle Ages, for example, children dressed—and were expected to act—like little adults. [4]Adolescence became a separate stage of life only fairly recently, when a teenage subculture appeared. [5]Before that, young people were "children" until about age 16. [6]Then they went to work, married, and had their own children. [7]Today, young adulthood has become a new stage of life, covering about ages 20 to 30. [8]And now that people live longer and spend many years in active retirement, older adulthood has also become a distinct life stage.

_____ 5. [1]Police raids on "massage parlors" are often reported in the newspapers. [2]Women are arrested for working as prostitutes. [3]Their clients risk arrest as well. [4]The prostitutes often have a long record of similar arrests. [5]A better way to solve this social problem might be to simply legalize prostitution. [6]It could be a woman's—or man's—right to sell her or his sexual services, if that is what she or he wants to do. [7]If prostitution were legalized, the business would be safer for everyone involved. [8]Prostitutes could be required to have regular health checks. [9]They would also have legal protection if their clients acted abusively.

FINDING MAIN IDEAS: Mastery Test 6

The main idea may appear at any place within each of the five paragraphs that follow. Write the number of each main idea sentence in the space provided.

_____ 1. [1]According to one researcher, the distance we like to keep between ourselves and other people depends on who the other people are. [2]The space within about one foot from us is "intimate" space. [3]We share it willingly only with loved ones. [4]If forced to share it with strangers (in a crowded elevator, for instance), we feel uncomfortable. [5]Between one and four feet away is our "personal" space, which we share with friends. [6]This is about how far apart we sit at a restaurant, for example. [7]Between about four and ten feet away is "social" space. [8]This is the distance we keep from strangers at parties and other gatherings. [9]Finally, over ten feet away is "public" space, a distance at which we can pretty much ignore others.

_____ 2. [1]A bullfighter usually kneels in front of the bull before a fight begins. [2]Audience members are amazed at his courage. [3]However, the truth is that by kneeling, the bullfighter tricks the bull into being gentle. [4]Among some animals, when two males fight, one can signal he gives up by taking a yielding position. [5]The animal drops to the ground and raises his backside. [6]This position tells the other male that he has won and thus reduces his instinct to fight. [7]For this reason, the bull thinks the kneeling bullfighter is giving up. [8]Therefore, the bull does not attack.

_____ 3. [1]The reason we shiver and get goosebumps when we are frightened has to do with our animal nature. [2]When animals see or hear something threatening, their fur stands on end. [3]This reaction makes them look larger and thus more dangerous to an enemy. [4]In addition, extra blood flows to their muscles, getting them ready for action. [5]Humans react in the same way. [6]When we sense danger, goosebumps appear where our fur would stand on end—if we had fur. [7]Also, since more blood is going to our muscles, less blood flows to our skin, making us feel cold. [8]We shiver, then, to get warm.

(Continues on next page)

_____ 4. ¹If you want to, you can jump in your car and *drive* to Alaska. ²The Alcan Highway (short for Alaska-Canada) stretches for 1422 miles from British Columbia, Canada, to Delta Junction, Alaska. ³Along the way, you'll see amazing mountains, ancient ice packs, and the occasional moose or grizzly bear. ⁴You'll stop at small frontier towns in the Yukon and meet all sorts of interesting people. ⁵However, you'll also have to deal with very rough patches of road the further north you go. ⁶Nearly everyone who drives the entire Alcan Highway experiences at least one flat tire along the way. ⁷Also, towns may be more than 100 miles apart and may contain little more than a closed gas station and an empty campground once you reach them. ⁸So, while driving the Alcan Highway can be an exciting adventure, it can also be a difficult journey.

_____ 5. ¹The Dionnes were the first quintuplets to survive their infancy. ²They were born on May 28, 1934, in a tiny Canadian town. ³The five identical girls were born to a poor farming couple who already had six children. ⁴The story of the Dionnes is a strange and even tragic one. ⁵The Canadian government took custody of the quints away from their parents. ⁶The government then built a sort of theme park called "Quintland," to house the five little girls. ⁷As many as 6,000 visitors a day visited Quintland, where they could watch the Dionnes through a one-way mirror. ⁸When they were 18, the girls moved back to their parents' home. ⁹But soon they broke off contact with their parents, claiming that their father was molesting them. ¹⁰As adults, the Dionnes were very poor, having never learned any way to support themselves. ¹¹They sued the Canadian government to share in the profits that it had made on Quintland.

This Chapter in a Nutshell

- To help make their ideas clear, writers use **signal words,** also known as **transitions**—words that carry the reader from one idea to the next.

- Typical addition words are *for one thing, second, also, another, in addition,* and *finally.*

- Typical time words are *first, next, then, after,* and *last.*

Yyou will become a better reader if you notice **signal words**. These are the words that writers provide to make the connections between their ideas clear. There are two common kinds of signal words, also known as **transitions**:

- Words that show addition
- Words that show time

Addition Words

Put a check (✓) beside the item that is easier to read and understand:

_____ I hate my job because of the long hours. My boss is often rude to me.

_____ I hate my job because of the long hours. Also, my boss is often rude to me.

As you probably noted, the second item is easier to understand. The word *also* makes it clear that the writer is presenting two reasons for hating his or her job. One reason is that the hours are long. *Another* reason is that the boss is rude. *Also* and words or phrases like it are known as addition words.

Addition words (and other signal words) are like signs on the road that guide travelers. They are also known as "bridge" words, carrying the reader across from one idea to the next:

I hate my job because of the long hours. , my boss is often rude to me.

Addition words tell us that writers are *adding to* their thoughts. They help writers organize their information and present it clearly to readers. In the cartoon on the right, the words *three ways* introduce a list, and the words *First, Second,* and *third* present each of the three ways to live longer.

"There are three ways to live longer. First, lose weight! Second, quit smoking! And third, stay out of the sun!"

Examples

The following examples contain addition words. Notice how these words introduce ideas that *add to* what has already been said.

- A good dinner and a glass of wine at the end of the day relax me. *In addition,* they make my problems seem smaller.

- Americans spend the biggest portion of their money on medical and dental care. The *next* biggest area of spending is on groceries.

- In 1870, the U.S. Constitution was amended to guarantee men of any race the right to vote. *Another* amendment in 1920 granted women the right to vote.

Below are some common addition words:

Addition Words

one	to begin with	in addition	last
first	another	next	last of all
first of all	second	moreover	final
for one thing	also	furthermore	finally

PRACTICE 1

Complete each sentence with a suitable addition word or phrase from the box below. Try to use each transition once. Then, in the spaces provided, write the letter of the transition you have chosen.

| **A.** also | **B.** another | **C.** finally |
| **D.** in addition | **E.** second | |

Hint: Make sure that each addition word or phrase that you choose fits smoothly into the flow of the sentence. Test each choice by reading the sentence aloud.

_____ 1. There are three reasons why top athletes make so much money. For one thing, they receive big salaries just for playing their sport. Second, they earn huge fees for personal appearances. _____, they make even more money by endorsing products.

_____ 2. Desert plants such as cactus store up water so they can survive long periods without rain. Desert animals _____ find a way to survive with little water.

_____ 3. Paper and plastics are two products that many communities ask people to recycle. _____ is used motor oil.

_____ 4. Bats are gentle creatures that will bite another animal only in self-defense. _____, a single bat can eat more than 1,200 mosquitoes an hour.

_____ 5. Many couples today are busier than ever. First of all, they must raise their own children. Their _____ responsibility is to care for aging parents.

PRACTICE 2

A. Below is a paragraph that is organized with the help of addition words. Underline the **three** addition words. They will help you then complete the outline of the paragraph.

> ¹A recent study suggested that parents should be on the lookout for stress in their children. ²There are several signs of stress in young people. ³Unusual tiredness in a child is one sign. ⁴Another is temper tantrums. ⁵And a third is the child forgetting known facts, which may result from mental exhaustion.

Main idea: There are several signs of stress in young people.

1. _____

2. _____

3. _____

B. Again, underline the **three** addition words. Then complete the outline of the paragraph.

> ¹Most people think of pizza as junk food, but pizza contains healthful ingredients. ²First of all, the crust is rich in B vitamins, which keep the nervous system humming smoothly. ³Also, the tomato sauce is an excellent source of vitamin A, which is essential for good vision, among other things. ⁴And finally, the mozzarella cheese contains protein and calcium, each of which supports good health in many ways, including keeping bones strong.

Main idea: Pizza contains healthful ingredients.

1. _____

_____

2. _____

_____

3. _____

_____

C. Once again, underline the **three** addition words. Then complete the outline of the paragraph.

> ¹Walking can be a rewarding experience. ²To begin with, walking lets you chat with your neighbors and see for yourself what's going on in your neighborhood. ³In addition, a brisk walk is an excellent and inexpensive form of exercise. ⁴Moreover, physical exercise such as walking acts as a natural anti-depressant.

Main idea: Walking can be a rewarding experience.

1. _____

2. _____

3. _____

Time Words

Check (✓) the item that is easier to read and understand:

___ I let the cooked turkey sit for thirty minutes. I carved it.

___ I let the cooked turkey sit for thirty minutes. Then I carved it.

The word *Then* in the second item makes the relationship between the sentences clear. *After* letting the cooked turkey sit for a while, the writer carves it. *Then* and words like it are time words.

I let the cooked turkey sit for thiry minutes. ***THEN*** , I carved it.

Time words tell us *when* something happened in relation to when something else happened. They help writers organize and make clear the order of events, stages, and steps in a process. In the cartoon on the right, the words *First, Then,* and *Finally* describe the sequence of three steps needed to open e-mail.

On the following page are some common words that show time.

"It's very simple. First you click on 'E-mail.' Then you enter your password. Finally, you click on 'Read mail.'"

Time Words

before	next	while	later
previously	soon	during	after
first	often	until	eventually
second	as	now	finally
third	when	then	last

Note: Additional ways of showing time are dates ("In 1850 . . ."; "Throughout the 20th century . . ."; "By 2018 . . .") and other time references ("Within a week . . ."; "by the end of the month . . ."; "in two years . . .").

Examples

The following items contain time words. Notice how these words show us *when* something takes place.

- I quickly shut the back door *after* the mouse ran out.
- *Before* their baby daughter was born, my sister and her husband were sure it was a boy.
- Some teenagers giggled loudly *during* the movie's love scenes. *Then* an usher asked them to leave.

PRACTICE 3

Complete each sentence with a suitable time word from the box. Try to use each transition once. Then, in the space provided, write the letter of the transition you have chosen.

A. after	**B.** before	**C.** then
D. until	**E.** when	

> *Hint:* Make sure that each time word or phrase that you choose fits smoothly into the flow of the sentence. Test each choice by reading the sentence aloud.

_____ 1. _____ John Kennedy served as a United States Senator from Massachusetts, he was elected president.

_____ 2. Here is a good way to prepare for a test: Study hard for an hour or so. _____ take a ten-minute break.

_____ 3. James had difficulty learning to swim _____ he learned how to float.

_____ 4. _____ Washington, D.C. was chosen, the capital of the United States was Philadelphia.

_____ 5. _____ she runs out of any grocery item, Gail writes it on her shopping list.

 PRACTICE 4

A. Below is a paragraph that is organized with the help of time words. Underline the **three** time words.

> [1]A psychologist placed a banana just outside the cage of a chimpanzee and a stick inside the cage. [2]Soon, the chimp grabbed the stick and poked it through the bars of the cage. [3]Next, the chimp dragged the banana within reach. [4]Finally, the chimp took the banana and ate it.

B. Below is another paragraph that is organized with the help of time words. Underline the **three** time words. Then complete the outline of the paragraph.

> [1]Take the following steps to find the right boyfriend or girlfriend. [2]First, trust your own instincts. [3]Don't be distracted by what your best friend thinks you should be looking for in a partner. [4]Your tastes are what matters here. [5]The next step is to widen your social circle. [6]Use Facebook, Instagram, and other social media as well as your phone, parties, clubs, church, and volunteer activities to be in touch with as many people as possible. [7]You're not going to run into the right person by sitting at home watching TV. [8]And last, don't settle for just anyone who is willing to date you. [9]If you're hanging onto a so-so relationship just so you aren't alone, you won't be ready if someone really special comes along.

Main idea: Use the following tips to find the right boyfriend or girlfriend.

1. _____

2. _____

3. _____

C. Underline the **five** time words. Then complete the outline of the paragraph.

¹Do you have a noticeable stain or burn in your carpeting? ²It's a problem you can correct. ³First, use a sharp utility knife to cut out the damaged area (but not the padding underneath). ⁴Second, cut a patch the same size and shape from a leftover piece of carpet or a spot of carpeting that's not noticeable, such as under a sofa. ⁵Next, cut a piece of cardboard a little larger than the patch. ⁶Then place the cardboard where you cut out the damaged piece of carpet. ⁷Last, glue the carpet patch to the cardboard.

Main idea: A noticeable stain or burn in a carpet can be corrected.

1. _____

_____

2. _____

_____

3. _____

_____

4. _____

_____

5. _____

_____

Two Final Points about Signal Words

1 Some signal words have the same meaning. For example, *also, moreover,* and *furthermore* all mean "in addition." Writers like to use different signal words to avoid repetition.

2 Certain words can serve as two different types of signal words, depending on how they are used. For example, the word *first* may be used as an addition word to show that the writer is presenting a list of details:

● My sister has some unusual shopping habits. *First,* she will never shop at a store unless there is a sale going on. *Moreover,* she . . .

First can also be used to signal a time order:

● The coach was unhappy with the way his team was playing. *First,* he called for a time-out. *Then* . . .

CHAPTER REVIEW

In this chapter, you learned how writers use signal words, also called transitions, to help make their ideas clear. You also learned two common kinds of signal words:

- **Addition words**

    — Writers use addition words to present a list of reasons, examples, or other details that support an idea. The items have no time order, but are listed in whatever order the writer chooses.

    — Words that signal addition include *for one thing, second, also, in addition,* and *finally.*

- **Time words**

    — Writers use time words to discuss a series of events or steps in the order in which they happen.

    — Words that signal time order include *first, next, then, after,* and *last.*

The next chapter—Chapter 8—will help you learn three other important kinds of signal words: words that show examples, contrast, and cause-effect.

 On the Web: If you are using this book in class, you can visit our website for additional practice with words that signal addition and time. Go to **www.townsendpress.com** and click on "Learning Center."

 REVIEW TEST 1

To review what you've learned in this chapter, complete each item by filling in the blank or writing in the letter of the correct answer.

1. Signal words are also known as ____transitions____. They are words or phrases (like *also* or *another* or *then* or *last of all*) that show the relationships between ideas.

_____ 2. TRUE OR FALSE? Signal words are like bridges that connect one idea with another.

3. Typical _____addition_____ words are *for one thing, also, moreover,* and *another.* Such words tell us the writer is presenting one or more ideas that add to the same line of thought as a previous idea.

4. Typical _____time_____ words are *then, next, later,* and *after.* They tell us when something happened in relation to when something else happened.

REVIEW TEST 2

A. (1–2.) Name the type of signal word used in each of the following cartoons.

"You really want to get into better shape? For one thing, spend less time on the couch. Also, quit snacking on garbage between meals. In addition, chase your tail more often."

"Let me see if I have this straight. I started out as an egg. Then, I became a tadpole. Next, a froglet. And eventually, the frog I am today?"

© 1998 Randy Glasbergen. www.glasbergen.com

___A___ 1. A. addition B. time   _____ 2. A. addition B. time

B. (3–4.) Fill in each blank with one of the signal words in the box. Use each word once. Then write the letter of the word in the space provide.

A. after	B. also

___B___ 1. An ideal apartment should be close to work and school. It should _____B_____ be in a safe area. In addition, it should be reasonably priced.

_A_   2. One way to start writing is to just get anything at all down on paper. Don't worry about spelling or punctuation or even making much sense. _____ you have broken the ice by getting a lot of words on the page, you can start to shape your paper.

C. (5–7.) Fill in each blank with an appropriate signal word from the box. Use each transition once.

soon	then	when

[1]A city in California made out a $26,000 check to Thomas Russell, a tax collector in the city. [2]But the check was mistakenly sent to an inmate by the same name. [3](5) _When_ it was delivered to the Tracy County jail, the inmate cashed the check, posted bond, and left jail. [4]Officials (6) _soon_ discovered their mistake. [5]They quickly tracked down the offender, and he was (7) _then_ put back in jail.

D. (8–10.) Fill in each blank with an appropriate signal word from the box. Use each transition once.

another	one	third

[1]Humans developed several physical features that make them differ from other animals. [2](8) _one_ human feature is the ability to stand and walk upright. [3]With their eyes at a high level, humans are able to see distant objects. [4](9) _Another_ distinctive human feature is their teeth and jaws. [5]Human beings have smaller, more even teeth than other animals. [6]A (10) _Third_ human feature is the most important: a large brain. [7]The human brain, for instance, is almost three times as large as the chimpanzee's.

Here is a chance to apply your understanding of signal words to a full-length reading. Maria Cardenas grew up in a family of migrant workers. The family moved from state to state, following the fruit and vegetable harvest. Maria became used to backbreaking labor, poverty, and violence. Her hard times, as well as her own lack of education, could have ended her hopes for a better life. But, as this selection will show, Maria has found the courage both to dream and to make her dreams become reality.

Read the selection and then answer the questions that follow. You'll find questions on vocabulary in context, main ideas, supporting details, and signal words.

Words to Watch

Below are some words in the reading that do not have strong context support. Each word is followed by the number of the paragraph in which it appears and its meaning there. These words are indicated in the selection by a small circle (°).

shattered (17): broken into pieces; destroyed
abducted (18): taken away by force
taunted (22): cruelly teased
overwhelmed (24): overpowered
briskly (24): in a lively manner
GED (24): general equivalency diploma (equal to a high-school diploma)
eligible (27): qualified

MIGRANT CHILD TO COLLEGE WOMAN

Maria Cardenas

1   As I walk into the classroom, the teacher gazes at me with her piercing green eyes. I feel myself shrinking and burning up with guilt. I go straight to her desk and hand her the excuse slip. Just like all the other times, I say, "I was sick." I hate lying, but I have to. I don't want my parents to get in trouble.

2   I'm not a very good liar. She makes me hold out my hands, inspecting my dirty fingernails and calluses. She knows exactly where I've been the past several days. When you pick tomatoes and don't wear gloves, your hands get rough and stained from the plant oils. Soap doesn't wash that out.

3   In the background, I can hear the students giggling as she asks her usual questions: "What was wrong? Was your brother sick, too? Do you feel better today?" Of course I don't

feel better. My whole body aches from those endless hot days spent harvesting crops from dawn to dusk. I was never absent by choice.

4   That year, in that school, I think my name was "Patricia Rodriguez," but I'm not sure. My brother and I used whatever name our mother told us to use each time we went to a new school. We understood that we had to be registered as the children of parents who were in the United States legally, in case Immigration ever checked up.

5   My parents had come to the States in the late '60s to work in the fields and earn money to feed their family. They paid eight hundred dollars to someone who smuggled them across the border, and they left us with our aunt and uncle in Mexico. My five-year-old brother, Joel, was the oldest. I was 4, and then came Teresa, age 3, and baby Bruno. The other kids in the neighborhood teased us, saying, "They won't come back for you." Three years later, our parents sent for us to join them in Texas. My little heart sang as we waved good-bye to those neighbor kids in Rio Verde. My father did love us!

6   My parents worked all the time in the fields. Few other options were open to them because they had little education. At first, our education was important to them. They were too scared to put us in school right away, but when I was 8, they did enroll us. I do remember that my first-grade report card said I was "Antonietta Gonzales." My father made sure we had everything we needed—tablets, crayons, ruler, and the little box to put your stuff in. He bragged to his friends about his children going to school. Now we could talk for our parents. We could translate their words for the grocer, the doctor, and the teachers. If Immigration came by, we could tell them we were citizens, and because we were speaking English, they wouldn't ask any more questions.

7   In the years to come, I often reminded myself that my father had not forgotten us like the fathers of so many kids I knew. It became more important for me to remember that as it became harder to see that he loved us. He had hit my mother once in a while as I was growing up, but when his own mother died in Mexico in 1973, his behavior grew much worse. My uncles told me that my father, the youngest of the family, had often beaten his mother. Maybe it was the guilt he felt when she died, but for whatever reason, he started drinking heavily, abusing my mother emotionally and physically, and terrorizing us kids. The importance of our education faded away, and now my papa thought my brother and I should work more in the fields. We would work all the time—on school vacations, holidays, weekends, and every day after school. When there were lots of tomatoes to pick, I went to school only every other day.

8   If picking was slow, I stayed home after school and cooked for the family.

I started as soon as I got home in the afternoon. I used the three large pots my mother owned: one for beans, one for rice or soup, and one for hot salsa. There were also the usual ten pounds of flour or *maseca*, ground corn meal, for the tortillas. I loved this cooking because I could eat as much as I wanted and see that the little kids got enough before the older family members finished everything. By this time there were three more children in our family, and we often went to bed hungry. (My best subject in school was lunch, and my plate was always clean.)

9   Other than lunchtime, my school life passed in a blur. I remember a little about teachers showing us how to sound words out. I began to stumble through elementary readers. But then we'd move again, or I'd be sent to the fields.

10   Life was never easy in those days. Traveling with the harvest meant living wherever the bosses put us. We might be in little houses with one outdoor toilet for the whole camp. Other times the whole crew, all fifty or one hundred of us, were jammed into one big house. Working in the fields meant blistering sun, aching muscles, sliced fingers, bug bites, and my father yelling when we didn't pick fast enough to suit him.

11   But we were kids, so we found a way to have some fun. My brother and I would make a game of competing with each other and the other adults. I never did manage to pick more than Joel, but I came close. One time I picked 110 baskets of cucumbers to Joel's 115. We made thirty-five cents a basket.

12   Of course, we never saw any of that money. At the end of the week, whatever the whole family had earned was given to my father. Soon he stopped working altogether. He just watched us, chatted with the field bosses, and drank beer. He began to beat all of us kids as well as our mother. We didn't work fast enough for him. He wanted us to make more money. He called us names and threw stones and vegetables at us. The other workers did nothing to make him stop. I was always scared of my father, but I loved him even though he treated us so badly. I told myself that he loved us, but that alcohol ruled his life.

13   I knew what controlled my father's life, but I never thought about being in control of my own. I did as I was told, spoke in a whisper, and tried not to be noticed. Because we traveled with the harvest, my brothers and sisters and I attended three or four different schools in one year. When picking was good, I went to the fields instead of school. When the little kids got sick, I stayed home to watch them. When I did go to school, I didn't understand very much. We spoke only Spanish at home. I don't know how I got through elementary school, much less to high school, because I only knew how to add, subtract, and multiply. And let's just say I got "introduced" to English writing skills and grammar. School was a strange foreign place where I went when I

could, sitting like a ghost in a corner alone. I could read enough to help my mother fill out forms in English. But enough to pick up a story and understand it? Never. When a teacher told the class, "Read this book, and write a report," I just didn't do it. I knew she wasn't talking to me.

14   In 1978, my mother ran away after two weeks of terrible beatings. Joel and I found the dime under the big suitcase, where she had told us it would be. We were supposed to use it to call the police, but we were too scared. We stayed in the upstairs closet with our brothers and sisters. In the morning, I felt guilty and terrified. I didn't know whether our mother was alive or dead. Not knowing what else to do, I got dressed and went to school. I told the counselor what had happened, and she called the police. My father was arrested. He believed the police when they said they were taking him to jail for unpaid traffic tickets. Then the police located my mother and told her it was safe to come out of hiding. My father never lived with us again although he continued to stalk us. He would stand outside the house yelling at my mother, "You're gonna be a prostitute. Those kids are gonna be no-good drug addicts and criminals. They're gonna end up in jail."

15   My father's words enraged me. I had always had a hunger for knowledge, always dreamed of a fancy job where I would go to work wearing nice clothes and carrying a briefcase. How dare he try to kill my dream! True,

Maria Cardenas today

the idea of that dream ever coming true seemed unlikely. In school, if I asked about material I didn't understand, most of the teachers seemed annoyed. My mother would warn me, "Please, don't ask so many questions."

16   But then, somehow, when I was 14, Mrs. Mercer noticed me. I don't remember how my conversations with this teacher started, but it led to her offering me a job in the Western clothing store she and her husband owned. I helped translate for the Spanish-speaking customers who shopped there. I worked only Saturdays, and I got paid a whole twenty-dollar bill. Proudly, I presented that money to my mother. The thought "I can actually do more than field work" began to make my dreams seem like possibilities. I began to believe I could be something more. The month of

my sixteenth birthday, Mrs. Mercer recommended me for a cashier's job in the local supermarket. I worked there for six weeks, and on Friday, January 16, 1981, I was promoted to head cashier. I was on top of the world! I could not believe such good things were happening to me. I had a good job, and I was on my way to becoming my school's first Spanish-speaking graduate. I thought nothing could go wrong, ever again.

17   But that very night, my dreams were shattered° again—this time, I thought, permanently. The manager let me off at nine, two hours early. I didn't have a ride because my brother was not picking me up until 11:00 p.m. But I was in luck! I saw a man I knew, a friend of my brother's, someone I had worked with in the fields. He was a trusted family friend, so when he offered me a lift, I said, "Of course." Now I could go home and tell everybody about the promotion.

18   I never made it home or to my big promotion. The car doors were locked; I could not escape. I was abducted° and raped, and I found myself walking down the same abusive road as my mother. My dreams were crushed. I had failed. In my old-fashioned Mexican world, I was a "married woman," even if I wasn't. To go home again would have been to dishonor my family. When I found I was pregnant, there seemed to be only one path open to me. I married my abductor, dropped out of tenth grade, and moved with him to Oklahoma.

"My father was right," I thought. 19 "I am a failure." But dreams die hard. My brother Joel was living in the same Oklahoma town as I was. He would see me around town, my face and body bruised from my husband's beatings. But unlike the workers in the fields who had silently watched our father's abuse, Joel spoke up. "You've got to go," he would urge me. "You don't have to take this. Go on, you can make it."

"No!" I would tell him. I was 20 embarrassed to have anyone know what my life had become. I imagined returning to my mother, only to have her reprimand me, saying, "What's the matter with you that you can't even stay married?"

But Joel wouldn't give up. Finally 21 he told me, "I don't care what you say. I am going to tell Mother what is going on."

And he did. He explained to our 22 mother that I had been forced to go with that man, that I was being abused, and that I was coming home. She accepted what he told her. I took my little girl and the clothes I could carry, threw everything into my car, and left Oklahoma for Florida. My husband taunted° me just as my father had my mother: "You'll be on food stamps! You can't amount to anything on your own!" But I proved him wrong. I worked days in the fields and nights as a cashier, getting off work at midnight and up early the next day to work again. I don't know how I did it, but I kept up the payments on my little car, I didn't go on food stamps, and I was happy.

23   But as Antonietta grew up and started school, I began to think my little triumphs were not enough. I was thrilled to see her learning to read, doing well in school. And when she would bring me her simple little books and trustingly say, "Read with me!" it filled me with joy. But I realized the day would come, and come soon, that I would be unable to read Antonietta's books. What would she think of me when I said, "I can't"? What would I think of myself?

24   Teaching myself to read became the most important goal in my life. I began with Antonietta's kindergarten books. I thought sometimes how people would laugh if they saw me, a grown woman, a mother, struggling through *The Cat in the Hat*. But with no one to watch me, I didn't care. Alone in my house, after my daughter was asleep, I read. I read everything we had in the house—Antonietta's books, cereal boxes, advertisements that came in the mail. I forced myself through them, stumbling again and again over unfamiliar words. Eventually I began to feel ready to try a real story, a grown-up story. But my fears nearly stopped me again. We lived near a library. Antonietta had asked again and again to go there. Finally I said "all right." We walked in, but panic overwhelmed° me. All those people, walking around so briskly°, knowing where to find the books they wanted and how to check them out! What was someone like me doing there? What if someone asked

me what I wanted? Too intimidated to even try, I insisted that we leave. I told Antonietta to use the library at her school. I struggled on in private, eventually earning my GED°.

25   The years passed, and I married a wonderful man who loved me and my daughter. He was proud that I had some real education, and he knew that I wanted more. But I couldn't imagine that going on in school was possible.

26   Then, in 1987, I was working for the Redlands Christian Migrant Association. They provided services for migrant children. One day, in the office, I spotted something that made my heart jump. It was a book called *Dark Harvest*. It was filled with stories about migrant workers. Although my reading skills had improved, I had still never read a book. But this one was about people like me. I began reading it, slowly at first, then with more and more interest. Some of the people in it had gone back for a GED, just as I had! Even more—some had gone on to college and earned a degree in education. Now they were teaching. When I read that book, I realized that my dream wasn't crazy.

27   My husband and I took the steps to become legally admitted residents of the United States. Then, my husband found out about a federal program that helps seasonal farm workers go to college. I applied and found I was eligible°. When I took my diagnostic tests, my reading, English, and math skills turned out to be seventh-grade

level. Not as bad as I thought! The recruiter asked if I would mind attending Adult Basic Education classes to raise my scores to the twelfth-grade level. Mind? I was thrilled! I loved to study, and in spite of a serious illness that kept me out of classes for weeks, my teacher thought I was ready to try the ABE exams early. Her encouragement gave my confidence a boost, and I found my scores had zoomed up to a 12.9 level.

28   Then, in the fall of 1994, I took the greatest step of my academic life. Proud and excited, I started classes at Edison Community College in Florida. Of course, I was also terrified, trembling inside almost like that scared little girl who used to tiptoe up to the teacher's desk with her phony absence excuses. But I wasn't a scared little kid anymore. My self-confidence was growing, even if it was growing slowly.

29   I laugh when I look back at that day I fled in terror from the library. My family and I might as well live there now. We walk in with me saying, "Now, we have other things to do today. Just half an hour." Three hours later, it's the kids saying to me, "Mom, are you ready yet?" But it's so exciting, knowing that I can learn about anything I want just by picking up a book! I've read dozens of how-to books, many of them about gardening, which has become my passion. I can't put down motivational books, like Ben Carson's *Gifted Hands* and *Think Big*. I love Barbara Kingsolver's novels. One of them, *The Bean Trees*, was about a young woman from a very poor area in Kentucky whose only goal, at first, was to finish school without having a child. I could understand her. But my favorite author is Maya Angelou. Right now, I'm re-reading her book *I Know Why the Caged Bird Sings*. She writes so honestly about the tragedy and poverty she's lived with. She was raped when she was little, and she had a child when she was very young. And now she's a leader, a wonderful writer and poet. When I see her—she read a poem at President Clinton's inauguration—I am very moved. And I can't talk about my life now without mentioning Kenneth and Mary Jo Walker, the president of Edison Community College and his wife. They offered me a job in their home, but so much more than that: they have become my friends, my guardian angels. I am constantly borrowing books from them, and they give me so much encouragement that I tell them, "You have more faith in me than I do myself."

30   Sometimes I have to pinch myself to believe that my life today is real. I have a hard-working husband and three children, all of whom I love very much. My son Korak is 11. Whatever he studies in school—the Aztecs, the rainforest, Mozart—he wants to find more books in the library about it, to learn more deeply. Jasmine, my little girl, is 7, and is reading through the *Little House on the Prairie* books. Like me, the children have worked in the fields, but there is little resemblance

between their lives and mine as a child. They are in one school the whole year long. They work at their own pace, learning the value of work and of money—and they keep what they earn. Antonietta, who inspired me to begin reading, is 17 now. Although she's only a junior in high school, she's taking college calculus classes and planning to study pre-med in college, even though her teachers have encouraged her to become a journalist because of her skill in writing.

31   And guess what! My teachers compliment my writing too. When I enrolled in my developmental English class at Edison, my teacher, Johanna Seth, asked the class to write a narrative paragraph. A narrative, she explained, tells a story. As I thought about what story I could write, a picture of a scared little girl in a schoolroom popped into my head. I began writing:

32   *As I walk into the classroom, the teacher gazes at me with her piercing green eyes. I feel myself shrinking and burning up with guilt. I go straight to her desk and hand her the excuse slip. Just like all the other times, I say, "I was sick." I hate lying, but I have to. I don't want my parents to get in trouble.*

33   I finish my narrative about giving my phony excuses to my grade-school teachers and hand it in. I watch Mrs. Seth read it and, to my horror, she begins to cry. I know it must be because she is so disappointed, that what I have written is so far from what the assignment was meant to be that she doesn't know where to begin to correct it.

34   "Did you write this?" she asks me. Of course, she knows I wrote it, but she seems disbelieving. "You wrote this?" she asks again. Eventually I realize that she is not disappointed. Instead, she is telling me something incredible and wonderful. She is saying that my work is good, and that she is very happy with what I've given her. She is telling me that I can succeed here.

An Update

35   And she was right. I graduated from Edison as a member of Phi Theta Kappa, the national academic honors society for junior colleges. I went on to Florida Gulf Coast University, where I earned my bachelor's degree in elementary education. I've had the pleasure of seeing my children make their successful ways in the world: Antonietta is a lawyer, Korak is a college student, and Jasmine is serving in the military. Most wonderfully of all, I am a third-grade teacher. My students are Hispanic, and many of them are the children of migrant workers, like me. But unlike me, they do not sit in the back of the classroom, scared and ignored. Unlike me, they do not hear that they will never do more than travel the country picking crops. They are growing up knowing that, like their teacher, they can stand on their own two feet. It is my great joy that I can help teach them that.

Maria Cardenas with her third-grade students

Questions about the Reading

For each question, write the letter of your answer in the space provided.

Vocabulary in Context

_____ 1. In the sentences below, the word *options* (ŏp′shənz) means
  A. opinions.
  B. pleasures.
  C. gifts.
  D. choices.

  "My parents worked all the time in the fields. Few other options were open to them because they had little education." (Paragraph 6)

_____ 2. In the sentence below, the word *reprimand* (rĕp′rə-mănd′) means
  A. scold.
  B. ignore.
  C. compliment.
  D. support.

  "I imagined returning to my mother, only to have her reprimand me, saying, 'What's the matter with you that you can't even stay married?'" (Paragraph 20)

_____ 3. In the sentences below, the word *intimidated* (ĭn-tĭm′ĭ-dā′ted) means
   A. thoughtful.
   B. bored.
   C. fearful.
   D. critical.

> "We walked in, but panic overwhelmed me. . . . What was someone like me doing there? What if someone asked me what I wanted? Too intimidated to even try, I insisted that we leave." (Paragraph 24)

Central Point and Main Ideas

_____ 4. Which sentence best expresses the central point of the entire selection?
   A. Maria's goal was to graduate from college and teach migrant children to achieve their dreams.
   B. With hard work and courage, Maria was able to overcome great difficulties to build a wonderful family and earn a college degree.
   C. Some books are filled with inspirational stories that can help us all.
   D. Maria's story shows us that certain skills, including writing and mathematical abilities, are necessary if we want to succeed in college.

_____ 5. The main idea of paragraph 10 is its
   A. first sentence.   C. third sentence.
   B. second sentence.   D. last sentence.

_____ 6. Which sentence best expresses the main idea of paragraph 26?
   A. In 1987, Maria worked for the Redlands Christian Migrant Association.
   B. The book *Dark Harvest* convinced Maria that her dream for a better education wasn't crazy.
   C. The Redlands Christian Migrant Association provided services for migrant children.
   D. The book *Dark Harvest* contained stories about migrant workers, including some who had gone on to college and became teachers.

Supporting Details

_____ 7. Maria's father began to drink heavily and abuse his wife more than ever after
   A. he lost his job.
   B. his children began going to school.
   C. Immigration came to the house.
   D. his mother died.

_____ 8. Maria was encouraged to leave her abusive husband by her
            A. mother.   C. brother.
            B. daughter.   D. employer.

Signal Words

_____ 9. The first word of the sentence below signals a relationship of
            A. addition.   B. time.

            "When the little kids got sick, I stayed home to watch them." (Paragraph 13)

_____ 10. The relationship of the second sentence below to the first is one of
            A. addition.   B. time order.

            "Proud and excited, I started classes at Edison Community College in Florida. Of course, I was also terrified. . . ." (Paragraph 28)

Discussion Questions

1. Maria's children worked in the fields, as their mother had. In what ways were those children's lives different from Maria's life when she was a child working in the fields?

2. Why do you think Mrs. Seth cried when she read Maria's narrative about giving phony excuses to her grade-school teacher? Why might Maria have thought that Mrs. Seth was disappointed with what she had written?

3. What do you think Maria means when she says she teaches migrant children that they can "stand on their own two feet"? What do you think *all* children must learn in order to "stand on their own two feet"?

Note: Writing assignments for this selection appear on page 509.

Check Your Performance			**SIGNAL WORDS I**
Activity	*Number Right*	*Points*	*Score*
Review Test 1 (4 items)	_____	× 5 =	_____
Review Test 2 (10 items)	_____	× 4 =	_____
Review Test 3 (10 items)	_____	× 4 =	_____
		TOTAL SCORE =	_____%

Enter your total score into the **Reading Performance Chart: Review Tests** on the inside back cover.

SIGNAL WORDS I: Mastery Test 1

A. Fill in each blank with an appropriate signal word from the box. Use each transition once. Then, in the space provided, write the letter of the signal word you have chosen.

A. also	**B.** first of all	**C.** in addition
D. until	**E.** while	

Hint: Make sure that each word or phrase that you choose fits smoothly into the flow of the sentence. Test your choices by reading each sentence to yourself.

_____ 1. To avoid drunk drivers, some people stay off the road late at night. They _____ stay home on New Year's Eve.

_____ 2. Some scientists worry that we will not pay enough attention to global warming _____ it is too late.

_____ 3. _____ he was digging in his garden, Lonnie discovered an old tin box full of coins.

_____ 4. That family really believes in volunteering. The mother delivers food to people in need, and the father works with the Boy Scouts on weekends. _____, their daughter plays the piano at nursing homes.

_____ 5. Be careful to avoid spreading bacteria when you are handling raw meat in the kitchen. _____, wash your hands frequently with soap and hot water. You should also scrub chopping boards, knives, and dishes immediately after using them.

(Continues on next page)

B. (6–9.) Fill in each blank with an appropriate signal word from the box. Use each transition once.

before	finally	then	when

¹Recently a man in Kansas got in trouble (6) _____ he created his own form of hot-air balloon. ²He strapped 42 weather balloons to a lawn chair and (7) _____ inflated the balloons. ³Sitting in the chair, he took off and climbed to 16,000 feet (8) _____ shooting some of the balloons with a BB gun. ⁴He descended faster than he expected and (9) _____ crashed into some power lines. ⁵He was uninjured, but spent the next few days in jail.

_____10. This paragraph uses
    A. addition words.
    B. time words.

SIGNAL WORDS I: Mastery Test 2

A. Fill in each blank with an appropriate signal word from the box. Use each transition once. Then, in the space provided, write the letter of the transition you have chosen.

A. after	**B.** also	**C.** during
D. moreover	**E.** second	

_____ 1. _____ buying his girlfriend a huge box of candy, Jared learned she was allergic to chocolate.

_____ 2. Duct tape was invented for use in plumbing. People _____ use it to mend toys, seal holes in garden hoses, create a secure grip on rakes, repair books, and for hundreds of other tasks.

_____ 3. The First Amendment in the Bill of Rights says that the government will not establish a state religion. The _____ Amendment guarantees the right of the people to bear arms.

_____ 4. _____ the Salem (Massachusetts) Witch Trials of 1692, 20 people were executed for supposedly being witches.

_____ 5. Alzheimer's disease is a cruel illness that robs its victims of their memories. _____, it sometimes causes drastic personality changes.

(Continues on next page)

B. Fill in each blank with an appropriate signal word from the box. Use each transition once.

during	last	next
then	to begin with	

¹Arranged marriages are still very common in much of the world, especially India. ²Most modern arranged marriages go through the same typical stages. ³(6) _____, the parents choose several possible mates for the adult child. ⁴(7) _____, meetings between the two families are scheduled. ⁵(8) _____ those meetings, the young people have their first chance to meet and chat. ⁶If they seem to like each other, the man and woman might (9) _____ spend some brief time alone, perhaps going for a walk in their neighborhood. ⁷(10) _____, the young people decide if they wish to marry, or to continue meeting other possible mates.

SIGNAL WORDS I: Mastery Test 3

A. (1–2.) Fill in each blank with an appropriate addition word from the box. Use each transition once.

another	one

¹The U.S. Census Bureau reports that close to 40 percent of the country's citizens live in states other than where they were born. ²Two main factors are involved. ³(1) _____ is economic. ⁴People who are looking for work tend to move where the jobs are. ⁵(2) _____ consideration is weather. ⁶People seem to enjoy the warmer states. ⁷This is especially true of senior citizens. ⁸When given the chance to move from a snowy state to a sunny state, many older Americans will do so.

B. (3–6.) Fill in each blank with an appropriate time word from the box. Use each transition once.

finally	first	second	then

¹People infected with rabies develop a series of alarming symptoms. ²At (3) _____ they feel achy and miserable, as if they were getting the flu. ³A (4) _____ symptom is that they begin behaving oddly. ⁴They may act extremely anxious, irritable, depressed, and even aggressive. ⁵They (5) _____ become extremely sensitive to sound, touch, and light. ⁶(6) _____ they develop hallucinations and seizures. ⁷Rabies is a dreadful disease that is almost always fatal.

(Continues on next page)

C. (7–9.) Fill in each blank with an appropriate signal word from the box. Use each transition once.

also	for one thing	furthermore

¹A steroid is a type of drug that is taken to build muscle and improve physical performance. ²A steroid can help an athlete compete in certain sports. ³However, the medical profession has raised various concerns about steroid use. ⁴(7) _____, a steroid can raise blood pressure. ⁵Studies have shown that it can (8) _____ cause violent mood swings. ⁶(9) _____, a steroid may lead to heart disease, liver cancer, and kidney failure. ⁷The dangers of using steroids far outweigh the benefits, which is why they are banned in most athletic contests.

_____ 10. This paragraph uses
    A. addition words.
    B. time words.

SIGNAL WORDS I: Mastery Test 4

A. (1–2.) Fill in each blank with an appropriate signal word from the box. Use each transition once.

after	during

¹Nuclear weapons have been used in war only twice, both times being in Japan (1) _____ World War II. ²On August 6, 1945, the United States dropped the first atomic bomb on Hiroshima, Japan. ³More than 140,000 people were killed, both by the bomb itself and from the radiation that followed. ⁴Three days later, a second bomb was dropped on another Japanese city. ⁵(2) _____ these two bombings, Japan surrendered unconditionally, and the war ended.

_____ 3. This paragraph uses
     A. addition words.   B. time words.

B. (4–5.) Fill in each blank with an appropriate signal word from the box. Use each transition once.

another	one

¹Books can be grouped in a variety of ways. ²(4) _____ familiar type is fiction. ³Fictional books are books whose contents are made up. ⁴The author invents all the characters and incidents. ⁵(5) _____ well-known type is the nonfiction book. ⁶In nonfiction, the author writes truthfully about real people and real events. ⁷There is a third type of book that falls somewhere between fiction and nonfiction. ⁸That is the historical novel. ⁹In a historical novel, the author writes about real people who lived at a particular time and place, but makes up what those people say and do.

_____ 6. This paragraph uses
     A. addition words.   B. time words.

(Continues on next page)

C. (7–9.) Fill in each blank with an appropriate signal word from the box. Use each transition once.

during	finally	then

[1]In 1968, a 3M Company scientist named Spencer Silver developed an unusual new glue. [2]The glue was strong enough to cling to objects, but weak enough that it could be removed and re-stuck elsewhere. [3](7) _____ the next few years, Dr. Silver tried to find a practical use for his strange new glue. [4]Nothing happened until the early 1970s. [5](8) _____ a co-worker of Dr. Silver's named Art Fry was sitting in church, wishing that he had a bookmark that would not either fall out of his hymnal or damage it. [6]He realized that Dr. Silver's adhesive would be the perfect solution. [7](9) _____, in 1979, 3M combined Dr. Silver's and Art Fry's ideas to create Post-It Notes. [8]The product has become one of 3M's biggest sellers.

_____ 10. This paragraph uses
    A. addition words.   B. time words.

SIGNAL WORDS I: Mastery Test 5

Read each textbook passage and then answer the questions that follow.

A. [1]To become a group leader, behave in certain ways in group discussions. [2]First, be well informed about the work. [3]Group members are more willing to follow someone who really knows the subject. [4]Second, work harder than anyone else in the group. [5]Leadership is often a question of setting an example, and you can do so with hard work. [6]Third, be open to an exchange of ideas with others in the group. [7]Listen to their ideas, and react with ones of your own. [8]Finally, help the group work together smoothly. [9]Make others in the group feel good about themselves, and give credit where it is due.

_____ 1. This paragraph uses
  A. addition words.
  B. time words.

2–3. Two of the transitions that signal major details of the paragraph are

_____ and _____.

4–6. Complete the outline of the selection.

Main idea: Your chances of becoming a group leader are increased if you behave in certain ways during group discussions.

1. _____

   _____

2. _____

   _____

3. _____

   _____

4. Help the group work together smoothly.

(Continues on next page)

B. ¹Although the exact cause of childhood obesity is not known, there are a number of theories. ²One cause may be a child's genes. ³A study of 540 adopted adults found that their weight was more like their biological parents than their adoptive ones. ⁴A second cause is environment. ⁵Children tend to eat the same kinds of foods and develop the same kinds of habits as the people around them. ⁶Third, heavier children are less active. ⁷But are they less active because they are fat, or do they become fat because they are less active? ⁸So far, there is no final answer. ⁹But some support the conclusion that children become fat because they are less active. ¹⁰Last of all, too much television may also be a factor. ¹¹According to studies, every hour a day spent watching TV results in a 2 percent increase in the frequency of obesity. ¹²Children who watch a lot of TV tend to eat more snacks, especially the high-calorie ones they see in ads. ¹³They are also less active than other children.

_____ 7. This paragraph uses
     A. addition words.
     B. time words.

  8–10. Complete the map of the selection.

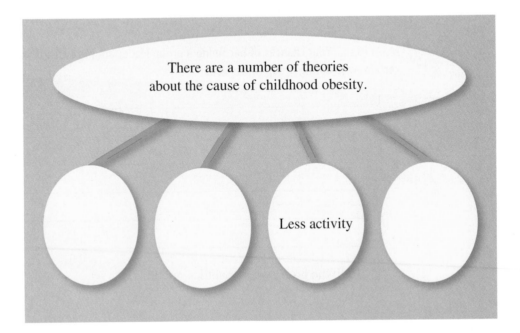

There are a number of theories
about the cause of childhood obesity.

Less activity

SIGNAL WORDS I: Mastery Test 6

Read each textbook passage and then answer the questions that follow.

A. ¹Perhaps surprisingly, physical good looks are only part of what makes us attractive to others. ²For one thing, attractiveness can change with age. ³How a person looks at the age of 17 is not always a sign of how he or she will look at age 30 or 50. ⁴Sometimes an average-looking adolescent, especially one with a warm, attractive personality, becomes a quite attractive middle-aged adult. ⁵Secondly, the longer we know and like someone, the more attractive we think that person is. ⁶Perhaps you can recall individuals who, as you grew to like them, became more attractive. ⁷Their physical imperfections were no longer so noticeable. ⁸Finally, love sees loveliness. ⁹The more in love a woman is with a man, the more physically attractive she finds him. ¹⁰And the more in love people are, the less attractive they find all others of the opposite sex.

_____ 1. This paragraph uses
  A. addition words.
  B. time words.

2–3. Two of the transitions that signal major details of the paragraph are

_____and _____.

4–5. Complete the outline of the selection.

Main idea: Physical good looks are only part of what makes us attractive to others.

  1. _____

     _____

  2. The longer we know and like someone, the more attractive we think that person is.

  3. _____

     _____

(Continues on next page)

B. ¹We communicate with each other for various reasons. ²One reason is to meet needs. ³Psychologists tell us that we are social animals; that is, we need other people just as we need food, water, and shelter. ⁴Two people may converse happily for hours gossiping and chatting about unimportant matters that neither remembers afterward. ⁵When they part, they may have exchanged little real information, but their communication met an important need—simply to talk with another human being. ⁶Another reason we communicate is to develop relationships. ⁷We get to know others through our communication with them. ⁸A third reason we communicate is to exchange information. ⁹We may be trying to decide how warmly to dress or whom to vote for in the next presidential election. ¹⁰All of us have countless exchanges that involve sending and receiving information.

_____ 6. This paragraph uses
   A. addition words.
   B. time words.

7–8. Two of the transitions that signal major details of the paragraph are

_____ and _____.

9–10. Complete the map of the selection.

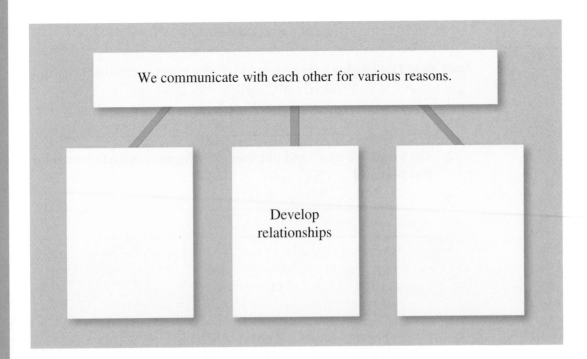

We communicate with each other for various reasons.

Develop
relationships

8 Signal Words II

This Chapter in a Nutshell

- To help make their ideas clear, writers use **signal words,** also known as **transitions**—words that carry the reader from one idea to the next.

  — Typical illustration transitions are *for example* and *for instance.*

  — Typical contrast transitions are *but* and *however.*

  — Typical cause and effect transitions are *reasons, because,* and *as a result.*

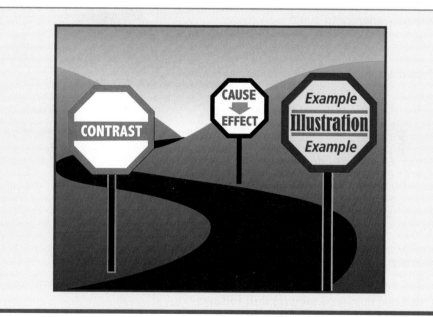

The previous chapter explained two common types of signal words (or *transitions*) that writers use to help make their ideas clear. This chapter looks at three other common types of signal words:

- Example words
- Contrast words
- Cause and effect words

Example Words

Check (✓) the item that is easier to read and understand:

____   Be careful when buying an old house. The plumbing, wiring, and roof may need to be replaced.

____   Be careful when buying an old house. For instance, the plumbing, wiring, and roof may need to be replaced.

The second item is easier to understand. The words *for instance* make it clear that the plumbing, wiring, and roof are among a number of things that may need to be replaced. *For instance* and other words and phrases like it are example words, also known as illustration words.

Example words tell us that a writer will provide one or more *examples* to make a given idea clear. In the cartoon on the right, the words *For example* are used to illustrate the woman's point about exercising.

Below are some common words that show examples:

"I do try to exercise. For example, I walk every day and carry ten-pound weights in my hands."

Example Words

(for) example	(for) instance	to illustrate
including	such as	

Examples

The following sentences contain example words. Notice how these words signal that one or more *examples* will follow.

● At least nine states get their names from rivers that flow through them. *For example,* Minnesota is named after the Minnesota River.

● Some English phrases don't make much sense to people just learning the language. *For instance,* if you tell a non-native speaker to "keep an eye out" for somebody, he probably won't know what you're talking about.

● President John F. Kennedy was famous for his sense of humor. *To illustrate,* once during a lecture he was asked how he had become a hero during World War II. He answered that he had no choice: "They sank my boat."

PRACTICE 1

Complete each sentence with a suitable example word or phrase from the box below. Try to use each transition once. Then, in the space provided, write the letter of the transition you have chosen.

A. for example	**B.** for instance	**C.** including
D. once	**E.** such as	

Hint: Make sure that each example word or phrase you choose fits smoothly into the flow of the sentence. Test each choice by reading the sentence aloud.

_A_ 1. Many health claims are made for certain foods. _____, olive oil is said to reduce heart disease.

_E_ 2. Nita's parents speak Spanish when they don't want their children to understand them, ____such as____ when they are planning a birthday party.

_B_ 3. Governments own some businesses. ____Such as____, local governments often own parking areas and water systems.

_C_ 4. Certain months of the year, _____ January, March, and June, are named for Roman gods.

_D_ 5. President Abraham Lincoln was famous for his honesty. _____, when he worked at a store, he walked several miles to return change to a customer.

PRACTICE 2

Very often textbook authors will define terms the reader may not know. Then, to make sure a definition is clear, an author may give one or more examples. Below are some paragraphs from textbooks. Read each and answer the questions that follow.

A. ¹A phobia is an irrational and extreme fear of some object or situation. ²One example is a fear of heights that is so extreme that one cannot drive over bridges without trembling. ³Other common phobias include fears of snakes, water, and enclosed places.

1. Which sentence gives a definition? __1__

2. Which sentence provides an example? __2__

B. ¹Functional illiteracy is the inability to read and write at a level required for success in daily life. ²The problem is wide-ranging. ³For instance, it is estimated that one in five adults is unable to read warning labels on containers of harmful substances. ⁴Other examples are the many adults that cannot read the headlines in a newspaper or fill out a job application. ⁵Yet another illustration of this problem is the half of the adult population in this country that is unable to read a book written at an eighth-grade level.

1. Which sentence gives a definition? _____*1*_____

2. Which sentence provides an example? _____*3*_____

C. The following paragraph has a definition-example pattern. Complete the map of the paragraph. First, write the definition in the heading. Then fill in the two missing supporting details—examples of the term that is defined.

¹Regeneration is the ability some animals have to renew lost body parts. ²This ability can come in very handy when a limb is lost in an accident or in a fight. ³For instance, an octopus can regrow lost tentacles. ⁴The sea star is another example of an animal that can regenerate. ⁵Even one leg of a sea star that includes part of the center of the body can regenerate a whole new body. ⁶Also, some lizards can regrow their tails. ⁷When such a lizard is caught by its tail, it releases the tail and runs away. ⁸A new tail is then grown.

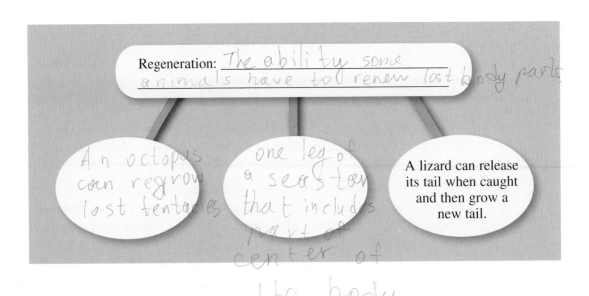

Regeneration: *The ability some animals have to renew lost body parts*

An octopus can regrow lost tentacles

one leg of a sea star that includes part of center of the body

A lizard can release its tail when caught and then grow a new tail.

Contrast Words

Put a check (✔) beside the item that is easier to read and understand:

___   The dog next door is lovable. She barks a lot at night.

___   The dog next door is lovable although she barks a lot at night.

The first item suggests that one of the lovable things about the dog is that she barks at night. The word *although* in the second item shows a contrast: the dog is lovable *even though* she barks so much at night. *Although* and words like it are contrast words.

Contrast words signal that a writer is pointing out differences between subjects. A contrast word shows that two things *differ* in one or more

"The trouble is that I like to spend money, but my wife likes to save it."

ways. Contrast words also inform us that something is going to *differ from* what we might expect. In the cartoon above, the word *but* contrasts the difference between the husband and wife.

Below are some common words that show contrast:

Contrast Words

but	instead	still	difference
yet	in contrast	as opposed to	different(ly)
however	on the other hand	in spite of	differs from
although	on the contrary	despite	unlike
nevertheless	even though	rather than	while

Examples

The following items contain contrast words. Notice how these words signal that one idea is *different from* another idea.

● Alberto was angry when he didn't get a raise. His wife, *however,* took the news calmly.

● Tarantulas are scary-looking, *but* they are actually quite harmless.

● A cup of coffee can give you a quick energy boost. *On the other hand,* coffee can also make you irritable and unable to sleep at night.

PRACTICE 3

Complete each sentence with a suitable contrast word or phrase from the box. Try to use each transition once. Then, in the space provided, write the letter of the transition you have chosen.

A. even though	**B.** however	**C.** in contrast
D. in spite of	**E.** rather then	

Hint: Make sure that each contrast word or phrase that you choose fits smoothly into the flow of the sentence. Test each choice by reading the sentence aloud.

___A___ 1. _____ the day started with sunshine, the weather forecast was for rain by evening.

___C___ 2. Dennis always votes Democratic, _____ to the other members of his family.

___D___ 3. _____ the long winters in Alaska, many people enjoy living there.

___E___ 4. _____ buying ready-made curtains, Elena made her bedroom curtains out of pretty sheets.

___B___ 5. Some cats will wait patiently to be fed. Others, _____, will follow their owner around the house meowing when they are hungry.

PRACTICE 4

A. Below is a paragraph that is organized with the help of contrast words. Underline the **two** contrast words. Then complete the outline of the paragraph.

> ¹There are two different views of the value of computers in the classroom. ²Some people feel that computers will soon take over many of the teachers' duties. ³One writer states, "Computers make do-it-yourself education downright efficient. ⁴Your child can probably learn spelling or arithmetic or a foreign language faster on a computer" than from a teacher in a crowded classroom. ⁵But others warn that too much technology may harm children. ⁶One psychologist says that computers, as well as video games and TV, may weaken children's language skills.

Main idea: There are two different views of the value of computers in the classroom.

    1. **Positive view:** _4_____

    2. **Negative view:** _____

B. Again, underline the **two** contrast words. Then complete the outline of the paragraph.

> ¹Doctors and scientists do not agree about when a person is truly dead. ²Some of them think that a person should be declared legally dead when blood circulation and breathing have stopped. ³Then organs that are still in good working order can be removed and donated to critically ill patients in need of a new liver, heart, or kidney. ⁴However, there are those who say that death does not occur until the entire brain stops functioning. ⁵These people admit that waiting for brain death means organs may stop working and not be in condition to be donated. ⁶But they point out that some individuals have awakened months after going into a state that seems like death.

Main idea: Doctors and scientists do not agree about when a person is truly dead.

    1. _2_____

    2. _4_____

C. Again, underline the **two** contrast words. Then complete the outline of the paragraph.

> ¹Do you like to gamble? ²If so, you have plenty of company. ³Whether it's making a friendly bet on a football game or visiting the Las Vegas casinos, many people like to gamble. ⁴For most people, gambling is a bit of harmless fun. ⁵They win or lose a few dollars at the card table or slot machine, and they enjoy the process. ⁶Yet for others, gambling is a serious addiction. ⁷Unlike most of us, they bet money they cannot afford to lose. ⁸Even if they win, they cannot stop; they then bet their winnings. ⁹Eventually they suffer a big loss and have to beg, borrow, or steal money to try to win it back. ¹⁰That sort of gambling has ruined many people's lives.

Main idea: There are two kinds of gamblers.

    1. _4_____

    2. _6_____

Cause and Effect Words

Check (✓) the item that is easier to read and understand:

_____ The baby refused to eat her breakfast. I was in a bad mood all morning.

__✓__ The baby refused to eat her breakfast. As a result, I was in a bad mood all morning.

In the first item, we are not sure of the relationship between the two ideas. Were there two problems: the baby refusing to eat and the bad mood? Or did the first problem cause the second one? The phrase *as a result* makes clear that the baby's behavior *caused* the bad mood.

Cause and effect words show that the writer is discussing one or more *reasons* or *results*. In the cartoon on the right, the word *because* explains the reason why the pig should be hired.

"You should hire me because I can really bring home the bacon."

Below are some common words that show causes and effects:

Cause and Effect Words

therefore	so	because (of)	thus
(as a) result	effect	(as a) consequence	results in
cause	explanation	consequently	lead to
affect	due to	since	reason

Examples

The following examples contain cause and effect words. Notice how these words introduce a *reason* for something or the *result* of something.

- Students who work full-time sometimes nap before classes *because* they are tired after work.
- One *reason* for our lower electric bills is that we use less air conditioning.
- The lifeguard thought she spotted a shark. *As a result*, the beach was closed for the rest of the day.

PRACTICE 5

Complete each sentence with a suitable cause and effect word from the box. Try to use each transition once. Then, in the space provided, write the letter of the transition you have chosen.

> *Hint:* Make sure that each cause or effect word that you choose fits smoothly into the flow of the sentence. Test each choice by reading the sentence aloud.

A. because	**B.** effect	**C.** result
D. so	**E.** therefore	

_____ 1. Drinking large amounts of carrot juice can _____ in a person's skin turning orange.

_____ 2. The contract offer made by management did not satisfy union members. _____, they decided to go on strike.

_____ 3. Scientists in the Antarctic no longer wear fur _____ they have discovered that quilted, layered clothing keeps them warmer.

_____ 4. Most baseball stadiums have lights _____ that night games can be played and day games can continue after dark.

_____ 5. American-style fast food has become popular all over the world. The _____ is that people around the world are developing American-style problems like diabetes, high blood pressure, and obesity.

PRACTICE 6

A. Below is a paragraph that is organized with the help of cause and effect words. Underline the **three** cause and effect words. Then complete the outline of the paragraph.

> ¹Researchers have learned that laughing can be good for you. ²Laughing relaxes the facial muscles, causing you to look and feel less tense. ³It also increases the oxygen in the brain, resulting in a lightheaded sense of well-being. ⁴In addition, laughing is a proven stress-reducer; it therefore decreases your chances of getting stress-related illnesses.

Main idea: Laughing can be good for you.

1. _____

2. _____

3. _____

B. Underline the **two** cause and effect words. Then complete the outline of the paragraph.

> ¹Changes at the end of the 1800s created more work for women. ²In both the home and the workplace, there was a greater emphasis on being clean. ³As a result, women spent more time washing, dusting, and scrubbing. ⁴Another change in the late 1800s was the availability of a greater variety of foods. ⁵Consequently, women spent more time on such food preparation as plucking feathers from chickens, roasting coffee beans, grinding whole spices and sugar, and cooking meals. ⁶By 1900, the typical housewife worked six hours a day on just two tasks: cleaning and meal preparation.

Main idea: Changes at the end of the 1800s created more work for women.

1. _____

_____

2. _____

_____

C. The following passage uses the cause-effect pattern. Complete the map of the paragraph on the following page: First write in the main idea. Then fill in the two missing supporting details.

> ¹Being unemployed can have harmful effects on health. ²In poor countries especially, unemployment may result in little or no medical care. ³The experience of unemployment itself can affect one's health. ⁴Studies have shown anxiety and depression can result from the loss of a job. ⁵Alcohol and drug abuse is another effect of unemployment. ⁶And being without work can also lead to high blood pressure and a rise in heart disease.

Being following can have harmful health effects.

| Especially in poor countries, little or no medical care | Anxiety and depression | | |

CHAPTER REVIEW

In this chapter you learned about three additional kinds of signal words that writers use:

- **Example words**

  — Writers may provide examples to help make an idea clear.

  — Words that signal examples include _for example_ and _for instance._

- **Contrast words**

  — Writers often discuss how two things are different from each other.

  — Words that signal contrast include _but_ and _however._

- **Cause and effect words**

  — Writers often discuss the reasons why something happens or the effects of something that has happened.

  — Words that signal causes include _reason_ and _because._

  — Words that signal effects include _therefore_ and _as a result._

The next chapter—Chapter 9—will develop your skill in making inferences about what you read.

On the Web: If you are using this book in class, you can visit our website for additional practice with words that signal examples, contrast, and cause and effect. Go to **www.townsendpress.com** and click on "Learning Center."

REVIEW TEST 1

To review what you've learned in this chapter, complete each item by filling in the blank.

1. This chapter presented more transitions—signal words or phrases like *for example, however,* and *therefore* that help carry the reader from one *(chapter, page, idea)* _____idea_____ to the next.

2. Typical *(example, contrast, cause and effect)* _____Examples_____ words are *such as, including,* and *for instance.* These words try to make a given idea clear.

3. Typical *(example, contrast, cause and effect)* _____Contrast_____ words are *but, on the other hand,* and *however.* These words tell us that two things differ in one or more ways. _____cause and effect_____

4. Typical *(example, contrast, cause and effect)* _____effect_____ words are *because, reason,* and *as a result.* These words tell us the reason why something happened or the results of something.

REVIEW TEST 2

A. Fill in each blank with one of the signal words in the box. Use each word once.

for instance	however	therefore

1. A stereotype is an overly generalized image of members of a group. One common stereotype, _____for instance_____, is the image of all professors as being absent-minded.

2. Researchers have discovered that people with certain speech problems lack feeling in their tongues. _____therefore_____, they have trouble placing their tongues in the correct position for certain sounds.

3. In the northern half of the world, the months of July through September are warmest. _____however_____, in the southern half of the world, those are the coldest months.

B. (4–5.) Fill in each blank with an appropriate signal word from the box. Use each transition once.

different	however

¹Glossy and flat paints have (4) ___different___ advantages. ²A glossy paint is easier to keep clean than a flat paint; (5) ___however___, a flat paint covers flaws in the wall better than a glossy one does. ³The cost for both paints is about the same. ⁴The choice of which is better depends on the buyer's need and preference.

(6–8.) Fill in each blank with an appropriate signal word from the box. Use each transition once.

example	for instance	such as

¹A mutant is a plant or animal with a brand-new characteristic. ²(6) ___for instance___, one mutant that was born not too long ago was a two-headed calf. ³Another (7) ___example___ was a recently hatched chicken with four legs. ⁴Some mutants turn out to be useful, (8) ___such as___ an orange plant that appeared in a field of normal white cauliflower. ⁵It led to the production of a new vegetable—an orange cauliflower.

C. (9–10.) Fill in each blank with an appropriate signal word from the box. Use each transition once.

as a result	reason

¹The United States Postal Service has set up a special room in several locations around the country. ²This room is known as the "Dead Letter Office." ³Here postal clerks open and read mail. ⁴Why do they open private mail? ⁵One (9) ___reason___ is that millions of letters are sent each year with wrong addresses and no return address. ⁶These letters are opened so that clerks can find out where to return the mail. ⁷Also, some envelopes are completely blank, with no address at all. ⁸(10) ___As a result___, postal clerks must also open these letters to try to discover where they should be sent. ⁹According to estimates, only 30 percent of the opened letters find their way to the sender or the person the letter was meant to reach.

REVIEW TEST 3

Here is a chance to apply your understanding of signal words to a full-length reading. The following selection tells what happens when the author decides to stop and move a cat lying in the middle of the road. It turns out the cat is still alive, and his day becomes a complicated one.

Read the selection and then answer the questions that follow. You'll find questions on vocabulary in context, main ideas, supporting details, and signal words.

Words to Watch

Below are some words in the reading that do not have strong context support. Each word is followed by the number of the paragraph in which it appears and its meaning there. These words are marked in the reading by a small circle (°).

grimaced (2): made a twisted face to express pain or disgust
ligament (5): a band of tissue which connects bones or supports organs
tendon (5): a tissue which connects muscles to bones and other parts of the body
good Samaritan (6): someone who helps others unselfishly
resignation (9): acceptance without resistance
dejected (11): depressed
pathetic (11): pitiful

LIFE OVER DEATH
Bill Broderick

1   My reaction was as it always is when I see an animal lying in the roadway. My heart sank. And a lump formed in my throat at the thought of a life unfulfilled. I then resolved to move him off the road, to ensure that one of God's creations did not become a permanent part of the pavement. Some might ask what difference it makes. If it's already dead, why not just leave it there? My answer is that I believe in death with dignity, for people and for animals alike.

2   So I pulled my car over to the side of the road and walked back to where the cat lay motionless. Two cars passed over him, managing to avoid running him over. With no other cars in sight, I made my way to the lifeless form just as a jogger went by. The

jogger grimaced° at the sight of the cat, blood dripping from his mouth. "How'd it happen?" he asked. I replied that I didn't know; he probably got hit by some careless driver. I just wanted to get him off the road. I reached down for the cat and got the surprise of my life. The little creature lifted his head ever so slightly and uttered a pitiful, unforgettable little "meow." He was still alive.

3   What was I going to do now? I was already late for work. All I had intended to do was move the cat off the road. I didn't need this. But I knew I had no choice. I sighed deeply, then reached down and carefully cradled the cat in my hands. I asked the jogger to open my car trunk and remove the things from a small box. Then I gently placed the cat in the box. He was in shock, so he probably could not feel the pain from his obvious injuries. "Kinda funny lookin', isn't he?" asked the jogger. I was annoyed by his question, but I had to admit that he was right. This cat looked peculiar. Not ugly, mind you. But he seemed to have a comical look on his face, even at such a dreadful time.

4   "What are you gonna do with him?" the jogger asked. I told him I would take the cat to the local vet and let him decide what to do.

5   The vet was only five minutes away. My wife and I had been taking our animals to him for several years, and I knew I could rely on him to do what was best for the cat. I took the cat into the reception room and placed it on the counter. As this was an emergency, the vet was summoned right away. He examined the cat thoroughly, listing the injuries for his assistant to write down. "Broken jaw, that'll have to be set. Two teeth broken. A couple more loose. Possible internal injuries, but they don't look too bad. Uh-oh. This doesn't look good. He doesn't appear to have any movement in his right front leg. Possible break, definite ligament° and tendon° damage."

6   The vet completed his examination, then looked at me and asked what I wanted to do. I knew what he meant. Did I want to have the cat "put to sleep"? I became uneasy. I clumsily explained that I was hoping to get advice from him on what to do. Fair enough. The jaw would have to be wired shut for six weeks, and the cat would have to wear a cast on his leg for three months. There was no way of knowing if the damage to the leg was permanent. He could have the cast removed and still not be able to use the leg. The cost of all the surgery would be high, but I would get a 50 percent "good Samaritan°" discount if I went ahead with it.

7   Now I was really at a loss. If I went ahead with the surgery, I'd be paying for a cat that wasn't mine, whose owner I'd probably never find, and who might end up with the use of

only three legs. And on top of it, this was one of the funniest-looking cats ever born. Black and white, spotted where it shouldn't be, twisted tail, and a silly half-smile on its face. I chuckled at that and the entire situation.

8   "What do you want to do, Bill?" asked the vet.

9   I shrugged my shoulders in resignation°. "Dan, I'll choose life over death every time. Let's give it our best shot."

10   I called back later in the day and learned that the surgery had been successful. "You can pick up your cat tomorrow morning," I was told. My cat. I started to say that he was not my cat, but I knew otherwise.

11   The next morning, my wife and I drove to the vet and picked up the cat. He looked ghastly. His jaw was now bandaged, and a cast covered one leg entirely and wrapped around his midsection. We were dejected°. But, as we drove him home, we began thinking that perhaps this cat was not as pathetic° as he looked. As frightened as he must have been, as much pain as he must have felt, he sat calmly in my wife's lap. He purred and stared out the window with his curious half-smile.

12   When we got home, we introduced him to our two Siamese cats, who stared in disbelief at this strange creature. They sensed it might be a cat, but they had never seen one like this. It took him very

little time to get used to his new surroundings. It took him longer to get used to the cast, which made even walking a chore. Surely he must have been embarrassed. After all, an animal normally able to glide around quietly should not make a scraping sound every time he moves.

13   In due time, the cast came off. To our relief, Pokey, as we now called him, had about 90 percent mobility in the leg. He got around okay, but he limped whenever he tried to move any faster than a slow walk.

14   All this occurred four years ago. Pokey is still with us today. In fact, he has become our most beloved cat. Because of his injury, he is strictly an indoor cat. This does not seem to bother him at all. It is hard to

believe that any cat has ever enjoyed himself more. Maybe it's because he had been slowed after being hit by a car, or perhaps he just has a special individuality. He is never bored. At times he will race around the house like he is leading the Indy 500. Or he'll leap into the air at an imaginary foe. Or he'll purr loudly at the foot of our bed, staring into space with that silly grin on his face. And he couldn't care less that he still looks funny.

It would have been easy to let 15 Pokey lie in the middle of the road. And it would have been just as simple to have the vet put him to sleep. But when I think of all the pleasure this cat has given us, and of how much fun he has living with us, I know the right decision was made. And I'd do it again in a second. I'll take life over death every time.

Questions about the Reading

For each question, write the letter of your answer in the space provided.

Vocabulary in Context

_____ 1. In the sentence below, the word *resolved* (rĭ-zŏlvd′) means
    A. forgot.
    B. hid.
    C. decided.
    D. drove.

    "I then resolved to move him off the road, to ensure that one of God's creations did not become a permanent part of the pavement." (Paragraph 1)

_____ 2. In the sentences below, the word *summoned* (sŭm′ənd) means
    A. paid.
    B. called for.
    C. written to.
    D. ignored.

    "As this was an emergency, the vet was summoned right away. He examined the cat thoroughly . . . ." (Paragraph 5)

_____ 3. In the sentences below, the word *ghastly* (găst′lē) means
   A. threatening.
   B. appealing.
   C. terrible.
   D. marvelous.

   > "He looked ghastly. His jaw was now bandaged, and a cast covered one leg entirely and wrapped around his midsection." (Paragraph 11)

Central Point and Main Ideas

_____ 4. Which sentence best expresses the central point of the selection?
   A. Drivers need to be alert to dangers on the road.
   B. Every life is valuable.
   C. Cats make wonderful pets.
   D. Pokey is strictly an indoor cat because of his injury.

_____ 5. Which sentence best expresses the main idea of paragraph 6?
   A. The author wanted to know if the damage to the cat's leg was permanent.
   B. The vet didn't know what to do with the cat.
   C. To help the author decide what to do, the vet explained what could be done for the cat and what it would cost.
   D. The author expected the vet to say that the cat should be "put to sleep."

_____ 6. Which sentence best expresses the main idea of paragraph 14?
   A. Pokey is beloved and enjoys life a great deal now.
   B. Pokey sometimes leaps into the air at imaginary enemies.
   C. Pokey must spend the rest of his life indoors.
   D. Pokey was injured four years ago.

Supporting Details

_____ 7. The author
   A. saw a car hit the cat.
   B. thought that the cat was ugly.
   C. was surprised that the jogger came by.
   D. was very surprised that the cat was still alive.

_____ 8. The author
   A. had heard about the vet.
   B. looked for the nearest vet.
   C. knew and trusted the vet.
   D. drove for hours till he found a vet.

Signal Words

_____ 9. In the sentence below, the word *but* signals
   A. an example.
   B. contrast.
   C. cause and effect.

   "The cost of all the surgery would be high, but I would get a . . . discount if I went ahead with it." (Paragraph 6)

_____ 10. In the sentence below, the word *because* signals
   A. an example.
   B. contrast.
   C. cause and effect.

   "Because of his injury, he is strictly an indoor cat." (Paragraph 14)

Discussion Questions

1. In the first paragraph, the author uses the expression "death with dignity." What do you think he means by that expression?

2. Why do you think that Pokey has become, in Broderick's words, "our most beloved cat"? Do you think Pokey's injuries had an effect on how the author ended up feeling about him? Why or why not?

3. Can—and should—something be done to make the world a better place for hurt and homeless animals like Pokey? Or should our priorities lie elsewhere? Explain your answer.

Note: Writing assignments for this selection appear on page 510.

Check Your Performance   **SIGNAL WORDS II**

Activity	Number Right	Points	Score
Review Test 1 (4 items)	_____	× 5 =	_____
Review Test 2 (10 items)	_____	× 4 =	_____
Review Test 3 (10 items)	_____	× 4 =	_____
		TOTAL SCORE =	_____%

Enter your total score into the **Reading Performance Chart: Review Tests** on the inside back cover.

SIGNAL WORDS II: Mastery Test 1

A. Fill in each blank with an appropriate signal word from the box. Use each transition once. Then, in the space provided, write the letter of the transition you have chosen.

A. as a result	**B.** but	**C.** for instance
D. however	**E.** so that	

_____ 1. Most people think winning the lottery would mean being rich for the rest of their lives, _____*but*_____ nearly half of all lottery winners run out of money within five years.

_____ 2. I stuffed steel wool into all the cracks in the kitchen area _____*so that*_____ bugs and mice could no longer get in.

_____ 3. Olympic events have certainly changed over the years. _____*for instance*_____, the 1904 games included such events as rock throwing, greased pole climbing, and mud fighting.

_____ 4. Many people believe that Harry Houdini drowned during a failed underwater escape. _____*However*_____, he actually died as a result of a hard punch to his stomach.

_____ 5. The baby was sick most of the night. _____*As a result*_____, the parents got very little sleep.

(Continues on next page)

B. (6–9.) Fill in each blank with an appropriate signal word from the box. Use each transition once.

caused	due to	lead to	result

[1]Teens and young adults lose hair for various reasons. [2]As part of the normal changes in the body, they can expect to lose about one hundred hairs per day. [3]Medical problems may (6) _____ more hair loss. [4]Abnormal hair loss may also be (7) _____ by undernourishment, so teens should be mindful of their diet. [5]Fevers can also (8) _____ in more hair falling out than usual. [6]Significant hair loss may also be (9) _____ allergic reactions to dyes or hair straighteners.

_____ 10. This paragraph uses
   A. example words.
   B. contrast words.
   C. cause and effect words.

SIGNAL WORDS II: Mastery Test 2

A. Fill in each blank with an appropriate signal word from the box. Use each transition once. Then, in the space provided, write the letter of the transition you have chosen.

A. although	**B.** because	**C.** example
D. for instance	**E.** instead	**F.** reason

_____ 1. _____ we think of spaghetti as an Italian food, it was probably first invented in China.

_____ 2. _____ of federal cutbacks, many schools have lost their physical education, art, and music programs.

_____ 3. A raptor is a bird that hunts and kills live animals. Hawks, eagles, and owls are _____s of raptors.

_____ 4. _____ of admitting he'd broken the vase, the little boy hid the pieces behind his grandmother's sofa.

_____ 5. Mary and Marie are identical twins with different birthdays. The _____ is that one girl was born before midnight and the other just after midnight.

_____ 6. Camping in the woods is not like sleeping in your bed at home. _____, you have to worry about insects, snakes, and about what to use as a bathroom in the middle of the night.

(Continues on next page)

B. (7–9.) Fill in each blank with an appropriate signal word from the box. Use each transition once.

consequently	due to	result

¹Pigs do not save money. ²They don't even save food. ³So why do we save our coins in things called "piggy banks"? ⁴Our use of the term "piggy banks" is actually (7) _____ a mistake. ⁵Back in the Middle Ages, metal was too expensive to be used for most household items. ⁶(8) _____, ordinary containers were made of an inexpensive earthen clay called "pygg." ⁷People would save their extra money in "pygg jars," which eventually became "pygg banks." ⁸Over the next few hundred years, people forgot that "pygg" meant clay, and began thinking of the word as "pig." ⁹Potters began making coin-holding containers in the shape of a pig. ¹⁰The (9) _____ was that the "piggy bank" was born.

_____10. This paragraph uses
    A. example words.
    B. contrast words.
    C. cause and effect words.

SIGNAL WORDS II: Mastery Test 3

A. (1–2.) Fill in each blank with an appropriate signal word from the box. Use each transition once.

different	however

[1]There are interesting differences between honeybees and bumblebees. [2]First of all, they have contrasting living circumstances. [3]Honeybees live in large colonies and need a lot of space to build their hives. [4]Bumblebees, (1) _____, live in small underground colonies and require little territory to nest. [5]Honeybees and bumblebees are also (2) _____ in their stinging behavior. [6]Honeybees will sting with little reason. [7]In contrast, bumblebees rarely sting, even if they are accidentally disturbed. [8]However, their sting is far more painful than that of a honeybee.

_____ 3. This paragraph uses
   A. example words.
   B. contrast words.
   C. cause and effect words.

(Continues on next page)

B. (4–6.) Fill in each blank with an appropriate signal word from the box. Use each transition once.

because of	resulted	therefore

[1]During the Middle Ages, people in Europe hated and feared ordinary house cats, which they thought were used by witches to contact demons. [2]Unfortunately, this fear of cats (4) _____ in many more deaths from the bubonic plague than should have occurred. [3](5) _____ their fear, people drove cats away from their houses and villages. [4]Rats were (6) _____ totally free to breed there and spread disease. [5]Millions of people died from the bubonic plague, which was carried by diseased rats. [6]If more cats had been allowed to stay, they could have killed many of these rats.

_____ 7. This paragraph uses
    A. example words.
    B. contrast words.
    C. cause and effect words.

C. (8–9.) Fill in each blank with an appropriate signal word from the box. Use each transition once.

example	for instance

[1]A "tell sign" is a nonverbal clue that a person may be lying. [2](8) _____, if a person is making more obvious hand gestures than normal, or scratching the head or neck, that person may not be telling the truth. [3]These gestures suggest a subconscious effort to rub out an untrue statement. [4]Another (9) _____ of a tell sign is a repeated shrugging of the shoulders, which may be a subconscious way to contradict what has been said.

_____ 10. This paragraph uses
    A. example words.
    B. contrast words.
    C. cause and effect words.

SIGNAL WORDS II: Mastery Test 4

A. (1–3.) Fill in each blank with an appropriate signal word from the box. Use each transition once.

consequence	result in	therefore

[1]When United States coins were originally produced, the dollar, half-dollar, 25-cent, and 10-cent coins were made of gold and silver. [2]People sometimes tried to enrich themselves by filing down the edges, which would (1) _____ their getting a little of the precious metal. [3](2) As a _____, the government began making those coins with ridged edges. [4]That way, it was obvious if someone had filed off some of the coin. [5]Later, the government stopped using precious metals for coins. [6]But blind people pointed out that the ridged edges on certain coins helped them to identify those coins by touch. [7](3) _____, dimes, quarters, half-dollars, and dollar coins still have ridged edges.

_____ 4. This paragraph uses
    A. example words.
    B. contrast words.
    C. cause and effect words.

(Continues on next page)

B. (5–6.) Fill in each blank with an appropriate signal word from the box. Use each transition once.

on the other hand	while

¹Do you consider yourself an introvert—or an extrovert? ²Introverts are people who gain energy from solitary activities. ³They often enjoy reading, writing, watching movies at home, or spending time with just one or two friends. ⁴Extroverts, (5) _____, draw energy from spending time with others. ⁵They like being with a crowd, taking part in group activities, and hanging out with lots of people. ⁶Introverts figure things out by thinking quietly about them, (6) _____ extroverts prefer to talk things out.

_____ 7. This paragraph uses
   A. example words.
   B. contrast words.
   C. cause and effect words.

C. (8–9.) Fill in each blank with an appropriate signal word from the box. Use each transition once.

example	for instance

¹A dictionary may seem solid and unchanging, like a rock. ²However, that is not the case at all. ³Dictionaries are constantly changing, just as language itself is. ⁴(8) _____, the latest edition of the *Merriam-Webster Dictionary* includes 10,000 words that the previous edition did not. ⁵One (9) _____ of a new word is *google*. ⁶It comes from the Internet search engine called Google. ⁷When someone says, "I googled for information about headaches," she means she spent time searching that topic on the Internet.

_____ 10. This paragraph uses
   A. example words.
   B. contrast words.
   C. cause and effect words.

SIGNAL WORDS II: Mastery Test 5

A. (1–5.) Fill in each blank with an appropriate signal word from the box. Use each transition once. Then complete the outline that follows.

because of	lead to	reason
result	so	

¹Most victims of house fires are poor people. ²In a very real sense, you could say that poverty is the (1) _____ that fires happen. ³Poor people tend to live in the oldest, most badly maintained buildings in a city. ⁴(2) _____ their poor maintenance, these houses often have faulty electrical wiring that can (3) _____ fires. ⁵Also, the poor often rely on open flames—whether using candles for light or gas stoves for heat. ⁶Any time there is an open flame nearby, a fire can easily (4) _____. ⁷Finally, poor people may not have money to spend on smoke detectors, (5) _____ they do not have any warning when a fire breaks out.

_____ 6. This paragraph uses addition words and
    A. example words.
    B. contrast words.
    C. cause and effect words.

7–9. Complete the outline of the selection.

    Main idea: Poverty can be seen as the cause of house fires.

    1. _____

    2. _____

    3. _____

(Continues on next page)

B. Read the following paragraph and answer the question that follows.

¹People hotly debate the issue of whether live animals should be used in testing medical products. ²People who oppose animal testing say there is no excuse for making animals experience the pain and fear that is associated with live testing. ³They say that animal testing is of limited value, since animals and humans respond differently to medications and medical procedures. ⁴On the other hand, supporters of animal testing say that many of the medicines and surgical procedures we use today would not exist without lab testing on animals. ⁵They claim that devices like heart and lung machines and pacemakers could never have been invented without animal testing.

_____ 10. This paragraph
    A. gives examples of animals that are used in product tests.
    B. contrasts two views on animal testing of medical products.
    C. states reasons why live animals should not be used to test medical products.

SIGNAL WORDS II: Mastery Test 6

A. Read the paragraph below. Then answer the question and complete the outline that follows.

> ¹Stress can lead to extreme behaviors. ²Some people react to stress by trying to escape from their problems through drug abuse. ³These people use drugs as a desperate way to deal with the difficulties of their lives. ⁴Another extreme behavior caused by stress is aggression, including child abuse and other violence between family members. ⁵Stress may also lead people to fall into a depression so deep that they fear it will never go away. ⁶The result is a suicide attempt.

_____ 1. This paragraph uses
   A. example words.
   B. contrast words.
   C. cause and effect words.

2–5. Outline the paragraph, writing in the main idea and the three major supporting details.

Main idea: _____

1. _____

2. _____

3. _____

(Continues on next page)

B. Read the following paragraph and answer the questions that follow.

¹Obsessive-compulsive behavior is a disorder in which people have repeated thoughts and actions they cannot control. ²One example involves an extreme fear of germs. ³After doing a routine action such as opening a book or eating a sandwich, one man would wash his hands for 15 minutes. ⁴Another instance of this disturbing disorder is a constant focus on money. ⁵One man was so consumed by the thought of becoming a millionaire at age 30 that he worked day and night. ⁶Eventually he collapsed and was taken to a hospital, where he tried to pull out his gold fillings and sell them to an attendant.

_____ 6. This paragraph uses
   A. example words.
   B. contrast words.
   C. cause and effect words.

7–10. Complete the map of the paragraph: Fill in the missing major and minor supporting details.

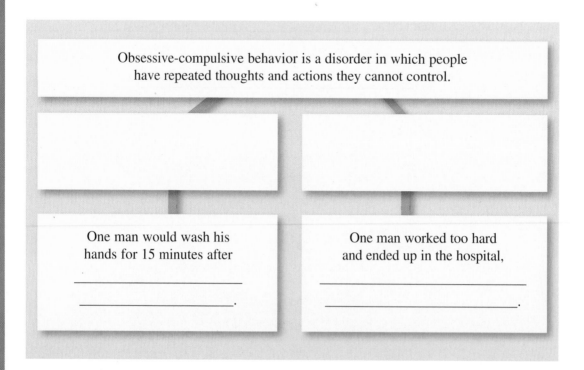

Obsessive-compulsive behavior is a disorder in which people have repeated thoughts and actions they cannot control.

One man would wash his hands for 15 minutes after _____ _____.

One man worked too hard and ended up in the hospital, _____ _____.

9 Inferences

This Chapter in a Nutshell

- Ideas are often suggested rather than being stated directly. We must **infer**, or figure out, those ideas.

- To make logical inferences, we must look closely at the information available and use our own experience and common sense.

Inferences are ideas that are not stated directly. They are conclusions that we come to based on what we see, hear, and read.

Look at the cartoon below. What can you figure out about it? Check (✓) the **two** inferences that are most logically based on the information suggested by the cartoon. Then read the explanation on the next page.

"Relax, Mom . . . it's macaroni."

_____ 1. The boy's mother approves of body piercings.

_____ 2. The boy had not warned his mother what he was going to do.

_____ 3. In the past, the boy had asked if he could get body piercings.

_____ 4. The boy did not really get body piercings.

_____ 5. The boy's mother has a few body piercings of her own.

Explanation

1. The boy's mother would not seem so shocked by her son's appearance if she approved of body piercings. Also, her son is telling her to relax, a sign that she is upset.

2. If the boy had warned his mother what he was going to do, her hair would not be standing on end and her eyes bugging out. She is clearly shocked by her son's appearance. You should have checked this item.

3. Nothing suggests that the boy had asked if he could get body piercings.

4. The boy is telling his mother that what appear to be body piercings are only macaroni. You should have checked this item.

5. Nothing in the picture or words suggests that the boy's mother has body piercings of her own.

With visual material such as cartoons, book covers, and photographs, we can infer a great deal from all the clues provided. With written material, we can "read between the lines" and pick up ideas the writer only suggests, or implies. This chapter will give you practice in making inferences from both visual and reading materials.

Inferences about Visual Materials

Cartoon

Look at the cartoon on the next page. Put a check (✓) by the **two** inferences that are most logically based on the information given in the cartoon. Then read the explanation that follows.

© Randy Glasbergen. www.glasbergen.com

BIOLOGY
QUIZ TODAY!

GLASBERGEN

"Class, who can tell me what I have preserved in this jar?
No, it's not a pig or a baby cow . . . it's the last student
who got caught cheating on one of my tests."

_____ 1. The class has just finished taking a test.

_____ 2. The specimen in the jar is really a baby pig.

_____ 3. The teacher is strict about cheating in his class.

_____ 4. The teacher wants his students to be afraid to cheat.

_____ 5. More students cheat in biology class than in other classes.

Explanation

1. Experience tells us that teachers give warnings like this *before* the test begins, not after.

2. We can safely assume that the specimen in the jar is not really a student, since teachers are not permitted to "preserve" students. It may be a baby pig, a baby cow, or just a "pretend" animal. However, we don't know exactly what it is.

3. From the stern warning the teacher gives the class as he holds up the jar, we can infer that he is strict about cheating in his class. You should have checked this item.

4. Holding up the preserved "cheating student" is a sign the teacher wants his students to be afraid to cheat. You should have checked this item.

5. Nothing in the cartoon suggests that students are any more likely to cheat in a biology class than in other classes.

Book Cover

Look at the following cover of a book titled *Surviving Abuse: Four True Stories* by Beth Johnson. Put a check (✓) by the **two** inferences that are most logically based on the information given on the cover.

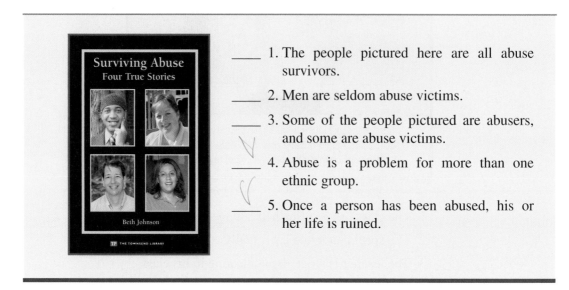

_____ 1. The people pictured here are all abuse survivors.

_____ 2. Men are seldom abuse victims.

_____ 3. Some of the people pictured are abusers, and some are abuse victims.

_____ 4. Abuse is a problem for more than one ethnic group.

_____ 5. Once a person has been abused, his or her life is ruined.

Explanation

1. The title *Surviving Abuse: Four True Stories* suggests that the four people pictured on the cover are all abuse survivors. You should have checked this item.

2. Two of the abuse victims are men and two are women. There is nothing to suggest that more women than men are victims of abuse.

3. The title indicates that the stories tell of surviving abuse, not being an abuser. Also, an abuser would not want to be pictured on the cover of a book.

4. The people on the cover represent three ethnic groups, suggesting that the problem of abuse cuts across all ethnic boundaries. You should have checked this item.

5. The smiling faces of the people on the cover suggest that being the victim of abuse need not ruin a person's life. So does the title, *Surviving Abuse.*

Photograph

Look at the following photograph. Put a check (✓) by the **two** inferences that are most logically based on the information given in the photograph.

_____ 1. The man is a drug addict.

_____ 2. The man is homeless.

_____ 3. The man is thinking about his past.

_____ 4. The man is trying to stay warm.

_____ 5. The man knows where he will sleep tonight.

Explanation

1. Although experience tells us that sometimes people who sleep in the streets are drug addicts, there is nothing in this photograph that tells us this man is a drug addict.

2. Common sense tells us that a man who has a home would not be sleeping on a street corner with all his apparent possessions nearby in a shopping cart. You should have checked this item.

3. We don't know either what the man is thinking about or even if he is sleeping.

4. That the man is bundled up and wearing a hood and hat and gloves and that he is sitting in the sunlight certainly suggests that he is trying to stay warm. You should have checked this item.

5. If the man knew where he would be sleeping that night, he might be less likely to be resting in the middle of the day.

A Final Comment about Visual Materials

As the preceding examples—the cartoons, the book cover, and the photograph—make clear, we live in a world full of images, and we make inferences about such visual materials all the time. In other words, making inferences is a skill all of us already possess. This chapter will now go on to strengthen your ability to make good inferences when reading.

Inferences about Reading Materials

You have already practiced making inferences while reading an earlier chapter in this book. Do you remember the following sentence from the "Vocabulary in Context" chapter?

> **Assets** such as good health, a loving family, and an enjoyable job make life worth living.

The sentence does not tell us exactly what *assets* means. However, it does suggest that assets are valuable things such as good health, a loving family, and an enjoyable job. We can then infer that *assets* means "things of value." For all the sentences in Chapter 3, you inferred the meanings of words by looking closely at the surrounding context.

In our everyday reading, we often "read between the lines" and pick up ideas that are not directly stated in print. To make such inferences, we use clues provided by the writer, and we also apply our own experience, logic, and common sense.

Inferences in Passages

✓ Check Your Understanding

Read the following passage and then check (✓) the **two** inferences that are most firmly based on the given information.

> [1]My wife is a murderer. [2]I got her a plant as a surprise one-month anniversary gift, and she proceeded to kill it. [3]She wasn't trying to kill it, but she doesn't exactly have a green thumb. [4]In the belief that all living things require water, she began flooding the plant on a daily basis. [5]"Be careful not to overwater it," I warned. [6]"Plants need air as well as water." [7]"Okay," she replied, and then dumped on another gallon of water. [8]The sicker the plant got, the more she watered it. [9]Finally, it melted away into an oozing heap. [10]One day I returned home to see that the plant and its pot had simply disappeared. [11]We had not been married that long yet, but I figured the safest thing to do was to say nothing.

_✓_ 1. The woman did not believe the man's advice.

____ 2. The women intentionally killed the plant.

_✓_ 3. The man knows more about plants than his wife does.

____ 4. The man is very angry at his wife.

____ 5. The man was surprised that the plant died.

Explanation

1. The woman continues to water the plant heavily after her husband's warning; she obviously did not believe his advice. You should have checked this item.

2. The man says that his wife wasn't trying to kill the plant, but that she simply lacks a green thumb. We can infer that she accidentally, not intentionally, killed the plant. The man states that his wife is a "murderer" for comic effect. People cannot "murder" plants.

3. Since the man knows that overwatering is not good for plants, he must know more about plants than his wife does. You should have checked this item.

4. The man says that "the safest thing to do was to say nothing." His words suggest that he fears her reaction if he says something about the dead plant. If he had been very angry at her, he probably would have said something.

5. The wife's continued overwatering of the plant, which the man notices and comments upon, suggests that he is not surprised that the plant died.

PRACTICE 1

Read each passage and then check (✓) the **two** inferences that are most firmly based on the given information.

A. ¹In the 1600s, the word *spinster* referred to any female. ²Spinning thread or yarn for cloth was something every woman did at home. ³By 1700, *spinster* had become a legal term for an unmarried woman. ⁴Such women had to work to survive, and spinning was their most common job. ⁵Before long, however, spinning was done in factories. ⁶*Spinster* then suggested someone who was "left over" or "dried up," just as the job of home spinning had dried up for women. ⁷Today, with so many women working and marrying later and later, most single women consider the word *spinster* an insult.

_____ 1. Women who could spin were thought to make especially good wives.

__✓__ 2. The word *spinster* was not originally an insulting term.

_____ 3. Today's single women should be proud to be called spinsters.

__✓__ 4. At one time in history, unmarried women were looked down upon.

_____ 5. Today, single women are no longer called spinsters.

B. ¹Sentenced to execution, some condemned American criminals have used their last moments to share a witty last word with observers. ²George Appel was electrocuted in 1928. ³Just before the switch was pulled, he joked with the onlookers: "Well, folks, soon you'll see a baked Appel." ⁴James W. Rodgers was shot by firing squad in 1960. ⁵When asked if he had a last request, he replied, "Why, yes—a bullet-proof vest." ⁶James French was sent to the electric chair in 1966. ⁷On the way to his execution, he caught the attention of a nearby reporter. ⁸"I have a terrific headline for you in the morning," he said; "French Fries." ⁹Jesse Bishop was sentenced to die by gas chamber in 1979. ¹⁰His last words were: "I've always wanted to try everything once . . . Let's go!"

_____ 1. Different methods of execution are used in the United States.

_____ 2. Appel, Rodgers, and Bishop were innocent of the crimes they were accused of.

_____ 3. Appel, Rodgers, and Bishop all wanted to die.

_____ 4. There are generally witnesses watching an execution.

_____ 5. People watching the executions were shocked by the convicted men's remarks.

C. ¹In 1857, a group of Egyptian salesmen tried to convince Congress that camels should be used in desert outposts in the West. ²The salesmen pointed out that a camel could carry up to 1,000 pounds more than an elephant. ³They said a camel's energy was almost limitless. ⁴As proof, they had a camel race a horse across difficult land covering 110 miles. ⁵The horse won the race, but died of fatigue shortly afterward. ⁶To show how much staying power the camel had, the salesmen had the camel run again the next day. ⁷The camel covered the same area at the same speed. ⁸The salesmen then pointed out how little water camels need. ⁹Camels barely sweat, and they regulate their body temperatures depending on the heat. ¹⁰Congress was convinced and bought 75 camels for soldiers to use. ¹¹However, soldiers hated the beasts and turned them loose in the desert. ¹²Most disappeared, but there are still occasional sightings of camels in remote desert regions today.

_____ 1. Camels are bad-tempered animals.

_____ 2. The Egyptian salesmen were trying to cheat Congress.

_____ 3. Camels could have been valuable in the American West.

_____ 4. Camels travel at a steady pace without using much energy.

_____ 5. The camels could never have survived in the American desert.

Inferring Main Ideas

Sometimes a paragraph does not have a main idea. In such cases, the writer has decided to let the supporting details suggest the main idea. The main idea is unstated, or **implied**, and you must **infer** it—figure it out—by deciding upon the point of the supporting details.

Asking two questions will help you to determine the writer's main idea:

- What is the topic, or subject, of the paragraph? In other words, what is the whole paragraph about?
- What is the main point being made about the topic?

The following paragraph has no stated main idea. Ask the two questions above to help you decide which of the four answers that follow the paragraph states the implied main idea. In the space provided, write the letter of that answer. Then read the explanation that follows.

> [1]When you have a relationship with someone, it is almost certain that you will argue now and then. [2]To keep an argument from causing hard feelings, listen to the other person's point of view. [3]Don't just hear what you want to hear, but focus on what the person is saying. [4]Also try to identify with his or her point of view as much as you can, remembering that a view other than your own may be valid. [5]Another way to keep an argument from causing hard feelings is to concentrate on behavior that is annoying you, not on the other person's character. [6]For example, say, "This bothers me a lot," not, "Only a stupid idiot would act the way you are!" [7]Finally, when the argument is over, put it behind you.

_____ The **unstated main idea** is:

   A. People often argue with each other.

   B. When you have a relationship with someone, you should try not to argue with him or her.

   C. There are guidelines you can follow to ensure that an argument does not cause hard feelings.

   D. The most important point in knowing how to argue is to put an argument behind you once it is over.

Explanation

If you answered the question "Who or what is the paragraph about," you probably found the topic: arguing. The next question to ask is "What is the main point being made about arguing?" To answer that question, consider the supporting details:

- The details of the paragraph are not about how often people argue or the importance of trying not to argue, so answers A and B are wrong.

- The details of the paragraph are specific guidelines for keeping an argument from causing hard feelings: "listen to the other person's point of view," "try to identify with his or her point of view," "concentrate on behavior that is annoying you, not on the other person's character," and "when the argument is over, put it behind you." Therefore answer C is correct—it makes a general statement that covers the specific guidelines listed.

- Answer D is wrong because it is too narrow: it is about only one of the guidelines.

 PRACTICE 2

The following paragraphs have implied main ideas, and each is followed by four sentences. In the space provided, write the letter of the sentence that best expresses the implied main idea.

_____ 1. ¹Because turnips were often eaten by the poor, other people often turned up their noses at them. ²Carrots were also once held in low esteem. ³They grew wild in ancient times and were used then for medicinal purposes. ⁴But they weren't considered fit for the table in Europe until the 13th century. ⁵Similarly, in the early 17th and 18th centuries, some Europeans considered potatoes fit only for animals. ⁶They were thought to cause leprosy in humans.

The **unstated main idea** is:
A. Vegetables are a healthy addition to any diet.
B. In previous centuries, some Europeans thought potatoes were unhealthy for humans.
C. Through the centuries, people have had mistaken ideas about certain vegetables.
D. While potatoes were once considered unhealthy, carrots were once used as medicine.

_____ 2. ¹A minister in Louisiana gave his cat away to a granddaughter who lived in New Orleans. ²Three weeks later, the cat showed up at the minister's home. ³It had traveled 300 miles and crossed the Mississippi and Red Rivers on its own. ⁴A German man took his cat on a family vacation from Germany to Turkey. ⁵At the border, the cat was nowhere to be found. ⁶However, two months and 1,500 miles later, the cat returned to his home in Germany. ⁷An American man took his cat with him when he moved from Utah to Washington. ⁸Soon after arriving in his new home, the cat disappeared. ⁹Over a year later, the cat showed up on the front porch of the man's Utah home 850 miles away. ¹⁰The man's former neighbors recognized the animal and offered him a new home.

The **unstated main idea** is:

A. Cats do not adjust well to new homes.
B. Lost pets are often found thanks to the kindness of people.
C. People should not get a cat unless they are sure they will not be moving.
D. Cats can have an incredible sense of direction.

_____ 3. ¹To become president of the United States, a person must be at least 35 years old. ²He or she must have lived in the United States for the last 14 years. ³In addition, he or she must be a natural-born citizen of the country. ⁴A convicted felon cannot be president of the United States.

The **unstated main idea** is:

A. There is an age limit to becoming president.
B. There are specific rules about who can become an elected official of a country.
C. The requirements for becoming a president of the United States are too limiting.
D. There are certain requirements for becoming president of the United States.

CHAPTER REVIEW

In this chapter, you learned the following:

- Making inferences is a skill we practice all the time with much of what we see and read.

- Important ideas in reading may not be stated directly, but must be inferred.

- To make good inferences, we must use the information presented, our own experience, and common sense.

The final chapter in Part One—Chapter 10—will deepen your ability to think in a clear and logical way.

On the Web: If you are using this book in class, you can visit our website for additional practice in making inferences. Go to **www.townsendpress.com** and click on "Learning Center."

REVIEW TEST 1

To review what you've learned in this chapter, answer each of the following questions by filling in the blanks.

1. To fully understand a cartoon, book cover, ad, or other visual image, we often must make ___*inferences*___

2. When we read, we often "read between the lines" and pick up ideas that are implied rather than directly ___*reading materials*___ *stated*

3. When making inferences, it is (*a mistake,* *useful*) _____ to draw upon our own experience as well as clues provided.

4. When the ___*main idea*___ of a paragraph is not stated directly, you can often figure it out by looking at the paragraph's supporting details.

REVIEW TEST 2

A. (1–2.) Put a check (✓) by the **two** inferences that are most logically based on the information given in the following cartoon.

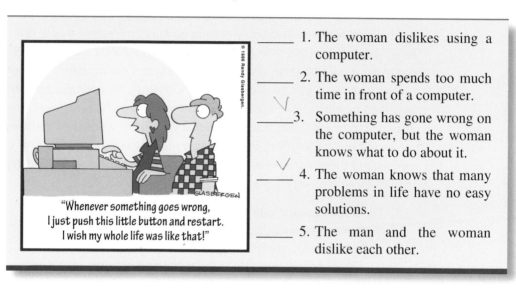

_____ 1. The woman dislikes using a computer.

_____ 2. The woman spends too much time in front of a computer.

_____ 3. Something has gone wrong on the computer, but the woman knows what to do about it.

_____ 4. The woman knows that many problems in life have no easy solutions.

_____ 5. The man and the woman dislike each other.

"Whenever something goes wrong, I just push this little button and restart. I wish my whole life was like that!"

B. (3–4.) Read the following passage and then check (✓) the **two** inferences that are most firmly based on the given information.

¹Because children have to attend school until they are 16, our classes are crowded with troublemakers who do not want to be there. ²These troublemakers make it difficult for serious students to get an education. ³Teachers must spend most of their time merely trying to keep the troublemakers under control, rather than actually teaching the good students. ⁴By the time a student is 13, it is clear whether he or she is serious about school or is only going to play the fool there. ⁵At that age, the troublemakers should be allowed to drop out, so that the good students can get on with their education.

_____ 1. Required attendance in school creates more problems than it solves.

_____ 2. Students today are creating more problems than they did in the past.

_____ 3. Students who are troublemakers at age 13 often mature and turn out to be good students.

_____ 4. If troublemakers were allowed to drop out at age 13, serious students would get a better education.

_____ 5. Students want to drop out of school because schools and teachers are not doing a good job.

C. Read the following paragraph and then, in the space provided, write the letter of the sentence that best expresses the implied main idea.

> ¹Most American parents wait until their children are at least two years old before teaching them how to use the toilet. ²Teaching infants to use the toilet early will help keep them comfortable and happy. ³The young children will not have to deal with irritating moisture and uncomfortable diaper rash. ⁴Early toilet training can also save parents and communities a lot of cash. ⁵Parents can save up to $3,000 on disposable diapers, and communities will not have to deal with the expenses caused by so much trash. ⁶In addition, toilet training may help parents form early bonds with their infants. ⁷Parents must pay close attention to their children's signals so that they know when their children need to use the toilet. ⁸By giving their children more attention and learning how to understand these signals, parents can start building a strong relationship with their children at a very early age.

_____ 5. The **implied main idea** of this paragraph is:
  A. It is extremely difficult to toilet-train an infant.
  B. Most parents are too busy to toilet-train an infant.
  C. There are real benefits to toilet-training children at younger ages.
  D. Forcing infants to use the toilet makes them angry and resentful of adults.

Here is a chance to apply your understanding of inferences to a full-length reading. The selection is by Dr. Ben Carson, who grew up poor with his single mother in inner-city Detroit. He was considered the "dummy" of his fifth-grade class until he realized he could learn and do well in school. Today, he is one of the world's most respected surgeons. In this excerpt from his book *The Big Picture*, he shares a message with young people of today.

Following the reading are questions on inferences. There are also questions on the skills taught in previous chapters.

Words to Watch

Below are some words in the reading that do not have strong context support. Each word is followed by the number of the paragraph in which it appears and its meaning there. These words are indicated in the selection by a small circle (°).

deplorable (2): wretchedly bad; miserable
cavernous (4): resembling a cave
spontaneous (5): unplanned; impulsive
graphically (8): vividly
gratification (8): satisfaction
bevy (9): group

DARE TO THINK BIG

Dr. Ben Carson

1   I do not speak only to parent groups. I spend a lot of time with students, such as those I encountered not long ago on a memorable visit to Wendell Phillips High School, an inner-city school on Chicago's south side.

2   Before I spoke, the people who invited me to the Windy City held a reception in my honor. There I met and talked with school officials and local religious leaders, many of whom informed me about the troubled neighborhood where the school is located. They indicated that gang influence was prevalent, living conditions were deplorable° in the surrounding public housing developments, dropout statistics were high, and SAT scores were low.

3   It sounded like a lot of other high schools I have visited around the country. Yet so dire were these warnings that, on the crosstown drive to the school, I could not help wondering what kind of reception I would receive from the students.

4   I need not have worried. When I walked into Wendell Phillips High School, its long deserted hallways gave the building a cavernous°, empty feel. The entire student body (1,500 to 2,000 strong) had already been excused from class and was assembled quietly in the school's auditorium. A school administrator, who was addressing the audience, noted my entrance through a back door and abruptly interrupted his remarks to announce, "And here's Dr. Carson now!"

5   All eyes turned my way. Immediately students began to applaud. Some stood. Suddenly they were all standing, clapping, and cheering. The applause continued the entire time I walked down the aisle and climbed the steps onto the auditorium stage. I couldn't remember ever receiving a warmer, more enthusiastic, or more spontaneous° reception anywhere in my entire life.

6   I found out later that a local bank had purchased and distributed paperback copies of my autobiography, *Gifted Hands*, to every student at Wendell Phillips. A lot of those teenagers had evidently read the book and felt they already knew me. By the time I reached the microphone, the noise faded away. I felt overwhelmed by their welcome.

7   I did what I often do when facing such a young audience. I wanted them thinking seriously about their lives and futures. So I quickly summarized my earliest years as a child, about my own

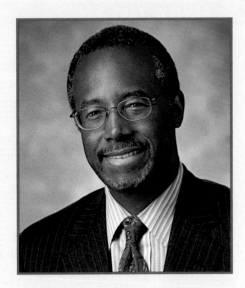

student days back at Southwestern High School in Detroit. I referred briefly to the incident when my anger nearly caused a tragedy that would have altered my life forever. I recounted my struggles with peer pressure, which sidetracked me for a time.

8   Then I talked about the difference between being viewed as cool and being classified as a lowly nerd. I find that serves as a graphically° relevant illustration for my message on delayed gratification°—a theme I hit almost every time I speak to young people.

9   The cool guys in every school are the ones who have earned a varsity letter in some sport—maybe several sports. They wear the latest fashions. They know all the hit tunes. They can converse about the latest blockbuster movies. They drive sharp cars and seem to collect a bevy° of beautiful girlfriends.

10   The nerds are the guys always hauling around an armload of books,

with more in their backpacks. They wear clean clothes—and often big, thick glasses. They even understand the science experiments. They ride the school bus, or worse yet, their parents drive them to school. Most of the popular girls would not be caught dead speaking to them in the hallway between classes.

11   The years go by, and graduation draws near. Often the cool guy has not done well in school, but his personality wins him a job at the local fast-food franchise, flipping hamburgers and waiting on customers. The nerd, who has won a scholarship, goes off to college.

12   A few more years go by. The cool guy is still flipping burgers. Maybe he has even moved up to Assistant Shift Manager by now. The girls who come in to eat lunch may notice and smile at him. He is still cool.

13   The nerd finishes up at college and does very well. Upon graduation he accepts a job offer from a Fortune 500 company. With his first paycheck, he goes to the eye doctor, who replaces those big, old, thick glasses with a pair of contacts. He stops at the tailor and picks out a couple of nice suits to wear. After saving a big chunk of his first few paychecks, he makes a down payment on a new Lexus. When he drives home to visit his parents, all the young women in the old neighborhood say, "Hey, don't I know you?" Suddenly, they do not want to talk to the guy behind the fast-food counter anymore.

14   The first guy—the cool guy—had everything back in high school. So what did he get for all that?

15   The other guy was not cool at all—but he was focused. Where did he go in the long run?

16   "And that," I told my audience, "is how we have to learn to think about life! With a long-term view. A Big-Picture perspective!"

17   Those students at Chicago's Wendell Phillips High School could not have been more attentive as I recounted the things this former nerd has seen and done. They listened to me explain and illustrate the incredible potential that resides in the average human brain. They even seemed receptive to my challenge that they begin to use those brains to plan and prepare for the future. So, as I wrapped up my talk by daring them to THINK BIG, I did something I had never done before, though I realized it could backfire if I had read this audience wrong. But since they had been such a responsive group, I decided to risk it.

18   I concluded by asking that auditorium full of high school students for a show of hands. "How many of you are ready, here today, to raise your hands and say to me, to your teachers, and to your peers, 'I want to be a nerd'?"

19   Although many of them laughed, almost all the students of Wendell Phillips High School raised their hands as they stood and applauded and cheered even louder than when I had walked in.

Questions about the Reading

For each question, write the letter of your answer in the space provided.

Vocabulary in Context

_____ 1. In the sentences below, the word *prevalent* (prĕv′ə-lənt) means
    A. absent.
    B. widely present.
    C. desirable.
    D. unimportant.

> "There I met and talked with school officials and local religious leaders . . . about the troubled neighborhood where the school is located. They indicated that gang influence was prevalent . . . ." (Paragraph 2)

_____ 2. In the sentences below, the word *dire* (dīr) means
    A. alarming.
    B. misleading.
    C. reassuring.
    D. amusing.

> "They indicated that . . . living conditions were deplorable in the surrounding public housing developments, dropout statistics were high, and SAT scores were low. . . . [S]o dire were these warnings that, on the crosstown drive to the school, I could not help wondering what kind of reception I would receive from the students." (Paragraphs 2–3)

Central Point and Main Ideas

_____ 3. Which sentence best expresses the central point of the entire selection?
    A. Dr. Ben Carson, a famous surgeon, was considered a nerd in high school.
    B. The student body of a tough inner-city high school listened politely to Dr. Ben Carson's talk.
    C. In a talk to high-school students, Dr. Ben Carson encouraged them to focus on long-term goals.
    D. Guys who earn varsity letters, know all the current music, and drive sharp cars seem to collect the most girlfriends in high school.

_____ 4. Which sentence best expresses the main idea of paragraph 13?
  A. The nerd does well in college and even lands a job with a Fortune 500 company.
  B. After a well-paying job lets him afford contacts, nice clothes, and a nice car, the nerd becomes more attractive to women.
  C. When the nerd graduates from college, he can afford a cool wardrobe.
  D. Later in life the cool guy is sure to envy the nerd's accomplishments.

Supporting Details

_____ 5. Dr. Carson arrived at Wendell Phillips High School
  A. worried about how the students would respond to him.
  B. confident that his speech would be a big success.
  C. favorably impressed by what he had heard from community leaders.
  D. very late.

_____ 6. The students at Wendell Phillips High School
  A. worked in fast-food restaurants.
  B. had unusually high SAT scores.
  C. skipped school on the day that Dr. Carson spoke.
  D. had been excused from class to hear Dr. Carson speak.

_____ 7. Peer pressure
  A. sidetracked Dr. Carson for a while during his teenage years.
  B. never affected Dr. Carson during his teenage years.
  C. was less of a problem during Dr. Carson's teen years than it is now.
  D. affected Dr. Carson in positive ways during his teenage years.

Inferences

_____ 8. From the article, the reader might conclude that
  A. Dr. Carson was considered cool in high school.
  B. Dr. Carson hardly ever speaks to parent groups.
  C. planning for the future can mean giving up some pleasure today.
  D. the visit to Wendell Phillips High School was Dr. Carson's first to Chicago.

_____ 9. Dr. Carson implies that
  A. girls in high school aren't impressed by cool guys.
  B. the cool guy in high school wasn't thinking about his future.
  C. the cool guy in school had a "Big Picture" perspective on his life.
  D. when the nerd got his first paycheck, he should have saved it instead of spending it on clothes and contact lenses.

_____10. What audience did Dr. Carson seem to have in mind when he wrote this essay?
   A. High-school administrators
   B. High-school students
   C. Parents of high-school students
   D. High-school dropouts

Discussion Questions

1. It doesn't seem likely that Dr. Carson, a highly educated adult, often uses words like "cool" and "nerd" in his own conversation. Why, then, do you think he chose to use such language in his speech at Wendell Phillips High School? What effect do you think it had on the students?

2. Although Dr. Carson was a good student, he admits that peer pressure and his own hot temper sometimes got in the way of his success. What are some obstacles—internal and external—that stand in the way of your being the best student you can be? What are some ways you might overcome these obstacles?

3. Dr. Carson speaks frequently to high-school students because he has learned something about life that he believes can be of value to them. If you were asked to give a single piece of advice to a group of younger students, what would you say?

Note: Writing assignments for this selection appear on page 511.

Check Your Performance   **INFERENCES**

Activity	Number Right	Points	Score
Review Test 1 (4 items)	_____	× 5 =	_____
Review Test 2 (5 items)	_____	× 4 =	_____
Review Test 3 (10 items)	_____	× 6 =	_____
	TOTAL SCORE	=	_____%

Enter your total score into the **Reading Performance Chart: Review Tests** on the inside back cover.

INFERENCES: Mastery Test 1

A. (1–3.) Look at the following book cover and then put a check (✓) by the **three** inferences that are most logically based on the information given on the cover.

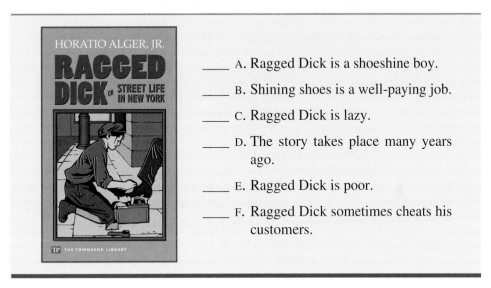

_____ A. Ragged Dick is a shoeshine boy.

_____ B. Shining shoes is a well-paying job.

_____ C. Ragged Dick is lazy.

_____ D. The story takes place many years ago.

_____ E. Ragged Dick is poor.

_____ F. Ragged Dick sometimes cheats his customers.

B. (4–7.) Put a check (✓) by the **two** inferences that are most logically based on each of the sentences below.

● When a blind man carries a lame man, both go forward.

_____ A. When people combine their strengths, they make progress.

_____ B. Only people with disabilities need the help of others.

_____ C. Disabled people should try to be as independent as possible.

_____ D. Nobody is perfect, but by working together, people can make up for each other's weaknesses.

(Continues on next page)

291

● If you get a lemon, make lemonade.

_____ E. Everyone gets more lemons in life than lemonade.

_____ F. Attitude and effort can turn around a bad situation.

_____ G. Sugar can make everything taste better.

_____ H. Even bitter things can be made into something sweet.

C. (8–10.) Read the following passage and then check (✓) the **three** inferences that are most firmly based on the given information.

¹Recently, a friend and I were at Universal Studios in Florida waiting to be seated for a show called *Raiders of the Lost Ark*. ²We stood there munching ice cream bars and people-watching when my eye was drawn to a tall woman near the front of our line. ³The woman, puffing away at a cigarette, looked to be in her late 50s. ⁴She was flashily dressed, with a beaded pink jacket and tight white pants, and her white-blonde hair was curled and styled like a young woman's. ⁵She smiled as she spoke to someone near her. ⁶With all of her makeup, she looked to me like a clown.

⁷"That woman near the front has no idea of how ridiculous she is," I commented to my friend. ⁸"She should act her age."

⁹Then the line started to move, and I noticed that she walked with a crutch. ¹⁰It hooked up under one arm and supported what was obviously a very weak leg. ¹¹The woman moved as briskly as she could, but still more slowly than other people. ¹²And then I realized that she was alone as I saw her take a seat by herself a few rows in front of us.

¹³The show started, but for quite a while I didn't pay any attention to it. ¹⁴Instead, I shook my head in self-disgust. ¹⁵And I thought about how many tests there are in our lives—how many chances we have to be either kind or cruel. ¹⁶On this particular test, I had just scored a zero.

_____ A. The woman injured her leg in an auto accident.

_____ B. The woman is trying to enjoy life despite her disability.

_____ C. The woman pitied herself because she had to use a crutch.

_____ D. The woman has a different idea of what it means to "act one's age" than the narrator.

_____ E. The narrator regrets that he prejudged the woman.

_____ F. The woman is a widow.

INFERENCES: Mastery Test 2

A. (1–3.) Look at the following cartoon and put a check (✓) by the **three** inferences that are most logically based on the information given.

THE JOKE'S ON YOU   by Phil Ryder & **YOU**

"Whoa...hold on a minute. You're not supposed to tell them the truth. For goodness
sake, man, you're a politician; show some
self-respect."

- Racer X • Jamaica Plain, MA

_____ A. Both men are politicians.

_____ B. The two men are brothers.

_____ C. The man who is speaking often lies to the public.

_____ D. The man who is listening will continue to tell the truth.

_____ E. The man who is listening is inexperienced.

_____ F. The audience is not interested in what the two men have to say.

B. (4–7.) Put a check (✓) by the **two** inferences that are most logically based on each of the sentences below.

● May your coffin be built out of the wood of a hundred-year-old oak tree, which I shall plant tomorrow.

_____ A. The speaker is wishing someone a long life.

_____ B. The speaker is an undertaker.

_____ C. The speaker is talking to a young person, perhaps a child.

_____ D. The speaker dislikes the person he or she is talking to.

(Continues on next page)

● You've got to do your own growing, no matter how tall your grandfather was.

_____ E. People with successful relatives have an easier time in life.

_____ F. Whatever your family background, no one can live your life for you.

_____ G. Family background is more important than character.

_____ H. The effort you make as an individual is more important than your family background.

C. (8–10.) Read the following passage and then check (✓) the **three** inferences that are most firmly based on the given information.

¹Sharon is a person whose life seems filled with conflict. ²I rarely talk with her without being reminded of that fact. ³For example, she constantly complains to me that people "do her wrong." ⁴"And I thought she was my friend!" is her constant complaint. ⁵Before I knew Sharon well, I sympathized with her incredible bad luck. ⁶Now, however, I think I understand the situation better. ⁷Sharon expects her friends to show her unconditional love and acceptance, no matter how she behaves. ⁸Even when she stands her friends up, tells them lies, and takes advantage of them, she is amazed when they withdraw their friendship. ⁹Despite her constant experience of losing friends, she doesn't realize that she is responsible for the situation.

_____ A. The writer has gained insight into Sharon's life, but Sharon hasn't.

_____ B. People like Sharon never change.

_____ C. Sharon has many good qualities.

_____ D. Sharon doesn't always treat her friends well.

_____ E. The writer no longer believes that Sharon's problems are due to bad luck.

_____ F. The writer of the passage is Sharon's sister.

INFERENCES: Mastery Test 3

A. (1–3.) Look at the following photograph and put a check (✓) by the **three** inferences that are most logically based on the information given.

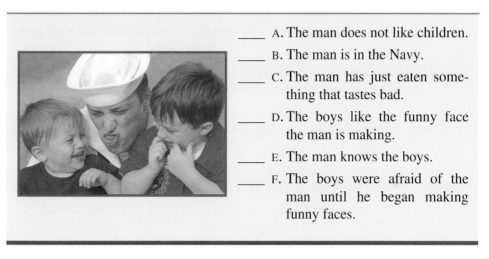

_____ A. The man does not like children.

_____ B. The man is in the Navy.

_____ C. The man has just eaten something that tastes bad.

_____ D. The boys like the funny face the man is making.

_____ E. The man knows the boys.

_____ F. The boys were afraid of the man until he began making funny faces.

B. (4–7.) Put a check (✓) by the **two** inferences that are most logically based on each of the sentences below.

- It is easier for a camel to go through the eye of a needle than it is for a rich man to enter the kingdom of heaven.

  _____ A. Rich men are favored by God.

  _____ B. Poor people are more likely to enter the kingdom of heaven than rich people.

  _____ C. Rich men should share their wealth with others.

  _____ D. Rich men don't care about entering the kingdom of heaven.

(Continues on next page)

● Kindness is the language which the deaf can hear and the blind can see.

_____ E. You don't need to see and hear to appreciate kindness.

_____ F. Kindness is a powerful form of communication.

_____ G. Only the disabled can truly appreciate kindness.

_____ H. People should be especially kind to deaf and blind people.

C. (8–10.) Read the following passage and then check (✓) the **three** inferences that are most firmly based on the given information.

> [1]At the very bottom of the American social ladder are the homeless. [2]They are people whose worldly goods fill a few shopping bags. [3]Social workers usually find that these people once were better off, but that some misfortune led to their losing their home. [4]An apartment building, for example, is sold to a developer, and its poor tenants are evicted. [5]A breadwinner loses his or her job because of a plant closing or a long illness. [6]A woman leaves an abusive husband but cannot afford an apartment of her own. [7]Whatever the cause, the result is the same: a person, a couple, a mother and her children, or an entire family living on the street. [8]Having fallen from a higher rung on the social ladder, many of the homeless are unable to regain their position.

_____ A. People become homeless for a variety of reasons.

_____ B. People are usually homeless for only a short period of time.

_____ C. Most homeless people are women.

_____ D. Homeless people are often unfortunate, not lazy.

_____ E. The cost of renting even a modest apartment is often more than poor people can afford.

_____ F. Homeless people usually only have themselves to blame for their homelessness.

INFERENCES: Mastery Test 4

A. (1–2.) Look at the following cartoon and put a check (✓) by the **two** inferences that are most logically based on the information given.

"Yes, I think I have good people skills.
What kind of idiot question is that?"

_____ A. The man is being interviewed for a job.

_____ B. The woman will probably hire the man.

_____ C. The woman asked the man a foolish question.

_____ D. The man probably does not have good people skills.

(Continues on next page)

B. (3–4.) Put a check (✓) by the **two** inferences that are most logically based on the passage below.

> ¹Although most everyone knows that eating sensibly and exercising regularly are the keys to healthy weight loss, the America fad diet industry continues to receive millions of dollars from people looking for a faster, easier solution. ²Eating sensibly and exercising regularly involve both education and commitment, neither of which is easy. ³And results, though proven, may not come quickly. ⁴Many people are anxious to lose weight right away. ⁵In addition, they are not willing to do the work that healthy eating and regular exercise require. ⁶That is why the fad diet industry continues to succeed every year. ⁷People want to believe there is a quick and easy fix. ⁸But no such pill, powder, or program has ever been found to match the success rate of a healthy lifestyle.

_____ A. Many Americans lack self-discipline when it comes to losing weight.

_____ B. Some fad diets are better than others.

_____ C. Americans tend to be impatient.

_____ D. If people ate sensibly, they wouldn't need to exercise.

C. In the space provided, write the letter of the sentence that best expresses the implied main idea in the paragraph that follows.

_____ 5. ¹To make your clothes last longer, avoid using the dryer. ²Over time, the heat will fade colors and weaken fabrics. ³Instead, hang your clothing to dry inside the house in cold weather and outside (but away from direct sunlight, which can also fade colors) when it's warm. ⁴Also, don't use bleach more than absolutely necessary. ⁵Bleach contains strong chemicals that can weaken fibers. ⁶Never store knitted clothes on hangers—the clothing can stretch out of shape. ⁷Instead, keep them folded in a drawer. ⁸Finally, get rid of stains promptly—if you let them set, they are much harder, if not impossible, to remove.

The **unstated main idea** is:
A. Most people don't know how to make their clothes last longer.
B. There are several ways to make your clothes last longer.
C. Dryers and bleach are bad for your clothes.
D. There are several reasons to avoid using your dryer.

INFERENCES: Mastery Test 5

A. Read each passage and check (✓) the **two** inferences that are most firmly based on the given information.

1–2. ¹Many people have suggested that opposites attract. ²People are more comfortable with those who look and act like themselves. ³They are naturally attracted to people that they can relate to. ⁴Ninety-nine percent of people marry someone who is of the same race. ⁵Seventy-five percent of people marry someone who is of the same religion. ⁶Most people marry someone who lives a short car ride away from their home and who has a similar level of attractiveness. ⁷People tend to marry someone who is within four years of their age, is around the same height as they are, and is in the same health. ⁸Rich people usually marry rich people, and poor people usually marry poor people. ⁹Smokers tend to marry other people who smoke. ¹⁰People who are outgoing, argumentative, or stubborn tend to end up with others who have those same qualities.

_____ A. Most people marry someone who is very similar to themselves.

_____ B. Marriages between people of different races and/or religions frequently end in divorce.

_____ C. Physical attraction is still one of the most important things to consider when choosing a mate.

_____ D. When it comes to marriage, opposites don't attract.

3–4. ¹Politicians who make the decisions to go to war are rarely personally affected by those decisions. ²They themselves do not do the fighting. ³They do not risk their lives on the battlefield. ⁴They do not run the danger of leaving their spouses widowed or their children parentless. ⁵Here's a suggestion. ⁶Before a politician can cast a "yes" vote to go to war, he or she should have to choose one member of his or her immediate family who will fight in that war. ⁷If politicians knew that a son or daughter, a brother or sister, would actually be part of the battle, they might find better ways to deal with the world's conflicts. ⁸As a result, there might be less war between countries and more peace.

_____ E. The writer believes that wars should be avoided.

_____ F. Most wars are unavoidable.

_____ G. Politicians need reminders that every person who dies in a war is a human being who probably has loved ones.

_____ H. Politicians have often risked their own lives in wars.

(Continues on next page)

B. In the space provided, write the letter of the sentence that best expresses the implied main idea in the paragraph that follows.

_____ 5. [1]Housework is the first thing to fall by the wayside in the time-pressured lives of professional women. [2]In a survey by a women's magazine, over 80 percent of full-time working women said the only way they could balance job, home, and family was to sacrifice high cleaning standards. [3]The next thing to get put on the back burner was sex. [4]Almost 75 percent said that by the end of the day, they or their spouses were too tired for anything but TV. [5]Fifty percent reported that friends and social occasions were third in line to get squeezed off the calendar.

The **unstated main idea** is:
A. Women who work full-time say they must sacrifice high cleaning standards.
B. According to a women's magazine survey, full-time working women would be better off if they took on part-time jobs instead.
C. Half of all full-time working women report that working full-time has meant less time for getting together with friends.
D. According to a women's magazine survey, full-time working women have to cut back on several customary activities.

INFERENCES: Mastery Test 6

A. After reading each passage, check (✓) the **two** inferences that are most firmly based on the information given.

1–2. ¹According to recent national studies, men are now less likely than women to get bachelor's degrees. ²And those men who do finish college take longer to get their degrees than women. ³Also, men get lower grades than women. ⁴The studies show that college men study less and socialize more. ⁵As a result, women are walking off with a higher share of the honors degrees. ⁶The enrollment of men is also down. ⁷Today they make up only 42 percent of the nation's college students. ⁸Women have also become a majority in graduate schools and professional schools.

_____ A. Women are more intelligent than men.

_____ B. Women are doing better in college than men are.

_____ C. The enrollment of men in colleges will continue to decline.

_____ D. In general, young women today take college more seriously than young men do.

3–4. ¹The famous writer Dorothy Parker (1893–1967) once ran into a movie star after the star's most recent and highly publicized suicide attempt. ²Parker patted the woman's arm and murmured, "Better luck next time." ³When Parker heard that President Calvin Coolidge, known as "Silent Cal," was dead, she asked, "How can they tell?" ⁴In her review of one Broadway play, she wrote that "*The House Beautiful* is the play lousy." ⁵And she remarked of the actress Katherine Hepburn in another play that she showed a range of emotions "from A to B."

_____ E. Dorothy Parker really wanted the "suicidal" movie star to kill herself.

_____ F. Parker thought that Katherine Hepburn's acting was dull.

_____ G. Katherine Hepburn never got over Parker's remark about her acting.

_____ H. Parker believed that bad plays and performances should be criticized.

(Continues on next page)

B. In the space provided, write the letter of the sentence that best expresses the implied main idea in the paragraph that follows.

_____ 5. [1]Patients should always be aware of a prescription drug's possible side effects. [2]Unexpected side effects, such as nausea or dizziness, can be frightening and even dangerous. [3]Consumers should ask, too, if they can take the medication along with other drugs they are using. [4]Some combinations of drugs can be deadly. [5]Finally, medication should always be stored in its own labeled bottle and never moved to another bottle. [6]Accidental mix-ups of drugs can have tragic results.

The **unstated main idea** is:
A. Consumers may use drugs carelessly.
B. Drugs can have dangerous side effects.
C. There are several guidelines for taking prescription medications safely.
D. To avoid tragic mix-ups, medications should always be stored in their own labeled bottles.

10 The Basics of Argument

This Chapter in a Nutshell

- A good thinker understands what it means to *make* a point.
- A good thinker understands what it means to *support* a point.

Look at the following cartoon and see if you can answer the questions that follow.

© 2002 by Randy Glasbergen.

GLASBERGEN

"I'm out in the fresh air and sunshine, my lungs are getting plenty of exercise, and I'm consuming a leafy vegetable . . . this has to be good for me!"

- What is the man's argument here? That is, what is his point?
- What is his support for his point?

Explanation

The man's point is that smoking is good for him. But his supporting reasons are *not* convincing ones. He's outside in the fresh air but putting cigarette smoke into his lungs, his lungs are not getting a healthy workout, and tobacco is not a leafy "vegetable." He makes a clear point—that smoking is good for him—but fails to support it. To make a good argument and prove a point, you must offer solid support.

Evaluating Arguments

A critical thinker is someone who can look at an **argument**—a point and its support—and decide whether the support is solid or not. Look at the following point:

> **Point:** It's more fun to watch movies at home than in a theater.

Now, is there solid support for this point? In other words, is the person who made it thinking clearly and logically? Let's say the person goes on to provide these details:

Support:

- When you are in a theater, you have to put up with rude adults and crying children.
- At home, you can "pause" a movie when you want to leave the room.
- It's great to watch movies in your pajamas while sitting in your favorite chair.

As you can see, the details do provide solid support for the point. They give us a basis for understanding and agreeing with the point that watching movies at home has its own special appeal.

This is a small example of what critical thinking is about: recognizing a point and deciding whether there is support that effectively backs up the point.

Practice in Evaluating Arguments

Point and Support

This first activity will review and sharpen your sense of the difference between a point and its support. As you learned earlier in the book, a **point** is a general idea; **support** is the specific information that backs up the point.

Check Your Understanding

Look at the following group of items. It is made up of a point and three statements that logically support the point. See if you can put a **P** in front of the point and an **S** in front of the three supporting statements.

_____ A. A six-foot snapping turtle lives on the bottom of the lake.

_____ B. Rattlesnakes have nests on the shoreline and often swim in the lake.

_____ C. Someone dumped scrap metal in the lake, and you could cut yourself badly.

_____ D. You should not go swimming in that lake.

Explanation

Statements A, B, and C all describe specific dangers of swimming in the lake. Statement D—that you should not swim in the lake—is the point that all of the other sentences support.

PRACTICE 1

In each of the following groups, one statement is the point, and the other statements are support for the point. Identify each point with a **P** and each statement of support with an **S**.

Group 1

_S_ A. Soda has no nutritional value.

_S_ B. Most cans of regular soda contain 10 teaspoons of sugar.

_S_ C. Caffeinated sodas make hyperactive kids even more hyper.

_P_ D. People should drink less soda.

Group 2

_S_ A. The puppy chewed on everything from my sneakers to the living room sofa.

_S_ B. It took the puppy weeks to learn that he was supposed to go outside, not on the kitchen floor.

_P_ C. The new puppy was very difficult to train.

_S_ D. At night the puppy would whine for hours, begging us to let him into our bedroom.

Group 3

_____ A. The majority of lottery winners are broke within five years.

_____ B. Family members often fight bitterly over how the money will be spent.

_____ C. Many lottery winners finally say they wish they had never won the money.

_____ D. Winning the lottery is not always a dream come true.

Logical Support I

Once you identify a point and its support, you need to decide if the support really applies to the point. The critical thinker will ask, "Is this support logical and relevant? Or is it beside the point?" In trying to make a point, people often bring up support that does not apply.

For example, say that a person claims that the people in the apartment next door are bad neighbors. To support that point, the person might say, "They play loud music late at night. In addition, they drive an old car." A critical thinker will realize that (1) playing loud music late at night may make them bad neighbors; (2) driving an old car does *not* make them bad neighbors. Driving an old car has nothing to do with whether or not they are bad neighbors. The first reason for disliking the people next door is relevant support, but the second reason is beside the point.

The following activity will sharpen your ability to decide whether evidence truly supports a point.

Check Your Understanding

Read the following point and the three items of "support" that follow. Then put a check (✓) next to the **one** item that logically supports the point.

Point: The teacher takes a personal interest in her students.

_____ A. [1]Her lectures are always well prepared, and she always follows her class syllabus. [2]When asked a question in class, she answers promptly and fully. [3]She has co-written a textbook on the subject that she's teaching.

_____ B. [1]She is lots of fun in class, always joking around and making wisecracks. [2]On Halloween, she came in dressed as a witch. [3]Once she handed out test booklets that said inside, "April fool!"

_____ C. [1]She has a one-on-one interview with each student at least twice a year. [2]She makes a point of knowing their families and often asks how their parents or siblings are doing. [3]If a student is having a special problem, she often visits him or her at home.

Explanation

A. The teacher described here knows her subject and is skilled at teaching, but nothing that she does shows that she takes a personal interest in her students. You should not have chosen this item.

B. The teacher described here is cheerful and fun-loving, but does nothing to show that she takes a personal interest in her students. You should not have chosen this item.

C. The teacher described here clearly goes out of her way to establish and maintain a personal connection to each of her students. If you checked the letter of this item, you were correct.

PRACTICE 2

Below is a point followed by three items of information. Put a check (✓) next to the **one** item that logically supports the point.

1. **Point: The applicant for the job did not seem as though he really wanted to be hired.**

    ___*B*___ A. ¹He showed up wearing brand-new blue jeans and a freshly ironed shirt. ²He greeted the receptionist politely and asked if he could have a cup of water while he was waiting to be interviewed. ³While he waited, he leafed through an old copy of *Time* magazine.

    ___✓___ B. ¹He arrived 15 minutes late for his interview, with no explanation. ²He looked rumpled and sleepy, as if he had just gotten out of bed. ³He answered the interviewer's questions with "Yeah" or "No." ⁴When the interviewer asked if he had any questions, he said, "Not really."

    ___C___ C. ¹He called the day before the interview to ask if he should bring anything along. ²When he arrived, he was 10 minutes early, and he brought flowers for the receptionist.³After the interview, he sent the interviewer a thank-you note.

2. **Point: My classmate, Gina, is very kind.**

    ✓ A. [1]When the rest of the class was making fun of the music teacher, she refused to join in. [2]When a boy from China joined the class, she did her best to make him feel welcome. [3]She is a volunteer math tutor after school.

    _____ B. [1]She's always looking at her face in her compact mirror. [2]She constantly worries that she's getting fat. [3]If someone wears the same thing she's wearing to class, she flips out. [4]She won't be seen in public without makeup.

    _____ C. [1]She participates in most classroom discussions. [2]She spends at least two hours a night on her homework. [3]She's doing an extra credit science project on solar energy. [4]She is a member of the National Honor Society.

3. **Point: Obesity is a growing health problem.**

    _____ A. [1]Thirty or so years ago, people were more active and, therefore, thinner because they didn't have computers and cable TV to sit in front of for hours on end. [2]There were also fewer fast-food restaurants and a smaller variety of junk food.

    _____ B. [1]Some diets are dangerous because they involve taking pills that contain large amounts of caffeine. [2]Other diets are unhealthy since they cut out necessary nutrients like fat and carbohydrates. [3]Most hazardous are diets that require starving one's self.

    ✓ C. [1]Because 30 percent of our population is very overweight, there has been a huge increase in physical problems such as type 2 diabetes and heart disease. [2]Emotional problems such as depression and anxiety have also increased. [3]As a result, the cost of health insurance has gone up.

Logical Support II

Check Your Understanding

Below is a point followed by five statements. Three of the statements logically support the point; two of the statements do not. In the spaces provided, write the letters of the **three** logical statements of support.

Point: Those parents are careless about their child's health and safety.

  A. They leave him alone in the house at night, sometimes not returning at all.

  B. They drop him off at the home of people they barely know, then disappear for days.

  C. They rarely take him to see the doctor or dentist.

  D. They never check to see if he has done his schoolwork.

  E. They do not allow him to have any pets.

Items that logically support the point: _____ _____ _____

Explanation

Items A, B, and C all support the point that the parents are careless about their child's health and safety. Items D and E do not directly involve the child's safety, so neither supports the point.

PRACTICE 3

Each point is followed by three statements that provide logical support and two that do not. In the spaces, write the letters of the **three** logical statements of support.

1. **Point:** Returning to school as an older student can be challenging.

  A. Studies show that more and more adults are returning to school.

  B. It takes a lot of work to re-learn study habits.

  C. Many older students have family and job responsibilities in addition to classes.

  D. Some older students are afraid of not "fitting in."

  E. It is never too late to gain new knowledge.

Items that logically support the point: _B_   _C_   _D_

2. **Point: Eating fish is good for your health.**

   A. Fish offers as much protein as beef, but with far fewer calories.

   B. Fish contains omega-3 fatty acids, which have been shown to reduce cholesterol and lower blood pressure.

   C. Fish is low in sodium and is a good source of vitamins and minerals.

   D. If fish is fried or prepared with a creamy sauce, it can have as many calories as beef.

   E. Because of overfishing by commercial fisheries, some popular ocean fish are becoming scarce.

   Items that logically support the point: ___A___   ___B___   ___C___

3. **Point: Workers in early American factories led difficult lives.**

   A. The average work day was 12 hours long.

   B. Early factory workers were paid pennies an hour.

   C. Female factory workers often worked in textile mills.

   D. The first American factories were built in the late 1700s.

   E. All workers on power machines risked accidents that could maim or kill.

   Items that logically support the point: ___A___   ___B___   ___E___

Making a Logical Point

This activity will develop your ability to look at evidence and then decide what point is supported by that evidence. This skill of coming to a logical conclusion is an important part of good thinking.

 ### Check Your Understanding

Look at the following three items of support:

Support:

- Although the boss gives very unclear directions for what he wants, he is furious if a job isn't done exactly as he intended.
- The boss has hired his lazy, incompetent niece, and no one is allowed to complain about anything she does.
- The boss takes two-hour lunches, while no one else is allowed to have more than a half hour.

Now check (✓) the **point** that is logically supported by the above evidence. Then read the explanation that follows.

_____ A. The boss is supportive of his family members.

_____ B. All bosses have their good and bad points.

_____ C. The boss does not care if his business succeeds or fails.

_____ D. The boss is an unpleasant person to work for.

Explanation

A. Only one of the supports mentions a member of the boss's family. You should not have chosen this point.

B. None of the supports says anything about the boss's good points, only his bad points, so you shouldn't have chosen this point.

C. The fact that the boss becomes furious if a job isn't done exactly as he intended indicates that he cares whether his business succeeds or fails. So you should not have chosen this point.

D. All the details support the statement that the boss is an unpleasant person to work for. It is the one you should have chosen as the point.

PRACTICE 4

For each group, read the three items of supporting evidence. Then check (✓) the point that is most logically supported by that evidence.

Group 1

Support:

- In heavily overpopulated areas, infants and children die at far above the average rate.
- The more overpopulated an area, the higher the crime rate.
- Noise pollution in overpopulated areas leads to psychological distress.

Point: Which of the following conclusions is best supported by all the evidence above?

___✓___ A. Overpopulation leads to a number of social problems.

_____ B. The life expectancy for adults in overpopulated places is lower than average.

_____ C. The majority of the world's cities are overpopulated.

_____ D. Overpopulation causes crime and disease.

Group 2

Support:

- Many American girls undereat in order to become or stay thin.

- Some young men take steroids to try to look more muscular.

- Adolescents who smoke cigarettes do so partly because smoking reduces appetite.

Point: **Which of the following conclusions is best supported by all the evidence above?**

_____ A. It is dangerous to use steroids without a doctor's prescription.

___✓___ B. Some young people risk their health for the sake of looking good.

_____ C. There are many reasons why young people should not smoke.

_____ D. Our society encourages girls to value their appearance above all else.

Group 3

Support:

- Drinking coffee improves my ability to concentrate.

- I enjoy having a cup of coffee while chatting with a friend.

- I love the taste and aroma of fresh coffee.

Point: **Which of the following conclusions is best supported by all the evidence above?**

_____ A. Much of the coffee we drink is produced in Central and South America.

_____ B. Drinking coffee can have unpleasant effects.

___⌐___ C. Sometimes when I drink coffee in the evening, I have a hard time falling asleep.

___✓___ D. Coffee is my favorite beverage.

CHAPTER REVIEW

In this chapter, you learned the following:

● A good argument is made up of a point, or a conclusion, and evidence to back it up.

● To think through an argument, you need to decide if each bit of evidence is relevant and logical.

● Sound thinking also includes looking at evidence and deciding what logical point, or conclusion, can be drawn from that evidence.

On the Web: If you are using this book in class, you can visit our website for additional practice in evaluating arguments. Go to **www.townsendpress.com** and click on "Learning Center."

REVIEW TEST 1

To review what you've learned in this chapter, fill in each of the blanks below.

1. A point is the (*main idea, evidence, logic*) _____ presented by a writer or speaker.

2. A good thinker is one who can look at an argument—a point and its support—and decide whether the _____ is solid or not.

3. In addition to asking "What is the point?" you must ask, "What is the _____support_____ for that point?"

4. Specific evidence is logical only if it truly supports the _____.

REVIEW TEST 2

A. (1–4.) In the following group, one statement is the point, and the other statements are support for the point. Identify the point with a **P** and each statement of support with an **S**.

_____ A. The first major improvement in automotive safety came in 1910 with the invention of safety glass windshields.

__V__ B. Automotive safety has improved over the years.

_____ C. Seat belts became standard in cars in the 1960s.

_____ D. Air bags became common in the 1980s.

B. (5.) Below is a point followed by three items of information. Put a check (✓) next to the **one** item that logically supports the point.

Point: Even though he's wealthy, my uncle is stingy.

__V__ A. He worked as a design engineer for IBM. He has a huge collection of books. He plays the piano. He can recite lines from Shakespeare off the top of his head.

__V__ B. He spends several hours a week clipping coupons. He buys day-old bread. He says he doesn't have cable TV because it costs too much. On the rare times we go out to restaurants, he gives the server a small tip.

_____ C. He doesn't like people from other countries. He thinks my sister should get married and have kids. He says things in this country have gone downhill since when he was young.

C. (6–8.) The point below is followed by three statements that provide logical support and two that do not. In the spaces, write the letters of the **three** logical statements of support.

Point: I need a bigger apartment.

A. There's barely enough room in the kitchen to turn around.

B. My living room is the size of a closet.

C. Because there's no storage space, boxes are piled on the floor.

D. My best friend has a huge apartment.

E. Rents are higher on this side of town.

Items that logically support the point: __A__   __B__   __C__

D. (9–10.) Read the three items of supporting evidence. Then check (✓) the point that is most logically supported by that evidence.

Group 1

Support:

- The drummer had no rhythm, and the lead guitarist was out of tune.
- The sound system was so bad that people were covering their ears.
- The singer forgot half the words.

Point: Which of the following conclusions is best supported by all the evidence above?

_____ A. Musicians are strange people.

___✓__ B. The concert was really bad.

_____ C. Practice makes perfect.

_____ D. Concerts are a great source of entertainment.

Group 2

Support:

- Lack of vitamin C leads to bleeding gums.
- People who lack iron in their diet may lose red blood cells and feel fatigue.
- A disease that causes slow bone growth results from a lack of vitamin D.

Point: Which of the following conclusions is best supported by all the evidence above?

_____ A. People long ago knew little about healthy eating.

___✓__ B. It is important to get enough vitamins and minerals in your diet.

_____ C. Citrus fruits (such as oranges) are a good source of vitamin C.

_____ D. Milk, which contains vitamin D and iron, is good for you.

Here is a chance to apply your understanding of argument to a full-length reading. Most Americans have dreadful diets. And with an obesity rate of over 30 percent, our bad food choices are killing us. Sometimes we make excuses for eating poorly, but often we don't really know how to eat right. This selection will show you how to eat better—and feel better. Following the selection are questions that cover all of the reading skills you've worked on in this book.

Words to Watch

Below are some words in the reading that do not have strong context support. Each word is followed by the number of the paragraph in which it appears and its meaning there. These words are marked in the reading by a small circle (°).

type 2 diabetes (1): a condition that occurs when the body can't use glucose
    (a kind of sugar) normally
deter (3): prevent
saturated (8): filled
skyrockets (11): goes up very quickly
distort (15): twist, mess up

THE SHOCKING STATE OF THE AMERICAN DIET
Adam Taylor

1   Today, the state of the typical American diet is beyond bad: it's deadly. Recent surveys revealed that more than 1,000 people *a day* die as a result of eating unhealthy foods. We've all heard that bad food choices can lead to weight gain and illnesses such as heart disease, cancer, and type 2 diabetes°. We all know that consuming too much fat and sugar can make us miserable and even shorten our lives. And yet we disregard the warnings. We keep eating garbage. We keep killing ourselves.

2   Just how bad *is* the American diet? Consider this: Two of the top five sources of calories in our diets are sweets and sodas. This means that at least 40 percent of most Americans' daily calories come from "foods" like cookies, candy, ice cream, and soft drinks. Doctors say that we should eat no more than six to nine teaspoons of sugar a day. Most of us eat at least 22 teaspoons! What's more, too much sugar is the number one cause of type 2 diabetes and obesity. Today nearly twenty million Americans suffer with type 2 diabetes. Worse still, more than one in three Americans are obese—extremely overweight.

3   However, warnings don't seem to deter° most of us. We continue feasting on sugar, processed foods, and bad fat. And everyone seems to have an excuse. Most Americans say they make poor food choices for three main reasons: 1) they don't like the taste of healthy food, 2) it's easier to eat fast foods and processed foods, and 3) they don't know how to eat healthily.

4   Excuse #1 is just that: an excuse. People who use this excuse like to insist that all "healthy" food is boring because it's mostly salads and fruit. In reality, there are endless delicious ways to prepare food that is good for you. Any quick search on the Internet for "healthy recipes" will bring up thousands of meal ideas, such as orange roasted salmon, baked honey mustard chicken, and vegetarian chili. People are often surprised at how much better healthy food actually tastes than fast and unhealthy food.

5   Those who use excuse #2 are correct. Sitting in a car and going through a drive-through or microwaving a frozen dinner in five minutes is easier than cooking dinner for a family. If this ease is worth losing possibly 10 to 20 years (or more) from your life, then by all means, continue being lazy. Doctors point out that those who eat mostly unhealthy food are three times more likely to die from cancer. Remember, however, that there are 10,080 minutes in a week. Most healthy meals take fewer than 30 minutes to prepare. And consider that the average American spends six to seven hours a day in front of TV and computer screens. Evidently, lack of time is not the problem: laziness is.

6   Finally, reason #3 is also not just an excuse. Many Americans truly do not know how to eat right. Millions of people have been raised in homes where healthy food was rarely prepared. It isn't surprising that as adults, they continue the same unhealthy habits.

7   Here's a simple guideline. There are five types of food that should be avoided. And nearly all these foods can be replaced by something that is healthy and tasty.

8   **Processed and fatty meats** may be some of the very worst foods you can put in your body. What is a processed meat? Any meat that is cured, smoked, or flavored has been processed. This includes bacon, sausage, ham, and most cold cuts. These meats are saturated° with fat and sodium. Worst of all, they are also packed with bad chemicals called nitrates and nitrites, which are used to make meats appear fresh (they're not). Even so, Americans eat roughly 5.7 *billion* pounds of bacon a year!

9   **White flour and added sugar** are in many of the foods that most of us consider to be "splurges." Cakes, pies, cookies, ice cream, and candy are full of sugar and white flour. White flour has been bleached and stripped

of any vitamins. It consists mainly of empty calories and zero nutrition. Instead of eating products that use white flour, look for whole grain and whole-wheat products instead.

10   Some people find it impossible to get through the day without *something* sweet, and that's all right. A few squares of dark chocolate and a handful of sweet berries are actually good for you. Half a carton of fudge and marshmallow ice cream is not. Think about your choices.

11   **All fried foods** are packed with bad fats and calories. As a basic rule, just say no to anything fried. When a food is fried in oil, calories triple and fat skyrockets°. Consider this: A large baked potato (7 oz.) has 220 calories and no fat. When that potato is cut up and turned into French fries, it contains 697 calories and 34 grams of fat! The same thing happens to fried meats. And frying vegetables changes something healthy into something unhealthy.

12   Avoiding fried foods is simple enough. Nearly any food that can be fried can also be baked, roasted, broiled, steamed, or grilled. The flavor of food prepared in any of these ways is fresher. And you are guaranteed to feel better after eating non-fried foods. By contrast, greasy foods can lead to digestion problems, including heartburn, nausea, and diarrhea.

13   **Sugar-sweetened drinks** cause more weight gain than any other food.

Even sports drinks and fruit-flavored iced teas contain huge amounts of sugar. A 20-ounce bottle of lemonade can contain as much sugar as two and a half Hershey's chocolate bars. And the average American consumes 45 gallons (that's 375 pounds!) of sweetened drinks a year.

14   The best choices are water or unsweetened drinks. If you just can't stand to drink non-sweet beverages, try soda water mixed with real fruit juice. This makes a tasty fruit soda that contains natural ingredients and very few calories.

15   Finally, **all artificial and processed foods** are bad for you. Artificial sugars used in diet drinks and artificial fats used in non-fat chips and dairy products are full of unhealthy chemicals. These chemicals distort° your body's natural response to sugars and fats. Remember that real sugar and real fats are not bad for you as long as you don't overdo them.

You are always better off choosing real ingredients in foods.

16   Processed foods are foods that are treated to preserve them, flavor them, or change their texture. Most canned, frozen, and boxed foods are processed. Here's a simple way to know if you're eating processed food. Take a look at the ingredients listed on the foods you buy. If you see five or more ingredients you have never heard of or can't pronounce, the item you're holding is a processed food.

17   Avoiding processed food is simple enough: buy *real food*—food with only one ingredient, the food itself! Buy as many *real* fruits, vegetables, meats, grains, and so on as possible. Prepare your own food instead of buying frozen dinners. Take a little more time. Every minute you put into creating a healthy meal may be a minute you're adding to your life and your family members' lives.

18   The hard truth is that for many of us, changing our diets will not be easy. Addictions to sugar, white flour, and fat are real. However, with focus and daily effort, you will discover how good healthy food can be. You will also begin to look and feel much better.

19   Remember that you are what you eat. You can choose what you will put into your body from this day on and what you will become. Choose to become a better you.

Questions about the Reading

For each question, write the letter of your answer in the space provided.

Vocabulary in Context

_____   1. In the sentences below, the word *disregard* (dĭs′rĭ-gärd′) means
A. believe.
B. ignore.
C. worry about.
D. display.

"We all know that consuming too much fat and sugar can make us miserable and even shorten our lives. And yet we disregard the warnings. We keep eating garbage." (Paragraph 1)

_____ 2. In the sentences below, the word *evidently* (ĕv′ĭ-dĕnt′lē) means
   A. strangely.
   B. confusingly.
   C. clearly.
   D. annoyingly.

   "Most healthy meals take fewer than 30 minutes to prepare. And consider that the average American spends six to seven hours or more a day in front of TV and computer screens. Evidently, lack of time is not the problem: laziness is." (Paragraph 5)

Central Point and Main Ideas

_____ 3. Which sentence best expresses the central point of the entire selection?
   A. Americans with bad diets use three excuses to justify eating poorly.
   B. Americans can choose what they eat, and better choices will keep us healthier.
   C. Grilling, roasting, or baking foods are healthy alternatives to frying foods.
   D. Some people eat sweets every day, and healthier treats can improve a bad diet.

_____ 4. Which sentence best expresses the main idea of paragraph 5?
   A. Most of us have plenty of time to prepare healthy meals.
   B. People are often lazy.
   C. There are 10,080 minutes in a week.
   D. Most Americans spend six to seven hours a day online and watching TV.

_____ 5. Which sentence best expresses the main idea of paragraph 15?
   A. Human bodies have a natural response to real fat and real sugar.
   B. Diet drinks and non-fat foods are made of harmful chemicals.
   C. Artificial and processed foods should not be included in a healthy diet.
   D. Sugar and fat in moderation are not bad for an otherwise healthy diet.

Supporting Details

_____ 6. According to the selection, more than one in three Americans suffer from
A. cancer.
B. heart disease.
C. diabetes.
D. obesity.

_____ 7. One way to improve an unhealthy diet is to
A. switch from butter to margarine.
B. eat real foods.
C. eat more red meat.
D. switch from berries to dark chocolate.

Signal Words

_____ 8. In the sentence below, the words _Instead of_ signal
A. addition.
B. an example.
C. contrast.
D. cause and effect.

"Instead of eating products that use white flour, look for whole grain and whole-wheat products instead." (Paragraph 9)

Inferences

_____ 9. We can infer from the selection that the author
A. is a doctor.
B. has already changed his diet to include healthy meals.
C. suffers from diabetes as a result of his unhealthy eating habits.
D. prefers to eat marshmallows and fudge instead of fruits and vegetables.

Argument

_____10. Write the letter of the statement that is the point of the following argument. The other statements are support for that point.
- A. There are certain foods that we should avoid in order to maintain a healthy diet.
- B. Processed and fatty meats may be some of the worst foods you can put in your body.
- C. White flour and added sugar contain no nutrition and are full of empty calories.
- D. Sugar-sweetened drinks create more weight gain than any other food.

Discussion Questions

1. Did anything you read in this selection surprise you? Explain.

2. Now that you've read "The Shocking State of the American Diet," do you plan to make any changes in your eating habits? If so, what changes might you make?

3. According to the selection, not only are artificial and processed foods "bad for us"; they can lead to disease and even death. Do you think that there should be laws against selling such dangerous foods? Why or why not?

Note: Writing assignments for this selection appear on page 512.

Check Your Performance   THE BASICS OF ARGUMENT

Activity	Number Right	Points	Score
Review Test 1 (4 items)	_____	× 5 =	_____
Review Test 2 (10 items)	_____	× 4 =	_____
Review Test 3 (10 items)	_____	× 4 =	_____
		TOTAL SCORE =	_____%

Enter your total score into the **Reading Performance Chart: Review Tests** on the inside back cover.

THE BASICS OF ARGUMENT: Mastery Test 1

In each of the following groups, one statement is the point, and the other statements are support for the point. Identify each point with a **P** and each statement of support with an **S**.

Group 1

_____ A. That neighborhood is a bad place to live.

_____ B. The schools do not have a good reputation.

_____ C. There is a lot of crime in the neighborhood.

_____ D. Gang members wearing different colors can be seen on the streets.

Group 2

_____ A. A number of problems are associated with credit cards.

_____ B. Having a credit card tempts people to spend far more than they should.

_____ C. Many credit cards charge a hefty annual fee and also charge penalties for late payments.

_____ D. More people fall victim to credit card fraud every year.

Group 3

_____ A. The Egyptians had no machinery or iron tools to cut the stones.

_____ B. Some of the stones used in the pyramids weighed several tons.

_____ C. 400,000 men worked each year for twenty years to build the Great Pyramid.

_____ D. The construction of the Egyptian pyramids was extraordinary.

Group 4

_____ A. Students can type and print out reports on a computer.

_____ B. The Internet provides an endless supply of information for research papers.

_____ C. Computers have made it easier for students to do their work.

_____ D. A computer can be used to take a class at home, rather than having to travel to campus.

(Continues on next page)

Group 5

_____ A. During the Civil War, soldiers faced many hardships.

_____ B. More soldiers died of disease during the Civil War than were killed in battle.

_____ C. In army hospitals, surgeons cut off injured limbs without the aid of painkillers.

_____ D. Soldiers had to wear woolen uniforms even in the heat of summer.

THE BASICS OF ARGUMENT: Mastery Test 2

A. (1–8.) In each of the following groups, one statement is the point, and the other statements are support for the point. Identify each point with a **P** and each statement of support with an **S**.

Group 1

_____ A. Shrimp is often served with the head still attached.

_____ B. For many people, raw fish is too scary-looking to eat.

_____ C. Raw octopus tentacles look like they're waving.

_____ D. Fish eggs are like spoonfuls of tiny eyeballs.

Group 2

_____ A. Drivers who fall asleep at the wheel are responsible for two out of every ten accidents.

_____ B. Too little sleep can contribute to dangerously high blood pressure.

_____ C. Getting too little sleep can have dangerous results.

_____ D. On-the-job accidents resulting from lack of sleep cost American industry $50 billion a year.

B. (9.) Below is a point followed by three items of information. Put a check (✓) next to the **one** item that logically supports the point.

Point: **Pursuing a dream is important.**

_____ A. Most people learn a lot about themselves when they go after what they really want. Even if their dreams don't come true, the experience will give them confidence and a better idea of what they want to do in life. People often regret not pursuing a dream.

_____ B. Dreams are usually unrealistic. It is hard for some people to face the fact that their dream of becoming a famous inventor, writer, or musician will never come true. It is better to be realistic than disappointed.

_____ C. As people get older, they are often unwilling to take the chances they might have taken when they were younger. Dreams of fame, fortune, and success begin to fade. Often, dreams are let go in favor of security and comfort.

(Continues on next page)

C. (10.) For the group below, read the three items of supporting evidence. Then put a check (✓) next to the point that is most logically supported by that evidence.

Support:

- Experiments have shown that convicts who are allowed to have pets become less violent.
- The attitude of patients in nursing homes improves when they have the opportunity to interact with cats and dogs.
- Children with mental and/or physical handicaps have benefited from learning to ride horses.

Point: Which of the following conclusions is best supported by all the evidence above?

_____ A. Everyone should own a pet.

_____ B. In general, cats require less care than dogs.

_____ C. Caring for a pet teaches responsibility.

_____ D. Animals have been shown to promote mental and physical health.

THE BASICS OF ARGUMENT: Mastery Test 3

A. Each point is followed by three statements that provide logical support and two that do not. In the spaces, write the letters of the **three** logical statements of support.

1–3. **Point:** I don't think we should take my car on a long trip.

    A. It stalls out in rainy weather.
    B. It has air conditioning and power windows.
    C. I recently had the muffler replaced.
    D. Whenever I shift gears, I hear a strange grinding sound.
    E. The odometer reads 174,286 miles.

Items that logically support the point: _____ _____ _____

4–6. **Point:** There are several reasons why women stay in abusive relationships.

    A. In some places, abused women can go to shelters when leaving an abusive relationship.
    B. Women are often economically dependent on their abusive partners.
    C. Abusive people must learn healthier ways of dealing with anger and frustration.
    D. Women fear that if they leave, their abusers will track them down and injure or even kill them.
    E. Some women with violent partners blame themselves for the abuse, instead of blaming their partners.

Items that logically support the point: _____ _____ _____

7–9. **Point:** There are several ways to tell an alligator from a crocodile.

    A. Alligators and crocodiles have stones and pebbles in their stomachs which help them grind up food.
    B. Both alligators and crocodiles lay eggs.
    C. In general, alligators have shorter snouts than crocodiles.
    D. When an alligator's jaws are closed, only the upper teeth can be seen.
    E. You can see a large bottom tooth on each side when a crocodile's jaws are closed.

Items that logically support the point: _____ _____ _____

B. (10.) Below is a point followed by three items of information. Put a check (✓) next to the **one** item that logically supports the point.

Point: My grandmother is lonely.

_____ A. She has cooked the entire Thanksgiving dinner for fifteen people for more than twenty years. She never complains about it, and, in fact, she seems to enjoy doing it.

_____ B. Most of her friends have retired and moved away. She has a hard time getting out and meeting new people because of her poor eyesight. Usually, she just sits at home and listens to the radio.

_____ C. Even when it's raining, she spends an hour in her garden every day. She has memorized the names of at least 200 plants and flowers. She even talks to her flowers to help them grow.

THE BASICS OF ARGUMENT: Mastery Test 4

A. (1–8.) In each of the following groups, one statement is the point, and the other statements are support for the point. Identify each point with a **P** and each statement of support with an **S**.

Group 1

_____ A. A common dream involves taking a test you haven't prepared for.

_____ B. Many people dream about being in public only half dressed.

_____ C. Many people dream of falling from a great height and trying to wake up before they hit the ground.

_____ D. Certain themes appear in many people's dreams.

Group 2

_____ A. Drunk drivers are thrown violently from vehicles because they often do not wear seat belts.

_____ B. Drunk drivers do not realize how fast they are going and get into accidents at high speeds.

_____ C. Intoxicated victims bleed more heavily because of alcohol in the bloodstream.

_____ D. Drunk driving accidents are the most deadly.

B. (9.) Below is a point followed by three items of information. Put a check (✓) next to the **one** item that logically supports the point.

Point: Nelson is unfriendly.

_____ A. His family moved a lot as he was growing up. He went to four different schools during high school. As soon as he made new friends, he often had to leave them behind.

_____ B. He shows no interest in relationships. Even though he gets invited to parties and other get-togethers, he rarely shows up. He never smiles or makes an effort to start a conversation with anyone.

_____ C. He volunteers at the local pet shelter and cares for abandoned cats and dogs. He has adopted several of the animals he's cared for. Some of his best friends are stray animals.

(Continues on next page)

C. (10.) For the group below, read the three items of supporting evidence. Then put a check (✓) next to the point that is most logically supported by that evidence.

> **Support:**
>
> ● Tickets to a movie theater cost more than renting a movie.
>
> ● Long lines and too few parking spaces can be problems at a theater.
>
> ● Rude people at a movie cough, laugh, or talk loudly.
>
> **Point:** Which of the following conclusions is best supported by all the evidence above?
>
> _____ A. Wide-screen televisions are becoming more popular.
>
> _____ B. Many theaters give a choice of 10 or more movies to see.
>
> _____ C. Watching a movie at home is better than going to the theater.
>
> _____ D. Watching a movie at home is one of life's great pleasures.

THE BASICS OF ARGUMENT: Mastery Test 5

A. Each point is followed by three statements that provide logical support and two that do not. In the spaces, write the letters of the three logical statements of support.

1–3. **Point:** The use of grades in school should be abolished.

    A. Students would learn for the sake of learning—not for the sake of grades.

    B. Teachers would have more time to spend on lesson planning.

    C. Some students may not be motivated without grades.

    D. The use of grades dates back to the 1500s.

    E. Grades don't always accurately measure a student's knowledge.

Items that logically support the point: _____ _____ _____

4–6. **Point:** Elephants are very intelligent animals.

    A. For years, hunters shot elephants to obtain the ivory from their tusks.

    B. Like chimps, elephants can recognize their reflections in mirrors.

    C. Elephants tear off branches of trees to use as fly swatters.

    D. Elephants have been seen keeping vigil over their dead companions.

    E. An elephant can live as long as sixty-five years.

Items that logically support the point: _____ _____ _____

7–9. **Point:** The great baseball player Roberto Clemente was a kind man.

    A. Roberto Clemente led the National League in batting average four times.

    B. Roberto Clemente often visited hospitalized children while traveling with his team, the Pittsburgh Pirates.

    C. In the off-season, Clemente spent much of his time involved in charity work.

    D. In 1972, Roberto Clemente was voted into the Major League Baseball Hall of Fame.

    E. Roberto Clemente died in a plane crash while taking relief supplies to earthquake victims in Nicaragua.

Items that logically support the point: _____ _____ _____

(Continues on next page)

B. (10.) For the group below, read the three items of supporting evidence. Then put a check (✓) next to the point that is most logically supported by that evidence.

Support:

● Medical advances such as vaccines and organ transplants have saved the lives of countless people.

● Pollution caused by cars and factories harms us and our environment.

● Sophisticated guns and bombs have killed millions of people in the 20th century alone.

Point: Which of the following conclusions is best supported by all the evidence above?

_____ A. Pollution is the biggest threat to human health today.

_____ B. Wars should be outlawed.

_____ C. Breakthroughs in science and technology have both helped us and harmed us.

_____ D. The future promises to bring new medical breakthroughs.

THE BASICS OF ARGUMENT: Mastery Test 6

A. (1–4.) In the following group, one statement is the point, and the other statements are support for the point. Identify the point with a **P** and each statement of support with an **S**.

_____ A. It is rude and distracting to use a cell phone while attending a concert or seeing a movie.

_____ B. Driving a car while using a cell phone is dangerous.

_____ C. There are times when cell phones should not be used.

_____ D. A student who uses a cell phone in class is not learning anything and is distracting others.

B. (5–7.) The point below is followed by three statements that provide logical support and two that do not. In the spaces, write the letters of the **three** logical statements of support.

Point: I am not the world's greatest housekeeper.

A. Piles of junk mail cover my desk and coffee table.

B. I would like to have my kitchen remodeled.

C. The inside of my refrigerator looks like an out-of-control biology experiment.

D. My house was built in 1951.

E. I only wash dishes when I run out of clean ones.

Items that logically support the point: _____   _____   _____

C. (8–10.) For each of the following groups, read the three items of supporting evidence. Then put a check (✓) next to the point that is most logically supported by that evidence.

Group 1

Support:
● Bats eat thousands of insects in an hour.

● Bats spread pollen to flowers and plants, which can then reproduce.

● Bats produce valuable fertilizer.

(Continues on next page)

Point: Which of the following conclusions is best supported by all the evidence on the previous page?

_____ A. Many people are frightened by bats.

_____ B. Some bats feed on animal or human blood.

_____ C. Researchers still have a lot to learn about bats.

_____ D. Bats are helpful to both plants and humans.

Group 2

Support:

● People who need new organs can get organ transplants.

● The polio vaccine has made getting polio almost unheard of.

● There are more effective ways to fight cancer.

Point: Which of the following conclusions is best supported by all the evidence above?

_____ A. The cost of medical care has skyrocketed.

_____ B. Young children are required to get certain vaccines.

_____ C. Unfortunately, not everyone can afford adequate medical care.

_____ D. Medical knowledge has greatly increased in the past century.

Group 3

Support:

● In the 1960s and 1970s, when murder rates were lower than today, the death penalty was hardly ever used.

● Today, the states that use the death penalty most also have the highest murder rates.

● Each death sentence costs taxpayers hundreds of thousands of dollars in appeals and lawyer's fees.

Point: Which of the following conclusions is best supported by all the evidence above?

_____ A. More criminals should receive the death sentence.

_____ B. Executions cost more than they are worth.

_____ C. Some states need to find ways to lower their murder rates.

_____ D. The death penalty costs too much and doesn't work.

Part Two

Ten Reading Selections

1 Learning to Read: The Marvel Kretzmann Story

Mary Sherry

Preview

Here is a true story about a person with a learning disability—she was unable to read for almost 20 years. Being good at math, she was passed on from one grade to the next. Although she was able to get a good job after high school, her problems with reading made life difficult. Eventually, she decided it was better to face her disability and conquer it. This is Marvel Kretzmann's success story.

Words to Watch

poised (18): calm and confident
self-esteem (19): confidence
brush-up (21): review
IQ (22): abbreviation for "intelligence quotient," one measure of intelligence
memos (26): short written reminders
thesaurus (26): a book of synonyms
illiterate (30): unable to read or write
floored (31): shocked
exudes (35): displays strongly

1   Imagine a world where you can't read the street signs. You have to find your way by using only landmarks. When you see a sign or road map, you can't understand it, even though it is written in your own language. And when people give you oral directions, you cannot write quickly enough to take useful notes.

2   In this world, getting around isn't your only challenge. You must struggle to read directions on packages of cake mixes and cleaning products. Figuring out the doses of over-the-counter medicines actually gives you a headache. You keep faulty products rather than return them to the store because you cannot fill out a refund slip. The only jobs you dare apply for are those that do not require any reading or writing.

3   This was Marvel Kretzmann's world for almost twenty years. It was a very small world because she feared

getting lost if she went beyond her place of work, familiar stores, and well-known routes to friends' and family's homes. She lived in daily fear that she would be asked to fill out a form or write something down for someone. Her world was a terrifying place.

4   Marvel's greatest fear of all was being found out. What if people knew that she could barely read and couldn't write at all?

5   Marvel was in the fifth grade when it became clear to her that she was far behind her classmates in reading and writing, and that she would never be able to catch up.

6   "I remember hearing giggles in the classroom as soon as I was called on to read out loud. The kids knew what was going to happen, and so did I. Any word with an "s" sound in it was sure to make me stumble. As I hesitated, my teacher would say the words for me, over and over, urging me to repeat after her. But all I could hear was the laughing in the background.

7   "Finally, the teacher would give up and say, 'We'll move on.' Even though I felt relief, I also felt embarrassed. I was pulled out of class for extra work, but by that time—as I realize now—it was too late. I was already labeled by classmates and teachers as 'slow.'

8   "But I was pretty good in math. This helped me get passed from grade to grade. It also helped me to hide how serious my problem was from my parents. I didn't want to bring the problem to their attention. As a ten-year-old, I was more interested in having fun than working hard on reading and writing."

9   Marvel had two close friends who accepted her for what she was, and is today: kind, generous, and a lot of fun. They would take notes for her and coach her through courses, and they helped cover her disability.

10   But those friends couldn't be with her all the time. Marvel recalls how in the large junior and senior high schools she attended, classmates soon caught on to her problem when the teacher asked students to take turns reading out loud. "Come on! Hurry up! She can't read!" she heard kids saying under their breath. Soon, rather than calling on students in order, up and down rows, teachers would skip around the class. That way, they wouldn't have to call on Marvel.

11   "In high school I learned to avoid classes that had writing assignments

and heavy reading. I took the easiest courses I could. I kept quiet and tried not to be noticed. I never volunteered in class. I earned the reputation of being a 'good' child. So many classes had multiple-choice tests that I usually could guess and get by. In fact, I remember one time when I was the only one in my class to get an A on an exam. I just did what I always did with those tests I couldn't understand. I went down the pages and marked this one or that one, guessing all the way!"

12   Marvel's ability to manage her life got better and better. She received her high-school diploma and enrolled in a technical school where she was trained as a dental assistant. A tutor helped her get through her classes. After finishing the program, she found a job. She liked being a dental assistant and discovered she was good at it. In this job, she was safe! She didn't have to write or read instructions to do her work.

13   Life outside of the dental office was another matter. Things she bought, such as appliances and other household items, came with instruction manuals. Expert at sewing, Marvel bought a fairly complicated sewing machine. "I thought I was going to lose my mind threading it and adjusting the tension. There were instructions in the manual, but they might as well have been in a foreign language.

14   "When I bought a computer, I practically burned out the phone lines dialing everyone I thought might be able to help me. I called the computer salesperson, friends, my sister, and 1-800-SOS-APPL day and night. I simply couldn't read the manual well enough to understand the computer's most basic uses. I would call and nervously ask, 'Why is this thing beeping at me? What did I do?' I needed to be walked though each disaster so I could keep on going."

15   The opportunities—and pitfalls—of the adult world seemed endless, requiring new and more complicated adjustments. Marvel wanted a checking account. Getting one was easy, because the bank officer simply asked her questions and filled out the forms. Marvel discovered, though, that writing out checks was stressful, especially when she had to do it in public. She developed a system of filling in store names on the checks at home or in the car before shopping— just so she wouldn't have to struggle in front of a clerk. Since spelling out "eleven" and "twelve" was always troubling, Marvel simply avoided writing checks for those amounts. As she shopped, she ran totals of her purchases in her head. Then she bought additional items or put some back on the shelves, just so the bill would be at least thirteen dollars or less than eleven.

16   Marvel's husband knew she had difficulty reading and writing, but he had no idea just how much difficulty.

He knew she had never been an "A" student, but he realized that she could manage things. For example, she addressed their wedding invitations from carefully printed lists. She wrote a form letter for her thank-you notes. Whenever a gift arrived, she copied that letter, simply filling in the blank for whatever the gift was. She had a "system," and it worked.

17   But sometimes she got caught. Once, Marvel won a radio contest sponsored by an insurance company. The prize was a free luncheon for all the people in her office at a restaurant of Marvel's choice. She stopped by a popular spot to check it out, thinking it would be a nice place to treat her fellow workers. A restaurant employee asked her to write down the name and address of the business so she could send a menu to Marvel's office. Marvel couldn't remember how to spell "Chicago"—the name of the street where her office is located. "I just blocked," she said. "I see 'Chicago' written out many times every day, but at that moment I froze. I turned and walked out—feeling defeated by such a simple thing as spelling 'Chicago.' I arranged to have the luncheon somewhere else."

18   Marvel Kretzmann tells about her struggle almost as though she were talking about someone else. She is upbeat, self-confident, poised°, open, and very friendly. Now in her late thirties, she realizes that difficulty reading and writing is a fairly widespread problem. "There are a lot of us out there," she says. "There are people who are afraid to travel because they can't read signs. Some won't apply for work because they can't fill out a job application. Others pretend they have left their glasses at home so they can take a form to someone who will read it to them. What is sad, though, is that many people assume people like us are lazy because we won't write things down in front of them. Sometimes, when they see us struggle, they think we simply don't concentrate, or worse, that we are worthless. Once, when I applied for a job, the person who interviewed me corrected my job application in front of me! Imagine how I felt! I told myself I couldn't work for that man, even if he offered me a job."

19   This remarkable openness and confidence did not come about by accident, nor did they come easily. After all, Marvel had spent years and years ashamed of her difficulty. How did she build her self-esteem° to such a high level? "I suddenly came face to face with the reality that life wasn't going to get any easier! In fact, it was getting harder." Marvel and her husband had bought a house, and she couldn't understand the legal papers involved. Furthermore, Marvel could see changes coming to the dental profession. One day her job would require taking notes and filling out forms. The thought also occurred to her that since she had no children,

there might not be anyone around to take care of her when she was old or to cover for her when she needed help with reading or writing.

20   So Marvel decided to go back to school.

21   She found a community adult-education program that offered brush-up° classes in academic subjects. There she found just what she needed and received small-group and individual instruction. The work was intense. Teachers trained to deal with special learning needs drilled Marvel in phonics, spelling, and reading. Marvel came to school right after work and usually got there before the teachers did. The staff members who arrived first always found Marvel deep in study in the hallway. Finally, they gave her a key to the classroom!

22   According to her teacher, Marvel's difficulties are typical of learning-disabled students. Such a person has a normal or an above-normal IQ°, but for some reason is unable to process math or reading and spelling. Unfortunately, the problem often isn't identified until the student is well beyond the grade levels where it could and should be more easily addressed. The problem is made worse by youthful reactions, such as bad behavior—or, in Marvel's case, extremely good behavior—and covering up.

23   Marvel is unhappy that she slipped through the system. "As an adult, I can see there were great gaps in communications between my teachers and my parents—and between me and my teachers, and me and my parents on this issue! I fell through all the cracks. My teachers failed to impress on my parents very early on that I was having trouble. I didn't want my parents to think I wasn't doing well. And I didn't have the guts to approach the teachers and say, 'Hey!' There were times I felt no teacher cared, as long as I didn't disrupt the class."

24   Marvel doesn't think much about the past, though. She is mastering her computer—by reading the instructions. She plans to attend school for another year or so to keep working on spelling and writing, "to keep it fresh." Since she went back to school five years ago, her reading has risen from the fourth-grade level to a level beyond high school.

25   Writing is still a chore, and reading is work, too. "I'm never going to write a book," Marvel says. "I can't even read a three-hundred-page novel in a week—it might take me a month or two. But that doesn't bother me. I know I have made real progress when I can set small goals and achieve them. I was so proud one time when my husband asked me to read a manual to him while he worked on my car. He looked up from under the hood and told me I was doing a great job and that school was really helping me!

26   "Thankfully, I can write letters now and make lists for shopping and for packing for vacations. I can take

notes and write memos° to others and know they will be understood. I have learned to use a lot of tools, including a dictionary, a thesaurus° (which I never knew existed), and a computer. I have also learned I need lots of quiet time to do these things well.

27   "I am able to read newspapers, magazine articles, and instruction manuals, even out loud if the situation calls for it. I feel more confident reading stories to my nieces and nephews and my friends' children. These are tremendous rewards—all the rewards I really need to make me feel good about going back to school.

28   "It hasn't been easy, despite all the wonderful help I've had. I will never forget my first night in a writing class after going to school for reading and phonics for a couple of years. The writing teacher gave the students fifteen minutes to write a short description about their favorite place. I could think of lots of places I would love to tell people about, but I couldn't write anything more than my name at the top of the paper! After the class, my teacher and I agreed I wasn't ready for this yet. I didn't feel defeated, though. I returned to the phonics and reading group. A few months later, I went back. By then I was able to handle the writing class. This class was another turning point for me. My teacher helped me break the silence. At last I was able to speak freely about the secret I had been hiding all these years. Now I feel good about writing something down and then reading it out loud."

29   Marvel believes it is important for her to encourage others who share her disability. "In the School for Adults, my teachers have asked me to reach out to people who they know have the same problem. I can spot them, too. They don't talk to anyone, they keep their heads buried in books they are struggling to read, and they never mix with the other students. Sometimes when I approach people who need a lot of help, they turn away because they don't want to admit how bad their problem is. I know how they feel. I also know that it is by taking many small steps that they will make progress. There are no miracles here, just a lot of hard work!

30   "Occasionally I am asked to speak to small groups about the School for Adults and how it helped me to meet this challenge. Sometimes I feel uncomfortable and feel I'm saying, in effect, 'Hi, I'm Marvel, and I am illiterate°!' However, I believe it is important to do what I can to get the word out to others who may benefit from the program.

31   "When school was ending last spring, several people in our study work group asked me if I would organize a little class for them during the summer. I was floored°! They were actually looking up to me! But I felt that if they thought I could help them, I knew they could push me, too, so why not? We met nearly every week

and practiced reading out loud, and we worked on pronunciation and word definitions."

32   How far has Marvel come? Not long ago she was invited to serve on the Advisory Council for the School for Adults. She sits as an equal with the school's director, teacher representatives, business owners, and others from the community.

33   At one meeting, the secretary was absent, and the chairman asked if someone would take notes for her. Without a moment's thought, Marvel said, "I will."

34   And she did!

An Update

35   Today, Marvel exudes° confidence. Although she is not reading thousand-page novels for entertainment these days or writing long reports, she has the confidence that comes from achieving a goal. She believes returning to school as an adult has made a real difference in her life.

36   Marvel continues to work as a dental assistant in the same practice. However, the practice has changed a great deal. The dentist who hired her decided to retire. New dentists with different procedures came into the practice. The office moved to a new location. The practice became paperless, yet, as Marvel exclaims, "There is more paperwork!"

37   However, Marvel still doesn't back down from the challenges that come with her job or her disability.

Computers are both her bane and her blessing. "You have to type into a computer, which means you have to spell," she says with a broad grin. She adds that her co-workers are helpful, and she lives out her conviction that you have to force yourself to do new things and continue to challenge yourself. Nonetheless, she won't give up her trusty "cheater books"— primarily her paperback dictionary.

38   In addition, Marvel believes her disability gives her a special advantage at work. She has discovered she has sensitivity to patients who may not be able to express their concerns adequately to the dentist. By gently asking questions, Marvel finds she helps dentist-patient communication. In an environment often clouded by anxiety and stress, Marvel brings calm. She takes great pride in her work, especially when she can use this special gift.

39   Outside of her professional life, Marvel has had to adapt to much change. She became involved with local land-use development proposals in her community and attended City Hall meetings, where she shared her ideas and was the spokesperson for her neighbors. This way of contributing to her community sparked a new interest that Marvel enjoys very much. Unfortunately she had to put these activities on hold. Her mother was diagnosed with Alzheimer's, and for 12 years before she died, Marvel was her caregiver.

An outgrowth of that experience was that she was asked to help start an Alzheimer's support group. Marvel served on her county's Grand Jury—another new experience. She says these have been opportunities to learn and opportunities to share her new knowledge. She is very practical and humble in recognizing her strengths.

40   Skilled at sewing, knitting, crocheting, crafts, and baking, Marvel is always working to improve these talents, too. She even turns to a computer for fun. "Surfing the Internet when you aren't a good speller can turn out to be, well . . . interesting," she says with a hearty laugh. "But I do it to learn stuff. I'm even on Facebook!"

To deal with her disability, Marvel 41 continues to use the strategies she learned when she returned to school as an adult. She has also found some new ones. She likes word hunt game books and electronic word games because they help improve her spelling. The computer makes her stretch her reading. On the rare occasions when she has to refuse a challenge, she can now say, "I'm not able to do that." She explains, "People are more accepting of this kind of disability now." As she says this, she becomes very quiet and thoughtful, and then smiles. "I don't have to pretend anymore."

Marvel at her sewing machine

Vocabulary Questions

A. Use context clues to help you decide on the best definition for each italicized word. Then, in the space provided, write the letter of your choice.

_____ 1. In the sentences below, the word *landmarks* (lănd′märks′) means
   A. street signs.
   B. familiar features of the surroundings.
   C. maps.
   D. written directions.

   "Imagine a world where you can't read the street signs. You have to find your way by using only landmarks." (Paragraph 1)

_____ 2. In the sentences below, the word *widespread* (wīd′sprĕd′) means
   A. unimportant.
   B. unusual.
   C. common.
   D. interesting.

   "... she realizes that difficulty reading and writing is a fairly widespread problem. 'There are a lot of us out there,' she says." (Paragraph 18)

_____ 3. In the sentences below, the word *intense* (ĭn-tĕns′) means
   A. rather easy.
   B. expensive.
   C. involving extreme effort.
   D. boring.

   "The work was intense. Teachers ... drilled Marvel in phonics, spelling and reading. Marvel came to school right after work..." (Paragraph 21)

_____ 4. In the sentence below, the word *disrupt* (dĭs-rŭpt′) means
   A. interfere with.
   B. attend.
   C. understand.
   D. skip.

   "There were times I felt no teacher cared, as long as I didn't disrupt the class." (Paragraph 23)

_____ 5. In the sentence below, the word *chore* (chôr) means
   A. fun activity.
   B. difficult task.
   C. mystery.
   D. surprise.

   "Writing is still a chore, and reading is work, too." (Paragraph 25)

B. Below are words, or forms of words, from "Words to Watch." Write in the one that best completes each sentence. Then write the letter of that word in the space provided.

A. brush-up	B. illiterate	C. memo
D. poised	E. self-esteem	

_____ 6. Although Marie was shy and giggly during her teens, she soon grew into a _____ and impressive young woman.

_____ 7. Before playing in the soccer game, Devon thought it wise to attend a _____ session on the rules.

_____ 8. The boss sent a _____ to all employees warning them that layoffs might soon occur.

_____ 9. Being able to figure out a complicated set of written directions is enough to boost anyone's _____.

_____ 10. If you are _____, it can be very difficult to get by in today's print-centered world.

Reading Comprehension Questions

Central Point and Main Ideas

_____ 1. Which sentence best expresses the central point of the selection?
A. Learning disabilities of all types can be overcome with hard work.
B. Marvel felt much shame and fear throughout her public-school education.
C. Through hard work, Marvel gradually overcame her learning disability and the shame and fear it caused her.
D. Students with learning disabilities should not have to attend the public schools in this country.

_____ 2. Which sentence best expresses the main idea of paragraph 12?
A. The first sentence
B. The second sentence
C. The third sentence
D. The last sentence

Supporting Details

_____ 3. The author states that in high school, she avoided classes that
      A. her close, helpful friends had not enrolled in.
      B. started early in the day.
      C. were too easy.
      D. had writing assignments and heavy reading.

_____ 4. According to one of Marvel's teachers, a typical learning-disabled student
      A. is poor at sports.
      B. has few talents.
      C. has an IQ of normal or above.
      D. has an IQ of normal or below.

_____ 5. Marvel is unhappy that she
      A. slipped through the public-school system.
      B. has never made the dean's list.
      C. is not paid more for her job as a dental assistant.
      D. never married.

Signal Words

_____ 6. In the sentence below, the words *such as* show a relationship of
      A. addition.
      B. contrast.
      C. time.
      D. an example.

> "Things she bought, such as appliances and other household items, came with instruction manuals." (Paragraph 13)

_____ 7. In the sentences below, the word *but* shows a relationship of
      A. addition.
      B. time.
      C. contrast.
      D. an example.

> "She had a 'system,' and it worked. But sometimes she got caught." (Paragraphs 16–17)

Inferences

_____ 8. Marvel's experience in the fifth grade suggests that
   A. children may not show sympathy toward other children with learning disabilities.
   B. elementary school teachers are quick to identify and help students who have trouble reading.
   C. the other students wanted to help Marvel learn to read better, but didn't know how.
   D. Marvel was not the only student in her class who had difficulty reading.

_____ 9. Paragraph 28 suggests that
   A. Marvel was not a very good student.
   B. Marvel did not allow short-term setbacks to keep her from learning to read and write.
   C. Marvel blamed her teacher for pushing her into a class she wasn't ready for.
   D. Marvel believed that the assignment to write about a favorite place was a silly one.

Argument

_____ 10. In the following group, one statement is the point, and the other statements are support for the point. Write the letter of the statement that is the **point** of the argument.
   A. People who are illiterate cannot read street signs or road maps.
   B. An inability to read limits a person's job opportunities.
   C. An inability to read makes it difficult for a person to function in today's world.
   D. Banking is difficult if one cannot read well enough to write checks.

Mapping

Complete the map of this selection by filling in the letters of the missing major details, which are scrambled below. Arrange the details in the order in which they occurred in Marvel's life. (Two of the items have already been filled in for you.)

Major Supporting Details Missing from the Diagram

A. Marvel learned to read at a level beyond high school.

B. Marvel decided to go back to school.

C. Marvel was in the fifth grade when she realized that she was far behind her classmates.

D. Marvel was trained as a dental assistant and then got a job as one.

E. Marvel avoided high-school classes that involved writing assignments and heavy reading.

F. Marvel was asked to join the Advisory Council of the School for Adults.

G. Marvel had two friends who took notes for her and coached her through her courses.

Central point: Marvel Kretzmann worked hard and eventually gained self-confidence and learned to read and write.

Discussion Questions

1. Should Marvel Kretzmann have been "passed from grade to grade" because she was good at math? Or should she have been made to stay at a lower grade until her reading and writing skills got better? Explain.

2. Do you know someone who has a learning disability? If so, how does that person's experience compare with Kretzmann's?

3. Kretzmann says that sometimes when she is called upon to speak to small groups, she feels "uncomfortable." Why do you think this is? Would you feel uncomfortable speaking to a group? Why or why not?

Note: Writing assignments for this selection appear on page 513.

Check Your Performance   **LEARNING TO READ**

Activity	Number Right	Points	Total
Vocabulary			
Part A (5 items)	_____	× 10 =	_____
Part B (5 items)	_____	× 10 =	_____
		SCORE =	_____%
Reading Comprehension Questions			
Central Point and Main Ideas (2 items)	_____	× 8 =	_____
Supporting Details (3 items)	_____	× 8 =	_____
Signal Words (2 items)	_____	× 8 =	_____
Inferences (2 items)	_____	× 8 =	_____
Argument (1 item)	_____	× 8 =	_____
Mapping (5 items)	_____	× 4 =	_____
		SCORE =	_____%

TOTAL SCORES: Vocabulary _____%   Comprehension _____%

Enter your total scores into the **Reading Performance Chart: Ten Reading Selections** on the inside back cover.

2 The Blind Vet
Gail Hoffman

Preview

When Nick returned home from the war in Afghanistan blinded by a bomb, he knew his life would never be the same. In so many ways, Nick would have to start all over again, and he wasn't certain he could do it. When Nick's friends slowly stopped coming by to see him, Nick fell into a sadness that threatened to destroy all his hopes. He wanted to give up. But one very special person refused to give up on Nick.

Words to Watch

rivulet (4): small stream
IED (6): improvised explosive device, a homemade roadside bomb that caused significant casualties in Iraq and Afghanistan
apprehension (8): fear
dwindled (9): decreased, became less
disheartened (13): saddened
sufficiently (23): enough

1   When Nick boarded the bus, everyone looked at him. A few people shook their heads in pity. It didn't seem right that such a young man should have so much trouble climbing the three short steps up to the bus aisle.

2   "Why does that man have that white stick?" a small girl asked her mother loudly.

3   "Shh!" the mother said quickly. "It's not polite to talk about him, honey. He's blind."

4   But Nick had heard the little girl. In fact, he could feel everyone's eyes on him even though he couldn't see them. Using his cane, Nick carefully measured the height of each step. Gripping the handrail with white knuckles, he slowly made his way to the aisle. Then he used his hands to feel his way. Gratefully, Nick eased into the first set of seats reserved for the disabled. A thin rivulet° of sweat trickled down Nick's forehead, and his hands shook.

5   *Okay. Relax.* Nick tried to calm himself down. *You'll be all right. You'll make it.*

6   Nick, barely 22, had been blind for just over a year. During a tour of duty in Afghanistan, the vehicle Nick had been riding in had run over an IED°. Nick remembered a bright flash, a terrible explosion, and the screams

351

of his comrades. Then, the bright color of his own blood in his eyes was the last thing Nick ever saw. Fragments of metal and glass had scarred his face and destroyed his eyes.

7   When he came home from the war, Nick was frightened. What would his friends think of him? Two of Nick's favorite pastimes had been cycling and playing basketball, and that's how he had met a lot of his friends. Now he wouldn't be able to do either. Would his friends even want to be around him anymore?

8   But Nick's biggest apprehension° was that his girlfriend, Kristen, would leave him. The two of them had been together since high school, and Nick had secretly planned on proposing to Kristen when he returned from Afghanistan. But he never dreamed that he'd be returning like this. Now Kristen would have to take care of him—if she even wanted to stay with him. *And why would she want to stay with him*, Nick wondered. Kristen was funny and smart. Plus, she was beautiful, with long red hair and bright green eyes. *She won't want to waste her time with some blind guy who can't even see her*, Nick thought bitterly. *She'll never marry me now.*

9   At first, Nick's friends came around a lot. They sat and talked with him, trying to get him to laugh at old jokes. They brought him foods he liked and often hung around for hours listening to music or reading the newspaper

to Nick. They rarely mentioned basketball or the upcoming cycling races they were training for—they thought this would make Nick sad. In fact, they rarely even mentioned Nick's blindness because it made them uncomfortable. And, in time, most of Nick's friends' discomfort with his blindness outweighed their concern for him. They ran out of things to talk about. One by one, the visits from Nick's friends dwindled°, and soon they had all faded away.

10   Now Nick became angry and depressed. He felt betrayed and abandoned by his friends, and he declined into self-pity. Nick might have sunk all the way to rock bottom if it had not been for Kristen. During that very difficult first year, Kristen never wavered in her devotion to Nick. She helped him in any way she could, even when Nick's frustration made it hard for her to help him.

11   "I'm blind!" he'd sometimes shout angrily. "Why are you ruining your life by staying with me? I'm no good anymore. Why don't you go find someone who can *see* you—someone who doesn't have to be treated like a baby?"

12   More than anything, Nick hated his loss of independence. He'd always prided himself on the fact that he was never afraid to try new things and go to new places. Sometimes on long weekend bike rides, Nick would make himself get lost intentionally just to see what kind of adventure it might turn into. Now he couldn't even walk to the corner store without Kristen's help.

13   Kristen knew that Nick needed to feel some sense of independence, or he would only become angrier and more disheartened°. As it was, he often spent entire days doing little more than listening to the radio, sleeping, and drinking beer—something he'd rarely done before. So when Kristen came across an article about a local center for disabled veterans, she mentioned it to Nick.

14   "It's a way for you to meet other men and women like yourself," Kristen explained. "And there's all kinds of help there to get you trained and prepared for a new career."

15   "Career?" Nick asked doubtfully. "What could I do without my eyes?"

16   Kristen walked over and took Nick's hands in hers. "A lot, Nick," she said quietly. "Why don't you go and find out?"

17   Nick agreed to give it a try. There was only one catch. The center didn't open until 9:00, and since Kristen had to be at work at 8:30, she would not be able to drive Nick there every day.

18   "Nick, the city bus stops right in front of the center," Kristen said carefully. "Why don't you learn how to take the bus?"

19   "Take the bus?" Nick replied angrily. "How would I even know where I was going? What if I get lost? I feel like you're abandoning me—just like all my friends did."

20   Kristen thought Nick might respond like this, so she had already figured out a plan. "Look," she said, "I'll make some arrangements at work. I'll ride the bus with you for a week or so until you get the hang of it. What do you think of that?"

21   It took a little more convincing, but Nick finally decided to try. And, actually, he was excited about the idea of something new—something he could do on his own.

22   And so, for a week and a half, Nick and Kristen took the bus together across town. She helped him use his cane to feel for the curb, the bus steps, and the aisle to his seat. They counted the number of stops it took to get from their apartment to the center, and when they arrived, Kristen helped Nick find the sidewalk that led to the

center's front door. If Nick stumbled or became confused, Kristen was there to smooth things over and encourage her boyfriend along.

23   Finally, Nick felt sufficiently° confident to ride the bus alone. He'd been enjoying the time spent at the center, and he was looking forward to being independent again. But now as Nick sat on the bus alone for the first time, he wasn't so sure. He heard the little girl ask her mother again what was wrong with the man with the funny cane. Nick took a deep breath and tried to concentrate.

24   *Two, three, four* . . . Nick counted the stops. Very carefully, he got off at the seventh stop. Just like every day with Kristen, Nick used his cane to walk over the curb and to the sidewalk to the center. His heart was pounding. What if he was going the wrong way? What if he fell? No one was there to help him.

25   "Hey, Nick! Good to see you." Relief flooded Nick. It was one of the instructors at the center. He'd made it!

26   At the end of his first week of riding alone, Nick was hardly nervous at all. Every day had gone well. Only one time had he tripped on the curb, but almost instantly the hand of a stranger had gripped his shoulder to keep him from falling. Nick had said thank you, but the stranger just patted him on the back.

27   Now as Nick carefully made his way down the steps of the bus, the bus driver said, "You sure are one lucky young man."

28   At first, Nick wasn't sure if the bus driver was talking to him. Why would anyone think he was lucky? "Me?" Nick asked.

29   "Yes, you!" the driver said with a friendly laugh.

30   "Why do you say that?"

31   "Well, to have someone looking out for you like that," the driver explained. "Making sure you're okay."

32   "What are you talking about?" Nick asked.

33   "You know," the driver said, sounding a little puzzled by Nick's question. "That pretty woman with the red hair—the one who has been standing on the corner waiting and watching for you every day this week. The one who caught you when you almost fell."

34   Nick was too stunned to say anything at first. Then tears filled his eyes behind his dark glasses.

35   The driver chuckled again and said, "I wish my wife cared that much about me!"

36   Nick smiled through his tears. "She's not my wife," he said quietly. "But she's going to be."

Vocabulary Questions

A. Use context clues to help you decide on the best definition for each italicized word. Then, in the space provided, write the letter of your choice.

_____ 1. In the sentences below, the word *trickled* (trĭk'əld) means
   A. waited.
   B. held.
   C. pulled.
   D. dripped.

   "Gratefully, Nick eased into the first set of seats reserved for the disabled. A thin rivulet of sweat trickled down Nick's forehead, and his hands shook." (Paragraph 4)

_____ 2. In the sentences below, the word *pastimes* (păs'tīms) means
   A. bad habits.
   B. responsibilities.
   C. enjoyable activities.
   D. promotions.

   "Two of Nick's favorite pastimes had been cycling and playing basketball, and that's how he had met a lot of his friends. Now he wouldn't be able to do either." (Paragraph 7)

_____ 3. In the sentences below, the word *declined* (dĭ-klīnd) means
   A. fell.
   B. climbed.
   C. became angry.
   D. refused.

   "Nick . . . felt betrayed and abandoned by friends, and he declined into self-pity. Nick might have sunk all the way to rock bottom if it had not been for Kristen." (Paragraph 10)

_____ 4. In the sentences below, the word *wavered* (wā'vərd) means
   A. gestured.
   B. hesitated.
   C. started.
   D. damp.

   "During that very difficult first year, Kristen never wavered in her devotion to Nick. She helped him in any way she could . . . . " (Paragraph 10)

_____ 5. In the sentence below, the word *intentionally* (ĭn-tĕn′shə-nəl-ē) means
   A. on purpose.
   B. quickly.
   C. every day.
   D. easily.

   "Sometimes on long weekend rides, Nick would make himself get lost intentionally just to see what kind of adventure it might turn into." (Paragraph 12)

B. Below are words, or forms of words, from "Words to Watch." Write in the one that best completes each sentence. Then write the letter of that word in the space provided.

A. apprehensive	B. disheartened	C. dwindles
D. rivulet	E. sufficient	

_____ 6. Although it hasn't rained a lot this spring, the rainfall will be _____ for the new crops.

_____ 7. The little girl became _____ when she discovered that Santa Claus wasn't real.

_____ 8. The ants were drawn to the _____ of honey leaking out of the honey jar.

_____ 9. Even though Hannah had practiced her speech, she was still _____ as she walked to the stage.

_____ 10. The longer I put off looking for a new job, the more my savings account _____.

Reading Comprehension Questions

Central Point and Main Ideas

_____ 1. Which sentence best expresses the central point of the entire selection?
   A. Nick, a blind vet, returns home from the war to find his world turned upside down.
   B. Kristen's solid devotion to Nick helps Nick through a very difficult time, proving that love can overcome even the greatest obstacles.
   C. Nick ultimately decides to marry Kristen after he realizes what she's done for him and how much she really loves him.
   D. The journey of the disabled veteran is a difficult one, and it is not unusual for friends to disappear just when the vet needs them most.

_____ 2. Which sentence best expresses the main idea of paragraph 8?
   A. Nick and Kristen had been very close before he was blinded, but now she was beginning to pull away.
   B. Nick was worried that if he couldn't even see Kristen's beauty, she wouldn't want to be with him.
   C. Nick suddenly realized that Kristen would probably not want to marry him now.
   D. Because he was blind, Nick feared that Kristen would leave him.

_____ 3. Which sentence best expresses the main idea of paragraph 9?
   A. Nick's friends felt reluctant to talk about his blindness, because it made them uncomfortable.
   B. Because Nick could no longer play basketball or cycle, his friends had to think of other things to do with him when they visited.
   C. Nick's friends came around fairly often, but Nick could tell they were going to slowly disappear.
   D. At first, Nick's old friends came to visit him, but because his blindness bothered them, they began to fade away.

Supporting Details

_____ 4. How long had Nick been blind by the time he was able to ride the bus alone?
   A. Three months
   B. Half a year
   C. A little over a year
   D. Two years

_____ 5. To help walk over curbs and climb the steps on the bus, Nick
   A. asked Kristen to help him.
   B. used his cane to feel for them.
   C. counted his footsteps.
   D. asked the bus driver to help him.

Signal Words

_____ 6. The word *so* in the sentence below signals a relationship of
   A. addition.
   B. time.
   C. contrast.
   D. cause and effect.

   "Kristen thought Nick might respond like this, so she had already figured out a plan." (Paragraph 20)

Inferences

_____ 7. We can infer that the bus driver
   A. had known Nick before he started riding the bus.
   B. was unwilling to help Nick when he boarded the bus.
   C. thought that Nick knew Kristen had been the one who caught him when he fell.
   D. does not get along well with his wife.

_____ 8. The reading suggests that
   A. Nick's friends should not be blamed for feeling uncomfortable and leaving him alone.
   B. the loss of his friends finally sent Nick over the edge.
   C. Nick was more angry than sad about losing his friends.
   D. true friendships with others can survive in spite of hardships.

_____ 9. From this selection, we can conclude that Kristen
   A. had never doubted she would remain Nick's girlfriend.
   B. often grew impatient with Nick's self-pity and anger.
   C. would have broken up with Nick if he had refused to go to the veterans' center.
   D. was worried, at first, about Nick taking the bus to the center alone.

Argument

10. In the following group, one statement is the point, and the other statements are support for the point. Identify the point with a **P** and each statement of support with an **S**.

   _____ A. Kristen encouraged Nick to start going to the disabled veterans' center.

   _____ B. Kristen showed her devotion to Nick in several important ways.

   _____ C. Kristen took time off from work to ride the bus with Nick.

   _____ D. Kristen waited on the corner to make sure Nick got to the center on his own.

Outlining

Prepare an outline of the story told in "The Blind Vet" by filling in the missing details, which are scrambled in the list below.

- Kristen helps Nick by taking the bus to the center with him.
- The bus driver tells Nick he's lucky to have someone looking out for him.
- Kristen suggests that Nick get training at a local center for disabled vets.
- Nick's friends come to visit at first, but then begin disappearing.

Central point: With his girlfriend's support, Nick, a blinded veteran, learns to cope with his disability.

1. At barely 22, Nick returns from war blinded by an IED.
2. Nick worries that his girlfriend, Kristen, is going to leave him.
3. _____

   _____

4. Nick becomes angry and depressed, even lashing out at Kristen.
5. Kristen realizes Nick needs to feel some sort of independence.
6. _____

   _____

7. _____

   _____

8. Nervously, Nick finally rides the bus alone to the center.
9. _____

   _____

10. Nick realizes that Kristen has been watching out for him every day during his first week riding to the center on his own.

Discussion Questions

1. Why do children stare at and talk loudly about people who, like the blind vet, are different in some way? Aside from the standard "It's not polite to stare/point/talk," how would you explain to a child why he or she should not stare or point at someone who looks different or behaves differently?

2. How do you think you would feel and react if one of your closest friends suddenly became disabled in some way? Would you find it difficult to be with him or her? Why or why not?

3. Consider this bit of scripture from the Bible: "Three things will last forever—faith, hope, and love—and the greatest of these is love." What do these words mean to you? How might they apply to "The Blind Vet"?

Note: Writing assignments for this selection appear on page 514.

Check Your Performance   THE BLIND VET

Activity	Number Right	Points	Total
Vocabulary			
Part A (5 items)	_____	× 10 =	_____
Part B (5 items)	_____	× 10 =	_____
		SCORE =	_____%
Reading Comprehension Questions			
Central Point and Main Ideas (3 items)	_____	× 8 =	_____
Supporting Details (2 items)	_____	× 8 =	_____
Signal Words (1 item)	_____	× 8 =	_____
Inferences (3 items)	_____	× 8 =	_____
Argument (1 item)	_____	× 8 =	_____
Outlining (4 items)	_____	× 5 =	_____
		SCORE =	_____%

TOTAL SCORES: Vocabulary _____% Comprehension _____%

Enter your total scores into the **Reading Performance Chart: Ten Reading Selections** on the inside back cover.

3 The Fist, the Clay, and the Rock
Donald Holland

Preview

Often the best teachers are the ones who challenge us the most. In this selection, the author describes such a teacher. Mr. Gery inspires his students to work hard by using nothing more than his fist, a lump of clay, a rock—and a few well-chosen words. Read how he does it.

Words to Watch

mound (1): pile
squashed (6): flattened
wand (11): magic stick
segued (17): moved smoothly onto another subject
vivid (17): strikingly bright; true to life

1 The best teacher I ever had was Mr. Gery, who taught twelfth grade English. He started his class with us by placing on the front desk a large mound° of clay and, next to it, a rock about the size of a tennis ball. That got our attention quickly, and the class quieted down and waited for him to talk.

2 Mr. Gery looked at us and smiled and said, "If there were a pill I could give you that would help you learn, and help you want to learn, I would pass it out right now. But there is no magic pill. Everything is up to you."

3 Then Mr. Gery held up his fist and kind of shook it at us. Some of us looked at each other. *What's going on?* we all thought. Mr. Gery continued: "I'd like you to imagine something for me. Imagine that my fist is the real world—not the sheltered world of this school, but the real world. Imagine that my fist is everything that can happen to you out in the real world."

4 Then he reached down and pointed to the ball of clay and also the rock. He said, "Now imagine that you're either this lump of clay or the rock. Got that?" He smiled at us, and we waited to see what he was going to do.

5   He went on, "Let's say you're this ball of clay, and you're just sitting around minding your own business, and then, out of nowhere, here's what happens." He made a fist again, and he smashed his fist into the ball of clay, which quickly turned into a half-flattened lump.

6   He looked at us, still smiling. "If the real world comes along and takes a swing at you, you're likely to get squashed°. And you know what? The real world *will* come along and take a swing at you. You're going to take some heavy hits. Maybe you already have taken some heavy hits. Chances are that there are more down the road. So if you don't want to get squashed, you're better off if you're not a piece of clay.

7   "Now let's say you're the rock, and the real world comes along and takes a swing at you. What will happen if I smash my fist into this rock?" The answer was obvious. Nothing would happen to the rock. It would take the blow and not be changed.

8   He continued, "So what would you like to be, people, the clay—or the rock? And what's my point? What am I trying to say to you?"

9   Someone raised a hand and said, "We should all be rocks. It's bad news to be clay." And some of us laughed, though a bit uneasily.

10   Mr. Gery went on. "OK, you all want to be rocks, don't you? Now my question is, 'How do you get to be

a rock? How do you make yourself strong, like the rock, so that you won't be crushed and beaten up even if you take a lot of hits?'"

11   We didn't have an answer right away, and he went on, "You know I can't be a fairy godmother. I can't pull out a wand° and say, 'Thanks for wanting to be a rock. I hereby wave my wand and make you a rock.' That's not the way life works. The only way to become a rock is to go out and make yourself a rock.

12   "Imagine you're a fighter getting ready for a match. You go to the gym, and maybe when you start, you're flabby. Your whole body is flab, and it's soft like the clay. To make your body hard like a rock, you've got to train.

13   "Now if you want to train and become hard like the rock, I can help you. You need to develop skills, and you need to acquire knowledge. Skills will make you strong, and knowledge is power. It's my job to help you with

language skills. I'll help you train to become a better reader. I'll help you train to be a better writer. But you know, I'm just a trainer. I can't make you be a fighter.

14   "All I can do is tell you that you need to make yourself a fighter. You need to become a rock. Because you don't want to be flabby when the real world comes along and takes a crack at you. Don't spend the semester just being Mr. Cool Man or Ms. Designer Jeans or Mr. or Ms. Sex Symbol of the class. Be someone. *Be someone.*"

15   He then smashed that wad of clay one more time, and the thud of his fist broke the silence and then created more silence. He sure had our total attention.

16   "At the end of the semester, some of you are going to leave here, and you're still going to be clay. You're going to be the kind of person that life can smush around, and that's sad. But some of you, maybe a lot of you, are going to be rocks. I want you to be a rock. Go for it. And when this comes"—and he held up his fist— "you'll be ready."

17   And then Mr. Gery segued° into talking about the course. But his demonstration stayed with most of us. And as the semester unfolded, he would call back his vivid° images. When someone would not hand in a paper and made a lame excuse, he would say, "Whatever you say, Mr. Clay" or "Whatever you say, Ms. Clay." Or if someone would forget a book, or not study for a test, or not do a reading assignment, he would say, "Of course, Mr. Clay." Sometimes we would get into it also and call out, "Hey, Clayman."

18   Mr. Gery worked us very hard, but he was not a mean person. We all knew he was a kind man who wanted us to become strong. It was obvious he wanted us to do well. By the end of the semester, he had to call very few of us Mr. or Ms. Clay.

Vocabulary Questions

A. Use context clues to help you decide on the best definition for each italicized
word. Then, in the space provided, write the letter of your choice.

_____ 1. In the sentences below, the word *sheltered* (shĕl′tərd) means
   A. protected.
   B. boring.
   C. exciting.
   D. dangerous.

   "'I'd like you to imagine something for me. Imagine that my fist is the
   real world—not the sheltered world of this school but the real world.'"
   (Paragraph 3)

_____ 2. In the sentences below, the word *obvious* (ŏb′vē-əs) means
   A. difficult.
   B. nearby.
   C. easy to see.
   D. confusing.

   "'What will happen if I smash my fist into this rock?' The answer was
   obvious. Nothing would happen to the rock. It would take the blow
   and not be changed." (Paragraph 7)

_____ 3. In the sentences below, the word *acquire* (ə-kwīr′) means
   A. to ignore.
   B. to prevent.
   C. to question.
   D. to get by one's own efforts.

   "'Now if you want to train and become hard like the rock, I can help
   you. You need to develop skills, and you need to acquire knowledge.'"
   (Paragraph 13)

_____ 4. In the sentence below, the word *wad* (wŏd) means
   A. mountain.
   B. lump.
   C. coating.
   D. package.

   "He then smashed that wad of clay one more time, and the thud of his
   fist broke the silence and then created more silence." (Paragraph 15)

_____ 5. In the sentence below, the word *lame* (lām) means
  A. reasonable.
  B. weak.
  C. amusing.
  D. crippled.

> "When someone would not hand in a paper and made a lame excuse, he would say, 'Whatever you say, Mr. Clay' or 'Whatever you say, Ms. Clay.'" (Paragraph 17)

B. Below are words, or forms of words, from "Words to Watch." Write in the one that best completes each sentence. Then write the letter of that word in the space provided.

| A. mound | B. segued | C. squashed |
| D. vivid | E. wand | |

_____ 6. After talking for a few minutes about the Bush presidency, our teacher _____ into a discussion of the 2008 presidential election.

_____ 7. The power-hungry dictator _____ all those who challenged his brutal policies.

_____ 8. The fairy tale was so _____ that when the child fell asleep, he dreamed about a house made of gingerbread and candy.

_____ 9. My little sister Vivien enjoys wearing a "magic" cape and waving her ruler around as if it were a _____.

_____ 10. That _____ of dirty clothes near the foot of the stairs really needs to be put in the washing machine.

Reading Comprehension Questions

Central Point and Main Ideas

_____ 1. Which sentence best expresses the central point of the selection?
   A. Mr. Gery forced his students to become fighters.
   B. Mr. Gery was good at getting his students to pay attention.
   C. Mr. Gery was not a mean person.
   D. Mr. Gery challenged his students to learn skills that would help them in the real world.

_____ 2. Which sentence best expresses the main idea of paragraph 6?
   A. Mr. Gery is in a bad mood.
   B. Mr. Gery wants his students to prepare themselves to take some heavy hits.
   C. Mr. Gery realizes that some of his students have already taken some heavy hits.
   D. Mr. Gery doesn't want his students to be like rocks.

Supporting Details

_____ 3. Mr. Gery compares his fist to
   A. a rock.
   B. a lump of clay.
   C. a magic wand.
   D. everything that can happen out in the real world.

_____ 4. Mr. Gery's job is to
   A. provide his students with shelter.
   B. help his students with language skills.
   C. train his students to become boxers.
   D. teach his students social studies.

Signal Words

_____ 5. Most of the signal words used in this selection are
   A. time words.
   B. addition words.

_____ 6. In the sentences below, the word *because* shows a relationship of
   A. contrast.   C. time.
   B. an example.   D. cause and effect.

   "'You need to become a rock. Because you don't want to be flabby when the real world comes along and takes a crack at you.'" (Paragraph 14)

_____ 7. The relationship of the second sentence below to the first sentence is one of
- A. contrast.
- C. time.
- B. cause and effect.
- D. addition.

> "'You're going to be the kind of person that life can smush around, and that's sad. But some of you, maybe a lot of you, are going to be rocks.'"
> (Paragraph 16)

Inferences

_____ 8. This selection suggests that
- A. students who have poor reading and writing skills may be unprepared for real life.
- B. reading and writing skills are less important than being physically tough when facing the real world.
- C. using a computer is the best way to develop good reading and writing skills.
- D. good teachers can make their students into fighters.

_____ 9. We can infer that the author
- A. was one of the students that Mr. Gery called "Mr. Clay" at the end of the semester.
- B. became a English teacher like Mr. Gery.
- C. thought Mr. Gery should have been harder on the class.
- D. learned a great deal from Mr. Gery.

Argument

_____10. Write the letter of the statement that is the **point** of the following argument. The other statements are support for that point.
- A. Mr. Gery challenged his students to become like rocks, not like clay.
- B. An inspiring teacher, Mr. Gery worked hard to motivate his students to succeed.
- C. Mr. Gery told his students that he'd help them train to become better readers and writers and then worked them hard.
- D. Mr. Gery teased his students when they didn't complete their assignments by calling them "Mr. Clay" or "Ms. Clay."

Outlining

Prepare an outline of "The Fist, the Clay, and the Rock" by filling in the missing details, which are scrambled in the list below.

- By the end of the semester, Mr. Gery has to call very few of his students "Mr. or Ms. Clay."
- Mr. Gery smashes his fist into the lump of clay.
- Mr. Gery calls students who don't do their work "Mr. Clay" or "Ms. Clay."
- Mr. Gery holds up his fist and asks the class to imagine that it is the real world.

Central point: Mr. Gery captures his students' attention and helps them to acquire language skills that that they will need in the real world.

1. Mr. Gery places a mound of clay and a rock on his front desk.

2. _____

_____

3. Mr. Gery asks the class to imagine that they're the lump of clay.

4. _____

_____

5. Mr. Gery asks his class to imagine what would happen if he smashed his fist into the rock.

6. Mr. Gery tells the class that if they want to train and become hard like a rock, he can help them develop their language skills.

7. _____

_____

8. _____

_____

Discussion Questions

1. What does Mr. Gery mean by saying that fists will come along in life? Give an example of a time you experienced a fist, or someone you know experienced a fist.

2. What does Mr. Gery mean by "clay"? What is the danger of being clay?

3. What does Mr. Gery mean by "rock"? How does a person become a rock?

Note: Writing assignments for this selection appear on pages 514–515.

Check Your Performance   THE FIST, THE CLAY, AND THE ROCK

Activity	Number Right	Points	Total
VOCABULARY			
Part A (5 items)	_____	× 10 =	_____
Part B (5 items)	_____	× 10 =	_____
		SCORE =	_____ %
Reading Comprehension Questions			
Central Point and Main Ideas (2 items)	_____	× 8 =	_____
Supporting Details (2 items)	_____	× 8 =	_____
Signal Words (3 items)	_____	× 8 =	_____
Inferences (2 items)	_____	× 8 =	_____
Argument (1 item)	_____	× 8 =	_____
Outlining (4 items)	_____	× 5 =	_____
		SCORE =	_____ %

TOTAL SCORES: Vocabulary _____ % Comprehension _____ %

Enter your total scores into the **Reading Performance Chart: Ten Reading Selections** on the inside back cover.

4

It's Not My Fault
Roger Kennedy

Preview

Oh, how we hate to admit we are wrong. In this essay, you'll learn some of the typical ways people try to avoid responsibility for their mistakes. Do you recognize yourself in any of these examples?

Words to Watch

humiliated (1): shamed
authority (6): power
scandal (7): a shameful event
conveniently (9): easily
engage (13): become involved

1   It's a fact. When we behave badly, we tend to make an excuse. And that excuse often involves blaming someone or something else for the mistakes we've made. Yeah, we know that taking responsibility for our actions is the right thing to do. But admitting that we are to blame makes us feel embarrassed and humiliated°. It's painful. Who wants to feel pain? So we come up with endless ways to hold others responsible for our own actions. Humans have been doing this for a very long time. Consider that the first humans presented in the Bible blamed a snake for their bad behavior!

2   What are some common ways in which we try to blame others? Take a look at the following examples:

3   At nearly 30 years old, Brian can't keep a job. He often gets in fights with his few friends. He lives a difficult life. Brian hasn't had an easy time of it. When he was a child, his parents fought all the time and went through a nasty divorce. Brian never received the love that he needed growing up. Worse yet, his father abused him. Today, Brian blames his parents for the way he's turned out. The last time he was fired from a job for getting to work late nearly every day, Brian complained to a friend that it wasn't fair.

4   "If my parents had raised me better, I'd be a better employee," he

griped. "My dad was the same way—he was out of work all the time. It's not my fault that I screwed up. I'm just doing what he taught me!"

5   Like Brian, many people reassign blame for their bad behavior to those who have hurt them. It's not hard to understand why. Sure, we're affected by painful things that have happened to us in the past. No doubt, those things influence the ways we live our lives and the choices we make. However, adults (like Brian) are in charge of their own lives. They can make their own decisions. They can also create changes and break old habits that may be holding them back. Allowing those who have hurt us in the past to still have control over our lives is always a bad idea. It is the lazy person's way out of taking control of his or her life.

6   Sometimes simply blaming parents or others with authority° isn't enough. Sometimes, we feel the need to blame a group of people or even *everyone* for our bad behavior. We find ourselves blaming "them" and "everybody else" to avoid admitting fault.

7   A classic example of this is the Lance Armstrong doping scandal°. In 2013, after years of hiding the truth, bicycling champion Armstrong finally admitted that he had used drugs in order to win seven Tour de France races. However, Armstrong would not admit that he had actually done anything wrong since doping was so pervasive and "everyone back then" was doping on the cycling circuit.

8   "If you took me back to 1995," Armstrong said in a 2013 interview, "I'd do the drugs again, because it was completely and totally widespread."

9   More than anything, the "Well, everyone else was doing it!" excuse is just a childish argument. Everyone has heard a child whine that a punishment isn't fair because Eric or Sara or Tomas "did it, too." As any parent would explain to a child, the fact that others behave badly is no excuse for doing something wrong.

This is a lesson that most of us learn in kindergarten. It is remarkable how many people conveniently° ignore it well into adulthood.

10 Sometimes people refuse to accept blame because, even though they know what they've done is wrong, it wasn't "*that* bad." They argue that other people have done far worse things, so they should not have to feel bad about their actions. This behavior was recently exhibited in Atlanta when 35 teachers were charged with changing answers on students' tests in order to make their schools appear more successful. Most of the teachers took responsibility and admitted guilt, but ten of the teachers refused.

11 "The judge gave them every opportunity to take responsibility for their actions," one witness said. "But they continued thinking that what they had done was not that bad."

12 As a result, the angry judge handed out stiff sentences, including lengthy prison time. Refusing to accept blame based on the idea that other people do worse things was just bad reasoning.

13 Finally, sometimes people refuse to admit that what they have done is wrong since someone did the same thing to them first. This "payback" excuse passes the blame back to the original wrongdoer. As opposed to the Golden Rule, this reasoning suggests that we should treat others exactly as badly as they treat us. And when we engage° in this kind of retribution, we should not be blamed for what happens since the other person "had it coming to him (or her)."

14 In Texas, the driver of a large pickup truck nearly rear-ended a small car when it suddenly cut in front of his truck in busy freeway traffic. The truck driver honked his horn and made rude gestures, but he couldn't get the small car out of his way. Finally, he decided to do a little payback. He whipped around the small car on the right and pulled directly in front of it. Then, as an added meanness, the driver of the truck put on his brakes for just a moment.

15 The driver of the small car had no time to react. She crashed into the back of the truck. The crash killed both her and her two-year-old daughter, whom she had been hurrying to the doctor. Although the driver of the truck expressed regret for what had happened, he stopped short of taking blame.

16 "This would have never happened at all if she hadn't cut me off in the first place," he replied when asked how he felt about what *he* had done.

17 Someone once wrote, "*It is a painful thing to look at your own trouble and know that you yourself and no one else has made it.*" Humans will do all sorts of things to avoid pain. We will often go to great lengths to find ways to blame someone else, *anyone* else, for the trouble we've created.

18   But consider what happens when we *do* take responsibility for our actions. Those around us often forgive us and even admire us. Sometimes, in spite of our mistakes, they wish they could be more like us. And then even better things happen: we gain a sense of self-respect and, with it, a sense of peace.

Vocabulary Questions

A. Use context clues to help you decide on the best definition for each italicized word. Then, in the space provided, write the letter of your choice.

_____ 1. In the sentences below, the word *griped* (grīpt) means

    A. complained.

    B. laughed.

    C. yelled.

    D. wondered.

> "The last time he was fired from a job for getting to work late nearly every day, Brian complained to a friend that it wasn't fair.
>
> "'If my parents had raised me better, I'd be a better employee,' he griped." (Paragraphs 3–4)

_____ 2. In the sentences below, the word *reassign* (rē'ə-sīn') means

    A. imagine.

    B. forget.

    C. explain.

    D. transfer.

> "'It's not my fault that I screwed up. I'm just doing what he taught me!'
>
> "Like Brian, many people reassign blame for their bad behavior to those who have hurt them." (Paragraphs 4–5)

_____ 3. In the sentences below, the word *pervasive* (pər-vā′sĭv) means
   A. unusual.
   B. widespread.
   C. illegal.
   D. secret.

> "Armstrong finally admitted that he had used drugs in order to win seven Tour de France races. However, Armstrong would not admit that he had actually done anything wrong since doping was so pervasive and 'everyone back then' was doping on the cycling circuit." (Paragraph 7)

_____ 4. In the sentences below, the word *exhibited* (ĭg-zĭb′ĭt-ĕd) means
   A. ignored.
   B. watched.
   C. shown.
   D. a problem.

> "This behavior was recently exhibited in Atlanta when 35 teachers were charged with changing answers on students' tests in order to make their schools appear more successful. Most of the teachers took responsibility and admitted guilt, but ten of the teachers refused." (Paragraph 10)

_____ 5. In the sentences below, the word *retribution* (rĕt′rə-byoo′shən) means
   A. thinking.
   B. game.
   C. anger.
   D. revenge.

> "This 'payback' excuse passes the blame back to the original wrongdoer. As opposed to the Golden Rule, this reasoning suggests that we should treat others exactly as badly as they treat us. And when we engage in this kind of retribution, we should not be blamed for what happens since the other person 'had it coming to him (or her).'" (Paragraph 13)

B. Below are words, or forms of words, from "Words to Watch." Write in the one that best completes each sentence. Then write the letter of that word in the space provided.

| A. authority | B. convenient | C. engaged |
| D. humiliated | E. scandal | |

_____ 6. The principal told Josh that if he _____ in another fight, he would be expelled.

_____ 7. When Carrie's boyfriend laughed at her new haircut, she felt _____ .

_____ 8. Any police officer would have the _____ to tell partygoers to quiet down.

_____ 9. The senator's affair with the married woman became a nationally famous _____ .

_____ 10. The airport is across the street from our hotel, making it _____ for us to get there early in the morning.

Reading Comprehension Questions

Central Point and Main Ideas

_____ 1. Which sentence best expresses the central point of the selection?
   A. Some people treat others poorly because others hurt them first.
   B. Blaming others is better than dealing with the pain of admitting wrongdoing.
   C. A popular way that people avoid responsibility is by blaming a group of people for bad behavior.
   D. Although it isn't admirable, people use a variety of excuses to avoid taking blame.

_____ 2. Which sentence best expresses the main idea of paragraph 3?

    A. Brian fights with friends and can't keep a job.

    B. Brian has had a hard life and blames his parents for his behavior today.

    C. When Brian was a child, his parents fought all the time and finally divorced.

    D. Brian's father abused him.

_____ 3. Which sentence best expresses the main idea of paragraph 9?

    A. The first sentence

    B. The second sentence

    C. The third sentence

    D. The last sentence

Supporting Details

_____ 4. Instead of blaming his parents for being fired from his job, Brian should

    A. blame his boss.

    B. consider looking for a different kind of job.

    C. take charge of his own life and make changes.

    D. realize that there are worse things that could happen.

_____ 5. Which response best expresses how Lance Armstrong defended his choice to use performance-enhancing drugs in 1995?

    A. "There are worse crimes."

    B. "Everyone else was doing it."

    C. "It's not my fault that I screwed up."

    D. "Other people put pressure on me."

_____ 6. What reasoning did the Atlanta teachers use to keep from admitting that what they had done was a mistake?

    A. They were getting back at the school system.

    B. Other teachers have done the same thing.

    C. Because they were underpaid, it was the school system's fault.

    D. There are certainly worse crimes than the crime they committed.

Signal Words

_____ 7. In the sentences below, the word *also* shows a relationship of
  A. cause and effect.
  B. time.
  C. addition.
  D. contrast.

> "[Adults] can make their own decisions. They can also . . . break old habits that may be holding them back." (Paragraph 5)

_____ 8. The relationship of the second sentence below to the first is one of
  A. cause and effect.
  B. time.
  C. contrast.
  D. an example.

> "'The judge gave them every opportunity to take responsibility for their actions,' one witness said, 'but they continued thinking that what they had done was not that bad.'
>
> "As a result, the angry judge handed out stiff sentences including lengthy prison time." (Paragraphs 11–12)

Inferences

_____ 9. The author implies that the first humans to blame others were
  A. teachers.
  B. the authors of the Bible.
  C. Adam and Eve.
  D. Brian and Lance Armstrong.

_____ 10. On the basis of the information in paragraphs 14–16, we can infer that the truck driver
  A. felt fully responsible for the death of the mother and her two-year-old daughter.
  B. had been acting deliberately to harm the mother and her two-year-old daughter.
  C. did not sustain any injuries as a result of the accident.
  D. had probably been drinking prior to the road rage incident.

Outlining

Prepare an outline of "It's Not My Fault" by filling in the missing details, which are scrambled in the list below.

- We call it "payback."
- Lance Armstrong used the "everyone else was doing it" excuse for doping during the Tour de France.
- We say "It wasn't that bad."
- Brian blames his parents for the way his life has turned out.

Central point: By using several excuses, we often avoid the pain of taking the blame for our mistakes.

1. We blame those who have hurt us in the past.
    a. Brian is unable to keep a job, often fights with friends, and is unhappy.

    b. _____
        _____

2. We say "Everybody does it."

    a. _____
        _____

    b. An athlete might insist that drug use was common in the 1990s, but this is a childish argument.

3. _____
    _____

    a. Teachers in Atlanta refused to admit guilt for changing students' answers, saying what they had done wasn't so bad.
    b. The judge in the Atlanta case was angry at the teachers' excuse and handed out stiff punishments.

4. _____
    _____

    a. A truck driver in Texas lost his temper when a woman cut him off in traffic.
    b. After causing an accident that killed the woman and her daughter, the truck driver said, "This would never have happened if she hadn't cut me off in the first place."

Discussion Questions

1. Think about a time when you admitted that you were wrong, when you were, in fact, to blame for something that went wrong. How did you feel after you accepted the blame? How did others treat you? Were you surprised by others' reactions?

2. What are some other common excuses people use to avoid blame? Are any of these reasons ever justified? Or are they simply excuses for bad behavior? Explain.

3. It is often said that we learn from our mistakes. But first we have to admit that we've actually *made* mistakes. Since these learning experiences are so valuable, what suggestions would you make to encourage people to take responsibility for their actions?

Note: Writing assignments for this selection appear on page 515.

Check Your Performance   IT'S NOT MY FAULT

Activity	Number Right	Points		Total
Vocabulary				
Part A (5 items)	_____	× 10	=	_____
Part B (5 items)	_____	× 10	=	_____
		SCORE	=	_____ %
Reading Comprehension Questions				
Central Point and Main Ideas (3 items)	_____	× 8	=	_____
Supporting Details (3 items)	_____	× 8	=	_____
Signal Words (2 items)	_____	× 8	=	_____
Inferences (2 items)	_____	× 8	=	_____
Outlining (4 items)	_____	× 5	=	_____
		SCORE	=	_____ %

TOTAL SCORES: Vocabulary _____% Comprehension _____%

Enter your total scores into the **Reading Performance Chart: Ten Reading Selections** on the inside back cover.

5 Joe Davis: A Cool Man
Beth Johnson

Preview

From age 14 on, Joe Davis followed a path that led him closer and closer to self-destruction. He lived in a world of drugs, guns, and easy money. In this world, he had no respect for himself or sympathy for others. Today Joe Davis is, in every way, a new man. Here is the story of how Joe saved his own life.

Words to Watch

option (6): choice
shown the ropes (10): shown how things should be done
rehabilitated (10): brought back to a good and healthy life
stickup man (11): someone who robs with a gun
went downhill (13): got worse
encountered (20): met
unruly (26): disorderly
hushed (27): quiet
yearn (37): want very much

1   Joe Davis was the coolest fourteen-year-old he'd ever seen.

2   He went to school when he felt like it. He hung out with a wild crowd. He started drinking some wine, smoking some marijuana. "Nobody could tell me anything," he says today. "I thought the sun rose and set on me." There were rules at home, and Joe didn't do rules. So he moved in with his grandmother.

3   Joe Davis was the coolest sixteen-year-old he'd ever seen.

4   Joe's parents gave up on his schooling and signed him out of the tenth grade. Joe went to work in his dad's body shop, but that didn't last long. There were rules there, too, and Joe didn't do rules. By the time he was in his mid-teens, Joe was taking pills that got him high and even using cocaine. He was also smoking marijuana all the time and drinking booze all the time.

5   Joe Davis was the coolest twenty-five-year-old he'd ever seen.

6   He was living with a woman almost twice his age. The situation

wasn't great, but she paid the bills, and certainly Joe couldn't. He had his habit to support, which by now had grown to include heroin. Sometimes he'd work at a low-level job, if someone else found it for him. He might work long enough to get a paycheck and then spend it all at once. Other times he'd be caught stealing and get fired first. A more challenging job was not an option°, even if he had bothered to look for one. He couldn't put words together to form a sentence, unless the sentence was about drugs. Filling out an application was difficult. He wasn't a strong reader. He couldn't do much with numbers. Since his drug habit had to be paid for, he started to steal. First he stole from his parents, then from his sister. Then he stole from the families of people he knew. But eventually the people he knew wouldn't let him in their houses, since they knew he'd steal from them. So he got a gun and began holding people up. He chose elderly people and others who weren't likely to fight back. The holdups kept him in drug money, but things at home were getting worse. His woman's teenage daughter was getting out of line. Joe decided it was up to him to discipline her. The girl didn't like it. She told her boyfriend. One day, the boyfriend called Joe out of the house.

7   BANG.

8   Joe Davis was in the street, his nose in the dirt. His mind was still cloudy from his most recent high, but he knew something was terribly wrong with his legs. He couldn't move them; he couldn't even feel them. His mother came out of her nearby house and ran to him. As he heard her screams, he imagined what she was seeing. Her oldest child, her first baby, her bright boy who could have been and done anything, was lying in the gutter, a junkie with a .22 caliber bullet lodged in his spine.

9   The next time Joe's head cleared, he was in a hospital bed, blinking up at his parents as they stared helplessly at him. The doctors had done all they could; Joe would live, to everyone's surprise. But he was a paraplegic— paralyzed from his chest down. It was done. It was over. It was written in stone. He would not walk again. He would not be able to control his bladder or bowels. He would not be able to make love as he had before. He would not be able to hold people up, then hurry away.

10   Joe spent the next eight months being moved between several Philadelphia hospitals, where he was shown the ropes° of life as a paraplegic. Officially he was being "rehabilitated°"—restored to a productive life. There was just one problem: Joe. "To be *re*habilitated, you must have been *habilitated* first," he says today. "That wasn't me." During his stay in the hospitals, he found ways to get high every day.

11   Finally Joe was released from the hospital. He returned in his wheelchair to the house he'd been living in when he was shot. He needed someone to take care of him, and his woman friend was still willing. His drug habit was as strong as ever, but his days as a stickup man° were over. So he started selling drugs. Business was good. The money came in fast, and his own drug use accelerated even faster.

12   A wheelchair-bound junkie doesn't pay much attention to his health and cleanliness. Eventually Joe developed his first bedsore: a deep, rotting wound that ate into his flesh, overwhelming him with its foul odor. He was admitted to Magee Rehabilitation Hospital, where he spent six months on his stomach while the ghastly wound slowly healed. Again, he spent his time in the hospital using drugs. This time his drug use did not go unnoticed. Soon before he was scheduled to be discharged, hospital officials kicked him out. He returned to his friend's house and his business. But then police raided the house. They took the drugs, they took the money, they took the guns.

13   "I really went downhill° then," says Joe. With no drugs and no money to get drugs, life held little meaning. He began fighting with the woman he was living with. "When you're in the state I was in, you don't know how to be nice to anybody," he says. Finally she kicked him out of the house. When his parents took him in, Joe did a little selling from their

house, trying to keep it low-key, out of sight, so they wouldn't notice. He laughs at the notion today. "I thought I could control junkies and tell them 'Business only during certain hours.'" Joe got high when his monthly Social Security check came, high when he'd make a purchase for someone else and get a little something for himself, high when a visitor would share drugs with him. It wasn't much of a life. "There I was," he says, "a junkie with no education, no job, no friends, no means of supporting myself. And now I had a spinal cord injury."

14   Then came October 25, 1988. Joe had just filled a prescription for pills to control his muscle spasms. Three hundred of the powerful muscle relaxants were there for the taking. He swallowed them all.

15   "It wasn't the spinal cord injury that did it," he says. "It was the addiction."

16   Joe tried hard to die, but it didn't work. A sister heard him choking and called for help. He was rushed to the hospital, where he lay in a coma for four days.

17   Joe has trouble finding the words to describe what happened next.

18   "I had . . . a spiritual awakening, for lack of any better term," he says. "My soul had been cleansed. I knew my life could be better. And from that day to this, I have chosen not to get high."

19   Drugs, he says, "are not even a temptation. That life is a thing that happened to someone else."

20   Joe knew he wanted to turn himself around, but he needed help in knowing where to start. He enrolled in Magee Hospital's vocational rehabilitation program. For six weeks, he immersed himself in discussions, tests, and exercises to help him determine the kind of work he might be suited for. The day he finished the rehab program, a nurse at Magee told him about a receptionist's job in the spinal cord injury unit at Thomas Jefferson Hospital. He went straight to the hospital and met Lorraine Buchanan, coordinator of the unit. "I told her where I was and where I wanted to go," Joe says. "I told her, 'If you give me a job, I will never disappoint you. I'll quit first if I see I can't live up to it.'" She gave him the job. The wheelchair-bound junkie, the man who'd never been able to hold a job, the drug-dependent stickup man who "couldn't put two words together to make a sentence" was now the first face, the first voice that patients encountered° when they entered the spinal cord unit. "I'd never talked to people like that," says Joe, shaking his head. "I had absolutely no background. But Lorraine and the others, they taught me to speak. Taught me to greet people. Taught me to handle the phone." How did he do in his role as a receptionist? A huge smile breaks across Joe's face as he answers, "I did excellent."

21   Soon, his personal life also took a very positive turn. A month after Joe started his job, he was riding a city bus to work. A woman recovering from knee surgery was in another seat. The two smiled, but didn't speak.

22   A week later, Joe spotted the woman again. The bus driver sensed something was going on and encouraged Joe to approach her. Her name was Terri. She was a receptionist in a law office. On their first date, Joe laid his cards on the table. He told her his story. He also told her he was looking to get married. "That about scared her away," Joe recalls. "She said she wasn't interested in marriage. I asked, 'Well, suppose you did meet someone you cared about, who cared about you, and treated you well. Would you still be opposed to the idea of marriage?' She said no, she would consider it then. I said, 'Well, that's all I ask.'"

23   Four months later, as the two sat over dinner in a restaurant, Joe handed Terri a box tied with a ribbon. Inside was a smaller box. Then a smaller box, and a smaller one still. Ten boxes in all. Inside the smallest was an engagement ring. After another six months, the two were married in the law office where Terri works. Since then, she has been Joe's constant source of support, encouragement, and love.

24   After Joe had started work at Jefferson Hospital, he talked with his supervisor, Lorraine, about his dreams of moving on to something bigger, more challenging. She encouraged him to try college. He had taken and passed the high-school general equivalency diploma (GED) exam years before, almost as a joke, when he was recovering from his bedsores at Magee. Now he enrolled in a university mathematics course. He didn't do well. "I wasn't ready," Joe says. "I'd been out of school seventeen years. I dropped out." Before he could let discouragement overwhelm him, he enrolled at Community College of Philadelphia (CCP), where he signed up for basic math and English courses. He worked hard, sharpening study skills he had never developed in his earlier school days. Next he took courses toward an associate's degree in mental health and social services, along with a certificate in addiction studies. Five years later, he graduated from CCP, the first member of his family ever to earn a college degree. He then went on to receive a B.A. in mental health from Hahnemann University in Philadelphia and an M.A. in social work from the University of Pennsylvania.

25   Today, Joe is employed as a psychotherapist at John F. Kennedy Mental Health Center in Philadelphia. He does his best to get into the "real world," the world of young men and women immersed in drugs, violence, and crime, Whenever he can, he speaks at local schools through a

program called Think First. He tells young people about his drug use, his shooting, and his experience with paralysis.

26   At a presentation at a disciplinary school outside of Philadelphia, Joe gazes with quiet authority at the unruly° crowd of teenagers. He begins to speak, telling them about speedballs and guns, fast money and bedsores, even about the leg bag that collects his urine. At first, the kids snort with laughter at his honesty. When they laugh, he waits patiently, then goes on. Gradually the room grows quieter as Joe tells them of his life and then asks them about theirs. "What's important to you? What are your goals?" he says. "I was still in school at age 40 because when I was young, I chose the dead-end route many of you are on. But now I'm doing what I have to do to get where I want to go. What are *you* doing?"

27   He tells them more, about broken dreams, about his parents' grief, about the former friends who turned away from him when he was no longer a source of drugs. He tells them of the continuing struggle to regain the trust of people he once abused. He tells them about the desire that consumes him now, the desire to make his community a better place to live. His wish is that no young man or woman should have to walk the path he's walked in order to value the precious gift of life. The teenagers are now silent. They look at this broad-shouldered black man in his wheelchair, his head and beard close-shaven, a gold ring in his ear. His hushed° words settle among them like gentle drops of cleansing rain. "What are *you* doing? Where are *you* going?" he asks them. "Think about it. Think about me."

Joe Davis is the coolest fifty-one-year-old you've ever seen.   28

An Update and a Goodbye

The original version of this article was published in 1996, in the Townsend Press book *Everyday Heroes*. At that time, Joe Davis was 39 years old.   29

The response to Joe's story was extraordinary. Over the years, many readers have contacted us to ask, "Whatever happened to Joe Davis?" In response, we updated his story several times in various Townsend Press books.   30

Here, we provide a final chapter.   31

After working as a therapist at John F. Kennedy Mental Health Center in Philadelphia, Joe spent almost twenty years as the coordinator of the "Think First" program at Magee Rehabilitation Hospital, the facility where he recovered from his gunshot wound. Through "Think First," he was able to visit a countless number of schools, juvenile detention centers,   32 prisons, gun courts, and anywhere else at-risk kids might be. There, Joe shared his story with young people. At each occasion he begged, scolded, lectured, laughed with, and loved those kids, urging them to avoid the mistakes that he had made.

33   Before leaving any such gathering, Joe would use his remarkable ability to zero in on a kid in special need of his message. He would slip his card into that boy's or girl's hand, saying, "I care. Call me. Anytime."

34   They did call him. And he was never too busy to listen. "Terri," he would tell his loving wife, when another middle-of-the-night phone call came from a stranger who had heard Joe speak, "I would meet a kid in a phone booth if I thought I could help."

35   Joe had the biggest, most loving heart in the world, but his battered body finally gave out. After two years of declining health, he passed away on August 15, 2015. He was three days short of his 60th birthday.

36   His funeral brought together an astonishing group of people. They were black, white, and brown. There were Christians, Jews, Muslims, and nonbelievers. Some had dropped out of high school; others had degrees from Ivy League universities. Some had done time in prison. Some worked in law enforcement.

37   All they had in common was that each had been touched by the miracle that was Joe's life. Each of them had experienced his ability to look past a person's exterior to something more important. When Joe met a person, he didn't see "troubled kid" or "college professor" or "ex-convict" or "addict." He saw people as we all yearn° to be seen—imperfect, struggling, but worthy of love. Because they felt that nonjudgmental love, people responded to Joe by wanting to be their best selves. They wanted to be worthy of Joe.

38   To the end, Joe Davis was a cool man.

Vocabulary Questions

A. Use context clues to help you decide on the best definition for each italicized word. Then, in the space provided, write the letter of your choice.

_____ 1. In the sentence below, the word *restored* (rĭ-stôrd′) means
  A. held back.
  B. punished.
  C. brought back.
  D. paid.

  "Officially he was being 'rehabilitated'—restored to a productive life." (Paragraph 10)

_____ 2. In the sentence below, the word *accelerated* (ăk-sĕl′ə-rā′td) means
  A. increased.
  B. grew less serious.
  C. disappeared.
  D. helped.

  "The money came in fast, and his own drug use had accelerated even faster." (Paragraph 11)

_____ 3. In the sentence below, the word *ghastly* (găst′lē) means
  A. quite small.
  B. very unpleasant.
  C. caused by a gun.
  D. illegal.

  " . . . he spent six months on his stomach while the ghastly wound slowly healed." (Paragraph 12)

_____ 4. In the sentences below, the word *notion* (nō′shən) means
  A. idea.
  B. joke.
  C. answer.
  D. cause.

  "When his parents took him in, Joe did a little selling from their house, trying to keep it low-key, out of sight, so they wouldn't notice. He laughs at that notion today. 'I thought I could control junkies . . . .'" (Paragraph 13)

_____ 5. In the sentence below, the word *immersed* (ĭ-mûrst′) means
  A. totally ignored.
  B. greatly angered.
  C. deeply involved.
  D. often harmed.

  > "For six weeks, he immersed himself in discussions, tests, and exercises to help him determine the kind of work he might be suited for." (Paragraph 20)

B. Below are words, or forms of words, from "Words to Watch." Write in the one that best completes each sentence. Then write the letter of that word in the space provided.

A. encountered	B. hushed	C. option
D. rehabilitated	E. unruly	

_____ 6. Mr. Barris is the meanest-looking man I've ever _____— his frown could freeze chili peppers.

_____ 7. Aunt Sarah _____ the children when their loud play made it hard for her to follow the soap opera.

_____ 8. His dad gave Carlos the _____ of working part-time in his store as a way of paying some of his college expenses.

_____ 9. The audience grew _____ after it was announced that the singer they had come to see had been delayed in traffic.

_____ 10. You'd never know it to look at him now, but the company president is a _____ drug addict.

Reading Comprehension Questions

Central Point and Main Ideas

_____ 1. Which sentence best expresses the central point of the selection?
- A. Most people cannot improve their lives after turning to drugs and crime.
- B. Joe Davis overcame a life of drugs and crime and a disability to lead a rich, productive life.
- C. The rules of Joe Davis's parents caused him to leave home and continue a life of drugs and crime.
- D. Joe Davis's friends turned away from him once they learned he was no longer a source of drugs.

_____ 2. A main idea may cover more than one paragraph. Which sentence best expresses the main idea of paragraphs 21–23?
- A. The first sentence of paragraph 21
- B. The second sentence of paragraph 21
- C. The first sentence of paragraph 22
- D. The first sentence of paragraph 23

_____ 3. Which sentence best expresses the main idea of paragraph 24?
- A. It was difficult for Joe to do college work after being out of school for so many years.
- B. Lorraine Buchanan encouraged Joe to go to college.
- C. Joe overcame a lack of academic preparation and eventually earned two college degrees and a master's degree.
- D. If students would stay in high school and work hard, they would not have to go to the trouble of getting a high-school GED.

Supporting Details

_____ 4. Joe Davis quit high school
- A. when he was 14.
- B. when he got a good job at a hospital.
- C. when he was in the tenth grade.
- D. after he was shot.

_____ 5. Joe tried to kill himself by
- A. swallowing muscle-relaxant pills.
- B. shooting himself.
- C. overdosing on heroin.
- D. not eating or drinking.

_____ 6. According to the selection, Joe first met his wife
   A. in the hospital, where she was a nurse.
   B. on a city bus, where they were both passengers.
   C. on the job, where she was also a receptionist.
   D. at the Community College of Philadelphia, where she was also a
      student.

_____ 7. Joe decided to stop using drugs
   A. when he met his future wife.
   B. right after he was shot.
   C. when he awoke from a suicide attempt.
   D. when he was hired as a receptionist.

Signal Words

_____ 8. The word *because* in the sentence below shows a relationship of
   A. addition.
   B. time.
   C. contrast.
   D. cause and effect.

   "'I was still in school at age 40 because when I was young, I chose the
   dead-end route many of you are on....'" (Paragraph 26)

Inferences

_____ 9. The author implies that
   A. Joe became a drug addict because his parents didn't care what
      happened to him.
   B. Joe tried hard to succeed in high school, but failed.
   C. Joe's parents turned their backs on him after he was shot.
   D. Joe was not as "cool" as he thought he was.

_____ 10. We can conclude that
   A. even longtime drug addicts like Joe can be rehabilitated.
   B. some drug addicts can never be rehabilitated.
   C. it's nearly impossible to go back to school after 17 years.
   D. there are few resources available for people who are recovering
      from addiction.

Outlining

Following is an outline showing major events in Joe Davis's life. Complete the outline by filling in the missing events, which are scrambled in the list below.

- Joe takes a job as a receptionist.
- Joe gets shot, which paralyzes him from the chest down.
- Joe starts selling drugs.
- Joe earns a college degree.

Central point: From a life of drugs and crime, Joe Davis turned his life around in several positive ways.

1. Joe leaves school.

2. _____

3. _____

4. Joe tries to commit suicide.

5. Joe gives up drugs and goes into a vocational rehabilitation program.

6. _____

7. Joe gets married.

8. _____

9. Joe earns a master's degree in social work.

10. Although he is gone, Joe is remembered as a man who touched many lives.

Discussion Questions

1. What do you think was the main turning point in Joe's life, and why do you think it happened?

2. Why do you think the students Joe spoke to laughed at him as he tried to share his honest thoughts? Why did they become quieter as he continued to speak of his life? What effect do you think his presentation had on these students?

3. Joe wanted young people to learn the lessons he did without having to go through what he went through. What lessons have you learned in your life that you would like to pass on to others?

Note: Writing assignments for this selection appear on page 516.

Check Your Performance   JOE DAVIS

Activity	Number Right	Points	Total
Vocabulary			
Part A (5 items)	_____	× 10 =	_____
Part B (5 items)	_____	× 10 =	_____
		SCORE =	_____ %
Reading Comprehension Questions			
Central Point and Main Ideas (3 items)	_____	× 8 =	_____
Supporting Details (4 items)	_____	× 8 =	_____
Signal Words (1 item)	_____	× 8 =	_____
Inferences (2 items)	_____	× 8 =	_____
Outlining (4 items)	_____	× 5 =	_____
		SCORE =	_____ %

TOTAL SCORES: Vocabulary _____ % Comprehension _____ %

Enter your total scores into the **Reading Performance Chart: Ten Reading Selections** on the inside back cover.

6 Rosa: A Success Story
Edward Patrick

Preview

This selection is about a woman who meets and conquers more obstacles than many of us have experienced. She does not spend a lot of time asking why these things are happening to her. She does what she must to make her life and the lives of her family better.

Words to Watch

plantation (1): large estate where crops are grown
to no avail (3): without success
trek (3): journey
conveyed (5): communicated
sentiment (5): attitude; thought
halting (6): awkward
preoccupied (16): not paying attention
collect myself (20): gain control of myself
immigrants (21): people who come to another country to live
oppressive (21): harsh and cruel

1   Up until six months before I met her, life for Rosa Perez had been easy. Her father was a wealthy plantation° owner in Nicaragua. Her family owned a large house with all the comforts of the rich. Then came the same type of violent civil war that has torn apart so many Latin American countries.

2   Rosa's father was identified as a supporter of the rebel cause, and the family's plantation was seized. During the government takeover, her father was shot and killed. Her mother gathered as much money as she could and fled with Rosa and her two younger brothers, Adolpho and Roberto. Their destination was the United States. Rosa's mother knew a man who knew another man who could get them through Mexico and across the U.S. border into Texas or California. There was nothing to worry about, they were told. Rosa believed it.

3   At first, things went smoothly. Twelve others joined Rosa and her family. The group had no trouble getting into and across Mexico. But just before they were to cross into

California, the guide said he could go no further. Another man would take them the rest of the way. Rosa's mother protested, but to no avail°. They were led across by a man they did not know. He told them to follow his every command. They must move quickly and silently or risk detection by the Border Patrol. It was a difficult trek°. It was dark. It was cold. Coyotes howled in what all hoped was the distance. Everyone was tired and frightened.

4   And then came the bright lights. Just as they were about to cross into the United States, the U.S. Border Patrol sighted the group and turned on the searchlights on their jeeps to track them down. People scattered. Rosa held on to Adolpho and Roberto. She looked back, but could not see her mother. "*Aqui. Ahora,*" commanded their guide, appropriately called a "coyote." Rosa blindly followed him and watched as the lights of the jeeps sped after the others. They waited quietly for what seemed like hours. Only when he was convinced that it was safe did their guide take the five who had managed to follow him the rest of the way. Eleven were not with them, including Rosa's mother.

5   I first saw Rosa three months after this nightmare. I arrived at my office early, wanting only to unwind from the freeway drive before my first class. I was annoyed that someone was standing outside my office so early in the morning. But I spoke with her, and soon realized that there was something special about this slender, dark-skinned young woman with large, expressive brown eyes. I didn't know then what it was I saw in her. Now I know she revealed an inner strength, conveyed° an unspoken sentiment° that "You don't know me, but you can believe in me." It was magnetic. I knew that I would help in any way I could.

6   Rosa wanted to learn English. She wanted to do more than just get by. Her halting° English told me she could manage that already. She wanted to be able to read and write the language so that she could provide for her brothers. My basic reading class had been

recommended to her. She asked what materials she could get to work on even before the semester started.

7   Eager students are always easy to work with, and Rosa proved to be one of my most enthusiastic students. She kept me on my toes and constantly challenged me. She prodded me to provide more information, additional examples, better explanations. If I used a word she didn't understand, she would stop me. She would make me explain it so that she and her classmates could grasp its meaning. If we looked for the main idea in a paragraph and her answer was different from mine, she insisted on giving the reasons why she felt she was right and I was wrong. I could not always convince her that my answer was better. But I always encouraged her to ask questions whenever she was confused or unconvinced. While I looked forward to the class she had enrolled in, I was always exhausted at its conclusion.

8   Rosa advanced from our basic reading classes to the more difficult study-skills class. Then she moved through the writing classes offered in the department. She enrolled in the Early Childhood Program at the college. This is a program which can lead to certification as a child-care worker. Her progress in her classes was reflected in a steady stream of A's and B's.

9   It took Rosa three years to complete the course work that she needed to graduate. I made plans to attend the graduation ceremonies where she would receive her associate's degree. She insisted that I attend the graduation party her friend Alberto was giving. I said I would be honored to go.

10   The ceremony was typical, with boring speeches made for proud accomplishments. The party was something special. Rosa had come a long way in the three years I had known her. She had made some wonderful friends, had found a decent job at a nearby day-care center, and had provided a good home for her two brothers.

11   Rosa greeted me when I arrived. She wanted for me to meet everyone there, and she hinted at a surprise she had for me.

12   "Dr. P, may I present to you my brothers, Adolpho and Roberto."

13   "*Mucho gusto,*" I began.

14   "Right," said the smaller brother. "Call me Bobby. Nice to meet you, Doc. Say, you don't mind if me and Al 'mingle,' if you know what I mean?"

15   I knew, and encouraged them to meet and greet the others— especially the young ladies—in attendance.

16   I commented on how quickly her brothers had adjusted to life in the States. But Rosa seemed preoccupied°. I was puzzled until I

saw that we were walking toward an older woman who had the same brown expressive eyes as Rosa. It was her mother.

17   Rosa's mother had been captured by the Border Patrol and deported to Nicaragua. There, she was jailed. Rosa had been depressed over her mother's lack of the freedom she and her brothers enjoyed. She had located her mother and worked for close to three years to get her released. I don't know all the details of how she did it. Perhaps it is best that I don't. At the moment I met her, I did not care at all about how she had attained freedom. I was just overjoyed that she was here with her children.

18   Rosa entered San Diego State University, some ninety miles away. As often happens with students who move on, I saw very little of her. She was working hard toward a degree in early childhood education, I was on leave for a year, and our paths rarely crossed. Sometimes she would come by right before Christmas or at the end of a school year. She stopped by the office again yesterday, with a purpose. She carried two babies in her arms. The six-month-old twins were hers. Their huge, expressive brown eyes told me that before she did.

19   Rosa proudly told what had happened in the five years since her graduation. I listened enthusiastically as she told me about receiving a Bachelor of Arts degree, marrying Alberto, opening a child-care center with him, and giving birth to their twin sons. "And now," she said, "I want to tell you their names. This is Alberto," she said, nodding toward the larger twin. Then she looked toward the smaller one. Her eyes smiled as much as her mouth. "He is smaller, yes, but obviously more intellectual. That is why we have chosen to name him Eduardo."

20   I gasped, tried to collect myself°, but did not succeed. Rosa came to the rescue. She calmly explained that Alberto and she decided to name the baby after me because of all the help I had provided when she needed it most. I babbled something about how proud I felt. It was true.

21   Some people, I know, object to the flow of immigrants° entering our country. They forget that almost all of us came to America from somewhere else. We need every so often to be reminded of success stories like Rosa's. Like many of our ancestors, she fled an oppressive° government and poor economic conditions. She then worked hard to create a new life for herself. Hers is not an uncommon story. Many others like her have come to enrich their lives, and they have enriched our country as well.

Vocabulary Questions

A. Use context clues to help you decide on the best definition for each italicized word. Then, in the space provided, write the letter of your choice.

_____ 1. In the sentence below, the word *detection* (dĭ-tĕk′shən) means
    A. assistance.
    B. trust.
    C. discovery.
    D. noise.

> "They must move quickly and silently or risk detection by the Border Patrol." (Paragraph 3)

_____ 2. In the sentences below, the word *prodded* (prŏd′ĭd) means
    A. urged.
    B. left.
    C. prevented.
    D. paid.

> "[Rosa] kept me on my toes and constantly challenged me. She prodded me to provide more information, additional examples, better explanations." (Paragraph 7)

_____ 3. In the sentence below, the word *reflected* (rĭ-flĕk′tĭd) means
    A. shown.
    B. given.
    C. sent back.
    D. hidden.

> "Her progress in her classes was reflected in a steady stream of A's and B's." (Paragraph 8)

_____ 4. In the sentence below, the word *deported* (dĭ-pôr′tĭd) means
    A. saved.
    B. forced out of the country.
    C. kept in the country.
    D. invited.

> "Rosa's mother had been captured by the Border Patrol and deported to Nicaragua." (Paragraph 17)

_____ 5. In the sentence below, the word *attained* (ə-tānd′) means

    A. remembered.

    B. lost.

    C. gained.

    D. defined.

> "At the moment I met her, I did not care at all about how she had attained freedom." (Paragraph 17)

B. Below are words, or forms of words, from "Words to Watch." Write in the one that best completes each sentence. Then write the letter of that word in the space provided.

A. conveyed	B. halting	C. oppressive
D. sentiment	E. trek	

_____ 6. In _____ English, Luis explained to me that he still had a number of relatives living in Mexico.

_____ 7. On September 11, 2001, TV and radio stations around the country _____ the shocking news that terrorists had attacked the World Trade Center.

_____ 8. When Mr. Davis retired from teaching after thirty-five years, many expressed the _____ that he had been one of the best teachers the school had ever had.

_____ 9. On our cross-country _____, we started in Brooklyn, New York, and ended in Los Angeles.

_____10. Forcing a prisoner to stand for hours in a freezing room is an _____ form of punishment.

Reading Comprehension Questions

Central Point and Main Ideas

_____ 1. Which sentence best expresses the central point of the selection?
   A. Civil wars have destroyed many countries.
   B. Like many immigrants fleeing oppression, Rosa came to America and made a successful life for herself.
   C. Rosa finally brought her mother to the United States.
   D. Rosa married and gave birth to twins, one of whom she named after the author.

_____ 2. Which sentence best expresses the main idea of paragraph 4?
   A. The Border Patrol turned on bright searchlights.
   B. Rosa held on to her brothers but couldn't see her mother.
   C. Rosa and her brothers successfully crossed the border, but her mother was among those who did not.
   D. The guide was very cautious and waited for what seemed like hours until it seemed safe to continue crossing the border.

_____ 3. Which sentence best expresses the main idea of paragraphs 6–7?
   A. Rosa's English was not very good.
   B. Rosa always asked questions in class.
   C. The author encouraged Rosa to ask questions.
   D. Rosa was a very eager student.

Supporting Details

_____ 4. Of the group escaping Nicaragua with Rosa and her family,
   A. all members began a new life in the United States.
   B. the majority began a new life the United States.
   C. only five managed to begin a new life in the United States.
   D. only Rosa succeeded in reaching the United States.

_____ 5. According to the reading, Rosa's
   A. brothers had trouble adjusting to life in the United States.
   B. mother spent about three years in a Nicaraguan jail.
   C. graduation party was boring.
   D. husband has never met the author.

Signal Words

_____ 6. The relationship between the two sentences below is one of
  A. addition.   C. an example.
  B. time.   D. contrast.

  "Rosa advanced from our basic reading classes to the more difficult study-skills class. Then she moved through the writing classes offered in the department." (Paragraph 8)

Inferences

_____ 7. We can conclude that Rosa
  A. came to America because she knew that she wouldn't have to work hard once she got here.
  B. believed that she would become rich in America.
  C. worked extremely hard to make a home for herself and her family in America.
  D. forgot about her mother in Nicaragua once she was in America.

_____ 8. We can infer that the author
  A. wishes that other immigrants were more like Rosa.
  B. thinks that there are too many immigrants flooding into America.
  C. realizes that he will probably never see Rosa again.
  D. deeply admires Rosa and other immigrants who are like her.

_____ 9. The selection suggests that
  A. it is easy to enter the United States illegally.
  B. it is risky to enter the United States illegally.
  C. few people attempt to enter the United States illegally.
  D. most of the people who attempt to enter the United States illegally are caught and sent back to where they came from.

Argument

_____10. Write the letter of the statement that is the **point** of the following argument. The other statements are support for that point.
  A. After fleeing war-torn Nicaragua, Rosa worked hard to become successful in America.
  B. Although Rosa could barely speak English when she began her college coursework, she received her associate's degree in three years.
  C. Rosa entered San Diego State University and received a Bachelor of Arts degree in early childhood education.
  D. Together with her husband, Alberto, Rosa opened a child-care center.

Mapping

Major events of the selection are scrambled in the list below. Write them in their correct order in the diagram on the next page.

- Rosa's education toward a bachelor's degree
- Rosa's escape to the United States
- Rosa's education toward an associate's degree
- Rosa's visit with the twins
- Rosa's graduation and party

Central point: Rosa is an example of the many immigrants who come to America to escape oppression and then work hard to become productive citizens.

Discussion Questions

1. As Rosa reached the border of the United States, she realized that her mother was not with her. Should she have looked for her mother, or was she right to cross into the United States when she did?

2. How did Rosa's education prepare her for her career? What interests and qualities would lead someone to want to work in childcare?

3. The author writes that "we need . . . to be reminded of success stories like Rosa's." Why do you think he feels this way? What can we learn from reading Rosa's story?

Note: Writing assignments this selection appear on page 517.

Check Your Performance   ROSA: A SUCCESS STORY

Activity	Number Right	Points	Total
Vocabulary			
Part A (5 items)	_____	× 10 =	_____
Part B (5 items)	_____	× 10 =	_____
		SCORE =	_____ %
Reading Comprehension Questions			
Central Point and Main Ideas (3 items)	_____	× 8 =	_____
Supporting Details (2 items)	_____	× 8 =	_____
Signal Words (1 item)	_____	× 8 =	_____
Inferences (3 items)	_____	× 8 =	_____
Argument (1 item)	_____	× 8 =	_____
Mapping (5 items)	_____	× 4 =	_____
		SCORE =	_____ %

TOTAL SCORES: Vocabulary _____ % Comprehension _____ %

Enter your total scores into the **Reading Performance Chart: Ten Reading Selections** on the inside back cover.

7 The Lady, or the Tiger?

Frank R. Stockton

Preview

Imagine you are given this choice: The true love of your life will either die a violent death or leave you for another lover. Which would you choose? This is the decision that the princess in the following story has to make.

Words to Watch

smooth (1): pleasing; polished
opposite (3): located directly across from
choir (5): group of singers, often in a church
gasped (10): sharply drew in breath
charm (11): the power to delight or attract
pausing (15): stopping
Paradise (20): Heaven

1   Once upon a time, there was a king. He had smooth°, polite manners. But in his heart, he was very cruel.

2   He was a man who had many ideas, and he was sure that all of his ideas were right. One of his ideas was that he should give his people entertainment that would educate them. Here his cruel nature truly showed through. He loved the stories of the Roman soldiers of old. Those soldiers would fight with wild beasts to entertain an audience. The king decided to have contests like these, but to give them a special twist. Here is what the king did.

3   The king built a huge stadium, where all the people of the kingdom could sit and look down on a sand-covered floor. When a man was accused of a crime, the king announced a holiday. Everyone came to the stadium. The king sat on his special golden throne. The accused man entered the stadium. After bowing respectfully to the king, the man walked to the opposite° side of the stadium. There he faced two doors, exactly alike. While all the people watched, the man opened one of those doors.

4   What was behind the door? That depended upon the man's choice. Behind one of them was something terrible. It was an angry, hungry tiger, who instantly jumped on the unlucky

man and tore him to pieces. The watching crowd would scream in horror, then walk home sadly.

5   But if he opened the other door, he found a beautiful lady. Then he and she were immediately married as a reward for his innocence. It didn't matter if the man was already married. It didn't matter if he happened to be in love with someone else. The king had to have his way. The stadium was quickly filled with a priest, a choir°, and dancing girls playing golden horns. With the sound of happy bells ringing, the marriage was performed and the prisoner was freed. Children threw flowers on his path as he led his new bride home.

6   To the king, this seemed perfectly fair. The accused man made his own choice. When he opened a door, he did not know whether he was about to be eaten or married. What happened was entirely up to him!

7   Now, the king had a beautiful daughter who was as stubborn and strong-willed as he was. The young princess had fallen in love with a handsome young man, who loved her as well. Unfortunately, her young lover was a commoner, not highly-born enough to marry the daughter of a king. So the two met in secret.

8   Of course, the king learned about his daughter's lover. He had the young man arrested and thrown into prison. The date for the trial was set. The king had his servants search for

the biggest and most ferocious tiger available. Other servants were sent out to find the most beautiful young lady in the kingdom.

9   Naturally, everyone was interested in this case. And everyone knew that the young man was guilty. He proudly admitted that he had loved the princess, and she admitted it as well. But the king didn't care about that. He still wanted his trial.

10   On the day of the trial, everyone came to the stadium. The king and his court took their places. Everything was ready. When the prisoner walked in, everyone gasped° and whispered admiring comments. He was so tall, so young, and so handsome! How sad that he might be dead soon!

11   The young man walked to the center of the stadium. He turned to bow to the king. But he did not look at the king. Instead, he looked straight at the princess, who sat

his eyes, he asked the silent question: "Which door?"

Her arm lay over the railing in front of her. She raised her hand ever so slightly and made a tiny, quick movement to the right. No one but her lover saw her. Every other eye in the place was fastened on him. 14

He turned and walked quickly to the doors. All the people held their breath. Without pausing° for a moment, he threw open the door on the right. 15

And now comes the point of the story. Did the tiger come out of the door? Or did the lady? 16

The more you think about the question, the harder it is to answer. Think about it, reader. Try to put yourself in the shoes of this jealous, strong-willed woman. She had lost her man. But who should have him now? 17

During the past weeks, she had often imagined him opening the door to the tiger. What horror! What cruel, sharp teeth! 18

But even more often, she had imagined him opening the other door. She burned with anger as she imagined him rushing to meet the woman, his eyes sparkling with joy. She imagined the happy shouts and laughter from the crowd, the ringing of the wedding bells, and her own scream of misery lost in all that noise. 19

Wouldn't it be better for him to die, and to go wait for her in Paradise°? 20

beside her father. Are you surprised that she was there? You should not be. Remember that she was as strong-willed as her father. From the moment that her lover was arrested, she had thought of nothing but her plan. She had used all her money, charm°, and power to learn the secret of the two doors. And she had succeeded. She knew which door hid the tiger, and which door hid the lady.

12   Not only that—she knew who the lady was. It was the prettiest of all the young girls in her own court, and the princess hated her. She imagined she had seen the girl and her lover look admiringly at one another. Once or twice she had seen the two speaking. With all the passion in her strong-willed heart, the princess hated the girl.

13   The moment her lover saw the princess's face, he saw that she knew the secret of the doors. With a flash of

21   And yet . . . that awful tiger! Those screams! That blood!

22   She had thought about her decision for many days and many nights. But she had finally made her choice. She knew for sure that when the moment came, she would move her hand to the right.

23   It is not an easy question, and I am not wise enough to answer it. And so I leave it to you to decide. Which came out of that door—the lady, or the tiger?

Vocabulary Questions

A. Use context clues to help you decide on the best definition for each italicized word. Then, in the space provided, write the letter of your choice.

____ 1. In the sentences below, the word *commoner* (kŏm'ə-nər) means
   A. prince.
   B. robber.
   C. rich man.
   D. ordinary person.

   "The young princess had fallen in love with a handsome young man, who loved her as well. Unfortunately, her young lover was a commoner, not highly-born enough to marry the daughter of a king." (Paragraph 7)

____ 2. In the sentence below, the word *ferocious* (fĕ-rō'shəs) means
   A. pitiful.
   B. violent.
   C. weak with hunger.
   D. greedy.

   "The king had his servants search for the biggest and most ferocious tiger available." (Paragraph 8)

____ 3. In the sentences below, the word *admiring* (ăd-mīr'ĭng) means
   A. nasty.
   B. intelligent.
   C. approving.
   D. silly.

   "When the prisoner walked in, everyone gasped and whispered admiring comments. He was so tall, so young, and so handsome! How sad that he might be dead soon!" (Paragraph 10)

_____ 4. In the sentences below, the word *passion* (păsh'ən) means

    A. love.

    B. respect.

    C. powerful emotion.

    D. interest.

> "She imagined she had seen the girl and her lover look admiringly at one another. Once or twice she had seen the two speaking. With all the passion in her strong-willed heart, the princess hated the girl." (Paragraph 12)

_____ 5. In the sentences below, the word *misery* (mĭz'ə-rē) means

    A. surprise.

    B. pleasure.

    C. sickness.

    D. deep unhappiness.

> "She burned with anger as she imagined him rushing to meet the woman, his eyes sparkling with joy. She imagined the happy shouts and laughter from the crowd, the ringing of the wedding bells, and her own scream of misery lost in all that noise." (Paragraph 19)

B. Below are words, or forms of words, from "Words to Watch." Write in the one that best completes each sentence. Then write the letter of that word in the space provided.

A. charm	B. gasp	C. opposite
D. pause	E. smoothly	

_____ 6. The salesman spoke to us so _____ that we almost bought a product we had no use for.

_____ 7. Sam _____ed when he saw that that his five-year-old nephew was playing with matches.

_____ 8. Beverly tried to _____ a co-worker into switching work shifts so she would be free to go to a party.

_____ 9. Every so often during the course of his talk, the speaker would _____ to take a drink of water.

_____ 10. In football, the two teams' goal posts stand at _____ ends of the field.

Reading Comprehension Questions

Central Point and Main Ideas

1. Which sentence best expresses the central point of the selection?
   A. A cruel king forces those accused of crimes to open one of two doors.
   B. A beautiful young princess falls in love with a commoner, but her father, the king, throws the young man into prison.
   C. A young princess decides whether to save her true love or see him torn apart by a tiger.
   D. The reader must decide whether a young princess will choose to let her lover marry another woman or see him torn apart by a tiger.

2. Which sentence best expresses the main idea of paragraph 12?
   A. The princess is jealous of a young girl in her own court.
   B. The princess has once seen the young girl and her lover look admiringly at one another.
   C. The princess knows that the young girl was the prettiest of all the young girls in her own court.
   D. Once or twice the princess has seen her lover speaking with the young girl.

Supporting Details

3. Which of his subjects does the king force to choose between the lady and the tiger?
   A. Known criminals.
   B. Men who had been accused of a crime.
   C. Unmarried men.
   D. Men who had spoken out against the king.

4. After entering the stadium, the young man immediately
   A. opens one of two doors.
   B. looks straight at the princess.
   C. begs the king for mercy.
   D. proudly admits to the king that he loves the princess.

Signal Words

5. In the excerpt below, the word *so* indicates a relationship of
   A. addition.
   B. time.
   C. cause and effect.
   D. contrast.

   > "Unfortunately, her young lover was a commoner, not highly-born enough to marry the daughter of a king. So the two met in secret." (Paragraph 7)

6. The relationship between the two sentences below is one of
   A. cause and effect.
   B. addition.
   C. an example.
   D. contrast.

   > "He proudly admitted that he had loved the princess, and she admitted it as well. But the king didn't care about that." (Paragraph 9)

7. In the sentences below, the word *when* indicates a relationship of
   A. addition.
   B. time.
   C. cause and effect.
   D. contrast.

   > "Everything was ready. When the prisoner walked in, everyone gasped and whispered admiring comments." (Paragraph 10)

Inferences

8. The story suggests that the young man
   A. does not trust the princess.
   B. trusts the princess to save his life.
   C. has never really been in love with the princess.
   D. is a common criminal.

_____ 9. We can conclude that the king

    A. does not care about the happiness of his subjects.

    B. has a strong sense of right and wrong.

    C. loves his daughter very much.

    D. secretly hopes that the young man would choose the lady rather than the tiger.

Argument

_____ 10. Write the letter of the statement that is the **point** of the following argument. The other statements are support for that point.

    A. The king forces men to marry the ladies behind the door even if the men are already married.

    B. The king throws his own daughter's lover in jail.

    C. The king does not care about the rights of others.

    D. The king orders unlucky men to be torn apart by tigers.

Summarizing

Complete the following summary of "The Lady, or the Tiger?" by filling in the blanks.

A **summary** of a reading is a brief statement of its main ideas. The details in a summary follow the order of the original selection. That means the first answer can be found toward the beginning of the selection, and the later answers will be found further along in it. Fill in the answers after looking back at the story to find any you're not sure of.

Once upon a time, a cruel king built a huge stadium and forced any man who had been accused of a crime to open one of two doors. Behind one door was a beautiful lady, _____

_____

Behind the other door was a tiger who would tear the unlucky man to pieces.

Now, the king had a strong-willed daughter who had fallen in love with a young commoner. When the king found out that the two were seeing each other, he _____

_____

The date for the trial was set. While this was happening, the princess

_____

She also learned that the lady behind the door was to be the prettiest girl in her court. She had once imagined that _____

_____ She hated the girl.

On the day of her lover's trial, her lover bowed to the king, and then looked straight at the princess. He knew _____

_____

When the princess motioned to the right, the young man threw open that door. Did the tiger come out of the door? Or did the lady? It is up to the reader to decide.

Discussion Questions

1. Do you think the tiger came out of the door, or the lady? Support your answer. If you were the princess, which door would you send your lover to?

2. The princess must choose between two strong feelings: love and jealousy. In your experience, which emotion is more powerful? Explain.

3. In this story, the princess must make an impossible choice in a "no-win" situation. Have you ever been faced with a difficult choice in which no matter what you decided, you would be unhappy? Explain.

Note: Writing assignments for this selection appear on pages 517–518.

Check Your Performance

THE LADY, OR THE TIGER?

Activity	Number Right	Points			Total
Vocabulary					
Part A (5 items)	_____	×	10	=	_____
Part B (5 items)	_____	×	10	=	_____
		SCORE		=	_____ %
Reading Comprehension Questions					
Central Point and Main Ideas (2 items)	_____	×	8	=	_____
Supporting Details (2 items)	_____	×	8	=	_____
Signal Words (3 items)	_____	×	8	=	_____
Inferences (2 items)	_____	×	8	=	_____
Argument (1 item)	_____	×	8	=	_____
Summarizing (5 items)	_____	×	4	=	_____
		SCORE		=	_____ %

TOTAL SCORES: Vocabulary _____% Comprehension _____%

Enter your total scores into the **Reading Performance Chart: Ten Reading Selections** on the inside back cover.

8 Dawn's Story
Nancy Kerns

Preview

Today, at the age of 39, Dawn Cogliser is a woman who appears to have it all—a loving husband and kids, a comfortable home in the suburbs, and an interesting job. Yet it wasn't so long ago that Dawn's life was full of abuse and addiction. Here is her story.

Words to Watch

cozy (1): comfortable
chaotic (4): out of control; disordered
reluctantly (6): unwillingly
molested (9): sexually abused
intercede (10): to speak out in support of somebody
stable (17): calm and steady; normal
humiliated (23): deeply embarrassed
illegitimate (33): born to parents who are not married
passivity (35): allowing to happen without doing anything
restraining order (45): a court order that commands someone to keep away from someone else

1 Dawn Cogliser's home is the definition of "warm and cozy°." The living room walls are a cheerful purple; the hallway is a deep burnt orange. An enormous soft chair is just the right size for an adult and child to snuggle in together. Children's artwork covers the walls; colorful balloons, left over from the previous day's birthday party, dangle everywhere. A friendly cat and a St. Bernard puppy wander through the house.

2 Dawn herself sits in a comfortable rocking chair. When her husband and three children come in the door, the kids pile on top of her as if she were a sofa.

3 Dawn lifts 18-month-old Zane high in the air. "Ooh, I love you so much!" she tells the giggling little boy as she plants kisses on his

tummy. "Could you be any sweeter?" She hugs 6-year-old Sage and pulls 3-year-old Jemma into her lap. All the children are chattering at once, telling their mother about their day. After a few minutes, their father, Bob, a gentle bear of a man with a dark beard, herds the kids towards the kitchen. "Mommy's busy right now. Let's get a snack," he tells them. "Thanks, honey," Dawn says, giving her husband's hand an affectionate squeeze.

4   Seeing Dawn today in such a peaceful setting, surrounded by her loving family, it is nearly impossible to imagine where she's come from. Looking at her—beautiful, strong, confident, and funny—an observer would think, "She's always had her act together." But most of Dawn's 39 years of life have been anything but quiet. She is the survivor of a chaotic°, abusive childhood; an adolescence spent mostly on the street; and a marriage filled with savage violence.

5   Looking back, it seems as though Dawn was marked for misfortune from the beginning. Her parents divorced when she was a baby. Her father went off to "do his thing" and left Dawn with her mother. Dawn's mother, a pretty 21-year-old, "wasn't especially motherly," Dawn says. She quickly tired of being responsible for the little girl and signed custody over to Dawn's paternal grandmother, Peggy, and Peggy's husband, Dan.

Peggy and Dan moved with Dawn to Germany, where Dan was in the service.

6   Dawn remembers her early life with her grandparents as "pretty normal." She had started kindergarten in Germany when her mother, who had remarried, decided she wanted her 6-year-old daughter back. She filed for a change of custody, which the courts granted. Dawn's grandparents reluctantly° returned the child to the States.

7   But any hopes that Dawn had of a normal family life with her mother and stepfather were soon destroyed. Her stepfather, Larry, was a tall, strong man with four daughters from a previous marriage. He also had a huge thirst for alcohol and a mean streak a mile wide. He beat his wife, he beat his daughters, and he beat Dawn. Soon Dawn's mother became physically violent as well. After Larry

would hit her, she would turn her built-up anger on her little daughter.

8   As the years went by, Larry's drunken rages and beatings turned into something even uglier. When Dawn's mother was out of the house, he would often drunkenly stumble into the bedroom Dawn shared with one of her stepsisters. There he would rape them, warning them that no one would believe them if they told.

9   Sure enough, when Dawn went to her mother for help, her mother slapped her across the face and told her never to repeat such lies again. (Incredibly, years later, she told Dawn that although she knew Larry molested° his own daughter, she didn't think he would do the same to her.)

10   Dawn's grandparents tried to intercede°. The rest of Dawn's childhood and teen years were filled with trips to family court and short-lived changes of custody. She bounced between her mother's home in Georgia and the home of her grandparents, who were now living in New Jersey. Occasionally she stayed with her father and his new wife and family in Pennsylvania, but a savage knock-down fight with her father, in which she was eventually thrown out into the snow with no coat or boots, ended that.

11   Nowhere felt like a safe place to be, and Dawn began going wild.

Hanging out on the streets was preferable to going home; the highs that drugs and alcohol provided were a welcome change from the turmoil of her life. What began to feel "normal" was staying in shelters, sharing apartments with prostitutes and drug dealers, or sleeping on friends' couches, in abandoned vehicles, and in makeshift sheds in the woods. "I felt at ease in the streets," she says today. "There, I wasn't trapped. Being homeless had its own dangers, but they were nothing compared to the dangers of living with my family."

12   Surprisingly, Dawn managed to stay in school, eventually earning her high-school diploma. School was a place to take a shower, get something to eat, and see her friends. "I didn't get much of an academic education," she says, "but I did get educated. I learned that I couldn't depend on anyone. My trust in my fellow human beings was just about nonexistent." The night of her high-school graduation in New Jersey, her friends presented her with a bottle of blackberry brandy and a bus ticket to upstate Pennsylvania. There she crashed with some friends in a low-income housing project until the landlord caught on and threw her out. For most of the next year, she was homeless, sleeping on friends' couches during the day and running the streets with drug dealers and prostitutes at night. Eventually her

grandmother came looking for her, and she returned to New Jersey.

13   Soon after, around the time of her 19th birthday, a friend invited her to a beer party. She wanted Dawn to meet someone. That someone was Den, a tall, good-looking factory worker. He and Dawn hung out that evening, and soon became a couple.

14   What did Dawn like about Den? She smiles at the question. "Oh, he was perfect," she answers, not meaning it. "He'd party. He was as big a pothead as I was a drinker."

15   Turning more serious, she adds, "I guess he was an escape. I felt like I was back at Square One, you know— back living with my grandparents, with absolutely no sense of any future for myself."

16   Dawn had always been an energetic, Type A person. "I always wanted to go, to do, to be something," she says. "I just had no idea what." She began working three jobs so she could afford a cheap apartment in a bad part of town. Soon Den moved in with her.

17   On the surface, Den's back-ground seemed far more stable° than Dawn's. He was the youngest of seven children born to an Irish Catholic farm family. By the time Dawn met him, his mother was working as a waitress, earning her own money, and she and her husband lived very separate lives within their house. But Den's sisters told Dawn that their earlier lives had been quite different. When Den's mother had been at home full-time raising her large family, her husband had frequent outbursts of anger and had hit her often. Although Den, the "baby," hadn't witnessed the beatings, Dawn later wondered how much of his father's behavior Den was imitating.

18   At first, living with Den was okay, by Dawn's standards. He was irritable if he'd run out of pot, or when he was hung over. He would call Dawn names, curse at her, or push her when he was in a particularly bad mood. But compared to what Dawn had lived with, these things were nothing. And getting high together was fun.

19   Then Den's mother became seriously ill. Although she had seven children, no one was available to help. So Dawn quit her jobs, as well as the beauty school she had begun attending, and she and Den moved in with his parents. Living in the basement of Den's family home, Dawn began to get another sense of his family. His father spoke little, but when he would come downstairs to do his laundry or Dawn would go upstairs to use the bathroom, he would mutter angrily that she and Den were sinning by living together. In response to his pressuring, the two got married.

20   Eventually Den's mother died, and the newlyweds bought a house together. For Dawn, having a house of her own was a dream come true. Finally, she believed, she was in a place that no one could throw her out of or take away from her. She loved the house fiercely and threw herself into decorating it, dreaming of filling it with children and finally having a happy family life.

21   But soon the house itself was her only source of pleasure. With every passing day, Den became more foul-tempered. "It was as if with each bit of added responsibility, he became more angry," Dawn says. "First we buried his mother. Then we bought the house. Bills came in. I was working nights. Anything out of the ordinary routine would set him off."

22   A favorite target was Dawn's weight. "Everything was 'you fat pig' this and 'you fat pig' that," she says. He told her she was fat, she was ugly, and that her family was grateful to him for having taken her off their hands. When she threatened to leave, he laughed at her. "No one else will ever want a fat pig like you," he told her.

23   Desperate and humiliated°, Dawn went through a stomach-stapling surgery in order to lose weight. During the surgery, her doctor discovered that the years of beatings from Larry and her mother had damaged her spleen. The organ needed to be removed. She healed badly from the surgery, developing pneumonia and then a blood infection. And she didn't lose weight.

24   "And the funny thing is," Dawn says today, "I look back at photographs of me from that time, and I was not fat."

25   Two years into their relationship, Den graduated from curses and pushes and name-calling to physical violence.

26   It was Dawn's 21st birthday. She wanted to go out to celebrate. Den didn't. Dawn called a girlfriend, and the two drove to the Jersey shore and bar-hopped until the early morning hours. When Dawn arrived home, loud, drunk and happy, Den was furious that she had gone out.

27   As she stood in her kitchen doorway talking with him, Den shoved her out of the way so he could get to the beer in the refrigerator. She objected. The two began shouting at each other. Den snapped. He landed a backhand blow to her jaw, shoved her down on the bed, and began choking her, all the time shouting abuse in her face. He then stormed out, going to his parents' house for the night.

28   The next day, when he returned, Den showed remorse. In tears, he apologized. "I'm so sorry," he said. Dawn hugged him and said it was all right. "I'll never hurt you again," he promised.

29   "Never again," though, was soon in coming. Once Den began to hit Dawn, he seemed powerless to stop. A bad day at work, a meal served late, running out of marijuana—anything could set him off. When Dawn became pregnant, he was wild with anger. "He definitely did not want to be a father," she says. "He was really bitter about how hard his mother had had to work to raise her kids, and he took that out on me." She soon lost the baby.

30   After Den's first punch to Dawn's face, he avoided that area. He specialized in body shots, so her bruises were covered by her clothing. But as their fifth year together rolled around, he crossed that line as well. During one beating, he battered her so badly that her face was deeply bruised and both eyes were blackened. In response, he went out and bought Dawn a tube of Dermablend, a special makeup created to cover bruises, scars and birthmarks.

31   "I was something he needed to disguise," Dawn says bitterly. "Just like we disguised our relationship and pretended we were a normal couple."

32   During all these years, Dawn's life with Den followed a predictable routine. Den got up in the morning, got high, went to the factory, got high at lunch, came home, had dinner, and got high. Dawn came home from her job at the local cable company and began drinking Jack Daniels as she prepared dinner. If Den was in a good mood, Dawn might share his marijuana. If not, he might beat her up. Eventually she'd drink enough to pass out for the night. On weekends, the pair might have a cookout with friends with whom they'd get drunk and high, occasionally with crank (methamphetamine) as well as marijuana.

33   Their friends did not concern themselves with Dawn and Den's troubles. Dawn's grandparents occasionally saw her with bruises on her face and told her not to tolerate Den's beatings, so she avoided them. When she became acquainted with her half-brother (an illegitimate° son of her father's) and became close friends with him, he was horrified to realize what was going on. On several occasions he contacted Den and threatened him if he didn't stop hurting Dawn. In response, Dawn says, "Den worked me over." On one occasion, she was asleep when the brother telephoned. She was awakened by the infuriated Den's fists slamming into her. Soon he insisted that her brother never again come to their house. Like the robot she was beginning to feel like, she obeyed.

34   "At first, I fought back," she says, sounding weary just at the memory. "I was strong, and he was a skinny

guy. But like I always say—crazy beats strong any day. Against that kind of crazy rage, I didn't have a chance."

35   And so she went on helplessly, day after day. She was drinking more heavily than ever, and if she allowed herself to think about the future, she assumed that she would not live much longer. Either Den would beat her to death, or she would take her own life. But finally an evening came that shook her out of her passivity°.

36   By the time Den got home from work that night, he was already drunk. Shaking her head in disgust, Dawn went on cooking dinner. He grabbed a beer out of the refrigerator and stumbled toward their bedroom. Soon she smelled the sweet odor of marijuana floating down the hallway. Then she heard Den cursing angrily; he had spilled his pot. Dawn put dinner on the table and sat down to wait for him.

37   Den emerged from the bedroom and began weaving unsteadily toward the kitchen. He stumbled over his own feet and responded by furiously punching his fist through the wall. When he reached the dining table, he glared down at the plate Dawn had set for him.

38   "From then on," Dawn reports, "everything felt like it was happening in slow motion."

39   Den sent his filled plate flying into the wall, then connected a hard backhand blow to Dawn's jaw. Swallowing her own blood, she ran from the table, but he pounced on her in the hallway and threw her to the floor. Under his ceaseless rain of blows, her pain grew so intense that she lost consciousness.

40   When Dawn opened her eyes, she was lying on the ground in the woods behind her house. Den had dragged her there. He was still sitting on top of her, but he wasn't hitting her. Instead, she felt something cold and metallic pressing against her throat. In a moment of sudden clarity, she realized it was the barrel of her own handgun, a .357 Magnum that she had bought years ago for protection. She tried to scream, but as if she were in a nightmare, no sound came out.

41   CLICK! Den had pulled the trigger. But she was still alive. Then she remembered—the last time she had cleaned the gun, she had not reloaded it.

42   When Den realized there were no bullets in the gun, he went mad with rage. Using the barrel of the gun as a hammer, he beat Dawn until she passed out once again.

43   Hours later, Dawn awakened. This time she was alone. She lay in the cold dirt sobbing until no more tears would come. Then she crawled out of the woods and to the driveway of her house, where her car was parked. She found the car key that

she always kept hidden under the fender.

44   A glance in the window confirmed that Den had passed out on the couch and would not hear her start the car. As she pulled away from the house, she took a look at herself in the rear-view mirror. She told the bloody, bruised, swollen woman looking back at her that she would never allow anyone to hurt her again.

45   Over the years, Dawn had called the police for help many times. But she had always refused to press charges against Den. This time she was ready. She drove to a pay phone, called the police, and then went into the station to file charges. The next time she saw her husband was in court. She left with a restraining order° against him and possession of the house.

46   "I walked out of the courtroom feeling terrific," she remembers. "But then a victim's advocate who was working with me took my arm. She said, 'Don't take the elevator down. He's probably waiting for you there. Instead, take the back stairs.' I thought, 'But . . . I have a restraining order! Why do I have to hide from him?'" It was Dawn's first hint that legal remedies might not be enough to keep her safe.

47   Dawn returned to her house, relieved to be able to live in it alone. She changed the locks and hoped that Den would be scared enough by her pressing charges that he wouldn't bother her again.

48   Her hopes ended two weeks later. It was a beautiful fall afternoon, and she was standing at the kitchen sink, washing dishes. She had left the front door open to let in the warm autumn air. Suddenly Den was standing in the kitchen, holding a potted plant and a pumpkin.

49   He sweetly said, "I know fall is your favorite time of year, so I brought you these. Let's go for a ride."

50   Dawn tried not to look as frightened as she felt. She knew—and Den knew—that their neighbors were all at work. No one would hear her if she screamed.

51   "I said, 'You're not supposed to be here.'" As soon as the words left her lips, Dawn saw the flash of a kitchen knife as it flew past her face. Certain she was going to die, she collapsed in a faint. When she woke up, she was alone. "I can only guess that my fainting scared him enough that he left," she says.

52   Whatever small sense of security Dawn had felt was gone. Den began calling her at work, threatening to kill her if she did not let him have the house. Her supervisor started taping her incoming phone calls, and she even got on the phone to let Den know that his threats were being recorded. Nothing had any effect.

Dawn realized that a restraining order was not enough to protect her from someone as violent and out of control as Den.

53 Meanwhile, friends had begun to rally around Dawn. One was a co-worker, Bob. He was everything that was foreign to Dawn: a kind man, a college-educated man, from a loving and stable family. "I couldn't imagine what he saw in me," Dawn says now. But he liked her, and he was worried sick about her. He and other friends told her, over and over, to leave her house and get Den out of her life.

54 For a long time, Dawn couldn't hear them. "For them, the worst thing was that Den would eventually kill me," she says. "But I was more afraid of being homeless than dying."

55 Finally, though, Bob said something that got through to Dawn. He told her, "That is not a home. That is just a house. You can get another house. But you can't get another life."

56 Dawn realized he was right. But by then, she was utterly exhausted and beaten down. In her words, "I was a zombie—just completely out of gas." She told her friends to do what they thought was best. They quickly found her an apartment, cleared out the house, and moved her belongings into her new place.

57 During the whole process, Dawn was numb. "I remember the afternoon they were carrying my stuff into the apartment," she says. "I was sitting on the tailgate of the truck, looking at them. One of them was an old friend from way back. He was a typical New Jersey 'piney,' covered with tattoos, with blond hair down to his waist. The other was Bob, this college graduate from a good home. It was as though I was seeing a vision of my past and my future."

58 As she sat on that tailgate, she saw kids riding their bikes and heard neighbors greeting each other. She felt enormously out of place. "It was total Norman Rockwell suburbia, and it freaked me out. All I could think about was, 'Where's the liquor store?'" As soon as her friends left, she went in search of it, even talking the owner into taking her out-of-town check for a giant bottle of Jack Daniels.

59 Leaving the house had its intended effect; Den stopped threatening her. But merely being away from her abuser did not heal Dawn. Like the survivor of a war, she was suffering from post-traumatic stress. She continued to drink heavily. Her sleep was interrupted by nightmares of Den coming for her with a gun. She imagined that when the houseplant hanging in the window swayed in the night breeze, it was Den reaching out to grab her. Doctors gave her sleeping pills and antidepressants, "but they just whacked me out."

60   Throughout this dark time, Bob was a constant, patient presence. He would sit by her bed at night, rubbing her head and talking quietly to her, not leaving until she fell asleep. In the morning, she would find a note from him, promising to call her later in the day. "And he always did," she says.

61   Dawn found a therapist that she trusted and worked hard on regaining a sense of optimism and trust. Slowly the terrifying visions faded, and Dawn felt herself returning to life. Her divorce from Den became final in 1991; about a year later, Bob asked her to marry him. Deeply in love, she accepted. Together, the couple bought a house—this time, a place that would be a true home for them both. They joyfully planned to fill it with children.

62   But Dawn soon learned that having a good husband and a safe home did not mean life would be stress-free. Pregnancy did not occur; doctors said Dawn might never be able to have children. Then she miscarried. All her old demons resurfaced, telling her, "You're worthless; you're a loser." She turned to her old comforter: alcohol. "I drank myself into oblivion," she confesses. "I'd come home from work, pull down the shades, and drink. It was a terrible time in our marriage." Realizing how close she was to losing everything she loved, she called her therapist and began seeing her again, sometimes with Bob. "We worked it through," she reports. "But without the help of someone from outside, who could talk to us both, I don't know if we would have made it." Dawn began attending Alcoholics Anonymous meetings. She's been "clean and sober" for nine years.

63   She and Bob decided to adopt. But shortly before their first appointment with an adoption agency, she became pregnant with their oldest child, Sage. Two years later, along came Jemma, and in another two years a second son, Zane, joined the family.

64   Today Dawn, her husband and kids, the cat and the dog are all living in what looks a lot like the "Norman Rockwell suburbia" that once scared and confused her so. There's even a white picket fence around the house. But Dawn never forgets where she came from. And she has dedicated herself to helping others who might be trapped in similar nightmares. Dawn is now employed as a case manager for a soup kitchen in Camden, New Jersey. She attends college and is working on her certificate in addictions counseling, and hopes to earn a master's degree eventually and practice as a clinical therapist.

65   But dearest to her heart is the organization she has founded,

"Healing Mama." (The organization's website is **www.healingmama.org**.) Its purpose is to support mothers who are recovering from addiction. "I started 'Healing Mama' because as a mother myself, I realized that there's nothing like a screaming baby at 3 a.m. to make you want to dive into that bottle," she explains. "But that wasn't an option for me, so when the kids were smaller, I began looking around for support. There were mothers' groups in our area, but when I went to their meetings, I felt so out of it. Those women's concerns weren't like mine."

66   Dawn sent out an e-mail to the mailing lists of a couple of moms' organizations she knew about. In it, she asked if there were other women interested in a group focusing specifically on the concerns of moms recovering from addiction while trying to "keep it together" for their families. To her astonishment, she received hundreds of responses, some from as far away as Australia. Using letters and essays from some of those women, as well as her own writing, Dawn put together the first six-page "Healing Mama" newsletter. Since then she has produced 11 issues of the newsletter, which has grown to 14 pages. Some are sent out to subscribers, but most Dawn gives away when she does public speaking about her experience as a battered, addicted woman.

67   Sitting today in the warmth of her comfortable home, surrounded by the people who love her, Dawn struggles to find words to describe her feelings about where her life's journey has brought her. With a look at her laughing children and smiling husband, this once homeless, addicted, beaten woman finally says, "Having all this—I am living a life beyond all my dreams."

An Update

68   When we last caught up with Dawn in 2008, she was in college, working as a case manager at a New Jersey soup kitchen, and thinking about going on to graduate school to become a mental health therapist.

69   Much has happened since then.

70   Dawn shifted her focus towards nursing. She earned her associate's degree and RN (registered nurse) certification, then completed her BSN (Bachelor's of Science in Nursing). But she wanted more. She enrolled in a master's program to become a nurse practitioner (NP). An NP is a highly skilled professional who can diagnose and treat patients. To obtain the experience she needed to earn her NP certification, Dawn and her family moved to Arizona, where Dawn worked in a clinic on a Navajo reservation.

71   Living on the "rez" for two years was an incredible experience for the

entire family. "I'd come home from work and find Bob and the kids out in the hogan"—a traditional Navajo dwelling—"helping the medicine man prepare for an event. We participated in coming-of-age ceremonies. At the Navajo Nation fair, we were down in the rodeo ring in the midst of the Apache Crown dancers. The dust from that event is still on my boots—I won't clean them off!"

72   After being certified as an NP, Dawn and the family moved to the mountain town of Grants Pass, Oregon, where she works as a family practitioner. Bob and the children (Zane, now 12; Jemma, 14, and Sage, 16) are all "smitten" with the beauty of the area.

73   In addition to her professional accomplishments, Dawn has set off on a journey of personal transformation. As a teenager and young adult, she struggled with eating disorders. Later, as she bore her children, her weight climbed to a dangerous level. "It got to the point that I thought, well, here I am, a mom to three wonderful kids like I always wanted, but I can't fully enjoy it because of my physical condition."

74   So Dawn began a "slow evolution" aimed at achieving better health. Gradually she cut all processed foods out of her diet and found physical activities that she loved—most of all, hiking in the wilderness. When we spoke, she had just completed a long hike in the Oregon mountains with a 25-pound backpack, and was planning a solo 23-mile overnight hike. She is fit, strong, and healthy.

75   Dawn emphasizes that she didn't go on a "diet." "I don't believe in diets," she says firmly. "I wanted to change how I lived my life, permanently. I follow a program of recovery that focuses on my whole health, body, mind and spirit. Today I have replaced negative coping skills with healthier things that allow me to live up to my highest potential. This not only lets me do the things I love in life, but to share that with my family. I am passionate about encouraging others, like my patients, to learn how to live a healthier lifestyle no matter what their circumstances." Her "Healing Mama" outreach continues, but now in the form of a Facebook page. "In the course of healing this mama," she says, "I've learned it's not about where we came from yesterday, or where we are going tomorrow. It's about where we are today."

Dawn hikes in the mountains near her Oregon home.

Vocabulary Questions

A. Use context clues to help you decide on the best definition for each italicized word. Then, in the space provided, write the letter of your choice.

_____ 1. In the sentence below, the word *turmoil* (tûr′moil) means
   A. positive effects.
   B. calm.
   C. confusion.
   D. excitement.

> "Hanging out on the streets was preferable to going home; the high that drugs and alcohol provided were a welcome change from the turmoil of her life." (Paragraph 11)

_____ 2. In the sentences below, the word *nonexistent* (nŏn′ĭg-zĭs′tənt) means
A. earned.
B. remembered.
C. gone.
D. personal.

"'I learned that I couldn't depend on anyone. My trust in my fellow human beings was just about nonexistent.'" (Paragraph 12)

_____ 3. In the sentences below, the word *imitating* (ĭm′ə-tā′tĭng) means
A. talking about.
B. hiding.
C. copying.
D. remembering.

". . . her husband had frequent outbursts of anger and had hit her often. Although Den, the 'baby,' hadn't witnessed the beatings, Dawn later wondered how much of his father's behavior Den was imitating." (Paragraph 17)

_____ 4. In the sentences below, the word *remorse* (rĭ-môrs′) means
A. pride.
B. anger.
C. surprise.
D. sadness and guilt.

"The next day, when he returned, Den showed remorse. In tears, he apologized. 'I'm so sorry,' he said. Dawn hugged him and said it was all right. 'I'll never hurt you again,' he promised." (Paragraph 28)

_____ 5. In the sentence below, the word *tolerate* (tŏl′ə-rāt′) means
A. refuse.
B. complain about.
C. put up with.
D. admit to.

"Dawn's grandparents occasionally saw her with bruises on her face and told her not to tolerate Den's beatings, so she avoided them." (Paragraph 33)

B. Below are words, or forms of words, from "Words to Watch." Write in the one that best completes each sentence. Then write the letter of that word in the space provided.

A. chaotic	B. cozy	C. humiliated
D. interceded	E. reluctantly	

_____ 6. Although our first apartment wasn't large, by selecting the right furnishings and curtains, we made it rather _____.

_____ 7. An orderly scene became _____ when a circus elephant left the parade and charged through the crowd.

_____ 8. Roger was _____ when a girl he asked for a date told him that she didn't find him attractive.

_____ 9. After a teacher _____ on my behalf, the school decided not to suspend me for wearing a clown suit to class.

_____ 10. When my alarm rang at 6 a.m., I _____ got out of bed.

Reading Comprehension Questions

Central Point and Main Ideas

_____ 1. Which sentence best expresses the central point of the selection?
   A. After surviving an abusive marriage, Dawn Cogliser found happiness as a suburban wife and mother.
   B. Dawn Cogliser's story demonstrates that it is possible to survive physical abuse and addiction and go on to lead a happy and productive life.
   C. Once homeless, addicted, and beaten, Dawn Cogliser is now studying to earn a master's degree and practice as a clinical therapist.
   D. Dawn Cogliser ran wild as a teenager, but now has a responsible job helping others.

_____ 2. The main idea of paragraph 32 is that

    A. Dawn and Den's life together revolved around substance abuse and Den's abuse of Dawn.

    B. Den and Dawn were both steady workers, despite their substance abuse.

    C. Dawn and Den's friends never realized how often Den was abusing Dawn.

    D. Dawn was an alcoholic.

Supporting Details

_____ 3. Dawn finally decided to press charges against Den after he

    A. badly bruised her face and blackened her eyes.

    B. gave her a tube of Dermablend to hide the bruises he had given her.

    C. began choking her on her 21st birthday.

    D. tried to shoot her, then beat her with the gun when he found that it was not loaded.

_____ 4. In order to finally get free of Den, Dawn followed Bob's advice and

    A. moved to another state.

    B. got a restraining order against Den.

    C. moved out of the house she loved.

    D. bought a .357 Magnum handgun.

_____ 5. Today Dawn is

    A. leading a healthy lifestyle.

    B. working as a family practitioner in Grants Pass.

    C. using Facebook to reach out to mothers who are recovering from addiction.

    D. all of the above.

Signal Words

_____ 6. The relationship of the second part of the sentence below to the first part is one of

    A. time.

    B. addition.

    C. contrast.

    D. cause and effect.

    "She began working three jobs so she could afford a cheap apartment in a bad part of town. Soon Den moved in with her." (Paragraph 16)

Inferences

_____ 7. On the basis of paragraph 17, we can infer that
    A. Dawn later suspected that Den became physically abusive in part because his father was.
    B. Dawn realized that Den's family was far happier than hers.
    C. Den was not affected by his parents' relationship.
    D. A lack of money was the chief reason for problems in Den's family.

_____ 8. Paragraphs 22–24 suggest that
    A. stomach-stapling surgery always helps a person lose weight.
    B. Dawn always knew she was fat.
    C. Den bullied Dawn into believing that she was fat and needed stomach-stapling surgery.
    D. Den was really the one who needed stomach-stapling surgery, not Dawn.

_____ 9. We can conclude from this selection that
    A. recovering from abuse and addiction is something a person must do on her own.
    B. once a person has been abused, she cannot be trusted to raise children.
    C. victims of abuse often numb themselves with drugs and alcohol.
    D. Dawn herself was to blame for the fact that Den abused her.

Argument

_____ 10. Write the letter of the statement that is the **point** of the following argument. The other statements are support for that point.
    A. A victim's advocate advised Dawn to avoid her abusive husband, Den, by taking the back stairway out of the courthouse.
    B. Several people aided Dawn as she tried to overcome a life of abuse and addiction.
    C. Dawn's second husband, Bob, gave Dawn love and emotional support.
    D. Dawn's therapist helped her regain a sense of optimism and trust.

Outlining

Prepare an outline of "Dawn's Story" by filling in the missing details, which are scrambled in the list below:

- Den continues to threaten Dawn, so Dawn lets him have the house and moves out.
- Dawn meets and marries Den, a factory worker.
- Dawn's stepfather Larry beats and rapes her.
- With the help of counseling and Alcoholics Anonymous, Dawn stops drinking.

Central point: Dawn's story shows that it is possible to overcome physical abuse and addiction and go on to lead a happy and productive life.

1. Dawn's parents divorce when she is a baby.

2. Dawn briefly lives with her grandparents, but is then returned to the custody of her mother, who has remarried.

3. _____

   _____

4. Dawn bounces between living with her mother and Larry, her grandparents, and her father.

5. For a while, Dawn is homeless.

6. _____

   _____

7. Dawn and Den buy a house, but Den begins to physically abuse Dawn.

8. When Den pulls a gun on her, which is fortunately not loaded, Dawn presses charges against him.

9. _____

   _____

10. Dawn marries Bob, a gentle college-educated man.

11. Suffering from post-traumatic stress, Dawn continues to drink.

12. _____

    _____

13. Today Dawn is a happily married mother of three, who helps others cope with abuse and addiction.

Discussion Questions

1. Imagine that you were describing Dawn and her story to someone you know. What kind of person would you say Dawn is? How did she create something positive out of having survived abuse?

2. Have you had any direct or indirect experience with abuse? How did the abuse eventually end, if it did end? Did the abuser stop doing it, or did the person being abused find the strength to stop it?

3. Statistics tell us that the problem of abuse is widespread in modern society. What are some of the reasons why this might be so? What can be done to help put an end to it?

Note: Writing assignments for this selection appear on page 518.

Check Your Performance   DAWN'S STORY

Activity	Number Right	Points		Total
Vocabulary				
Part A (5 items)	_____	× 10	=	_____
Part B (5 items)	_____	× 10	=	_____
		SCORE	=	_____ %
Reading Comprehension Questions				
Central Point and Main Ideas (2 items)	_____	× 8	=	_____
Supporting Details (3 items)	_____	× 8	=	_____
Signal Words (1 item)	_____	× 8	=	_____
Inferences (3 items)	_____	× 8	=	_____
Argument (1 item)	_____	× 8	=	_____
Outlining (4 items)	_____	× 5	=	_____
		SCORE	=	_____ %

TOTAL SCORES: Vocabulary _____% Comprehension _____%

Enter your total scores into the **Reading Performance Chart: Ten Reading Selections** on the inside back cover.

9 Knowledge Is Power

Anna-Maria Petričić

Preview

When Anna-Maria Petričić was a student in Croatia, she read the words "Knowledge is real power." She wasn't sure what they meant, but she felt that their message was an important one. This is the story of the author's struggle to unlock the secret of those words.

Words to Watch

essence (1): central part
dismayed (4): discouraged
objective (5): unaffected by personal feelings
certified (8): guaranteed to be true
terse (9): short and direct
pretentious (10): meant to show off
imprinted (10): fixed
formidable (13): difficult
shrouded (16): covered
resolved (16): firmly decided
earnestly (17): seriously
steadfast (17): firm
quest (21): search
ascended (22): climbed
valedictorian (25): the student with the highest grades in a class, who gives a farewell speech at graduation

1 "Knowledge is real power," stated the bold letters on a bookmark showing Superman soaring upward from between two blocks of books. As I read this, a wave of energy swept over me. I studied the bookmark, trying to comprehend its exact meaning. It seemed like the essence° of life was revealed on that small piece of red and blue paper. But, as a teenager in high school, I had no idea what it meant. I only knew that this great excitement I was experiencing had something to do with knowledge.

I wanted the power that knowledge brought. For that to happen, I knew I had to attend college. I also knew that this would not be easy.

2 As a high-school student in Sisak, a town near Zagreb, Croatia, all I heard were horror stories about college. "First you sweat preparing for the entrance exams. If you survive that and are lucky enough to be accepted into college, you must deal with your teachers. They will be your enemies for the next four years. The first lesson they teach is that they will do everything they can to crush your confidence, to break your spirit, to make you quit." Such tales were commonly whispered in the high-school hallways by students aspiring to go to college.

3 I was shocked. Surely these stories could not be true. College was supposed to build my confidence in the process of attaining knowledge. Teachers were supposed to encourage me with their wisdom and compassion. They should prepare me for all challenges, not turn me against learning. The more I heard the whispers, the more convinced I became that I must not attend college in my homeland. If I wanted knowledge, I must attend a university in America.

4 I read all I could about colleges in the United States. I was dismayed°. The costs were staggering. Then I read about a small private university

in Iowa that was offering work-study scholarships for international students. The school would cover tuition, room, and board in exchange for a twenty-hour-per-week work commitment. In return, students had to show the university that they had sufficient funds in the bank for health insurance and personal expenses. Including airfare from Croatia to America, I calculated that I would need $2,000 per year.

5 I could hardly contain myself. I dashed into the kitchen that cold winter evening to proudly announce the news to my mother. "I am going to school in America!" My mother looked up at me while still working at the foamy sink full of dirty dishes. "Yes? And who is going to pay for that?" My mother's voice was heavy yet coolly objective°. In my excitement, I overlooked the fact

that my mother hardly made enough money to provide for our immediate needs. I brushed that thought aside, not willing to let it spoil my enthusiasm. I wanted my mother's support. Everything else would work out somehow.

6   I eagerly wrote a letter of inquiry to the American university. Within a couple of weeks, I received a thick envelope. My mother stood beside me while I ripped it open and spread the contents on the table. I picked up the letter on top. It was from the dean of the College of Arts and Sciences. I was blinded with tears as I read the words of encouragement and warm invitation to attend the college. I felt that at this school, my desire for education would be sacredly cherished and respected. My educational heaven was waiting in America. To get there, I knew that I had to be prepared to wage a long, hard battle. And I had to start now.

7   When she saw how understanding the university was, my mother took a strong stand of support. She vowed to do all she could to help make my dream become reality. She pointed to a row of dictionaries on the bookshelf. I reached for the Croatian-English dictionary and began the first of many long, difficult, and sometimes discouraging steps.

8   Although my English was quite good, the application forms sent by the college included many words I didn't understand. After a few hours of trying to interpret meanings and of translating, my head was spinning. I needed to take the Test of English as a Foreign Language (TOEFL) and the Scholastic Aptitude Test (SAT). I also needed to send a certified° translation of my high-school transcripts. The application deadline was in April. I was not even going to get my high-school diploma until June. Suddenly, everything was moving so fast. I couldn't keep up. "Maybe I should postpone this until next year," I thought. We had little money, and I wasn't even sure I could get accepted. I could attend the University of Zagreb for a year, and then transfer the units. My mother suggested that I send a letter to the admissions officer explaining the situation.

9   After sending the letter, I went to a branch of the University of Zagreb to get information about the entrance exams. I waited for an hour in a small, crowded room thick with cigarette smoke. Two ladies behind the admissions desk provided meager answers to students' questions. The women were apparently upset that all these students were wasting their precious gossip time. Their sharp, terse° responses offered no help. Instead, they managed to make the students feel guilty for even asking. I gave up

in my attempt to find out about the entrance exams.

10   As I walked toward the exit, I stopped to observe the college students who were in the hallway. They wore torn jeans, and they spoke in pretentious° sentences. Their eyes were dull, and they had lifeless smiles imprinted° on pale faces. Burning cigarette butts between their fingers were their only well-defined feature. I did not know whether to feel pity for them or for myself. As I left the building, I was both disappointed and humiliated. I had been there for only an hour, and I wondered how I would feel after four years of classes here. My dream had spoiled me. I wanted the luxury of being treated like a human being, and I knew just the place where that would happen.

11   Shortly, I received a new letter from my admissions officer in Iowa that provided encouragement. He asked me to continue my application process and said that I should not worry about my high-school transcripts. They could be mailed as soon as I graduated. What was needed at this time were my test results.

12   A month later, I took the TOEFL and SAT at the American school in Zagreb. I had studied hard and was satisfied with my performance. The results of both tests were sent directly to the university in America.

When the admissions officer received them, he called me to offer congratulations. I had done well. My application was almost complete. Besides my transcripts, which I knew would not be a problem, I needed only one more thing: the money.

13   My mother joined forces with me in this last, but most formidable°, obstacle. She borrowed money from a friend and deposited it in my account so that I could obtain the bank's confirmation that I had the funds required by the university. However, at the last minute, my mother's friend decided that he needed his money back. I was forced to withdraw the money.

14   When I returned home from the bank, I found my mother unwrapping our old paintings, works of art by Vladimir Kirin, a famous Croatian artist who was now deceased. Mother had collected his work for as long as I can remember and had planned to open an art gallery in the artist's memory. As I walked across the room, my mother's words stopped me in my tracks. "You have to write an ad for the weekend paper," she said. These paintings meant more than anything to my mother. Yet she was prepared to sell them so that I could live my dream.

15   The ad was placed. All we had to do was wait for the phone calls. But none came. After two weeks, we ran the ad again, but nothing happened.

16   I suddenly felt afraid. Even though I could see myself walking around the campus of my new college, even though I could visualize my new classrooms and teachers, it was all still just a dream. I felt like I was looking at slowly dissolving fog. The dream world was fading away, leaving the old, gray reality. I was trapped in truth that I could not accept. I became paralyzed as I imagined myself slowly sinking into ignorance and despair. I would become one of those lifeless, gray faces that walked daily to the bus station through the smog-shrouded° streets. I would work with people who can only afford to think about survival, people who see no values beyond the crispness of bills in their wallets. The ignorant world threatened to swallow me. Though scared to death, I resolved° not to yield. I was not just fighting for money; I was fighting for principle. I would not live a life of deliberate humiliation. I refused to expect from life only as much as others thought I should expect. I alone was responsible to make the best of my life. I had to continue my fight.

17   For the first time in my life, I earnestly° prayed for myself. I went to church in the early afternoon when I knew nobody would be there. My wooden-soled shoes echoed on the cold floor that led to the main altar. I knelt down and prayed. I prayed for money. That humiliated me because I have always thought it was selfish to pray for myself. My prayers had always been devoted to my friends, family, and to those who suffered. I never prayed for anything for myself because I believed that if God took care of the world, I would be taken care of. Now, I prayed for the most selfish thing of all, and I hated myself for it. Full of shame, I prayed, my eyes steadfast° on the ground. Finally, I gained enough strength to look up at the crucifix. I surrendered completely. I forgot all of my thoughts, and my mind began to flow toward some new space. The pressure dissolved. I felt as if I'd been let out of prison. I was free. My guilt and shame were gone, and my heart was beating with a new force. Everything was going to be fine.

18   In the meantime, my mother continued to search for funds. She called an old friend who owned a jewelry store. He had known me since I was a little girl and bragged that he would do anything for me. He fell silent when he heard my mother's request. He was sorry, but he had just invested all of his money in a new project. He tried to comfort my mother. "I would teach her myself if she were my daughter," he boasted. "School in America. Who does she think she is? She doesn't need college. A woman shouldn't be

too smart. She can marry either of my two sons. I promise she will have the freedom to go to church whenever she wants. What more could she need?" Struggling to remain civil, my mother thanked him sarcastically and walked away.

19 Time was slipping by. I had already obtained a United States visa, and I had made my air reservation. The travel agent found a cheap student rate. Despite strict regulations, she was willing to sell me a one-way ticket. My hopes were raised, but even the low-cost ticket had to be paid for. And there was precious little time.

20 That evening, my mother, brother, grandmother, and I gathered in the living room of our small apartment. I stared at the wall. My brother leaned against the doorway, cursing fate. My grandmother tightly held her prayer book, her lips moving slowly. Gloomy silence threatened to break down the walls. Then, as if by magic, words I did not think about came from my lips. "Mother, what about a credit card?" Unlike in America, it was not easy to obtain a credit card in Croatia. Yet my mother knew an influential officer of a local bank. Could he help us? My mother sighed and acknowledged that it was worth a try. Once again my hopes were raised.

21 I returned home from school the next day to find a sense of calm that our household had not known for weeks. Before I had a chance to ask, my mother smiled and nodded her head. My prayers had been answered. My quest° for knowledge was to become a reality.

22 Later that summer, I was on a flight to America. As the plane ascended° into the clouds, my thoughts turned from the quickly disappearing city I was leaving to the destination I knew so little about. I suddenly realized that I was all alone. I was on my own. Everything that happened from that moment on would be the result of my own actions. I was not afraid. My dream had come true, and I was about to begin living a different reality.

23 That reality turned out to be all that I wanted: loving teachers, a real chance to pursue knowledge, and wonderful friends from all over the world. My life as a college student is better than I ever dreamed. It has not been easy. In my job with the University Food Service, I have had to work very hard. I have also had to deal with some irresponsible and uninterested students who refuse to carry out their assignments or pretend they don't understand simple instructions. I must remind myself that this is the only way to keep my scholarship. But my work has many rewards. I have become assistant director of Food Services. I have also received the

first Outstanding Student-Employee Award presented by the university, and my work has been recognized by the Board of Trustees.

24   And I have begun the study of literature. This has opened up a new world for me. Every reading assignment, each class discussion has deepened my understanding of life. I am getting to know myself. I can feel the power growing inside me as I complete each assignment. I am beginning to live the magic of knowledge. In everything I learn, I find the same lesson: I can never know everything, but with what I know, I can accomplish anything. The old Superman bookmark is pasted on my door: "Knowledge is real power." Now I know what it means.

An Update

25   Shortly before this story's original publication, I graduated from Maharishi University of Management in Iowa, with a B.A. in Literature, *summa cum laude*, and valedictorian° of my class. Two days after completing my last class, I moved to Los Angeles to pursue my dream of becoming a writer.

26   One would expect that a young woman with the courage and wherewithal to leave home and country in order to attend college in America would easily make her way in Los Angeles. Well, I didn't know what culture shock was until I got to the West Coast. The traffic, the people, the high cost of living . . . Did I mention the traffic? Although I'd gotten my driver's license in Iowa, I'd never actually driven a car. And even if I had, I wouldn't have been prepared for the LA freeways.

27   I worked as a writer in Los Angeles (and a personal assistant, a bookkeeper, a healer, a creativity workshop leader, and whatever else it took to support a writer's life). After a few years, I met a man who was so determined to win my heart that he wouldn't take no for an answer. The other thing my husband was determined to do was to see me write and publish a novel. I have published three along with a number of novellas. We like to joke that he made me marry him, and I'm glad he did. Sixteen years later, our marriage thrives, although we haven't escaped challenges, including the fateful day in 2011 when both of us were laid off. Although terrifying, the loss of our jobs made us alert to new opportunities. I was offered a job at my alma mater as the executive director of the alumni department. Back to Iowa we went.

28   Three years later, another desire reappeared in my imagination. Just like many years before, as a schoolgirl in Croatia, I wanted to become a teacher of English as a Second Language (ESL). As I write this update, I'm in college again, this time as a graduate student of linguistics at the University of Iowa.

I work as a teaching assistant in the ESL department, and I teach academic reading to international students. It is sometimes hard to believe that my very own students can now read this essay, which was originally published 20 years ago. I'm honored by this privilege and wish that many, many students find inspiration in my story.

Vocabulary Questions

A. Use context clues to help you decide on the best definition for each italicized word. Then, in the space provided, write the letter of your choice.

_____ 1. In the sentence below, the word *comprehend* (kŏm′prĭ-hĕnd′) means
  A. forget.
  B. write down.
  C. understand.
  D. pass by.

  "I studied the bookmark, trying to comprehend its exact meaning." (Paragraph 1)

_____ 2. In the sentence below, the word *aspiring* (ə-spīr′ĭng) means
  A. paying.
  B. hoping.
  C. remembering.
  D. forgetting.

  "Such tales were commonly whispered in the high-school hallways by students aspiring to go to college." (Paragraph 2)

_____ 3. In the sentence below, the word *attaining* (ə-tān′ĭng) means
  A. recognizing.
  B. creating.
  C. pleasing.
  D. gaining.

  "College was supposed to build my confidence in the process of attaining knowledge." (Paragraph 3)

_____ 4. In the sentences below, the word *meager* (mē'gər) means
  A. complicated and difficult.
  B. complete.
  C. careful.
  D. brief and inadequate.

  "Two ladies behind the admissions desk provided meager answers to students' questions. The women were apparently upset that all these students were wasting their precious gossip time." (Paragraph 9)

_____ 5. In the sentence below, the word *civil* (sĭv'əl) means
  A. outraged.
  B. feminine.
  C. polite.
  D. superior.

  "Struggling to remain civil, my mother thanked him sarcastically and walked away." (Paragraph 18)

B. Below are words, or forms of words, from "Words to Watch." Write in the one that best completes each sentence. Then write the letter of that word in the space provided.

A. ascended	B. dismayed	C. essence
D. pretentious	E. steadfast	

_____ 6. Janelle was _____ when steam began pouring from the radiator of her car.

_____ 7. If you ask me, women who dress their dogs in designer outfits are being awfully _____.

_____ 8. Even though his friends make fun of him, Anthony is _____ in his belief that the earth has been visited by flying saucers.

_____ 9. The _____ of my grandfather's advice to me was that the more education I get, the better off I will be.

_____10. Derek started off as a clerk in the company, but after 15 years, he had _____ to the rank of vice-president.

Reading Comprehension Questions

Central Point and Main Ideas

_____ 1. Which sentence best expresses the central point of the selection?
   A. There are big differences between Croatia and America.
   B. Education is better in the United States than in Croatia.
   C. By not giving up, the author has achieved the college experience she dreamed of and can now pass on to her students.
   D. Colleges and universities should provide more low-cost opportunities for foreign students.

_____ 2. Which sentence best expresses the main idea of paragraph 2?
   A. The author spent her high-school years in Croatia.
   B. As a high-school student, the author heard horror stories about college.
   C. The author was told that college entrance exams were very difficult.
   D. The author was warned that college teachers would be her enemies.

_____ 3. Which sentence best expresses the main idea of paragraph 23?
   A. Even though she has become a successful college student, the author is disappointed with life in the United States.
   B. Despite difficulties, the author has found life as a student in the United States rewarding.
   C. The author's hard work in Food Services has paid off with an award and official recognition.
   D. The author must work hard to keep her scholarship.

Supporting Details

_____ 4. According to the author,
    A. one of her mother's friends was able to help her go to college in the United States.
    B. selling precious paintings helped her raise the money she needed.
    C. the University of Zagreb was willing to offer her a scholarship.
    D. she was able to raise the money to begin college in the United States through a credit card.

_____ 5. When the author's mother called an old friend who owned a jewelry store,
    A. he promised to help.
    B. he said he had just invested his money in another project.
    C. he said he would have helped if Anna-Maria were a boy instead of a girl.
    D. he promised to give Anna-Maria jewelry if she married one of his sons.

Signal Words

_____ 6. The sentence below expresses a relationship of
    A. cause and effect.
    B. addition.
    C. contrast.
    D. time.

    "I never prayed for anything for myself because I believed that if God took care of the world, I would be taken care of." (Paragraph 17)

_____ 7. The relationship of the second sentence below to the first sentence is one of
    A. addition.
    B. time.
    C. contrast.
    D. cause and effect.

    "In my job with the University Food Service, I have had to work very hard. I have also had to deal with some irresponsible and uninterested students . . . ." (Paragraph 23)

Inferences

_____ 8. Paragraph 23 suggests that the author
  A. nearly dropped out of school because of her job with the University Food Service.
  B. dislikes most American college students.
  C. found it very easy to balance work and studying.
  D. worked much harder than some American college students.

_____ 9. This selection suggests that college teachers in Croatia
  A. are more intelligent than college teachers in America.
  B. are less intelligent than college teachers in America.
  C. do not encourage their students to succeed.
  D. have less training than college teachers in America.

Argument

_____ 10. Write the letter of the statement that is the **point** of the following argument. The other statements are support for that point.
  A. Anna-Maria's mother borrowed money from a friend and deposited it in her daughter's bank account.
  B. Anna-Maria's mother put some paintings she owned up for sale to raise money for her daughter's education.
  C. Anna-Maria's mother tried hard to provide funds so that her daughter could go to college in America.
  D. Anna-Maria's mother obtained a credit card to help pay for her daughter's college expenses.

Mapping

The following scrambled statements make up a summary of the selection. Complete the map on the next page by writing the statements in their correct order.

- Anna-Maria decides to go to college.

- She decides that going to a special college in the United States would be better than attending the University of Zagreb.

- Finally in the United States, Anna-Maria has found her new life to be all that she had hoped for.

- As a high-school student, Anna-Maria is inspired by the words "Knowledge is real power."

- After much struggle, Anna-Maria and her family find the money needed to get her to the United States.

Central point: With persistence and support, Anna-Maria Petričić has achieved the education she wished for.

Discussion Questions

1. The author writes that when she went to high school, students told horror stories about college. When you were in high school, what was your view of college? Has your view of college changed since then? If so, in what ways?

2. At the conclusion of the selection, the author writes that she now knows the meaning of the words "Knowledge is real power." What does that statement mean to you?

3. The author had to work while going to school. Are you working while attending school? If so, how do you make time in your life for both responsibilities?

Note: Writing assignments for this selection appear on page 519.

Check Your Performance   **KNOWLEDGE IS POWER**

Activity	Number Right	Points	Total
VOCABULARY			
Part A (5 items)	_____	× 10 =	_____
Part B (5 items)	_____	× 10 =	_____
		SCORE =	_____ %
Reading Comprehension Questions			
Central Point and Main Ideas (3 items)	_____	× 8 =	_____
Supporting Details (2 items)	_____	× 8 =	_____
Signal Words (2 items)	_____	× 8 =	_____
Inferences (2 items)	_____	× 8 =	_____
Argument (1 item)	_____	× 8 =	_____
Mapping (5 items)	_____	× 4 =	_____
		SCORE =	_____ %

TOTAL SCORES: Vocabulary _____% Comprehension _____%

Enter your total scores into the **Reading Performance Chart: Ten Reading Selections** on the inside back cover.

10 What I Believe
John Langan

Preview

Sometimes we get caught up in day-to-day life, and we may take the wonder of our lives for granted. However, amazing stories of human kindness, strength, and love surround us. In this selection, the author reminds us, through a few of these amazing stories, just how awesome and mysterious our existence is.

Words to Watch

instincts (1): feelings
precious (3): prized
escorted by (9): along with
aced (9): did very well on; earned an A
unaffordable (10): costing too much
existence (13): life

1   People are truly remarkable, and the world is a truly mysterious place. Some of the mystery is the voice inside us that tells us to be kind to others and to treat others as we would ourselves want to be treated. It is the voice that says, "Love thy neighbor as thyself." On an almost daily basis, my religious instincts° are engaged by this voice and by the extraordinary behavior of people in the world around us. Here are just three examples:

2   **1.** A disturbed young racist shoots and kills nine people during a Bible-study class in Charleston, South Carolina. Still, the daughter of one of the victims finds it in her heart to say the following to this hate-filled man at his bond hearing:

3   "I forgive you. You took something very precious° away from me. I will never get to talk to her ever again. I will never be able to hold her again, but I forgive you, and have mercy on your soul. You hurt me. You hurt a lot of people. If God forgives you, I forgive you."

4   Many of the other victims said

similar things. Flowers piled up in front of the church where the killings took place, and in the midst of the flowers, someone placed a handwritten sign: "Darkness cannot drive out darkness; only light can do that. Hate cannot drive out hate; only love can do that."

5   The amazing grace and mercy in these reactions is beyond understanding. We are left in awe and wonder at such extraordinary humanity.

6   **2.** The author Alice Trillin tells a story of volunteering at a camp for children with disabilities. Alice was especially good friends with a little girl she called by her initial, L. L. had genetic diseases that kept her from growing normally and from digesting food. She had difficulty walking. She had to be fed through a tube at night. Still, the little girl was, in the author's words, "the most optimistic, most enthusiastic, most hopeful human being I had ever encountered." As Alice became closer to the little girl, she grew more curious about L. What had given her such strength, such joy and optimism? What was her secret? Then one day at camp, while the children were playing a game, L. asked Alice to hold her mail. On top of the pile was a note from L.'s mother. Alice glanced at it and saw the words that L.'s mother had written to her daughter. "If God had given us all the children in the world to choose from, L., we would only have chosen you."

Just as humans are capable of amazing forgiveness, they are capable of amazing love, and in the presence of it, we are left with awe and wonder and a sense of the great mystery in life.   7

3. The columnist Nicholas Kristof writes about a little Vietnamese girl whom he describes as "one of the mightiest people I've met, at 94 pounds. She has a towering presence, at a bit more than five feet tall."   8

The eighth of nine children in a very poor farming family in the Mekong Delta, she shone in school. However, her mother demanded— unsuccessfully—that she drop out of primary school and earn money as a live-in housemaid in distant Ho Chi Minh City. In eighth grade, her mom burned her schoolbooks to try to force her to drop out. But she borrowed books and continued to excel. She persevered even when her parents again burned her books in 12th grade. And as she graduated from high school, she prepared secretly for the college entrance examination. Her mother learned of this and lashed out, "I hope you fail the exams." Other students arrived at the exam location escorted° by cheering, doting parents. She arrived alone, sobbing. Still, she aced° the exam.   9

With no money from her parents, college seemed unaffordable°, but she saved every penny she could. She had long worked every vacation—   10 sometimes in a factory job by day and in a duck soup restaurant by night. At college, she confined herself to a food budget of $3.50—*per week*. Malnourished, she toppled over three times in the middle of class in a dead faint.

11   Professors and students discovered that she was starved and basically penniless—leaving her feeling humiliated. But it was a turning point because her teachers and classmates responded with kindness, sympathy, and help. She was then able to eat enough to keep from fainting in public. She shares a small room with two other young women, all sleeping on the floor next to each other. She studies until midnight, and then sets her alarm for 4 a.m. to resume studying. Her parents have now come around. They see she will soon become an English teacher and the best-paid member of the extended family.

12   Such heroic strength is an inspiration to the human spirit. Her amazing grace, along with the forgiveness and love in the previous examples, make me stand in awe. I am fully aware the world has many such stories. They reveal truths of the soul and heart that are beyond the power of reason to understand.

13   Not knowing about life after death, I believe in life before death. This world, this existence°—it's all a mind-blowing mystery. We know in the deepest parts of our hearts that life is ever so precious and fragile. We hear a voice within us that says we must do our best to care for one another and to never stop seeking truth. We know that one day we will be dust and ashes, and at the same time we know that we are in the midst of wonder. We are, as Shakespeare said, "such stuff as dreams are made of."

Vocabulary Questions

A. Use context clues to help you decide on the best definition for each italicized word. Then, in the space provided, write the letter of your choice.

_____ 1. In the sentences below, the word *humanity* (hyōō-măn'ĭ-tē) means
A. strangeness.
B. questions.
C. kindness.
D. anger.

"The amazing grace and mercy in these reactions is beyond understanding. We are left in awe and wonder at such extraordinary humanity." (Paragraph 5)

_____ 2. In the sentences below, the word *optimistic* (ŏp'tə-mĭs'tĭk) means
A. cheerful.
B. sad.
C. silly.
D. strange.

"Still, the little girl was, in the author's words, 'the most optimistic, most enthusiastic, most hopeful human being I had ever encountered.' As Alice became closer to the little girl, she grew more curious about L. What had given her such strength, such joy ...?" (Paragraph 6)

_____ 3. In the sentences below, the word *persevered* (pûr'sə-vîrd') means
A. became angry.
B. kept trying.
C. kept a secret.
D. asked for help.

"But she borrowed books and continued to excel. She persevered even when her parents again burned her books in 12th grade. And as she graduated from high school, she prepared secretly for the college entrance examination." (Paragraph 9)

_____ 4. In the sentence below, the word *doting* (dōt'ĭng) means
A. bored.
B. curious.
C. tearful.
D. loving.

"Other students arrived at the exam location escorted by cheering, doting parents." (Paragraph 9)

_____ 5. In the sentences below, the word *malnourished* (măl-nûr′ĭsht) means
   A. sick with a fever.
   B. very underfed.
   C. badly injured.
   D. embarrassed.

> "At college, she confined herself to a food budget of $3.50—*per week.* Malnourished, she toppled over three times in the middle of class in a dead faint." (Paragraph 10)

B. Below are words, or forms of words, from "Words to Watch." Write in the one that best completes each sentence. Then write the letter of that word in the space provided.

A. **aced**	B. **existence**	C. **instincts**
D. **precious**	E. **unaffordable**	

_____ 6. Ben's friend told him to go into the dark cave, but Ben's _____ told him not to.

_____ 7. I'd love to live right on the beach, but the houses there are _____.

_____ 8. After studying the driver's handbook for a month, Beth _____ her written driving exam.

_____ 9. Although they aren't worth much, my great-grandmother's gardening tools are _____to me.

_____ 10. During its five-year _____, a hummingbird may fly more than 8,000 miles to and from its winter nesting spot.

Reading Comprehension Questions

Central Point and Main Ideas

_____ 1. Which sentence best expresses the central point of this selection?
   A. The author believes we should love our neighbors as we love ourselves.
   B. People who are able to forgive those who have hurt them are remarkable.
   C. The author is inspired and awed by three examples of extraordinary love, forgiveness, and strength.
   D. We don't know what happens after death, so we should live life to the fullest.

_____ 2. Which sentence best expresses the main idea of paragraph 6?
   A. L. was optimistic even though she was very sick.
   B. Alice Trillin could not figure out how L. could be so hopeful when she was so sick.
   C. L. was at a camp for children with disabilities when Trillin met her.
   D. L.'s optimism was the result of her mother's love for her.

_____ 3. Which sentence best expresses the main idea of paragraph 9?
   A. In spite of her parents' discouragement, the young girl succeeded in gaining an education.
   B. The girl's parents told her to drop out of school, and when she didn't, they burned her books twice.
   C. Because the family was poor, the parents wanted the girl to leave school and work.
   D. The support and love that other parents showed to their children made the girl cry.

Supporting Details

_____ 4. The daughter of one of the victims of the racist Charleston mass murderer said that if
   A. other relatives of victims could forgive the murderer, then she could too.
   B. God could forgive the murderer, then she could too.
   C. light can drive out darkness, then love can drive out hate.
   D. it were up to her, she would sentence the murderer to life in prison.

_____ 5. The little girl L. was at a camp for children with disabilities because
   A. she was volunteering to help other children.
   B. her parents could no longer take care of her at home.
   C. her parents did not want her to attend school anymore.
   D. she had genetic diseases that kept her from growing normally.

_____ 6. In order to have enough money for college, the Vietnamese girl
      A. saved nearly every penny she earned.
      B. sometimes worked both a day job and a night job.
      C. confined herself to a food budget of $3.50 a week.
      D. All of the above.

_____ 7. Why have the Vietnamese girl's parents finally "come around"?
      A. They are proud of her courage and hard work.
      B. They realize she is soon going to be a well-paid English teacher.
      C. They are impressed that her professors and classmates have helped her out.
      D. They realize that their daughter has an amazing spirit and heroic strength.

Signal Words

_____ 8. The sentence below expresses a relationship of
      A. an example.
      B. cause and effect.
      C. contrast.
      D. time.

      "I will never be able to hold her again, but I forgive you …" (Paragraph 3)

Inferences

_____ 9. This selection suggests that
      A. it is quite rare to witness selfless acts of kindness.
      B. the author has no religious beliefs.
      C. amazing and heroic people are, in fact, all around us.
      D. it is often terribly difficult to rise above tragedy and pain.

_____ 10. When the author writes that the young Vietnamese woman's parents "have now come around. They see she will soon become an English teacher and the best-paid member of the extended family," we can infer that the parents
      A. have changed their minds because they now realize their daughter will earn good money.
      B. have changed their minds because the daughter is now well educated.
      C. regret being unkind to their daughter.
      D. will now encourage their other children to go to college.

Mapping

Events and stories presented in "What I Believe" are scrambled in the list below. Write them in the diagram in the order in which they appear in the selection.

- A Vietnamese girl works and struggles to achieve her dream of a college education.
- Alice Trillin reads a wonderfully loving note to L. from her mother.
- A Vietnamese girl's parents cruelly discourage her from obtaining an education.
- Alice Trillin wonders how L. can be so optimistic in spite of her disease.
- A racist kills nine people, but many of the victims' relatives forgive him.

Discussion Questions

1. The author tells three stories of "extraordinary behavior of people in the world around us." Which story did you find most impressive? Why?

2. Many of the relatives of the Charleston murders forgave the gunman. Would you be able to forgive someone if he or she killed someone you loved? Why or why not?

3. The author comments on the "mystery" of this world and the lives we live. What do you find to be mysterious about life? What is difficult for you to understand, explain, or believe? What inspiring stories have *you* heard about or witnessed—or even been involved in?

Note: Writing assignments for this selection appear on page 520.

Check Your Performance   WHAT I BELIEVE

Activity	Number Right	Points	Total
Vocabulary			
Part A (5 items)	_____	× 10 =	_____
Part B (5 items)	_____	× 10 =	_____
		SCORE =	_____ %
Reading Comprehension Questions			
Central Point and Main Ideas (3 items)	_____	× 8 =	_____
Supporting Details (4 items)	_____	× 8 =	_____
Signal Words (1 item)	_____	× 8 =	_____
Inferences (2 items)	_____	× 8 =	_____
Mapping (5 items)	_____	× 4 =	_____
		SCORE =	_____ %

TOTAL SCORES: Vocabulary _____ %   Comprehension _____ %

Enter your total scores into the **Reading Performance Chart: Ten Reading Selections** on the inside back cover.

Part Three

Relationships
and
Combined Skills

1 Relationships Tests

To think clearly and logically and have good comprehension, you need to understand relationships between ideas. The tests that follow will help you strengthen your understanding of the common types of relationships that have been explained in Chapters 7 and 8 of this book.

RELATIONSHIPS: Test 1

Here are some words that express relationships between ideas:

But (which means "however")
I liked Lola very much. *But* I did not love her.
Or: I liked Lola very much. *However,* I did not love her.

Because (which means "due to" or "the reason that")
Because I worked for ten hours straight, I was very tired.
Or: Due to working for ten hours straight, I was very tired.
Or: I was very tired. *The reason* was *that* I had worked for ten hours straight.

Therefore (which means "so" or "as a result")
My car would not start. *Therefore,* I decided to take a bus.
Or: My car would not start, *so* I decided to take a bus.
Or: My car would not start. *As a result,* I decided to take a bus.

Also (which means "and" or "in addition" or "moreover")
I wrote a paper for one of my classes. *Also,* I studied for an exam.
Or: I wrote a paper for one of my classes, *and* I studied for an exam.
Or: I wrote a paper for one of my classes. *In addition,* I studied for an exam.
Or: I wrote a paper for one of my classes. *Moreover,* I studied for an exam.

Then (which means "next" or "after")
In the morning, I drank some orange juice. *Then* I ate some oatmeal.
Or: In the morning, I drank some orange juice. *Next,* I ate some oatmeal.
Or: In the morning, I drank some orange juice. *After* that, I ate some oatmeal.

For each item below, write in the logical connecting word that describes the relationship between the two ideas.

1. **and, but, so**   Robert forgot to comb his hair, _____ he is wearing two different socks.

2. **and, but, so**   I would have sent you a text, _____ I don't have your number.

3. **and, but, so**   The sky grew very dark, _____ thunder boomed overhead.

4. **and, but, so**   Julia needed more vitamin C in her diet, _____ she bought a bag of oranges.

5. **also, then, because**   Nobody ate dessert _____ the meal had been so big.

6. **Also, Then, However**   Nikki left the front door unlocked. _____, she left a window open.

7. **Also, Then, However**   I closed my eyes. _____, I jumped off the high dive.

8. **Therefore, However, In addition**   I don't mind most bugs. _____, I am terrified of spiders.

9. **Therefore, However, In addition**   The roses are beautiful. _____, they smell very sweet.

10. **Therefore, However, In addition**   Nobody was paying attention. _____, the teacher suddenly announced a pop quiz.

RELATIONSHIPS: Test 2

For each item below, write in the logical connecting word that describes the relationship between the two ideas.

1. ***and, but, so***   My shirt is wrinkled, _____ my shoes are muddy.

2. ***and, but, so***   I'd like to eat that giant donut, _____ I'm trying to lose weight.

3. ***and, but, so***   Carlos wanted to surprise his grandmother, _____ he sent her flowers.

4. ***and, but, so***   Erin likes to cook fancy meals for friends, _____ she cooks simple meals for herself.

5. ***Also, Then, Because***   _____ hail damaged the peach trees, there is a shortage of peaches this year.

6. ***Also, Then, However***   Owning a pet teaches a child responsibility. _____, it helps a child learn kindness.

7. ***Also, Then, Because***   The first step is to make a plan. _____ you must follow that plan.

8. ***Therefore, However, In addition***   My phone was turned off. _____, I didn't realize you had texted me ten times.

9. ***Therefore,***
   However,
   In addition

   We will need 50 hot dogs for the picnic. _____,
   we will need two watermelons.

10. ***Therefore,***
    However,
    In addition

    I'd be glad to drive you to the reunion. _____,
    you'll have to help pay for gas.

RELATIONSHIPS: Test 3

For each item below, write in the logical connecting word that describes the relationship between the two ideas.

1. ***and, but, so*** I couldn't see the teacher, _____ I moved closer to the front of the classroom.

2. ***and, but, so*** My little brother believes in ghosts, _____ he also is afraid of vampires.

3. ***and, but, so*** Public speaking can be stressful, _____ there are ways to make it easier.

4. ***and, but, so*** The roads were too icy to drive on, _____ Michael canceled his trip.

5. ***Also, Then, However*** The crowd cheered for five minutes. _____, the band rushed back onto the stage for an encore.

6. ***Also, Then, Because*** Remember to put your napkin on your lap. _____, do not chew with your mouth open.

7. ***Also, Then, Because*** _____ the movie was so dull, the woman behind us started snoring.

8. ***Therefore, However, In addition*** Most of us eat too much sugar. _____, we tend to eat too much fat.

9. ***Therefore,***   I'm afraid of heights. _____, flying in an
   However,   airplane doesn't seem to bother me.
   In addition

10. ***Therefore,***   Ike stayed up until 3 a.m. watching zombie movies.
    However,   _____, he could barely stay awake in class.
    In addition

RELATIONSHIPS: Test 4

For each item below, write in the logical connecting word that describes the relationship between the two ideas.

1. ***but, then, and***   I love to play poker, _____ I'm not very good at it.

2. ***however, so, because***   The toilet overflowed, _____ I called the plumber.

3. ***Therefore, In addition, But***   Kara studied very hard. _____, she did well on the test.

4. ***Also, Then, Because***   The conductor raised his arms. _____, the orchestra began to play.

5. ***Therefore, Moreover, Because***   _____ I forgot her birthday, my girlfriend isn't speaking to me.

6. ***Also, Then, Due to***   Grandmother has a dog named Chico. _____, she has a cat named Chaco.

7. ***However, Next, So***   First, Ruben washed his hands. _____, he started to make dinner.

8. ***Then, Because, In addition***   It is dangerous to drink and drive. _____, it is just as dangerous to text and drive.

9. ***However,***
   As a result,
   Moreover

   It was raining very heavily earlier this evening. _____, the game started two hours late.

10. ***Therefore,***
    However,
    Also

    Gilbert isn't good at basketball. _____, he is excellent at soccer.

RELATIONSHIPS: Test 5

For each item below, write in the logical connecting word that describes the relationship between the two ideas.

1. ***But, However, In addition***   The car needs an oil change. _____, it needs a new air filter.

2. ***So, Then, Also***   Renee e-mailed her application for the job. _____ she waited nervously for a reply.

3. ***Therefore, But, However***   Edwin and Briana are both tall. _____, their children will probably be tall, too.

4. ***after, but, due to***   May is usually a beautiful month, _____ this year it has been cold and rainy.

5. ***Therefore, Also, Because***   _____it rained overnight, I don't have to water the flowers.

6. ***also, then, however***   Mimi speaks English and Vietnamese. She _____ knows American Sign Language.

7. ***also, so, because***   The babysitter canceled at the last minute, _____ Elise couldn't go to the party.

8. ***The reason is, After, So***   My brother has to attend summer school. _____ that he failed math.

9. ***However,***
As a result,
Moreover

Too much coffee can make you nervous. _____, it can stain your teeth.

10. ***Therefore,***
However,
In addition

I'd love to go get ice cream with you. _____, I have to stay home with my baby sister.

2 Combined-Skills Tests

Following are 15 tests that cover the skills taught in Part One and reinforced in Part Two of this book. Each test consists of a short reading passage followed by questions on any of the following: vocabulary in context, main ideas, supporting details, signal words, inferences, and argument.

COMBINED SKILLS: Test 1

Read the passage below. Then, in the space provided, write the letter of the best answer to each question that follows.

¹Many of us would probably pay huge amounts of money for everyday pleasures that are often taken for granted. ²Imagine that you had ten million dollars. ³You would probably pay at least two million dollars to always have a guaranteed good night's sleep that would leave you feeling refreshed and great when you wake up in the morning. ⁴To be forever free from pain (especially if you have had to deal with constant pain from headaches or an aching body), you would gladly part with three million. ⁵To know that good friends would always be there for you, you might not hesitate to give up another two million dollars. ⁶And in exchange for having satisfying work that you were good at and cared about and that paid you well, you would surrender your last three million.

 _____ 1. In sentence 3, the word *guaranteed* means
  A. possible.
  B. necessary.
  C. sure.
  D. costly.

 _____ 2. In sentence 5, the word *hesitate* means
  A. be slow to act.
  B. want.
  C. think.
  D. expect.

_____ 3. The sentence that best expresses the main idea of the passage is
  A. sentence 1.
  B. sentence 2.
  C. sentence 3.
  D. sentence 6.

 _____ 4. According to the passage, satisfying work is work that
  A. pays huge amounts of money.
  B. you are good at, that you care about, and that pays you well.
  C. few other people are skillful enough to do.
  D. puts you in charge of many other people.

_____ 5. According to the passage, freedom from pain is especially important to
  A. millionaires.
  B. the elderly.
  C. people who have had to deal with constant pain.
  D. poor people.

_____ 6. The passage suggests that
  A. millionaires often spend large amounts of money to buy life's simple pleasures.
  B. millionaires lead more enjoyable lives than people who aren't millionaires.
  C. not everyone experiences a good night's sleep, pain-free living, good friends, and satisfying work.
  D. you would need more than ten million dollars to buy some of life's simple pleasures.

_____ 7. We can conclude from this passage that
  A. ten million dollars is not really a lot of money.
  B. it is more important to get a good night's sleep than to have good friends.
  C. you would need more than ten million dollars to buy simple pleasures.
  D. we should be thankful for life's simple pleasures.

_____ 8. Three of the items below are supporting details for an argument. Write the letter of the statement that represents the **point** of the argument.
  A. Most people would gladly pay two million dollars to be certain of getting a good night's sleep.
  B. Freedom from pain would be worth three million dollars to most people.
  C. Most people would gladly pay millions to enjoy life's simple pleasures.
  D. To most people, having satisfying work would be worth three million dollars.

COMBINED SKILLS: Test 2

Read the passage below. Then, in the space provided, write the letter of the best answer to each question that follows.

¹A community college can be a better fit for some students than a four-year university. ²Why is this the case? ³First, class schedules are much more flexible. ⁴Because 80 percent of community college students work full-time or part-time, classes meet at night and on weekends. ⁵Next, hundreds of community colleges can be found right in the middle of—you guessed it: communities. ⁶These colleges are easy to access by car or local transit systems. ⁷If students don't want to or can't afford to go away to college, community college is an excellent choice. ⁸Community colleges also offer a wide range of course choices. ⁹There are classes in arts, sciences, humanities, business, and social science. ¹⁰In addition, there are practical training and certificate programs. ¹¹These include medical assistance, auto mechanics, and home health care. ¹²Such programs can quickly lead to employment. ¹³Finally, after graduation, students can transfer to four-year schools. ¹⁴Applying to and transferring into a B.A. or B.S. program can be easy. ¹⁵In some cases, it is even guaranteed.

  1. In sentence 3, the word *flexible* means
   A. easily changed to fit one's needs.
   B. easy to understand.
   C. expensive and time-consuming.
   D. confusing and frightening.

  2. In sentence 6, the word *access* means
   A. do well in.
   B. get to.
   C. walk past.
   D. afford.

  3. The main idea of the passage is stated in
   A. sentence 1.
   B. sentence 3.
   C. sentence 7.
   D. sentence 8.

_____ 4. Eighty percent of students at community colleges
   A. work full-time or part time.
   B. transfer to four-year schools.
   C. have dropped out of a four-year school.
   D. live within a mile of their community college.

_____ 5. Community colleges offer certificate programs and practical training that
   A. can lead to acceptance at four-year schools.
   B. cost more than other degree programs.
   C. are far more interesting than many traditional degrees.
   D. can lead to jobs after graduation.

_____ 6. The relationship of sentence 5 to sentence 4 is one of
   A. addition.
   B. contrast.
   C. an example.
   D. time order.

_____ 7. When the author comments on the flexible schedules at community colleges, he is implying that
   A. most students prefer night classes.
   B. schedules are not as flexible at four-year schools.
   C. night and weekend classes may not be a good idea.
   D. students should probably not work and go to school at the same time.

_____ 8. Three of the items below are supporting details for an argument. Write the letter of the statement that represents the **point** of the argument.
   A. Tuition is lower at community colleges than at four-year colleges.
   B. Night and weekend classes allow students to keep their jobs and still go to school.
   C. Students can save money by going to community colleges.
   D. Students can live at home while attending classes.

COMBINED SKILLS: Test 3

Read the passage below. Then, in the space provided, write the letter of the best answer to each question that follows.

¹People who are poor in the material sense can be rich in other ways. ²Kara King, for instance, had lost her job and her health. ³She had cancer, whose treatment had taken her hair; and without money to see a dentist, she'd lost her teeth. ⁴She needed a bone marrow transplant. ⁵Her husband, Tom, was also out of work. ⁶Badly needing a pleasant outing, Tom and Kara and their children scraped together enough money to afford dinner at a local truck stop. ⁷Over their meal, they talked about the challenges facing them, but they also joked and laughed and enjoyed each other's company.

⁸When the meal was over, Kara asked for the check. ⁹Then their waitress told her that a man sitting at the counter had already paid for their meal. ¹⁰Kara was offended and told the waitress, "I don't take charity." ¹¹But the waitress just shrugged.

¹²On the ride home, Kara kept thinking about what had happened, and she became even angrier. ¹³She had lost almost everything, but she still had her pride. ¹⁴So once she was home, she called the truck stop and demanded to know who had paid the bill. ¹⁵The waitress said, "He's still here," and handed him the phone.

¹⁶The man turned out to be a long-distance trucker, far from his own family. ¹⁷Kara asked him indignantly why he had paid for their meal, and he told her. ¹⁸"He had never heard a family discuss problems that openly," Kara reported, "and he just wanted to do something for us. ¹⁹This man couldn't believe we could laugh at life like that." ²⁰The trucker went on to tell Kara, "I counted. ²¹Your children said they loved you 20 times." ²²When she heard that, Kara's anger dissolved: "I broke down, and I cried."

_____ 1. In sentence 1, the word *material* means
    A. cloth.
    B. physical.
    C. expensive.
    D. selfish.

_____ 2. In sentence 22, the word *dissolved* means
    A. got confused.
    B. went away.
    C. mixed.
    D. increased.

_____ 3. Which sentence expresses the main idea of this selection?
A. A stranger can often brighten someone's life.
B. Kara became angry when she learned a stranger had paid for her family's meal.
C. Family affection and love are worth far more than money.
D. Kara has had a very difficult experience.

_____ 4. The family did not have much money because
A. the father refused to look for work.
B. there were a lot of children to support.
C. they had spent all of their money on a new house.
D. both parents had lost their jobs.

_____ 5. What made Kara cry?
A. Her cancer had made her weak and dependent.
B. She was told that her children had said they loved her 20 times during dinner.
C. She was angry that a total stranger had treated her like a charity case.
D. Cancer had taken away everything from her but her pride.

_____ 6. The relationship of sentence 9 to sentence 8 is one of
A. time.
B. addition.
C. an example.
D. contrast.

_____ 7. We can infer from this selection that Kara
A. is a strong person.
B. feels sorry for herself.
C. often tells jokes to avoid thinking about her situation.
D. will not survive her cancer.

_____ 8. The truck driver's comments and actions suggest that he
A. often eavesdrops on families eating dinner.
B. wishes he could have had dinner with Kara and her family.
C. misses his own family while on the road.
D. is a cancer survivor.

COMBINED SKILLS: Test 4

Read the passage below. Then, in the space provided, write the letter of the best answer to each question that follows.

> [1]Traditionally, men preferred to be the only breadwinners in their families. [2]Men, however, have discovered several benefits to having a working wife. [3]First of all, of course, a working wife's income can raise her family's living standards. [4]Also, men with working wives are more free to try changing careers. [5]The woman's income can tide the family over economically during his career change. [6]Third, should a husband lose his job, some of the problems of unemployment are offset by his wife's earnings. [7]Among other things, her earnings provide him with the luxury of search time to locate the best job opportunity. [8]Finally, sharing the burden of earning a living has allowed men to discover the joys of fatherhood. [9]In earlier times, fathers were so busy earning a living that they had little chance to know their children.

_____ 1. In sentence 6, the words *offset by* mean
  A. made worse by.
  B. created through.
  C. shown in.
  D. made up for.

_____ 2. The main idea of the passage is stated in
  A. sentence 1.
  B. sentence 2.
  C. sentence 3.
  D. sentence 9.

_____ 3. According to the passage, in the past
  A. no women worked outside the home.
  B. women wanted their husbands to be the family's sole breadwinner.
  C. men wanted their wives to work outside the home, but few employers would hire them.
  D. fathers were so busy earning a living that they had little chance to know their children.

_____ 4. The relationship of sentence 2 to sentence 1 is one of
      A. cause and effect.
      B. contrast.
      C. time.
      D. an example.

_____ 5. The relationship of sentence 8 to sentence 7 is one of
      A. cause and effect.
      B. time.
      C. addition.
      D. an example.

_____ 6. We can conclude from this passage that
      A. in the past, most men stayed in the same job all their lives.
      B. women often earn more than men.
      C. women often earn less than men.
      D. most men want to go back to the old days when they were the sole breadwinners of their families.

_____ 7. We can infer from this passage that
      A. without a wife's income, most families would fall into poverty.
      B. in the past, many children spent more time with their mothers than with their fathers.
      C. in the past, most children never saw their fathers.
      D. with both parents working, children now see little of either parent.

8. In the following group, one statement is the point, and the other statements are support for the point. Identify the point with a **P** and each statement of support with an **S**.

    _____ A. Having a working wife frees men to try changing careers.

    _____ B. Having a working wife raises a family's standard of living.

    _____ C. Men have discovered several benefits to having a working wife.

    _____ D. Having a working wife enables men to discover the joys of fatherhood.

COMBINED SKILLS: Test 5

Read the passage below. Then, in the space provided, write the letter of the best answer to each question that follows.

¹Sometimes it seems as though there is nothing you can do to make the world a better place. ²After all, the world is huge and complex. ³And the problems its seven billion people deal with seem infinite. ⁴War and starvation are widespread. ⁵Terrorists murder innocent people. ⁶Hatred, prejudice, and fear tear lives and entire communities apart. ⁷And the fact is that many of these same problems have been around for centuries. ⁸You may at times feel hopeless. ⁹What on earth can you possibly do to turn these horrors around? ¹⁰The honest answer is: not much. ¹¹No one individual has the power to end wars or find the solution to widespread hunger and poverty.

¹²Does that mean there is nothing you can do to make the world a better place? ¹³Hardly. ¹⁴While one single person's actions may not solve a world problem, if every individual did at least one small good thing every day, things would get better. ¹⁵Perhaps you cannot end loneliness among the elderly, but you can spend some time with an aged friend or relative. ¹⁶You cannot end hatred, but you can show love in hundreds of small ways. ¹⁷Smile at a stranger. ¹⁸Plant flowers. ¹⁹Help the bagger at the market. ²⁰Simply listen to a friend who is troubled talk about her problems. ²¹Remember that things can indeed be changed. ²²No darkness on earth has to be eternal. ²³It may not be lit up by one small flame, but millions of small flames can help drive the darkness out.

_____ 1. In sentence 3, the word *infinite* means
    A. interesting.
    B. confusing.
    C. unimportant.
    D. endless.

_____ 2. In sentence 22, the word *eternal* means
    A. forever.
    B. strange.
    C. obvious.
    D. inside.

_____ 3. Which sentence best expresses the main idea of the selection?
    A. There is very little one person can do to change the world.
    B. Our world is huge, complex, and full of problems.
    C. We can make the world a better place.
    D. We can show love in many small ways.

_____ 4. There are more than _____ people in the world.
       A. seven million
       B. seven billion
       C. 100 million
       D. 100 billion

_____ 5. If every individual did at least one small good thing every day,
       A. things would get better.
       B. big problems still could not be solved.
       C. he or she would feel better about his or her life.
       D. things would get worse.

_____ 6. The relationship of sentence 17 to sentence 16 is one of
       A. contrast.
       B. an example.
       C. time.
       D. cause and effect.

_____ 7. The passage suggests that
       A. the author is disappointed with most people.
       B. world problems are not that big.
       C. not everyone does one small good thing every day.
       D. things will never get better.

8. In the following group, one statement is the point, and the other statements are support for the point. Identify the point with a **P** and each statement of support with an **S**.

     _____ A. We can plant flowers.

     _____ B. We can show love in many little ways.

     _____ C. We can listen to a friend talk about her problems.

     _____ D. We can smile at a stranger.

COMBINED SKILLS: Test 6

Read the passage below. Then, in the space provided, write the letter of the best answer to each question that follows.

¹Many NBA basketball players may look like giants, but the tallest human who ever lived was nearly two feet taller than the average NBA star. ²Robert Wadlow (1918-1940) grew to the height of just under nine feet by the time he was 21 years old. ³However, perhaps as impressive as his height was Robert's quiet determination to be seen as an ordinary and likable young man, rather than a freak of nature. ⁴At age 13, Robert towered above his classmates at seven feet, four inches, but he did his best to blend in by becoming a Boy Scout and making friends through his everyday interests in stamp collecting and photography. ⁵By the time Robert was 18, he was more than eight feet tall. ⁶Strangers would stare, whisper, and even run from him, screaming in fear. ⁷Rather than reacting angrily, Robert made an effort to speak kindly and quietly to everyone he met, even those who appeared afraid of him. ⁸In time, his friendly ways earned him the nickname "The Gentle Giant." ⁹Throughout his brief life, Robert continued to try to move attention away from his height and focus on his education, hobbies, and friends. ¹⁰Sadly, medical complications related to his size claimed his life at 22. ¹¹Upon his death, his family honored the wish Robert had had to be seen as normal. ¹²They had all of his clothes and personal items destroyed so that they would not be collected and displayed in a "freak" show.

_____ 1. In sentence 10, the word *complications* means
  A. practices.
  B. decisions.
  C. problems.
  D. improvements.

_____ 2. Which statement best states the main idea of the passage?
  A. Robert Wadlow, the tallest human who ever lived, wished to be seen as an ordinary and likable young man, not as a freak of nature.
  B. Robert Wadlow, who grew to the height of just under nine feet, was the tallest human being who ever lived.
  C. Even though he was extremely tall, Robert Wadlow had rather everyday interests.
  D. Throughout his brief life, the "Gentle Giant," Robert Wadlow, struggled to overcome people's fear of him.

_____ 3. Robert Wadlow's interests included
   A. playing basketball.
   B. weight lifting.
   C. stamp collecting and photography.
   D. performing as "The Gentle Giant" in plays.

_____ 4. Upon his death, Robert Wadlow's parents honored his wish to be seen as normal by
   A. refusing to discuss his life with anyone outside the family.
   B. destroying his clothes and personal items so that they would not be collected and displayed in a freak show.
   C. publishing Robert's autobiography.
   D. burning all their photographs of Robert.

_____ 5. The relationship of sentence 3 to sentence 2 is one of
   A. addition.
   B. an example.
   C. contrast.
   D. cause and effect.

_____ 6. This passage suggests that
   A. Robert liked to impress people with his great height.
   B. it was difficult for some people to view Robert as normal.
   C. Robert knew that his life would be brief.
   D. Robert's own family looked upon him as a freak.

_____ 7. We can conclude from this passage that
   A. Robert actually did not mind being treated like a freak.
   B. Robert was bitter at the treatment he received from others.
   C. Robert was sensitive and patient.
   D. Robert wanted to play professional basketball.

_____ 8. Three of the items below are supporting details for an argument. Write the letter of the statement that represents the **point** of the argument.
   A. Robert Wadlow became a Boy Scout.
   B. Robert Wadlow spoke kindly and quietly to everyone he met, even those who appeared afraid of him.
   C. Robert Wadlow wished to be seen as normal.
   D. Robert Wadlow tried to get people to focus on his education, hobbies, and friends rather than his height.

COMBINED SKILLS: Test 7

Read the passage below. Then, in the space provided, write the letter of the best answer to each question that follows.

¹When a forest burns, we expect to see firefighters trying to stop the flames. ²Despite past practices, park officials today sometimes allow forest fires to burn, or they even set fires themselves. ³During the 1900s, forest fires were put out immediately. ⁴That meant that fires did not grow very large. ⁵They didn't burn up all the dead trees and plants on the forest floor. ⁶So when a fire did start, a huge amount of fuel—those dead trees—was waiting right there on the ground. ⁷Today, officials sometimes let small fires burn. ⁸These fires clean up the forest floor. ⁹This periodic cleanup is part of the cycle of nature. ¹⁰Sometimes, officials go a step further. ¹¹They actually direct firefighters to set legal fires to get rid of dead trees and also to kill off aggressive trees. ¹²Aggressive trees are trees that grow quickly and block the sun from other trees and plants. ¹³When these trees burn, more sunlight gets through for smaller plants. ¹⁴The smaller plants prosper, and so do the animals that eat those smaller plants. ¹⁵In fact, research shows that an area has three times as many plants and animals after a fire as before a fire. ¹⁶The managers at Yosemite National Park in California burn more than 2,500 acres every single year.

_____ 1. In sentence 9, the word *periodic* means
    A. happening from time to time.
    B. happening every day.
    C. rare.
    D. terrible.

_____ 2. In sentence 14, the word *prosper* means
    A. die out.
    B. grow smaller.
    C. stay as they are.
    D. do very well.

_____ 3. The main idea of this passage is found in
    A. sentence 1.
    B. sentence 2.
    C. sentence 7.
    D. sentence 16.

_____ 4. According to the passage, an area of forest has
     A. three times fewer plants and animals after a fire as before a fire.
     B. twice the number of plants and animals after a fire as before a fire.
     C. about the same number of plants and animals after a fire as before a fire.
     D. three times as many plants and animals after a fire as before a fire.

_____ 5. One reason for letting small fires burn is that
     A. they quickly become big fires.
     B. they make it easier for aggressive trees to take over the forest.
     C. they clean up the forest floor.
     D. it is a waste of manpower to put them out.

_____ 6. The relationship of sentence 2 to sentence 1 is one of
     A. contrast.
     B. an example.
     C. cause and effect.
     D. addition.

_____ 7. The relationship of sentence 6 to sentence 5 is one of
     A. contrast.
     B. addition.
     C. cause and effect.
     D. time.

_____ 8. We can conclude from this passage that
     A. firefighters would rather put out small forest fires than large forest fires.
     B. there are more legal forest fires today than there were during the 1900s.
     C. during the 1900s, great forest fires occurred because there were many dead trees and plants on the forest floor.
     D. all of the above.

COMBINED SKILLS: Test 8

Read the passage below. Then, in the space provided, write the letter of the best answer to each question that follows.

> ¹In India, boys are valued as gifts from God. ²Girls, however, are considered at best a disappointment. ³Centuries of tradition determine that boys be given better treatment throughout life. ⁴In their parents' house, they are, for instance, fed first so that they get the largest portions and choicest bits of food. ⁵In the recent past, strangling newborn girls was common in rural India, where there was not enough food to go around. ⁶Today, although the outright murder of girl babies may occur less often, female children are done away with in other ways. ⁷For instance, a baby girl who falls ill is often left untreated. ⁸On the other hand, her family would do anything possible to get medical care for their male children.

_____ 1. Which sentence best states the implied main idea of the selection?
   A. The way girls are treated has been improving in India.
   B. In India, boys have traditionally been favored over girls.
   C. In the past, newborn girls were sometimes strangled in rural India.
   D. Indian families do everything possible to get medical care for their male children.

_____ 2. According to the passage, the treatment of girls was worst in
   A. Indian cities.
   B. today's India.
   C. rural India.
   D. wealthy Indian families.

_____ 3. Indian parents display their preference for boys over girls by
   A. feeding their sons first.
   B. giving their sons the largest portions.
   C. giving their sons the choicest bits of food.
   D. all of the above.

_____ 4. The relationship of sentence 7 to sentence 6 is one of
   A. contrast.
   B. an example.
   C. addition.
   D. time.

_____ 5. The relationship of sentence 8 to sentence 7 is one of
   A. contrast.
   B. time.
   C. cause and effect.
   D. an example.

_____ 6. This passage suggests that in India
   A. girls have often been seen as an economic burden.
   B. many more girls are born than boys.
   C. parents were harshly punished for strangling newborn girls.
   D. there are far more adult males than females.

_____ 7. We can conclude from this passage that
   A. in India today, the economic position of women has greatly improved.
   B. most Indian parents do not want their sons to marry.
   C. India is a country with large numbers of poor people.
   D. even in India today, baby girls die more often than baby boys.

8. In the following group, one statement is the point, and the other three statements are support for the point. Identify the point with a **P** and each statement of support with an **S**.

   _____ A. In India, baby girls who fall ill are often left untreated, while parents will do anything possible to get medical care for their sons.

   _____ B. In India, boys are fed first and get the largest portions of food.

   _____ C. In India, boys are favored over girls.

   _____ D. In India, baby girls are sometimes strangled.

COMBINED SKILLS: Test 9

Read the passage below. Then, in the space provided, write the letter of the best answer to each question that follows.

[1]Two of America's most beloved presidents were assassinated— Abraham Lincoln and John F. Kennedy. [2]There are a number of striking coincidences in President Lincoln's and President Kennedy's lives. [3]Lincoln was elected president in 1860, 100 years before Kennedy was elected president. [4]Both had a vice president named Johnson. [5]Andrew Johnson was Lincoln's vice president. [6]Lyndon Johnson was Kennedy's. [7]Both Johnsons were Southern Democrats who had served in the U.S. Senate. [8]Andrew Johnson was born in 1808, and Lyndon Johnson was born in 1908. [9]Furthermore, both Lincoln and Kennedy supported racial equality and were advocates of civil rights. [10]Both were shot in the head, both on a Friday and in the presence of their wives. [11]John Wilkes Booth, Lincoln's killer, was born in 1839, a hundred years before Kennedy's killer, Lee Harvey Oswald, was born. [12]Both assassins were themselves killed before they could be brought to justice.

_____ 1. In sentence 2, the word *striking* means
    A. hitting.
    B. dull.
    C. common.
    D. remarkable.

_____ 2. In sentence 9, the word *advocates* means
    A. victims.
    B. critics.
    C. supporters.
    D. historians.

_____ 3. The main idea of the paragraph is stated in
    A. sentence 1.
    B. sentence 2.
    C. sentence 3.
    D. sentence 10.

_____ 4. According to the paragraph, both Lincoln and Kennedy
   A. were born in Illinois.
   B. had the same birthday.
   C. had a vice president who had served in the Senate.
   D. were Southerners.

_____ 5. TRUE OR FALSE? Both Lincoln and Kennedy were killed by men who themselves were killed before they could be put on trial for murder.

_____ 6. The relationship of sentence 9 to the sentences before it is one of
   A. time.
   B. an example.
   C. contrast.
   D. addition.

_____ 7. We can conclude that
   A. both Lincoln and Kennedy were assassinated because of their support for civil rights.
   B. both Andrew Johnson and Lyndon Johnson were part of an assassination plot.
   C. Booth and Oswald did not share the feelings of love that most Americans had for these two presidents.
   D. few Southerners were glad when Lincoln and Kennedy were assassinated.

_____ 8. We can infer that
   A. the deaths of John Wilkes Booth and Lee Harvey Oswald left many unanswered questions.
   B. Booth and Oswald acted alone in carrying out their assassinations.
   C. neither Andrew Johnson nor Lyndon Johnson was a believer in civil rights.
   D. both Booth and Oswald were killed to protect others who were involved in the assassinations.

COMBINED SKILLS: Test 10

Read the passage below. Then, in the space provided, write the letter of the best answer to each question that follows.

¹Everyone knows doctors wear white coats. ²Medical students even take part in a White Coat Ceremony to celebrate their career choice. ³But why exactly do doctors wear them? ⁴The white coat has become a symbolic doctor's uniform for several reasons. ⁵To begin with, the color white is associated with good health. ⁶Doctors and nurses in the 1800s often wore black coats and uniforms. ⁷Patients often died then, and people connected the color black with death and mourning. ⁸Doctors didn't like that connection, so they began wearing white in the early 1900s. ⁹Another reason for wearing white was that it was associated with science. ¹⁰Around the same time, other doctors started wearing white coats because they looked like scientists' lab coats. ¹¹Doctors wanted to remind people that medicine was a science. ¹²Finally, white coats set doctors apart from other people. ¹³The white coat was a sign that the doctor was not your friend or neighbor or a member of your family. ¹⁴Today, the white coat is a sign of a doctor's skill in dealing with health issues, just as a police uniform is a sign of an officer's authority to enforce the law.

_____ 1. In sentence 5, the word *associated* means
   A. connected.
   B. described.
   C. explained.
   D. organized.

_____ 2. In sentence 14, the word *authority* means
   A. lack of control.
   B. kindness.
   C. confusion.
   D. power.

_____ 3. The main idea of this passage is found in
   A. sentence 1.
   B. sentence 2.
   C. sentence 4.
   D. sentence 14.

_____ 4. According to the passage, people in the 1800s
      A. knew that chances were good that doctors would be able to cure them.
      B. connected doctors who wore black with death and mourning.
      C. preferred doctors who wore white to doctors who wore black.
      D. suggested to their doctors that they wear white clothing, not black.

_____ 5. Doctors started to wear white coats
      A. in the mid-1800s.
      B. in the late 1800s.
      C. within the past 50 years.
      D. in the early 1900s.

_____ 6. The signal words used for this passage are mainly
      A. time words.
      B. addition words.
      C. contrast words.
      D. example words.

_____ 7. The passage suggests that in the 1800s
      A. doctors weren't very successful at healing people.
      B. medical science was nearly as advanced as it is today.
      C. doctors didn't try very hard to heal their patients.
      D. doctors killed most of their patients.

_____ 8. Three of the items below are supporting details for an argument. Write the letter of the statement that represents the **point** of the argument.
      A. In the 1800s, scientists wore white lab coats.
      B. People connected black with death and mourning.
      C. Doctors had good reasons for switching from black to white coats.
      D. The color white was associated with health.

COMBINED SKILLS: Test 11

Read the passage below. Then, in the space provided, write the letter of the best answer to each question that follows.

[1]Doctors race against the clock in order to perform organ transplants. [2]They have to find a proper recipient and then fly the organ to wherever that person lives. [3]Doctors refrigerate the organs, but, for example, a refrigerated heart stays fresh for only four hours. [4]They can't freeze the organs because ice crystals form and damage the tissue. [5]That's why researchers are studying the common U.S. and Canadian wood frog. [6]The wood frog has "freeze tolerance." [7]In the winter, it becomes basically a frog-shaped ice cube. [8]About 2/3 of the water in its body freezes, and it looks dead. [9]But it's not. [10]The frog's liver makes glucose, a natural sugar that acts like antifreeze. [11]It makes some of the frog's body water remain liquid and limits the ice formation in the frog. [12]It also keeps the cells from shrinking, so that ice crystals don't tear the tissue. [13]When the temperature warms up, the frog simply thaws out and hops away. [14]Researchers would like to make that happen in donor organs. [15]If doctors could freeze organs, medical teams would have more time to transport them. [16]Many more lives would be saved. [17]Keeping organs fresh is a major obstacle to organ transplants, but wood frogs just might help researchers solve that problem.

_____ 1. In sentence 2, the word *recipient* means
   A. someone who learns something.
   B. someone who gives something.
   C. someone who receives something.
   D. a means of transportation.

_____ 2. In sentence 6, the word *tolerance* means
   A. interest.
   B. ability to put up with something.
   C. disability.
   D. dislike for something.

_____ 3. The sentence that best expresses the main idea of the passage is
   A. sentence 1.
   B. sentence 2.
   C. sentence 5.
   D. sentence 17.

_____ 4. Scientists can't freeze organs because
   A. ice crystals form and damage the tissue.
   B. the organs are needed right away for transplants.
   C. it is currently against the law to do so.
   D. no method has been found to safely thaw them out.

_____ 5. The relationship between sentence 9 and sentence 8 is one of
   A. contrast.
   B. time.
   C. cause and effect.
   D. addition.

_____ 6. We can infer from this passage that at present
   A. there is little need for transplanted organs.
   B. most transplanted organs are human hearts.
   C. some organs don't get to the people who need them in time.
   D. in the future, fewer people will need organ transplants.

_____ 7. We can conclude from this passage that
   A. in the future, it may be possible to freeze human organs.
   B. some organs can be frozen while others can't.
   C. wood frogs are only one of many animals which have "freeze tolerance."
   D. human beings can be trained to have "freeze tolerance."

8. In the following group, one statement is the point, two statements are support for the point, and one statement is unrelated to the point. Identify the point with a **P**, each statement of support with an **S**, and the unrelated statement with an **X**.

   _____ A. The glucose in a wood frog's body limits ice formation during freezing weather.

   _____ B. The glucose in a wood frog's body keeps the cells from shrinking during freezing weather.

   _____ C. Glucose is also produced by plants.

   _____ D. Glucose is a sugar which helps the wood frog survive freezing weather.

COMBINED SKILLS: Test 12

Read the passage below. Then, in the space provided, write the letter of the best answer to each question that follows.

> [1]There are real differences between people with high self-esteem and those with low self-esteem. [2]Researchers have found that people with good self-concepts tend to be more accepting of others. [3]They are also more accepting of their own failures. [4]However, they fail less, since they tend to be better achievers than people with low self-esteem. [5]High self-esteem is also related to independence and open-mindedness. [6]People with positive self-images will be more willing to accept criticism and suggestions. [7]On the other hand, persons with low self-esteem are sensitive to criticism and blame themselves whenever things go wrong. [8]And because they lack confidence, they will give in to pressure and can often be easily influenced. [9]They also seek flattery and criticize others in order to improve their self-images.

_____ 1. The main idea of the passage is found in
   A. sentence 1.
   B. sentence 2.
   C. sentence 3.
   D. sentence 5.

_____ 2. According to the passage, people with high self-esteem
   A. blame themselves when things go wrong.
   B. often criticize others.
   C. are very sensitive to criticism.
   D. are more accepting of their own failures.

_____ 3. According to the passage, people with low self-esteem
   A. are usually independent and open-minded.
   B. easily give in to pressure.
   C. fail less than other people.
   D. like to flatter others.

_____ 4. The relationship of sentence 7 to sentence 6 is one of
   A. an example.
   B. cause and effect.
   C. addition.
   D. contrast.

_____ 5. The relationship between the two parts of sentence 8 is one of
    A. contrast.
    B. cause and effect.
    C. time.
    D. an example.

_____ 6. This passage suggests that people with high self-esteem
    A. never fail.
    B. are more likely to feel anger toward members of different ethnic groups and races.
    C. are harder to bully than people with low self-esteem.
    D. have a hard time recovering from setbacks.

_____ 7. This passage suggests that people with low self-esteem
    A. are more likely to follow leaders who express anger toward others.
    B. are more likely to succeed than people with high self-esteem.
    C. can never develop high self-esteem.
    D. are very accepting of different ethnic groups and races.

8. In the following group, one statement is the point, and the other three statements are support for the point. Identify the point with a **P** and each statement of support with an **S**.

    _____ A. People with high self-esteem tend to be better achievers than people with low self-esteem.

    _____ B. People with high self-esteem share several positive personality traits.

    _____ C. People with high self-esteem tend to be open-minded and independent.

    _____ D. People with high self-esteem are more willing to accept criticism and suggestions.

COMBINED SKILLS: Test 13

Read the passage below. Then, in the space provided, write the letter of the best answer to each question that follows.

¹Studies show that rich people give away a smaller percentage of their incomes than poor and middle-income Americans do. ²It's as if well-off people decided, "I've got mine, and that's all that matters." ³Where does such a cold attitude come from? ⁴One reason might be the theory of "trickle-down economics." ⁵This theory suggests that if the government gives more benefits to the wealthy, the rich will spend more. ⁶The benefits will then eventually "trickle down" to poorer people by creating more jobs for them. ⁷However, research shows that this theory doesn't work. ⁸In fact, it has caused the poor to become poorer. ⁹Other studies have shown that wealthy people often feel they have a "right" to their money, and that less wealthy people are somehow to blame for not being born rich. ¹⁰Finally, many wealthy people exist in a bubble of privilege. ¹¹They live near other wealthy people, go to school with wealthy people, and socialize with wealthy people. ¹²They have never been anything but wealthy and cannot imagine ever being in need. ¹³Poor and middle-income people, by contrast, do know what it is to be in need. ¹⁴Unlike many rich people, they can imagine themselves slipping into real poverty. ¹⁵Therefore, they are more generous with what little they have. ¹⁶They know that someday they, too, might need a helping hand.

_____ 1. In sentence 6, the word *eventually* means
   A. immediately.
   B. sooner or later.
   C. sadly.
   D. never.

_____ 2. Which sentence best expresses the main idea of this selection?
   A. Wealthy people can often be unkind and coldhearted.
   B. Poorer people are more likely to be generous than wealthy people, because they know what it's like to be poor.
   C. There are certain reasons why wealthy people are often less generous than poorer people.
   D. Poor and middle-income people are more thoughtful than the wealthy.

_____ 3. The theory of "trickle-down economics" is that if the government gives the wealthy more benefits, the wealthy will spend
   A. more money.
   B. less money.
   C. their money on themselves.
   D. more time helping the poor.

_____ 4. Some wealthy people live in a "bubble of privilege" because they
   A. are uncomfortable being around poor people.
   B. are always near other wealthy people.
   C. refuse to be more generous with their money.
   D. have a "right" to their money.

_____ 5. Some wealthy people feel that less wealthy people
   A. are usually foolish with their money.
   B. need to work harder.
   C. are their equals.
   D. are to blame for not being born rich.

_____ 6. The relationship of sentence 4 to sentence 3 is one of
   A. contrast.
   B. addition.
   C. time order.
   D. an example.

_____ 7. The relationship of sentence 7 to the three sentences before it is one of
   A. addition.
   B. time.
   C. an example.
   D. contrast.

_____ 8. We can infer from this selection that
   A. most wealthy people are not very nice.
   B. many wealthy people have no contact with poorer people.
   C. it is likely that most wealthy people will give more money in the future.
   D. most poorer people do not like wealthy people.

COMBINED SKILLS: Test 14

Read the passage below. Then, in the space provided, write the letter of the best answer to each question that follows.

[1]Many people think that in order to lose weight, they must exercise a lot. [2]Of course, exercise is good for us for many reasons. [3]However, to be successful at losing weight, eating less is far more important than exercising more. [4]To begin with, exercise consumes fewer calories than many people think. [5]For example, 30 minutes of hard exercise, such as running or swimming, burns only 300 to 350 calories. [6]In addition, most people are probably not going to do strenuous exercise every day or for 30 minutes at a time. [7]Instead, they will probably exercise about 90 minutes a week, working off around 1000 calories. [8]That entire exercise regimen could be wiped out by drinking one 12-ounce soda a day. [9]For most people, it is much easier to cut out one soda a day than to exercise every other day. [10]Furthermore, exercise increases appetite, making it harder to stick to smaller portions. [11]Finally, people who spend 45 minutes or more at a gym after work often complain that they then do not have time to cook. [12]The fast food or restaurant meal they eat instead more than cancels the benefits of any time spent in the gym. [13]Certainly, getting fit is a huge part of a healthy life. [14]But to lose weight, eating less and healthier is more important.

_____ 1. In sentence 4, the word *consumes* means
    A. brings out.
    B. uses up.
    C. shuts down.
    D. puts away.

_____ 2. In sentence 8, the word *regimen* means
    A. ruler.
    B. army.
    C. class.
    D. program.

_____ 3. The main idea of the passage is stated in
    A. sentence 1.
    B. sentence 2.
    C. sentence 3.
    D. sentence 14.

_____ 4. Thirty minutes of hard exercise
    A. is hardly worth doing.
    B. burns about 300 to 350 calories.
    C. is less than most Americans exercise every day.
    D. can burn off a 12-ounce soda.

_____ 5. Many people complain that after spending 45 minutes at the gym, they
    A. don't have time to cook.
    B. are in pain.
    C. have not burned as many calories as they are consuming.
    D. feel as though they've wasted their time.

_____ 6. The relationship of sentence 10 to sentence 9 is one of
    A. contrast.
    B. cause and effect.
    C. an example.
    D. addition.

_____ 7. This passage suggests that
    A. most people need to go on a diet.
    B. most people have an easier time eating less food than exercising.
    C. unless you have time to exercise an hour a day, exercise is pointless.
    D. spending time in a gym leads to eating more fast food.

8. In the following group, one statement is the point, and the other statements are support for the point. Identify the point with a **P** and each statement of support with an **S**.

    _____ A. After a gym workout, many people undo its effects by grabbing a fast-food meal.

    _____ B. Exercise increases appetite.

    _____ C. Exercising more is not as good for weight loss as is eating smaller, healthier meals.

    _____ D. Exercise burns fewer calories than many people think it does.

COMBINED SKILLS: Test 15

Read the passage below. Then, in the space provided, write the letter of the best answer to each question that follows.

¹The United States has one of the highest divorce rates in the world, with more than one million divorces a year. ²There are several reasons why divorce is more common today than it was in the past. ³One reason is that women are less financially dependent on their husbands. ⁴Even with children, they manage to go to school and train for positions in today's job market. ⁵With their own income, they are not trapped at home as they were in the past. ⁶Another reason for divorce is less opposition. ⁷Legally, it is easier to obtain a divorce than was the case with earlier generations. ⁸There is less religious opposition as well, and less of a social stigma. ⁹Divorced people, who were once the subject of whispers and scandal, are now all around us. ¹⁰A third reason for the increase in divorce is that people expect more from marriage now. ¹¹They want their mates to enrich their lives, help them develop their potential, and be loving companions and good sexual partners. ¹²They are not as willing as their parents were to settle for less. ¹³Finally, men and women today are more realistic. ¹⁴If a marriage does not work out, they are more ready to simply accept that fact. ¹⁵Perhaps the marriage is not meant to be, they may decide, and to try to continue it might only damage both of them as well as their children. ¹⁶The talk shows and newspaper and magazine articles are full of stories about people who go on to make new beginnings in their lives. ¹⁷Couples in unhappy marriages are prompted to react in a similar way: better to put a bad experience to an end, and to make a new start in life.

_____ 1. In sentence 8, the word *stigma* means
   A. approval.
   B. shame.
   C. reaction.
   D. interest.

_____ 2. The main idea of the selection is stated in
   A. sentence 1.
   B. sentence 2.
   C. sentence 9.
   D. sentence 17.

_____ 3. People now expect their marriages to provide them with
      A. loving companions and good sexual partners.
      B. a mate who will cook and clean for them, if they are men.
      C. a mate who will be the breadwinner, if they are women.
      D. all of the above.

_____ 4. According to the selection, some people are prompted to end unhappy marriages by
      A. greedy divorce lawyers.
      B. stories about people who go on to make new beginnings in their lives.
      C. church leaders who advise them that their marriage was not meant to be.
      D. pressures put upon them by their children.

_____ 5. The relationship of sentence 13 to sentence 12 is one of
      A. addition.
      B. cause and effect.
      C. an example.
      D. time.

_____ 6. This selection suggests that in the past
      A. most people were happily married.
      B. married people were more realistic than they are today.
      C. the American divorce rate was about the same as it is today.
      D. a lot of people felt trapped in unhappy marriages.

_____ 7. We can conclude from this selection that
      A. the American divorce rate will continue to rise.
      B. many people who stay married now do so because they want to, not because they have to.
      C. the American divorce rate will begin to decline.
      D. divorced people should be treated with whispers and scandal.

_____ 8. The author's attitude toward divorce seems to be that it is
      A. too common in the United States.
      B. to be avoided at all costs.
      C. disgraceful.
      D. better than staying in an unhappy marriage.

SAMPLE ANSWER SHEET

Use the form below as a model answer sheet for the 15 combined-skills tests on the preceding pages.

Name _____ Date _____

Section _____ SCORE: (Number correct) _____ x 12.5 = _____ %

COMBINED SKILLS: Test ____

1. _____

2. _____

3. _____

4. _____

5. _____

6. _____

7. _____

8. _____

Appendixes

Pronunciation Guide

Each word in Chapter 3, "Vocabulary in Context," is followed by information in parentheses that shows you how to pronounce the word. (There are also pronunciations for the vocabulary items that follow the readings in Parts One and Two.) The guide below and on the next page explains how to use that information.

Long Vowel Sounds

ā	pay
ē	she
ī	hi
ō	go
o͞o	cool
yo͞o	use

Short Vowel Sounds

ă	hat
ĕ	ten
ĭ	sit
ŏ	lot
o͝o	look
ŭ	up
yo͝o	cure

Other Vowel Sounds

â	care
ä	card
îr	here
ô	all
oi	oil
ou	out
ûr	fur
ə	ago, item, easily, gallop, circus

Consonant Sounds

b	big
d	do
f	fall
g	get
h	he

Consonant Sounds *cont.*

j	jump
k	kiss
l	let
m	meet
n	no
p	put
r	red
s	sell
t	top
v	very
w	way
y	yes
z	zero
ch	church
sh	dish
th	then
th	thick
zh	usual

Note that each pronunciation symbol above is paired with a common word that shows the sound of the symbol. For example, the symbol ā has the sound of the *a* in the common word *pay*. The symbol ă has the sound of the *a* in the common word *hat*. The symbol ə, which looks like an upside-down *e* and is known as the schwa, has the unaccented sound in the common word *ago*. It sounds like the "uh" a speaker often says when hesitating.

Accent marks are small black marks that tell you which syllable to emphasize as you say a word. A bold accent mark (′) shows which syllable should be stressed. A lighter accent mark (′) in some words indicates a secondary stress. Syllables without an accent mark are unstressed.

Writing Assignments

A Brief Guide to Effective Writing

Here in a nutshell is what you need to do to write effectively.

Step 1: Explore Your Topic through Informal Writing

To begin with, explore the topic that you want to write about or that you have been assigned to write about. You can examine your topic through **informal writing**, which usually means one of three things.

First, you can **freewrite** about your topic for at least ten minutes. In other words, for ten minutes, write whatever comes into your head about your subject. Write without stopping and without worrying at all about spelling or grammar. Simply get down on paper all the information about the topic that occurs to you.

A second thing you can do is to **make a list of ideas and details** that could go into your paper. Simply pile these items up, one after another, like a shopping list, without worrying about putting them in any special order. Try to accumulate as many details as you can think of.

A third way to explore your topic is to **write down a series of questions and answers** about it. Your questions can start with words like *what, why, how, when*, and *where*.

Getting your thoughts and ideas down on paper will help you think more about your topic. With some raw material to look at, you are now in a better position to decide on just how to proceed.

Step 2: Plan Your Paper with an Informal Outline

After exploring your topic, plan your paper, using an informal outline. Do two things:

- **Decide on and write out the point of your paper.** It is often a good idea to begin your paragraph with this point, which is known as the **topic sentence**. If you are writing an essay of several paragraphs, you will probably want to include your main point somewhere in your first paragraph. In a paper of several paragraphs, the main point is called the **central point**, or **thesis**.

- **List the supporting reasons, examples, or other details that back up your point.** In many cases, you should have at least two or three items of support.

Step 3: Use Transitions

Once your outline is worked out, you will have a clear "road map" for writing your paper. As you write the early drafts of your paper, use **transitions** to introduce each of the separate supporting items you present to back up your point. For instance, you might introduce your first supporting item with the transitional words *first of all.* You might begin your second supporting item with words such as *another reason* or *another example.* And you might indicate your final supporting detail with such words as *last of all* or *a final reason.*

Step 4: Edit and Proofread Your Paper

After you have a solid draft, edit and proofread the paper. Ask yourself several questions to evaluate your paper:

1 Is the paper **unified**? Does all the material in the paper truly support the opening point?

2 Is the paper **well supported**? Is there plenty of specific evidence to back up the opening point?

3 Is the paper **clearly organized**? Does the material proceed in a way that makes sense? Do transitions help connect ideas?

4 Is the paper **well written**? When the paper is read aloud, do the sentences flow smoothly and clearly? Has the paper been checked carefully for grammar, punctuation, and spelling mistakes?

Writing Assignments for the Twenty Readings

Note: Your instructor may also permit you to write a paper that is based upon one of the discussion questions that follow each reading.

Part One Readings

A Parent Gets a Reading Lesson

1. What attitude did your parents take toward reading? How did their attitude affect your own? Write a paragraph in which you explain how their attitudes and your own are alike or different. Here is a sample topic sentence:

   Although reading was not important to my parents, I have always liked to read.

   In your paragraph, explain how you could tell what your parents' attitude about reading was, from their actions and comments. Then explain your own attitude about reading. Comment on whether the attitudes are the same or different, and in what ways.

2. What did you think of the mother in "A Parent Gets a Reading Lesson"? Did you have a good impression of her, a bad impression, or a mixed impression? Write a paragraph that explains what you thought of her and why. Use examples from the essay to back up the impression that you formed.

Discovering Words

1. Write a paragraph about one of your significant early memories of reading. Maybe it involves being read to by a parent or teacher. Maybe it's about reading the back of a cereal box at breakfast. Maybe it's about a favorite childhood book. Or maybe it's about the frustration of trying to read in school.

   Begin your paragraph with a sentence that summarizes the memory you are writing about. Here are some examples:

   One of my best early memories of reading is of Grandpa reading me stories.

   When I was very young and realized I could read street signs, I felt wonderful.

   Fear and confusion are what I felt when I tried to read in elementary school.

Follow your first sentence with a description of what happened and how you felt about it. Be sure to include details that will help your reader understand when and where this event occurred.

2. Malcolm X writes that reading made him feel free. What activity makes you feel especially free? Is it reading, as with Malcolm? Walking alone through the city? Driving your car? Running? Dancing? Painting? Making music?

   Write a paragraph that explains what makes you feel free. Use descriptive words that help the reader experience what you experience. Everyone has a different understanding of what it means to feel free, so be sure to explain what it is about this experience that is so appealing to you.

One Less Sucker Lives

1. In "One Less Sucker Lives," the author describes how she was taken advantage of by a con man who told her a hard-luck story. When have you been taken advantage of by someone who, like the con man, appealed to your trust or generosity and then treated you unfairly? Write a paragraph about what happened. Begin with a topic statement that explains when you were taken advantage of and who did it, like this:

   Last summer, my cousin Terrence took advantage of me.

   Just last week, a young woman in the train station took advantage of me.

   As you write your paper, explain how the person approached you and what he or she did to gain your trust. Describe what the person then did to take advantage of you. Explain why you feel that you were not treated fairly. Conclude by writing how you now feel about the person who took advantage of you.

2. Jeanne Smith says that the encounter with the con man taught her a lesson—to be less trusting and more cynical. Write a paragraph about an incident that taught you a lesson. Your topic sentence should briefly mention both the incident and the lesson. An example:

   A scary incident last summer taught me to be more careful about locking my apartment door.

   In the paragraph, tell the story of what happened in time order, from beginning to end. Conclude by explaining what lesson you learned from it, and how you have applied that lesson to your life.

Classroom Notetaking

1. Draw a line down the middle of a notebook page. On the top left-hand side, write, "Things I do." On the top right-hand side, write, "Things I don't do." In the first column, list the notetaking tips from the selection that you already use. In the second column, list those things you don't do now, but according to the article, might help you take better notes.

   Then write a paragraph that explains how the notetaking tips that you *do* use help you. For the tips you *don't* use, explain which ones you'd like to try, and why.

2. The author says that the best lecturers "combine knowledge with showmanship" and "can make any subject . . . leap vividly to life." Write a paragraph about a teacher you have had who is both well-informed and entertaining. Provide at least two detailed illustrations of how this teacher has kept your attention. Come to some conclusion about how the teacher's attitude affected your learning.

   Or, instead, write a paragraph describing a teacher who was unbelievably boring. Provide several detailed examples of how this teacher failed to be informative and entertaining. In your conclusion, tell about how your learning in that class was affected.

Winning the Job Interview Game

1. "Winning the Job Interview Game" gives excellent advice on how to make a great impression at a job interview. But how do you go about "Losing the Job Interview Game"? Write a comical paragraph in which you advise job applicants on how to make the worst possible impression. Look at "Winning the Job Interview Game" for ideas: for instance, write about the worst way to dress, the worst way to answer questions, and so on.

2. Of all the people you know personally—that is, not celebrities that you've just read or heard about—whose job would you most like to have? Why? Write a paragraph on that topic. Your topic sentence might be something like this:

   Of all the people I know, my uncle Bernie has the best job.

   Develop your paragraph by explaining who the person is, how you know him or her, and what job he or she holds. Then explain what it is about the job that makes it desirable to you.

Learning Survival Skills

1. What career plans have you made so far? Write a paragraph about your plans and how your college classes relate to those plans. If you are not sure yet about your career choice, write about a likely possibility.

   In your paragraph, describe your interests and how they have led to your plans for a career. Then explain how your program of study will contribute to your success. Here are some sample topic sentences for such a paragraph:

   > My interest in animals and science has led me to enroll in a program to become a veterinary assistant.

   > Because I have always loved art and design, I am earning a degree in graphic arts.

   > I intend to earn a double degree in horticulture and business because my dream is to have my own landscaping company.

2. Coleman writes, "To not be open to growth is to die a little each day." Whom do you know who seems to have chosen slow death over growth and positive change? Here are a few examples of behavior by people who refuse to take advantage of opportunities for growth:

   - They skip class and miss assignments, even though they are in danger of flunking out of school.

   - They refuse to take on added responsibilities at work, even though these could lead to a higher salary or a more interesting job.

   - They hang onto self-destructive habits such as overeating, watching too much TV (or some other form of addiction), or spending time with the wrong people.

   Write a paragraph about how the person you have chosen has decided not to grow. In the paragraph, introduce the person, and explain how you know him or her. Next, describe the harmful behavior. Be specific. For example, don't just say someone spends too much time with the wrong people—give a detailed example or two of people who are negative influences and why they are negative. You might conclude by suggesting some positive behavior changes that person could make and how they would help him or her.

Migrant Child to College Woman

1. Throughout her life, Maria Cardenas has forced herself to do things that were very difficult for her. For example, she made herself learn to read on her own. She forced herself to begin college, despite her fears. She did these things because she believed the long-term benefits would be more important than any short-term discomfort.

   When have you made yourself do something difficult, even though it would have been easier not to? Maybe it's been one of these:

   - Apologizing for something you did wrong
   - Starting a new class or job
   - Moving to a new town
   - Speaking up for yourself to someone who was treating you badly

   Write a paragraph about what you did and why. In it, answer these questions:

   - What did I do that was difficult?
   - Why did I find doing it so hard or frightening?
   - Why did I think doing it would be worthwhile?
   - How did I feel about myself after I'd done it?

2. Maria feels a strong drive to help migrant children. She wants to help them learn to speak English and to "stand on their own two feet."

   If you were offered the chance to help a particular group of people, who would it be? What kind of help would you most like to offer them? Write a paragraph in which you explain what group you would help, why you'd like to help them, and, finally, what you would do to help the people in this group.

   Or instead, if you are now a volunteer with a particular group, write a paragraph about your experiences with that group. Tell why you decided to volunteer, what you actually do, and what your rewards are from the experience. Remember to give specific examples from your experience to support your general points.

Life Over Death

1. Think of an animal that has played a role in your life. Perhaps it was a pet in your own home or in the home of someone you visited frequently. Perhaps it was a neighborhood animal that you often observed outdoors. Write a paragraph about one characteristic of that animal, such as any of the following:

   - Cleverness
   - Stupidity
   - Laziness
   - Playfulness
   - Stubbornness
   - Loyalty

   Begin with a topic sentence that names the animal and the characteristic. For instance, that sentence might be similar to this one:

   My sister's kitten, Muffin, is the most affectionate animal I've ever known.

   Then, describe two or three specific events or behaviors that are good examples of the characteristic you have chosen.

2. The author of "Life Over Death" felt he "had no choice"—that he *had* to help the injured cat. For this assignment, write a letter to the author telling him about a time you also did something because you thought it was the only right thing to do. A topic sentence for this letter could be worded something like this:

   When my sister lost her job, I had no choice—I had to invite her and her children to live with me for a while.

   After your topic sentence, describe the situation that you faced, and then explain the decision you made. Conclude by telling what finally happened.

Dare to Think Big

1. Ben Carson mentions that when he was in high school, peer pressure "sidetracked me for a time." Have you found peer pressure to be a negative influence in your life? A positive influence? Or has it not been an influence at all? Write a paragraph describing your experience with peer pressure. Begin with a statement of your topic, like this:

   > For me, peer pressure has been a positive influence on my life.

   Then develop your paragraph by describing who your peers were, how they influenced you, and how you responded to their influence. Give at least two specific examples of how the influence of other young people affected you. For instance, you might write: "Because my best friend signed up for a summer tutoring program, I decided to sign up as well."

2. Write a paragraph in which you contrast a "cool guy" and a "nerd" that you're acquainted with. Tell how they are different in three categories. For instance, you might talk about how they dress, how they walk, their attitude towards school, how they speak, their interests, how they spend their spare time, etc. In each category, be very specific about how the two individuals are different.

The Shocking State of the American Diet

1. Write about your favorite meal. Using the five food categories from the selection, determine if your favorite meal is healthy or unhealthy. If the meal is unhealthy, explain one or two ways that you could improve it. For example, could you substitute healthier options? Grill the meat instead of frying it? Drink water instead of soda? If the meal is healthy, explain why. For example, does it include fruits and vegetables? Is the bread made of whole grains? Does it contain fewer than five unfamiliar ingredients?

   Be sure that your topic sentence names specific foods and states whether or not they are healthy. For example, a topic sentence could be something like the following:

   > My favorite meal—macaroni and cheese with a tall glass of chocolate milk—isn't as bad as fast food or fried food, but it could be improved.

   After your topic sentence, describe the reasons that the meal is healthy or the ways that you could improve it. Conclude by stating one positive result that could happen if you change to—or stick to—healthier eating habits.

2. The author of the selection writes, "The hard truth is that for many of us, changing our diets will not be easy. Addictions to sugar, white flour, and fat are real. However, with focus and daily effort, you will discover how good healthy food can be. You will also begin to look and feel much better."

   Discovering benefits from change isn't limited to food choices. Write a paragraph about a time in your life that you had to work hard to change an unhealthy habit, addiction, or behavior. Maybe you wanted to stop biting your fingernails or to quit smoking. In the paragraph, clearly state the habit, addiction, or behavior, and then explain the actions you took that enabled you to change. Also include the names and relationships of anyone who may have supported you or helped you. Lastly, include what you discovered about yourself through the process. For example, if you quit smoking, perhaps you discovered your own strength and willpower. Or maybe you learned to appreciate the outdoors without needing to smoke a cigarette.

Part Two Readings

Learning to Read: The Marvel Kretzmann Story

1. When Marvel realized her life was getting more difficult rather than easier, she returned to school—a decision that changed her life. Like Marvel, we all have made decisions that changed our lives, such as the decision to do any of the following:

   - Marry or divorce
   - Have a child
   - Get a new job
   - Move to another town
   - End a destructive relationship
   - Go back to school

   Write a paragraph about a life-changing decision you have made and its effects. In your paper, answer the following questions:

   - What decision did I make?
   - Why did I make it?
   - What happened to me as a result of my decision?
   - If I had it to do over again, would I make the same decision?

   Begin by choosing a decision you might wish to write about. Next, check to see if you have enough supporting details to write about that decision. To do so, you might write down the above questions and list as many answers to each as you can think of.

2. Marvel is surprised to find herself looked up to by fellow students who also have difficulty reading. However, she realizes that if *they* think she can help them, she probably *can* help them—and also help herself.

   Whom do you know (perhaps yourself?) who has struggled with an obstacle and was later able to help others with that same problem? Write a paragraph that includes the following:

   - The person's problem
   - How he or she learned to deal with it
   - How that person later helped someone else deal with the same problem

The Blind Vet

1. Has someone ever believed in you and patiently urged you on in spite of your own self-doubt or frustration? This person could be a friend, teacher, coach, or parent. Write a paragraph about this experience. Be sure to provide specific details as you answer these questions in your paragraph:

   - Who helped you?
   - Why were you feeling doubtful or frustrated?
   - How did this person help you?
   - What was the outcome?
   - What did you learn from this experience?

2. Hoffman writes, "More than anything, Nick hated his loss of independence." Most of us take our ability to do whatever we want for granted. We never question being able to take a trip, drive a car, or even make lunch for ourselves, since it's what we're used to. For Nick, being unable to go on long, adventurous bike rides and try new things was particularly upsetting. What would you miss most if you no longer had your independence due to some kind of disability? Write about one or two aspects of your life that you would particularly miss if, like Nick, you had to rely on others to take care of you. Be sure to describe each activity and explain why it is so important to you.

The Fist, the Clay, and the Rock

1. The author writes of Mr. Gery, "[He] worked us very hard, but he was not a mean person. We all knew he was a kind man who wanted us to become strong." Write a paragraph about an adult in your life who, like Mr. Gery, was tough but kind. In your paragraph, tell who the person was, what his or her relationship was to you, and why you considered him or her "tough but kind." Provide at least one example that shows the person's toughness and kindness.

   Start with your main point, which might be something like this:

   Mr. D'Angelo, my boss at the supermarket, was a tough but kind man.

   The paragraph that began like this would go on to describe why Mr. D'Angelo impressed the writer as being both tough and kind. ("He expected me to work hard, but he always let me know that he appreciated me.") The paragraph would include at least one detailed example of a time Mr. D'Angelo showed the writer both his toughness and his kindness.

2. Mr. Gery warned his students that life would give them some "heavy hits." Write a paragraph about a heavy hit you've taken in life—something that happened that was very difficult to deal with.

Begin by stating what the "hit" was. For example:

Life gave me a heavy hit when my aunt died in a car accident.

In your paragraph, give a detailed account of what happened. Be sure to explain why the incident was personally difficult for you. In the case of the topic sentence above, for instance, the writer might say, "My aunt took care of me whenever my mother was at work. She was like a second mom in my life."

It's Not My Fault

1. As is pointed out in this selection, many of us use excuses for our behavior when we make mistakes. Write about one incident in the past when you—or someone you know—tried to avoid blame for a mistake. What was the mistake? What did you or the other person do or say to try to avoid blame? Finally, what was the outcome?

2. In this selection, Brian blames his parents for his failures in life. Some adults, in fact, blame everything from lack of education to the cost of living for why their lives are not going the way they want them to go. Do you know people like Brian, who, although they are adults, refuse to grow up and take responsibility for their lives? Write about one or more of these people. What or whom do they blame for their failures? As a result, what are their lives like? What is one thing each of them could do to turn their lives around?

Joe Davis: A Cool Man

1. Like Joe Davis, many of us have learned painful lessons from life. And like him, we wish we could pass those lessons on to young people to save them from making the same mistakes. Write a letter to a young person in which you use your own experience as a lesson. Begin with a topic sentence stating the lesson you'd like to teach, as in these examples:

   > My own experience is a lesson on why it's a bad idea to get involved with drugs and the people who take them.

   > I hope you can learn from my experience that dropping out of high school is a big mistake.

   > I know from firsthand experience that teenage girls should not let their boyfriends pressure them into a sexual relationship.

   As you develop your letter, describe in detail the hard lesson you learned and how you learned it.

2. One of Joe's goals was to regain the trust of the friends and family members he abused during his earlier life. Have you ever given a second chance to someone who treated you poorly? Write a paragraph about what happened. In your paragraph, answer the following questions:

   - What did the person do to lose your trust? Was it an obviously hurtful action, like physically harming you or stealing from you, or something more subtle, like embarrassing you or hurting your feelings?

   - Why did you decide to give the person another chance? Did the person apologize? Did you decide the mistreatment was not as bad as you first thought?

   - What happened as a result of your giving the person a second chance? Did he or she treat you better this time? Or did the bad treatment start over again?

   Conclude your paragraph with one or more thoughts about what you learned from the experience.

Rosa: A Success Story

1. Edward Patrick writes, "Almost all of us came to America from somewhere else." What do you know about your family's arrival in this country? Write a paragraph that tells what you know about your first relatives in the United States. Answer as many of the following questions as you can:

   - Who were your first relatives in the United States?
   - Where did they come from?
   - When did they arrive?
   - Why did they come to the United States?
   - What was life in the U.S. like for them at first?

   If you don't know much about your first relatives in the United States, write instead about the earliest generation you do know about.

2. Rosa's college classes prepared her for a career in childcare. If you want your education to lead to a specific career, write a paragraph about that career and why you've picked it. Give specific examples of the type of work you'd like to do and why. If you're not sure about the career you want, write about one or two that you're considering. Your topic sentence for this paragraph might be worded like either of these:

   I'm aiming for a career in accounting for several reasons.

   Although I haven't made a final decision, I'm considering the pros and cons of a career as a chef.

The Lady, or the Tiger?

1. Pretend the story ends with paragraph 15. The final sentence is, "Without pausing for a moment, he threw open the door on the right." Now, write your own ending to the story. What happened after the young man threw open the door? Use your imagination! In your version of the ending, write more than what happened immediately. Consider answering some of these questions: Why did what happened happen? How did the crowd react? How did the princess and king react?

2. "The Lady, or the Tiger?" is about a difficult decision that a princess had to make. Write a paragraph about a time you had to make a difficult decision. Begin with a sentence that describes the decision you faced, like this:

   When my parents divorced, I had to decide whether to live with my mother or my dad.

   In the paragraph, explain why the decision was difficult for you. Describe the good and bad points that either choice would have. For instance, the writer of the above paragraph about living with her father or mother might write, "If I lived with my mother, I would stay in my familiar house in my own neighborhood. On the other hand, my mom and I argued a lot." After describing the alternatives, tell the reader what you decided and why. Conclude your paragraph by saying how you now feel about your decision.

Dawn's Story

1. Dawn Cogliser has learned some painful, important lessons in life—lessons about addiction, abuse, and channeling her energy in positive directions. Now she's trying to pass on those lessons through her public speaking and her "Healing Mama" newsletter.

   Like Dawn, just about everybody has learned lessons that others could benefit from. What is a lesson you would like to pass on? Write a letter in which you use your own experience to teach a lesson. You may address it either to a particular person (for example, a younger sibling or a friend) or to a category of people (for example, high-school students). Begin your letter with a topic sentence that states the lesson you'd like to teach, like this:

   My experience has taught me that it's a bad idea to stay with an abuser.

   I hope others will learn from my experience to stay away from drugs.

   A life lesson that I would like to pass on is that eventually, lies always catch up with you.

   As you develop your letter, describe in detail the lesson you learned and how you learned it.

2. Dawn's experience has influenced her choice of a career. Hoping to help other people deal with addiction and abuse, she took classes to become a therapist and, eventually, a nurse practitioner. If you want your education to lead to a specific career, write a paragraph about that career and why you've chosen it. Provide specific examples of the work you'd like to do and why. If you are not sure about the career you want, write about one or two that you are considering. Begin your paragraph with a topic sentence similar to one of these:

   There are several reasons why I am planning to become a dental hygienist.

   I am considering a career as either a police officer or a small business owner.

Knowledge Is Power

1. The author would not have been able to attend a college in the United States without the support of her mother. Who has helped you most in your quest for an education? That help may be very practical—such as paying bills or providing a place to stay—or it may be emotional support and encouragement. Write a paragraph explaining who this person is. Give specific examples of how he or she has helped you. Here are some sample topic sentences for this assignment:

   > By reassuring me when I get discouraged, my husband is my greatest supporter as I seek an education.

   > My boss has been the biggest help to me since I started college, because he (*or* she) has allowed me to work on a flexible schedule and has helped me with some expenses.

2. Anna-Maria was inspired by a bookmark that said, "Knowledge is power." Choose another familiar saying, such as one of the following:

   - A stitch in time saves nine.
   - Too many cooks spoil the broth.
   - A little knowledge is a dangerous thing.
   - A fool and his money are soon parted.
   - Fools rush in where angels fear to tread.
   - The acorn doesn't fall far from the tree.
   - One bad apple can spoil the whole bunch.

   Write a paragraph about an incident from your own experience that demonstrates the truth of the saying you choose. Begin with a topic sentence that mentions both the saying and the incident, like this:

   > The time my brother won a large sweepstakes prize showed the truth of the saying "A fool and his money are soon parted."

   Then describe the incident in detail. Be sure to emphasize the relationship between the saying and what happened. Conclude by restating the saying as it applies to the incident, for example:

   > In this case, my brother certainly played the fool in being so quickly separated from his money.

What I Believe

1. The author begins his essay by pointing out that "people are truly remarkable." He then proceeds to present three examples of just how remarkable people can be—even when they are faced with sorrow, illness, and hardship. Have you ever known someone who, in his or her own way, was also "truly remarkable"? What did this person do? Write a paragraph that tells this person's story. And remember—a remarkable person does not have to be famous or a superhero. He or she, as the author points out, may simply be "an inspiration to the human spirit."

2. In concluding his essay, the author writes, "Not knowing about life after death, I believe in life before death." What happens after death is, to many people, one of life's biggest mysteries. To many others, however, what happens after death is no mystery at all—their religious beliefs offer explanations and reassurances. What are your feelings about what happens to us after we die? Have your feelings about death affected the way you live your life? In what way(s)? Write a paragraph that explores these questions. Remember that you do not have to "answer" the question of what happens after we die—simply express what you think and feel. Your paragraph may, in fact, lead you to ask further questions.

Limited Answer Key

An important note: To strengthen your reading skills, you must do more than simply find out which of your answers are right and which are wrong. You also need to figure out (with the help of this book, the teacher, or other students) *why* you missed the questions you did. By using each of your wrong answers as a learning opportunity, you will strengthen your understanding of the skills. You will also prepare yourself for the review and mastery tests in Part One, the reading comprehension questions in Part Two, and the relationships tests and combined-skills tests in Part Three, for which answers are not given here.

Answers to the Practices in Part One

2 Dictionary Use

Practice 1
1. campus, canary, cancer
2. holdup, holiday, hog
3. letter, lettuce, level
4. railroad, raise, raincoat
5. sharp, shapely, shampoo

Practice 2
1. revise
2. kidnap
3. please
4. believe
5. really
6. schoolteacher
7. writing
8. library
9. definitely
10. across

Practice 3
1. frag•ment, 2
2. in•jec•tion, 3
3. com•pli•cate, 3
4. in•sen•si•tive, 4
5. com•mu•ni•ca•tion, 5

Practice 4
1. A
2. A
3. A
4. B
5. B
6. B
7. B
8. A
9. B
10. B

Practice 5
2. miracle, 2
3. offense, 2
4. intelligent, 2
5. reliable, 2

Practice 6
1. 2; first
2. 3; second
3. 3; first
4. 4; second
5. 4; second

Practice 7
1. verb, noun
2. noun, verb
3. verb, noun
4. verb, noun
5. adjective, noun, verb

Practice 8
1. parties
2. wrote, written
3. lives
4. spoke, spoken
5. littler, littlest

Practice 9
1. Definition 1
2. Definition 1
3. Definition 2

3 Vocabulary in Context

Practice 1: Examples

1. *Examples:* the thumbs-up sign, hands on the hips, a shrug of the shoulders; A
2. *Examples:* quotations which were never said, events that never occurred; C
3. *Examples:* burping, loud talking, playing around; A
4. *Examples:* exercising daily, eating nutritious foods; C
5. *Examples:* coughing, sighing, scraping of chairs; B

Practice 2: Synonyms

1. admit
2. unwilling
3. ridiculous
4. fearful
5. false idea

Practice 3: Antonyms

1. *Antonym:* simple; C
2. *Antonym:* famous; A
3. *Antonym:* unrelated; B
4. *Antonym:* out of order; B
5. *Antonym:* criticized; C

Practice 4: General Sense of the Passage

1. B
2. A
3. C
4. B
5. B

4 Main Ideas

Practice 1

1. goldfish: S
   parakeet: S
   pet: G
   dog: S
   cat: S

2. square: S
   circle: S
   triangle: S
   shape: G
   diamond: S

3. up: S
   down: S
   direction: G
   sideways: S
   north: S

4. soda: S
   beer: S
   orange juice: S
   beverage: G
   water: S

5. high-risk job: G
   astronaut: S
   firefighter: S
   policeman: S
   miner: S

6. sleeping bag: S
   sheet: S
   pillow: S
   blanket: S
   bedding: G

7. "hello": S
   greeting: G
   a wave: S
   "hi": S
   open arms: S

8. screech: S
   noise: G
   crash: S
   off-key music: S
   sirens: S

9. jump: S
   command: G
   stop: S
   move: S
   sit down: S

10. jail: S
    hanging: S
    suspension: S
    fine: S
    punishment: G

Practice 2

Answers will vary. Here are some possibilities:

1. Jennifer Lopez, George Clooney
2. tiger, elephant
3. table, sofa
4. cake, pie
5. New York, Las Vegas
6. New Year's Day, Independence Day
7. basketball, football
8. canary, swan
9. broccoli, carrots
10. Mars, Venus

Practice 3

1. SD	3. T
SD	SD
T	MI
MI	SD

2. SD	4. MI
SD	T
MI	SD
T	SD

Practice 4

1. *Topic:* B
2. *Main idea:* Sentence 1

3. *Topic:* C
4. *Main idea:* Sentence 6

5. *Topic:* B
6. *Main idea:* Sentence 2

7. *Topic:* C
8. *Main idea:* Sentence 7

5 Supporting Details

Practice 1

1. SD	3. MI
MI	SD
SD	SD

2. SD	4. SD
SD	SD
MI	MI

Practice 2 *(Wording of outlines may vary.)*

Passage 1

1. Don't make a big deal of the mistake.
2. Use humor.
3. Ask for help.
   Ex.—Tell the waiter, "Sorry; I need some help cleaning up here."

Words that introduce a list: different ways

Words that introduce
   First major detail: One
   Second major detail: Another
   Last major detail: third

Passage 2

1. The delinquent group
2. The academic subculture
3. The fun subculture
   a. Interested in their social status
   b. Focus on material things like clothes and cars

Words that introduce a list: three subcultures

Words that introduce
   First major detail: first
   Second major detail: next
   Third major detail: Last of all

Practice 3 *(Wording of map items may vary.)*

Passage 1

Words that introduce a list: four most popular hobbies

Words that introduce
   First major detail: one
   Second major detail: second
   Third major detail: next
   Fourth major detail: final

Passage 2

Go to class and take a lot of notes.	Study regularly.	Use test-taking strategies.
Be there and write down that material.	Learn new material daily.	Answer easier questions first.

Words that introduce a list: several suggestions

Words that introduce
   First major detail: To begin with
   Second major detail: Another
   Third major detail: Finally

6 Finding Main Ideas

Practice 1

1. *Main idea:* Sentence 1
2. *Main idea:* Sentence 2
3. *Main idea:* Sentence 3
4. *Main idea:* Sentence 1

Practice 2

1. *Main idea:* Sentence 7
2. *Main idea:* Sentence 1
3. *Main idea:* Sentence 2
4. *Main idea:* Sentence 1

7 Signal Words I

Practice 1

1. C Finally
2. A also
3. B Another
4. D In addition
5. E second

Practice 2 *(Answers may vary.)*

A. Main idea: *There are several signs of stress in young people.*

1. Unusual tiredness (*Addition word:* one)
2. Temper tantrums
   (*Addition word:* Another)
3. Forgetting known facts
   (*Addition word:* third)

B. Main idea: *Pizza contains healthful ingredients.*

1. The crust is rich in B vitamins.
   (*Addition word:* First of all)
2. The tomato sauce is an excellent source of vitamin A. (*Addition word:* Also)
3. The mozzarella cheese contains protein and calcium. (*Addition word:* finally)

C. Main idea: *Walking can be a rewarding experience.*

1. Lets you chat with neighbors
   (*Addition word:* To begin with)
2. Excellent and inexpensive form of exercise (*Addition word:* In addition)
3. Natural anti-depressant
   (*Addition word:* Moreover)

Practice 3

1. A After
2. C Then
3. D until
4. B Before
5. E When

Practice 4 *(Wording of answers may vary.)*

A.

1. Soon
2. Next
3. Finally

B. Main idea: *Use the following tips to find the right boyfriend or girlfriend.*

1. Trust your own instincts.
   (*Time word:* First)
2. Widen your social circle.
   (*Time word:* next)
3. Don't settle for just anyone who is willing to date you.
   (*Time word:* last)

C. Main idea: *A noticeable stain or burn in a carpet can be corrected.*

1. Cut out the damaged area with a sharp utility knife. (*Time word:* First)
2. Cut a patch the same size and shape from leftover carpet or from an unnoticeable spot. (*Time word:* Second)
3. Cut a piece of cardboard a little larger than the patch. (*Time word:* Next)
4. Place the cardboard where you cut out the damaged piece of carpet.
   (*Time word:* Then)
5. Glue the carpet patch to the cardboard.
   (*Time word:* Last)

8 Signal Words II

Practice 1

1. A. For example (*or* B. For instance)
2. E. such as
3. B. For instance (*or* A. For example)
4. C. including
5. D. Once

Practice 2

A. *phobia*; definition—sentence 1; example —sentence 2 (*or* 3)

B. *functional illiteracy*; definition—sentence 1; example—sentence 3 (*or* 4 *or* 5)

C. *Regeneration*: the ability to renew lost body parts

An octopus can regrow lost tentacles.

One leg of a sea star that includes part of its center can regenerate a whole new body.

Practice 3 (*Answers may vary.*)

1. A. Even though
2. C. in contrast
3. D. In spite of
4. E. Rather than
5. B. however

Practice 4 (*Answers may vary.*)

A. Main idea: *There are two different views of the value of computers in the classroom.*

1. They will help children learn faster and more efficiently.
2. They will get in the way of children's learning. *Or:* They may weaken children's language skills.
   (*Contrast words:* different, But)

B. Main idea: *Doctors and scientists do not agree about when a person is truly dead.*

1. Some think death occurs when blood circulation and breathing stop.
2. Others say death occurs when the entire brain stops functioning.
   (*Contrast words:* However, But)

C. Main idea: *There are two kinds of gamblers.*

1. Gamblers who have harmless fun
2. Gamblers who are addicted and who ruin their lives
   (*Contrast words:* Yet, Unlike)

Practice 5 (*Wording of answers may vary.*)

1. C. result
2. E. Therefore
3. A. because
4. D. so
5. B. effect

Practice 6 (*Wording of answers may vary.*)

A. Main idea: *Laughing can be good for you.*

1. It relaxes the facial muscles.
2. It increases the oxygen in the brain.
3. It reduces stress.
   (*Cause and effect words:* causing, resulting, therefore)

B. Main idea: *Changes at the end of the 1800s created more work for women.*

1. A greater emphasis on being clean caused women to spend more time washing, dusting, and scrubbing.
2. The availability of a greater variety of foods resulted in women spending more time on food preparation.
   (*Cause and effect words:* As a result, consequently)

C. Main idea: Being unemployed *can have harmful health effects.*

Increased alcohol and drug abuse

High blood pressure and rise in heart disease

9 Inferences

Practice 1

A. 2, 4
B. 1, 4
C. 3, 4

Practice 2

1. C
2. D
3. D

10 The Basics of Argument

Practice 1

Group 1
A. S
B. S
C. S
D. P

Group 2
A. S
B. S
C. P
D. S

Group 3
A. S
B. S
C. S
D. P

Practice 2

1. B
2. A
3. C

Practice 3

1. B, C, D
2. A, B, C
3. A, B, E

Practice 4

Group 1: A
Group 2: B
Group 3: D

Acknowledgments

Text Credits

Broderick, Bill. "Life Over Death." Reprinted by permission.

Cardenas, Maria. "Migrant Child to College Woman." Reprinted by permission.

Carson, Dr. Ben. "Dare to Think Big." Taken from *The Big Picture* by Dr. Benjamin Carson, with Gregg A. Lewis. Copyright © 1999 by Benjamin Carson. Used by permission of Zondervan. www. zondervan.com

Coleman, Jean. "Learning Survival Skills." Reprinted by permission.

Herndon, Lucia. "A Parent Gets a Reading Lesson." Reprinted with the permission of the *Philadelphia Inquirer*. Copyright © 2015. All rights reserved.

Hoffman, Gail. "The Blind Vet." Reprinted by permission.

Holland, Donald. "The Fist, the Clay, and the Rock." Reprinted by permission.

Johnson, Beth. "Joe Davis: A Cool Man." Reprinted by permission.

Kennedy, Roger. "It's Not My Fault." Reprinted by permission.

Kerns, Nancy. "Dawn's Story." Reprinted by permission of Dawn Cogliser.

Langan, John. "What I Believe." Reprinted by permission.

Malcolm X, with Alex Haley. "Discovering Words." From *The Autobiography of Malcolm X* by Malcolm X and Alex Haley, copyright © 1964 by Alex Haley and Malcolm X. Copyright © 1965 by Alex Haley and Betty Shabazz. Used by permission of Random House, Inc.

Patrick, Edward. "Rosa: A Success Story." Reprinted by permission.

Petričić, Anna-Maria. "Knowledge Is Power." Reprinted by permission.

Prentergast, Marcia. "Winning the Job Interview Game." Reprinted by permission.

Ryder, Phil. Cartoon on page 293. Reprinted by permission.

Sherry, Mary. "Learning to Read: The Marvel Kretzmann Story." Reprinted by permission.

Smith, Jeanne R. "One Less Sucker Lives." Reprinted by permission.

Taylor, Adam. "The Shocking State of the American Diet." Reprinted by permission.

White, Robin. "Classroom Notetaking." Reprinted by permission.

Photo Credits

Part One

Chapter 1, p. 22 © SIBSA Digital Pvt. Ltd./Alamy; Chapter 2, p. 58 © Marion S. Trikoso/Library of Congress; Chapter 3, p. 92 © photographee.eu/fotolia; Chapter 4, p. 125 © Monkey Business/fotolia; Chapter 5, p. 158 © Elenathewise/fotolia; Chapter 6, p. 186 © Flirt/SuperStock; Chapter 7, pp. 219 and 224 courtesy Beth Johnson; Chapter 8, p. 254 © Peter Gudella/Shutterstock; Chapter 9, p. 286 courtesy The Carson Scholars Fund; Chapter 10, p. 318 © Kaycco/fotolia.

Part Two

Chapter 1, pp. 338 and 344 courtesy Marvel Kretzmann; Chapter 2, p. 352 © Image Source/Shutterstock; Chapter 3, p. 362 © Stephen Rees/Shutterstock; Chapter 4, p. 371 © UK Stock Images Ltd./Alamy; Chapter 5, p. 382 courtesy Terri Davis; Chapter 6, p. 394 © snowwhiteimages/fotolia; Chapter 7, p. 404 © Casther/fotolia, p. 405 © Urvadnikov Sergey/fotolia; Chapter 8, pp. 414 and 425 courtesy Dawn Cogliser; Chapter 9, p. 433 courtesy Cheryl Fusco Johnson; Chapter 10, p. 448 © Rob Bartee/Alamy.

Index